ARTEM KUDELIA PHD

Psychotherapy Fundamentals

Complete Guide

First edition

This book was professionally typeset on Reedsy.
Find out more at reedsy.com

Contents

Foreword

Students often inquire about the existence of a psychotherapy guide that combines scientific rigor with an accessible presentation, a progressive orientation, and forward-looking innovation, while maintaining a respectful attitude towards the psychotherapeutic principles and achievements of the past.

In doing so, they emphasize their interest in a textbook that does not cultivate and develop only one approach (even if it is comprehensive and detailed!), built solely on the traditions of a single (albeit great!) psychotherapeutic school.

The need for a publication that encompasses a wide range of psychotherapeutic approaches and provides a clear exposition of the corresponding issues is evident.

Moreover, students express their desire to read not just an author who systematizes the achievements of others (even if it is done masterfully), but someone whose didactic, methodological, and epistolary abilities rest on a solid foundation of their own substantial psychotherapeutic experience.

The author of this book cannot be classified as an orthodox psychotherapist. On the contrary, they view psychotherapeutic problems through the prism of a "panoramic lens," weighing, comparing, exploring possibilities, and highlighting the limitations of each described psychotherapeutic approach.

As one becomes acquainted with the textbook's text, with its thorough description of approaches, techniques, and specific methods, one gradually realizes the thought: "Indeed, the author has tried all of this, received feedback, and reflected on it in their psychotherapeutic practice! Well, if not everything, then at least the majority."

The declarative statements and factual material of this book have been greatly multiplied by the value of that very "procedural experience" that can only be gained through conscientious and honest engagement in real psychotherapy.

Undoubtedly, psychotherapy is an art that is not granted to everyone and requires dedicating one's entire life to it. However, the author convincingly argues that psychotherapy is also a "science situated in the intersecting space between medicine, psychology, and philosophy." Yet, it is a distinct science. Scientific understanding of psychotherapy employs a different "language" from academic psychology discourse. Psychotherapy, as a science, operates with different "units" of analyzing the psyche and relies on its own logic of constructing psychological knowledge, distinct from academic approaches. Traditional university psychologists and psychotherapists even have different authorities. While the latter would insist on including B.F. Skinner, Jean Piaget, K. Lewin, U. Michell, L.S. Vygotsky, and others in the Top 100 Greatest Psychologists of Modern Times (see the ranking conducted by 1,750 members of the American Psychological Association in 2001), the former cannot imagine the structure of psychological science without M. Erickson, C. Rogers, R. Laing, A. Beck, I. Yalom, and others.

Working with this book, students (even if they do not plan to become psychotherapists in the future, which is the majority) will understand that every interaction between a practical psychologist and a client is unique. Not only the client but the psychologist themselves is unique. They will grasp that in studying the psyche, one can deal not only with a sample in which individual characteristics of the people included dissolve and the individuals themselves become "objects." They deal with unique personalities and individuality. Students will discover that the most significant psychological knowledge is often fundamentally unquantifiable, not expressible in numbers, but revealed through personal observations. They take on the character of that very "personal knowledge" described by M. Polanyi. Students will notice that psychological knowledge acquired through psychotherapy practice is, in most cases, unverifiable, meaning its reliability does not meet the criteria of reliability, validity, and statistical significance. The verification of this knowledge is based on the wealth of the psychotherapist's experience, their authority within the psychotherapist community, the number of cases in which real help was provided to patients, and so on. At the very least, enthusiastic students engaged in psychotherapy will learn to approach calmly the conclusion of V.M. Allakhverdov: "*None of the fundamental propositions of psychoanalysis have received any convincing empirical confirmation*" (2003).

By familiarizing themselves with the content of this book, students will be able to refine their image as professionals in the field they are mastering.

In the current era of blurring traditional positivist orientations in academic psychology within modern postclassical science, this image represents a psychologist who successfully combines academic scientific activity with practical psychotherapeutic work. They will fully understand the message of the renowned psychologist and psychotherapist Fedor Vasilyuk, who proclaimed that "there is nothing more theoretical than good practice" (F. V. Vasilyuk, 1996).The book holds great value for aspiring psychotherapists as it extensively covers the most important psychotherapeutic approaches of today. The book is characterized by:

- Incorporation of the latest scientific developments when describing each psychotherapeutic school.
- The accessibility of language and the use of established concepts and terms commonly employed by specialists.
- The materials in each book of the series are presented in a clear and comprehensive manner, following the structure of "methodological vector, theoretical context, most prominent representatives and their biography, facts that significantly influenced the development of the approach, most important concepts of the approach, goals of psychotherapy, and issues with proven efficacy within this approach, as well as the specificity of working with patients of various psychopathological profiles. Additionally, literature for in-depth study of the approach is provided."

- The aim is to focus the reader's attention on their own personal growth and awaken their interest in "trying out" a particular type of psychotherapy.

This publication and the continuation of books in the series make it easier to compare different psychotherapeutic approaches, assess their strengths and weaknesses, and recognize the common aspect that unites them all: the humane endeavor to relieve human suffering and enable individuals to attain happiness.

Preface

This educational publication explores the fundamental approaches in psychotherapy. The "**Psychology and Psychotherapy: Theories and Practices**" series extensively covers the history of these approaches, along with their theoretical and practical aspects. It can serve as a textbook for courses such as "Fundamentals of Psychological Counseling," or "Fundamentals of Psychotherapy." It is intended for psychologists, medical professionals, psychology students, and readers with a wide range of interests. *This initial book sets the foundation for the entire series.*

Acknowledgments

I would like to express my gratitude to my psychology and psychotherapy teachers who have paved the way and established a solid foundation of knowledge. Furthermore, I extend my immense appreciation to patients, colleagues, friends, and all individuals who have directly or indirectly contributed to the writing of this book.

BONUS: Get Your Free Resources Now

I'm excited to share a **free eBook** and **exclusive access** to **psychological resources** with you. To get started, scan the QR code or visit psychemaster.com/psychotherapy-fundamentals

What You'll Get:

- **Free eBook**: Explore advanced psychotherapeutic techniques and approaches that complement the insights.
- **Interactive Learning**: Engage with exercises and quizzes to solidify your understanding of complex theories.
- **Latest Research**: Stay updated with the most recent findings in the field of psychotherapy and integrative therapy approaches.
- **Continuous Support**: Get consistent tips, strategies, and motivation to assist you in staying focused and excelling in your studies and practice.

Maximize your understanding of psychotherapy!

1

Introduction

In the modern world of psycho-technologies, there are hundreds of different schools of psychotherapy that belong to the entire spectrum of existing personality theories and physiological concepts.

Often, a particular form of psychotherapy originates from a specific psychological or medical school. In some cases, psychotherapy was inseparable from medicine, while in others, it had its own specific theoretical constructs that could even contradict the existing biological model of human behavior and perception.

Psychotherapy, as a medical discipline that involves the use of words as an auxiliary or primary means of treatment, has existed since ancient times. Its roots can be traced back to the traditions of ancient shamanism in various cultures, which emerged thousands of years before the birth of Christ.

By employing various verbal and ritual-behavioral methods, shamans were sometimes able to create remarkable changes in their clients, whether it was the treatment of an illness, physical wounds, mental disorders, or the solution of social problems. It is precisely archaic shamanism that represents a certain form of proto psychotherapy, and it takes on different forms in various parts of the world in accordance with the cultural peculiarities of the contexts.

The psychosocial role of the **shaman** represented an evolutionary leap for ancient societies, distinguishing human tribes qualitatively from packs of other animals. In any animal pack, there is a hierarchy with a leader and subordinates, and there may be some degree of partial division of activities, at least based on age and gender criteria. Mutual aid and support can exist within animal packs in the event of a predator attack or encountering a difficult situation, and there may be various instinctive actions related to attempts at self-healing from certain illnesses. However, in the animal kingdom, even among higher primates and dolphins, there is no social role for a shaman as a being to whom other members of the pack turn for help with their problems.

The role of a shaman is multifaceted and archetypal, evolving over time and taking on new specific forms in various social spheres of activity and professions: healer, philosopher, chemist, musician, and blacksmith—roles that often derive from the shamanic image in the collective consciousness of the social group.

Originally, verbal healing had almost exclusively trance connotations without any rational basis. The shamans sang songs, chanted, summoned spirits, sought healing and blessings, and expelled dark forces from the patient's body. In the grand scheme of the ancient human worldview, which was constructed on a pre-rational, mythical level that did not rely on any foundation of rational thinking and the pursuit of objective truth, this was largely sufficient. The shaman was considered a conduit for spirits and Gods, and his words were not disputed by other members of society.In different social niches, the shaman possessed no less, and sometimes greater, power than the tribal chief, once again demonstrating the formation of a hierarchical structure distinct from that of animals. Carl Jung suggested that it was the shamanic image that became the primary imprint engraved in the human collective unconscious, manifesting in the form of the archetype of the sage—a collective group projection of wisdom, knowledge, spirit essence, understanding of the world, and the ability to heal.

The tribal shaman served as psychosocial support for the group members, reducing the level of anxiety and creating complexes of special meanings in life. It can be said that, at a profound level, the shaman fulfilled a projective fatherly and motherly role for the adult members of the tribe when their parents were either deceased or, for various reasons, unable to provide constructive advice related to their current life situation.

About five thousand years ago, archaic shamanism gradually began to consolidate, and the oral transmission of psychospiritual knowledge transitioned into a religious form, in which the role of the shaman underwent a number of changes and became more structured and cohesive.

Both the early shamanic role and the later role of the **priest** continued to serve the function of facilitating the connection between members of a social group and the realm of knowledge, wisdom, elevated meanings, and deceased ancestors, thus creating a behavioral metaphor for the neurophysiological connections between different regions of the human brain. If we were to draw an analogy between a social group and the human brain, we believe that shamanism would embody the process of creating numerous new connections among different brain regions with completely distinct functional characteristics.

The myths and metaphors in which shamans lived gradually found embodiment in humanity's aspiration to objectively perceive and understand the world, not only through the psycho-spiritual revelations of certain members of the social group upon whom the rest of the individuals were highly dependent but also through two other forms of knowledge: logical deduction and experimental testing. The process of shamanism transitioning into a religion reflected a crisis in finding a common denominator among the scattered beliefs existing within the social culture. This transition essentially created a second evident branch of power in the social sphere, thereby significantly distancing spiritual and religious concepts from human consciousness.

We can offer the metaphor that the crisis of transitioning from fragmented shamanism to a consolidated religious organization is akin to the process of maturing and transitioning from early childhood to adolescence, where some aspects of infantile perception of the world are still retained, but the organization of a child's behavior in society is qualitatively different.Formally, the beginning of attempts to perceive the world through objective rational thinking can be traced back to ancient Greece and the ancient Greek philosophers, who were able to construct rational conclusions, lay the foundations for the science of logic, and serve as vivid examples of independent thinking without subordination to authoritative proof. The Socratic dialectic can be considered a clear example of this, as can the philosophical activities of Socrates' contemporaries and his disciples.

The method of understanding the world through the prism of logical deduction and experimental experience was quite new for humans at that time, and it took centuries of attempts to synthesize the irrational and rational ways of understanding the world to arrive at a relatively common ground. Similar internal tensions between philosophers and scientists continued until the 19th century.

An interesting example of such transitional thinking processes were the conclusions of the medieval Christian philosopher-thinker Augustine, who, in one of his works, pointed out "three things that God cannot do." The first is to sin; the second is to create a copy of Himself; and the third is to create a triangle whose sum of angles would exceed 180 degrees. In principle, we believe that this aphorism can be interpreted as a form of irony from Augustine, who clearly hinted that faith in the psycho-spiritual context should not exceed the boundaries set by the laws that exist in the elementary rules of logic, algebra, geometry, and other sciences.

This represents another crisis of adolescence in the understanding of reality when a child gradually becomes aware that there are real rules in the adult world, and the ability to enter it directly is linked to the ability to let go of infantile attachments to old forms of belief inherent in earlier stages of human development. However, this period passes gradually. Even scientists at the end of the 19th century could still reluctantly depart from religious notions about the structure of the world and reality.

The realization of this internal conflict is perfectly demonstrated by the slowness with which Charles Darwin entered the scientific world with his theory of evolution. In an era when, despite the existing objective methods and objective philosophy of understanding reality in the scientific world, many scientists could persist in the ideology of the creation of the world in seven days, perceiving the religious position not as a metaphor but quite literally.

Rationalization in the scientific context gained more momentum in the 19th and 20th centuries, reflecting a specific stage of civilization's development and maturation. Nevertheless, even in such ultra-objective sciences as physics, there has always been room for myth, which allowed for the construction of new hypotheses, the destruction of old dogmas, and the discovery of new unsolved mysteries of nature.

Psychotherapy, as a **science**, is situated in the overlapping space between **medicine**, **psychology**, and **philosophy**. It has formed a deeper alliance with myth due to the problematic nature of obtaining truly pure objective information, as in physics or chemistry.

Almost all existing personality theories in the fields of psychotherapy and psychology are more related to philosophy than to scientifically established facts. If we were to list the various names of well-known psychoanalysts and other psychotherapists of different orientations, we would find that the majority of their theories are based on subjective experience. They constructed their methodology for working with patients based on their subjective experience of interacting with reality.

The validity of different therapeutic approaches began to be considered a fixed statistical fact years after the spread of a particular psychotherapeutic orientation to the general public. The response to the subjectivity of one psychotherapist is met with the subjectivity of another. And very often, one can observe a clear tendency to reject the philosophy of one's opponent more due to personal reasons than objective ones.

Searching solely for the problem in the patient's pure physiology did not provide the necessary answers. The actual cause of the majority of mental disorders is almost impossible to identify with typical infectious or viral diseases. Naturally, various, sometimes mutually exclusive, theories of the emergence and formation of certain disorders arose.

For example, Ken Wilber's integrative theory allows us to consider various illnesses and peculiarities of psychological processes based on a minimum of four basic sectors:

- "**I** - Individual Interior" (subjective/experiential "I" or mind)
- "**It** - Individual Exterior" (objective/material "it" or form/body)
- "**We** - Collective Interior" (inter-subjective "we" or shared values/-culture)
- "**Its** - Collective Exterior" (inter-objective "its" social environment)

Ken Wilber's Matrix

	Interior	Exterior
Individual	**I** - Individual Interior	**It** - Individual Exterior
Collective	**We** - Collective Interior	**Its** - Collective Exterior

The "**I** - Individual Interior" sector is primarily associated with psychological processes, subjective experiences, and the world of philosophical ideas, which only partially reflect a clear objective reality. Through this sector, for example, we can examine the influence of psychological formations such as sexual complexes on the formation of behavior related to the symptomatology of various behavioral anomalies and deviations.

Discussing the internal motivation of an individual and commenting on the relationship between behavior and personality instances, such as the superego, ego, or id, without recognizing their dependence on the activity of specific brain regions, this sector creates a specific map for interpreting reality, which is more akin to religious myth, and the objectivity of experience often becomes a minor addition rather than the main pillar of the concept.

It may seem that the position of this sector is alien to modern science, but when it comes to psychology and psychotherapy, we find that this is not the case. Only a relatively small part of them is based on purely objective experience. A large amount of information is practically used without being tied to an objective criterion. And only years or decades later can precedents arise to make certain parts of the theory and practice objective.

Psychoanalysis is a vivid example of this. Its concepts of defense mechanisms have been used as ideas in practice for over 50 years without formal statistical confirmation of their validity. Most other aspects of psychoanalysis have suffered the same fate. And we are talking about a very large branch of psychotherapy that has been studied by hundreds of medical scientists for decades. The form of verbal therapy, based on the philosophical conclusions and observations of Freud and his disciples, determined the way of looking at mental disorders and interacting with them.

Debates regarding the etiology of various mental disorders continue to this day between subjectively oriented analysts and objectively oriented physiologists, whose opinions converge very slowly and gradually. For example, a psychoanalyst, in the course of several decades of practice, observes that people with schizophrenia develop specific relationships with their mothers, which may predispose them to the emergence and course of symptoms. The analyst can refine their interpretation and profiling skills to the point where they can confidently describe the peculiarities of a person's relationships with parental figures and the specifics of their development simply by observing their behavior for a few minutes. Their map constantly validates itself with new experience gained in their work.However, when we try to statistically and critically record this information, we sometimes find that what the analyst does is more of an art than a science. It is similar to teaching someone how to draw. You can teach someone to draw well, but it is extremely difficult to determine the specific criteria present in the paintings of Salvador Dali, Paul Renoir, Edgar Degas, or Vincent van Gogh in order to pass on the inherent talent of the master to someone else.

Similar problems have often arisen in psychotherapy in the field of hypnotic suggestion, where various researchers have tried to discover statistics on how many people are capable of entering a hypnotic trance and how many are not. What we know from our practice is that the quality of hypnotic suggestion is influenced by a significant number of criteria inherent in both the hypnotherapist and the patient, as well as the environment in which they are located. The method of work itself and the duration of hypnotization will significantly affect the quality of hypnotic suggestion.

If we want to obtain truly objective data in this context, we may encounter a number of difficulties. The psychopathological profile of the hypnotized individual is one of the key stumbling blocks. Since the depth of the hypnotic trance that can be induced in a person depends on their psychopathological profile, it can be a determining factor when collecting accurate statistics in this context. For example, based on our observations, individuals with a demonstrative accentuation of personality can be hypnotized in one form or another in almost 100% of cases, while individuals with paranoid accentuation are rarely hypnotizable or only enter a shallow trance. These accentuations depend on the activity of different brain regions.

If we create statistics on the percentage of hypnotizable individuals without providing data on how many people in the sample have specific accentuations, our data may formally tell us nothing. It may only provide very generalized information that is difficult to apply in practice.

We have observed that in many countries, the main concepts of recognized therapeutic approaches in the medical community may have a philosophical-practical inclination or contradict certain aspects of the basic traditional medical model of interpreting physiological processes. Humanistic, existential, transpersonal, and other psychotherapy approaches can serve as explicit examples.The effectiveness of therapy itself is often measured after a certain period of time following its implementation in clinical conditions. There are remarkable examples in the history of psychology and psychotherapy where psychologists, medical professionals, and therapists who have gained recognition in their field and whose methods have been approved for use by various medical institutions in many countries can center their perspectives not only on abstract philosophical concepts but also on elements of ancient shamanism and religious traditions. The theories of synchronicity and archetypes by Carl Jung, for instance, stand as vivid examples.

In these theories, the concept of the interconnectedness of various events unfolding in space and time, inherent in shamanistic beliefs, and the image of the primordial form through which notions of the divine are glimpsed, become central in different aspects of therapeutic practice.

Stanislav Grof, a psychiatrist with over 50 years of experience, describes in his books examples of thousands of his patients experiencing perinatal events. Neurologists in any country may argue that pre-birth experiences cannot be accurately recorded in the brain due to the lack of myelination of the axons in the cerebral cortex. And this is not to mention his descriptions of patients' experiences of past incarnations, which currently do not fit within the framework of the scientific paradigm.

This is what we are dealing with. There are numerous accounts of patients' experiences. Through analyzing this experience, we can draw conclusions and generalizations that can form a solid foundation for psychotherapeutic practice. However, as soon as a psychotherapist, similar to Jung or Grof, attempts to relate their findings to existing understandings of consciousness and the body in today's science, we find that complete integration is often unattainable, especially in key aspects of the theories. And we are talking about two medical professionals, titans of psychotherapy in the last 100 years. If we were to comment on psychologists and philosophers who have made significant contributions to the development of psychotherapy, we would often find even less inclination from them to seek a connection between the practical philosophy of psychotherapy and strict physiological criteria. This is an obvious fact that is often overlooked.

However, this indicates that their practical philosophy is directly related to the "**I** - Individual Interior" sector, as defined by Ken Wilber. What can be attributed to objective physiological, chemical, and other scientific criteria, according to Wilber, needs to be considered through the second sector of his matrix, the "**It** - Individual Exterior" sector.It is within this sector that modern medicine attempts to describe the majority of existing illnesses, attributing them to the activity of bacteria, viruses, infections, and injuries, while carefully avoiding abstract philosophical concepts of morality, defense mechanisms of the psyche, unconscious complexes, and similar aspects that belong to the "**I** - Individual Interior" sector.

The sector of the "**It** - Individual Exterior" is easier to deal with; it encompasses scientific facts from pure sciences. Most people consider the facts in this sector to be scientifically valid, accurate, and correct. It is within this sector that we can create experiments that can be reproduced by others. This sector does not accept mere personal observation of things that cannot be observed repeatedly by others.

For example, the work of a psychotherapist is mostly one-on-one, where the therapist, using elementary processes of induction and deduction, may attempt to map out the manifestation of symptoms and cognitive errors created by the individual and identify causal relationships between the present and the past in order to understand what may currently condition the symptom. For instance, psychoanalysis by S. Freud was created based on such observations, conclusions, and inferences.

If we try to examine it through the lens of the "**It** - Individual Exterior" sector, it would appear to us as practical philosophy with no connection to real scientific facts. However, as soon as we attempt to translate its key terms into the language of neurophysiology, it can reveal itself to us in a new, unexpected, and truly scientific guise. For instance, the concept of the moral super-ego can be interpreted as the left prefrontal cortex, associated with the ability to exhibit volitional qualities, maintain socially acceptable behavior, set goals, and achieve them. The concept of the "Id", interpreted in psychoanalysis as a complex of unconscious aggressive and sexual impulses, may find its neurophysiological parallel in the activity of the hypothalamus, primarily responsible for aggressive, sexual, and feeding behaviors. The concept of rapport in hypnosis can be interpreted as the manifestation of the activity of the trust neurotransmitter oxytocin. The sense of empathy will find its analog in the activity of the anterior cingulate gyrus of the brain, while depressive disorders will correspond to a decrease in the levels of dopamine and serotonin neurotransmitters. Anxiety and fear will be linked to the hyperactivity of the amygdala and adrenal glands, which synthesize adrenaline.Thus, we see that each sector is akin to a language of communication in which people belonging to various professional orientations are accustomed to conversing. However, the ability to view any personality or bodily process through the prism of different interpretive languages inherent in different sectors opens up a vast number of new possibilities and space for synthesizing the experiences of generations with diverse professional orientations. We observe that each sector merely operates as a language for interpreting reality, not reality itself. Even what we consider scientifically recognized facts are nothing more than a way to talk about a particular fragment of reality.

Gregory Bateson considered a sign of madness in a person their certainty that one interpretation of the world can be the ultimate truth, and he regarded the criterion of normality and sanity as the ability to use at least two different maps of reality in everyday life. Equating interpretation with reality is akin to equating a restaurant menu with real food. Following this principle, in our work, we will strive to examine psychotherapy through the prism of four different sectors, which formally serve as distinct maps for describing reality and between which bridges should have long been built. Unfortunately, the overwhelming majority of textbooks on psychotherapy currently view it through the lens of the first or second sector—the "**I** - Individual Interior" and the "**It** - Individual Exterior", which significantly reduces its meaningful aspects and potential. Psychotherapy is rarely considered in the context of the third and fourth sectors: the "**We** - Collective Interior", which allows for seeing the socio-cultural prerequisites for the formation of mental disorders, and the "**Its** - Collective Exterior", which reveals the influence of the political and economic system in a country on people's mental health and how changes in these spheres can condition its improvement or deterioration. The

"**We** - Collective Interior" sector can provide a unique way of viewing the diversity of symptoms through the lens of cultural values. What may be a soul ailment in one nation may be deemed completely appropriate and normal behavior in another. Values and beliefs can not only differ depending on culture but can sometimes have completely opposite or reverse interpretations. Any attempt to understand the pathological nature of a person's behavior based on the values of a single culture (for example, Western or Eastern) will lead to a reduced and narrow understanding of the subject. Similar to the dimensions of the four basic sectors by Ken Wilber, within the cultural sector, one can attempt to form a meta-cultural perspective on symptoms and their treatment, not based on the ideology of a single culture but by comparing one culture to another and trying to understand which system of therapeutic beliefs may better correspond to different ethnic characteristics. Such integration into a meta-positive position is, in my opinion, a natural evolutionary step in the development of the psychotherapeutic process.

The position of theoretical synthesis will primarily aim to create a kind of Integrative Operational System within the psychotherapist's consciousness, enabling the practical integration of theoretical developments in completely different areas of activity and finding ways to shape the psychotherapeutic process at various levels: psychological, philosophical, medical, chemical, cultural, sociological, economic, and political.

The subject matter of the fourth sector—the "**Its** - Collective Exterior" for psychotherapy—is somewhat of a "dark forest," yet it is precisely the state of a large social system in a country that fractally reflects the health of smaller fractals within the system, such as the sum of cultures existing in the country, families within different cultures, and individuals within the family system. The fractal organization of this structure can provide not only a unique perspective and multidimensional perception of the problem context but also enable the transfer of practical methods from one context to another.

Let's consider a vivid example: Few people realize that the relationships between the leader of a large system and their subordinates generally reflect the psychodynamics of each family system belonging to the larger system. The attitude towards the father figure in a family extends to the male boss in a company; colleagues often project sibling transferences if the individual has any, and subordinates may reflect children's dynamics. This is a highly generalized model of representation in which there are numerous interpretative criteria, but the direction of attention alone can create an entirely new methodology for relationships. In such a methodology, a psychotherapeutic method aimed at correcting the neurotic condition of an individual can lead to constructive changes, for example, in the economic and political state of the country. This may initially sound utopian, but in our work, we will strive to conduct a detailed analysis of the possibility of drawing such parallels, which makes this work interesting not only for psychologists, psychotherapists, and medical professionals but also for a wide range of readers.

The next issue we will address in the context of this book series is the positioning of verbal psychotherapy as a distinct professional path that is only partially related to medicine, psychology, sociology, philosophy, anthropology, and cybernetics. More precisely, it has direct relevance to them but at the same time, it stands apart from them.

As we have come to realize from Ken Wilber's concept, the process of education in the psychology faculty pays much more attention to the "**I** - Individual Interior" sector, while in medical school, it focuses on the "**It** - Individual Exterior." A psychologist will have philosophical notions about symptoms, whereas a medical professional will focus on physiological aspects. An anthropologist will provide us with abundant information from the cultural context "**We** - Collective Interior," while legal experts and economists will contribute from the broader social perspective "**Its** - Collective Exterior."

In our view, it is only through the integration of multiple sectors that we can arrive at the most effective methods of work. Therefore, it is necessary to establish the profession of psychotherapist as a separate category, encompassing the best aspects related to this subject from psychology, medicine, philosophy, and other disciplines while excluding topics unrelated to psychotherapy within those disciplines. To the best of our knowledge, such separation and segregation of the psychotherapist profession are gradually being implemented in some universities in various Western countries. The pace at which this trend will reach other regions of the world is unknown, but in my opinion, at least theoretical attempts should be made to initiate movement in this direction.Another interesting piece of evidence supporting this concept is that some renowned leaders and creators of various psychotherapy methods are medical professionals, while others are psychologists. On the one hand, we can observe the tendency of medical professionals to confine psychotherapy strictly within their realm of competence. However, paradoxically, we also witness the same medical professionals applying methods and techniques developed by psychologists in clinical settings. I have witnessed numerous such situations. In this case, it is clearly necessary to abandon double standards and recognize the specificity of psychotherapeutic knowledge as interdisciplinary and integrative.

In this work, I would like to apply a slightly unconventional approach to exploring the main themes of psychotherapeutic science. Most often, textbooks on general psychotherapy simply provide a list of existing therapeutic schools: who created them, what is their history of development, and what are their basic theoretical concepts and technical arsenal? Their analytical comparison and the evident fact that different types of psychotherapy are more suitable and appropriate for treating certain disorders while less suitable for others are usually overlooked. Another problem is the criteria for selecting which directions in psychotherapy to include in the textbook, considering that as of 2000, over 700 directions in psychotherapy were registered worldwide. A textbook is not elastic, and typically, it can adequately accommodate only 10–15 of the most popular directions, with brief mentions of some others. I have chosen a slightly different style of presentation, where we examine vectors of psychotherapy within the books of the series instead of focusing on specific directions.

In my view, a vector represents a category that can include a group of therapeutic directions sharing key values and beliefs, forming the basis for the theoretical framework and technical arsenal of a particular method. Many dozens of different therapy schools can be encompassed within a single psychotherapeutic vector.

Conversely, one therapy school may utilize different vectors. A simple example would be the cognitive and behavioral vectors, which employ entirely distinct theoretical and practical foundations. However, the resulting intersection of these schools, such as cognitive-behavioral therapy, can be interpreted through the prism of both corresponding vectors.

Some integrative forms of psychotherapy, like NLP-psychotherapy, can integrate almost all known vectors, allowing for the application of multidisciplinary psychotherapeutic methodologies. On the other hand, we can observe schools that are exclusively tailored to one psychotherapeutic vector, rejecting the methodologies of others. Whether this is good or bad remains a philosophical question.However, in our work, which aims to adopt an integrative approach to the diversity of experiences, we will accept and consider all existing paradigms in psychotherapy as viable and acceptable to varying degrees. At the same time, one significant factor is the personality of the psychotherapist who applies a given method, filtering and refracting it through the lens of their own personality.

In this work, we will emphasize eleven fundamental vectors of psychotherapy, which, in my opinion, are divided into five dichotomies, reflecting the fact that the conceptual basis of some vectors has a diametrically opposite focus of attention compared to others.

Furthermore, one book of the series will be dedicated to the integrative and eclectic vector in psychotherapy, capable of uniting different theoretical and practical knowledge accumulated in various psychotherapy schools.

The first such dichotomy is the psychoanalytic and hypnotic vectors in psychotherapy.

Psychoanalytic and Hypnotic Approaches

The psychoanalytic vector in psychotherapy emphasizes mindfulness and conscious introspection of past experiences. It focuses on analyzing the dynamics of morality and instinct in consciousness and behavior, rejecting suggestion as a primary therapeutic method. On the other hand, the hypnotic vector, in its original form, prioritizes suggestion as the main catalyst for change and often overlooks psychodynamics and preceding trauma in relation to symptoms. Some practitioners attempted to merge analytical principles with hypnosis, leading to the development of methods like hypnoanalysis. However, conflicts emerged as different practitioners held opposing views and approaches.

For instance, Pierre Janet, an opponent of Freud, employed hypnoanalysis to work with a young girl experiencing painful menstrual periods. Through hypnotic regression, Janet discovered that the girl associated her first period with something bad and dirty. In an extreme attempt to relieve the pain, she immersed herself in cold water. Although her periods ceased temporarily, they returned as heavy and painful when she was 15. Janet decided to implant false memories by suggesting that she had only stood next to the barrel during that incident. Surprisingly, the pain syndrome disappeared during her next menstrual period. Janet's unconventional approach sparked controversy, with critics accusing him of practicing therapy through lies, contrasting it with Freud's emphasis on acknowledging the truth.

Non-analytically oriented hypnotherapists often construct hypnotherapy based on suggestion, guiding the patient from the problematic context to an opposite state. Hypnotherapist K. K. Platonov, for example, describes a case where he induced a severely depressed man, whose wife had left him, into a hypnotic state. Platonov then suggested that the patient should redirect his attention to the future, stop thinking about his ex-wife, seek a new partner, and find joy in life. This approach disregards psychoanalytic psychodynamics entirely. Nevertheless, practitioners like Platonov have reported successful hypnotic interventions and observed long-term positive dynamics in their patients, validating the effectiveness of their work.

The existence of contradictory beliefs and practices in different psychotherapy systems highlights the challenge of determining absolute truth. Ken Wilber, through a comparative analysis of various schools of psychology and psychotherapy, proposes an integrative model that accepts different, sometimes conflicting, beliefs as elements of a spectrum. Each therapeutic approach possesses its own validity within a specific range of meanings. Like different colors of a rainbow, various theories and practices in psychotherapy serve as maps, each representing a unique perspective. When viewed collectively, they offer different lenses through which to understand the world, contributing to a common meta-meaning.

In conclusion, the field of psychotherapy encompasses diverse approaches and perspectives, each with its own value and relevance. The integrative model encourages the utilization of various therapeutic theories and techniques, similar to different medical treatments that prove most effective when applied in appropriate contexts. Recognizing that each theory represents a piece of the broader psychotherapeutic landscape allows for a comprehensive understanding and application of different approaches.

Provocative and Humanistic Therapies

Humanistic psychotherapy, created by Carl Rogers as an alternative to authoritarian psychoanalysis and behaviorism, became part of the broader humanistic movement in America in the mid-1960s and early 1970s. This period witnessed a gradual rejection of segregation based on race and sexual orientation. It was a time of hippies, LSD-25, marijuana, and a refusal to participate in the military in favor of love and world peace. Practices such as yoga, Buddhism, and Hinduism gained popularity. Overall, it was a tangible manifestation of democracy.

Rogers changed the term "patient" to "client," metaphorically comparing psychotherapy to a dance in which the client leads. He believed that all the necessary resources for change already exist within the client, and the therapist's role is simply to provide conditions of acceptance, warm support, and tissue paper. These changes were widely accepted and became particularly popular as they embodied the spirit of humanization.

However, the limitations of humanistic methods in addressing severe neurotic and psychotic disorders were soon realized. Nonetheless, the humanistic approach was crucial at that time to counter the oppressive nature of authoritarianism in psychotherapy and introduce a new element into the spectrum of therapeutic communication. Paradoxically, this rebellion within the humanistic tradition gave rise to another rebellion, led by a figure named Frank Farrelly.

Farrelly, a psychiatrist, began experimenting with deliberately non-humanistic methods, which he later referred to as "provocative." He infused humor and irony into psychotherapy, turning therapy sessions into unique stand-up acts. He eliminated pompousness but reintroduced authority in a sarcastic manner, finding that many humanistic principles, such as empathy, acceptance, and respect, when turned inside out, could yield remarkably strong and original results. Contrary to expectations, he emphasized the contradictory and multifaceted nature of human beings.

Independently of Farrelly, the American hypnotherapist Milton Erickson also employed provocative methods, albeit in a different way. Erickson primarily used provocative situations or assignments that involved specific post-hypnotic suggestions, rather than engaging in direct provocative dialogue with his patients. While Farrelly openly challenged schizophrenics in hospitals, provoking them to realize that there are people even more insane than themselves, including their psychiatrist, Erickson would adapt to an aggressive girl in a ward, joining her in tearing apart bed sheets and ripping the heating radiator from the wall. Then, in agreement with the nurse, he would tear off the girl's gown in the corridor, provoking her to exclaim that such behavior is likely not allowed. The styles differ slightly, but the essence remains the same. It is worth noting that Erickson never referred to his method as "provocative."

Another notable dichotomy, both in terms of meaning and approach, can be observed between behavioral psychotherapy on one side and existential psychotherapy and transpersonal therapy on the other. While the latter is not a mere copy of the former, it largely embodies the same spirit of psychotherapy, exploring philosophical, abstract, spiritual, and transpersonal realms.

Behavioral and Existential, Transpersonal Therapies

Here we can gradually begin to note that the overwhelming majority of psychotherapy approaches emerged in opposition to their predecessors. Psychoanalysis emerged as a rebellion against hypnotic suggestion, behaviorism as a rebellion against psychoanalysis, humanism as a rebellion against psychoanalysis and behaviorism, and the existential and transpersonal movements as a rebellion against the excessive materialism of psychoanalysis and behaviorism. It is difficult not to recognize that opposition is the driving force behind progress. However, until it starts to seriously contradict objective reality by asserting that the methodology of one school is true and all others are harmful, it remains a valid point. It should be added that the opposition between two other approaches—cognitive and somatic—can significantly influence an individual's mental state. Cognitive therapists focus on cognitive errors made by people in the thinking process, while somatic psychotherapists become preoccupied with releasing the patient's muscular armor and assisting in the expression of various suppressed emotions that form the basis of neurotic and even psychotic processes.Behavioral therapy formally began with an experiment conducted on an 11-month-old boy named Albert. This experiment resembled a form of abuse, and it is unlikely that it could be conducted in the modern scientific world for ethical reasons. The boy was shown a white rat and then subjected to strong, fear-inducing strikes on a metal gong behind him. After a certain number of repetitions of this procedure, the boy started crying at the sight of the rat without the gong strikes. His negative reactions extended to inanimate, white, fluffy objects.

Scientists have concluded that the reverse process is possible, and they are capable of instilling positive states into previously recorded negative reactions. All of this is in line with the philosophy of radical behavioral reductionism, which denies the existence of anything in consciousness that cannot be seen, heard, or felt. Reductionist behavioral theories in psychotherapy found their place largely thanks to the ultra-objective theories of this method and the ability of these methods to bring about actual changes in the personalities of patients. However, without taking into account the multidimensionality of personality, the value-motivational apparatus, the goals of the individual, and their emotions, the behavioral method could sometimes transform from psychotherapy into a rather sophisticated form of abuse. This happened in the 1950s with aversive-reversive therapy, which was actively attempted in Europe and America for the treatment of homosexuality. At that time, individuals accused of homosexuality were given the opportunity, or rather forced, to undergo aversive-reversive therapy, in which they were induced to vomit and subjected to electric shocks while being shown images of naked people of the same sex as themselves and then forced to masturbate to images of people of the opposite sex. If we consider this method now, it is quite easy to conclude that success in some cases is possible only if the homosexual individual consciously desires to reshape their symptoms. However, this procedure, as far as we know, was often involuntary. Moreover, the coercive format not only failed to change a person's sexual orientation but could also lead to significant additional problems.

Currently, some outdated behavioral methods are still being used in certain clinics. However, more often than not, this approach is combined with other styles of psychotherapy, such as cognitive and hypnotic techniques.The existential and transpersonal dimensions of psychotherapy focus on exploring deep philosophical and psycho-spiritual meanings that exist within the patient's personality (if such meanings can be discovered). Although each dimension touches upon slightly different sectors of therapeutic work, existential therapy primarily emphasizes the attempt to create a special high-level abstract meaning of life that can organize the individual's personality and enable more effective regulation of emotional states.

The awareness of beliefs and values related to death, isolation, freedom, inner emptiness, love, and wholeness permeates the existential approach, transforming the psychotherapeutic session into a philosophical conversation—an intricate, sophisticated, and sometimes elevated discourse, which, however, often remains inaccessible to certain clients due to either their low intellectual level or underdeveloped abstract thinking, which are frequently synonymous. Human rationality is directly linked to the ability to generalize acquired information through experience or observation into abstract categories. The great meaning of life reflects these abstractions.

For some individuals, an abstract understanding of life must be reached independently through conversation and reflection. Others yearn for the sharing of abstract concepts by those around them. This should simply be accepted as an objective reality. Consequently, it is rare to find existential psychotherapy applied in clinical settings where rapid and clear procedures are necessary to accommodate the flow of patients. Moreover, it should be noted that the existential dimension is often absent from these procedures. Instead, there are specific meanings that require attention and rules of interaction with the patient to achieve the desired effect.

Some authors who pioneered existential psychotherapy gained their experience and insights under harsh circumstances. For instance, Viktor Frankl, an Austrian psychiatrist, neurologist, and psychologist, was imprisoned in three Nazi concentration camps from 1942 to 1945. During his time in the camps, he devoted almost all his efforts to assisting fellow inmates while secretly working against the Nazis. In such conditions, Frankl discovered that people are driven and maintain their will to live not only by their sexual desires or the pursuit of power but also by the search for meaning in their existence, which becomes a determining factor for survival on the brink of life and death. Frankl believed that an objective perspective on the suffering endured could help individuals survive in difficult situations. In 1945, he was liberated from the concentration camp by Allied forces, and in 1946, he became the head of the Vienna

Neurological Clinic. The work he did in the camp provided him with a strong impetus for the development of his theory, which he successfully put into practice.Despite the remarkable theoretical and philosophical developments in existential therapy, in our subjective opinion, it is only applicable to a portion of patients who are willing to undergo change on a high philosophical and abstract level. At the same time, it is essential to acknowledge that the pure application of various psychotherapeutic approaches can yield similar results: good applicability to individuals possessing a particular personality profile, while showing almost complete inadaptability to representatives of other profiles.

A striking example of such a mismatch can be found in some theories of gestalt psychotherapy, where its founder, Frederick Perls, encountered patients with schizoid profiles—individuals who primarily live through cognitive processes rather than bodily sensations and emotions—and referred to them as "paper people," often refusing to work with them as a result. Sigmund Freud set very high intellectual requirements for undergoing psychoanalysis. In the realm of hypnotic suggestion, individuals suffering from paranoid disorders often do not receive the necessary help. Hypnotherapists, with great sympathy and enthusiasm, will speak more about hysteroid and demonstrative personalities than about paranoids, who, in 99% of cases, are incapable of entering a full hypnotic state.In an attempt to create a map of an integrative theoretical approach in psychotherapy, we have discovered that different approaches correspond well to different psychopathological profiles and are largely oriented towards some of them. Understanding this correlation can be a great help in forming a complex set of meta-beliefs that reveal the methodology of the correct profile-based application of therapeutic toolsets inherent in various schools of psychotherapy. In our work, we will pay much attention to this theme so that the reader can grasp key concepts about the combination of methods with different profile characteristics. However, it is worth emphasizing that it is not the vector or school of psychotherapy that engages in treatment but rather the doctor, psychologist, or philosopher who filters the method through the prism of their own personality. The personal factor in psychotherapy greatly influences the process and must be taken into account.

In the transpersonal vector, we can see attempts to integrate Western and Eastern philosophies into a unified concept that can be applied for psychotherapeutic purposes. In this vector, the attitude towards ancient forms of philosophy and religion is based on the perception of them as different forms of protopsychology and their ability to partly serve as theoretical and practical foundations for this method of psychotherapeutic practice. Due to this, the methodology of transpersonal psychotherapy may deviate from notions of rationality and scientificity. Although at times the excessive esotericism of transpersonal psychotherapy is nothing more than an alternative description of reality, it can suit individuals who share it perfectly.

The module in psychotherapy associated with the transpersonal aspect was established by Carl Gustav Jung, who started propagating his concepts about the collective unconscious and its archetypes in the early 20th century. Jung describes an interesting case from his practice when he worked at the Burghölzli Clinic. One patient suffering from schizophrenia beckoned him to the window, pointed at the sun, and began talking about seeing a solar phallus hanging from the sun and being surrounded by a solar wind.

Jung remembered his patient's strange fantasies and returned to them about five years later. Archaeologists discovered a hidden library in Egypt, and the manuscripts found there were sent to various scholars for research. Several such manuscripts ended up in the hands of Carl Jung.

In one of the manuscripts, Jung found a description of an ancient ritual performed by a priest of the Mithras cult, which was active in the East before the rise of Christianity. In this description, Jung found phrases that perfectly matched the schizophrenic patient's fantasies from Burghölzli. It depicted the sun that he was looking at, the solar phallus hanging from it, and the solar wind blowing it.For Jung, this situation was similar to the story of Isaac Newton, who had an apple fall on his head and, according to legends, "discovered" the gravitational force of the Earth. After this incident, Jung began to discover that what had previously been considered the nonsensical delusions of mentally ill individuals could be very clear material, which the patients themselves most likely couldn't have known with a high probability.

Jung observed many similar coincidences, which led him to actively study religion and alchemy in order to effectively recognize and find correspondences between the experiences of patients and the structural elements of myths and legends. Later, Jung discovered that the collective unconscious could actively manifest itself through the prism of dreams, which could be subjected to analysis.

However, Jung never referred to his work as transpersonal psychotherapy. One of the formal pioneers of both transpersonal psychology and psychotherapy can be considered Stanislav Grof, who, as a medical doctor and Freudian psychoanalyst, came to a similar understanding and representation of the intrapersonal processes of patients while working with holotropic breathwork. Observing the states described by patients after undergoing holotropic psychotherapy, he became increasingly convinced of Jung's correctness, his concepts of the collective unconscious, and the manifestation of archetypes in each individual. The key was the altered state of consciousness during mental illness, patients' dreams, or other altered states of consciousness produced by specific breathing techniques.

The anti-psychiatric vector has a strong inclination towards existential philosophy. It pays a lot of attention to the idea of illness as an alternative form of health that has not found constructive socialization.

Cognitive and Somatic Therapies

The creator of cognitive psychotherapy is Aaron Beck, who introduced the concept that patients create certain cognitive errors in their thinking process, distorting their behavior and the states they experience. Cognitive psychotherapy aims to change and transform such incorrect and illogical thoughts and beliefs in individuals, as well as various forms of stereotyping that may occur in perception. A cognitive psychotherapist can help a patient reformulate old thinking strategies or develop better ones that lead to more constructive, positive states and personal balance. Unlike psychoanalytically oriented therapists, cognitive psychotherapists pay much less attention to early childhood experiences and focus the therapy process on the present. The way you think and perceive reality at this moment is the primary focus of attention in their work. In my opinion, cognitive psychotherapy and its methods are more effective as a complement to psychoanalytic work than contradicting it. Aaron Beck's cognitive therapy is one of the most recognized in the scientific community and finds wide application in clinical practice.

Albert Ellis's Rational-Emotive Therapy, which developed separately and independently from Beck's cognitive psychotherapy, largely duplicates its key focuses of attention and principles of work. Ellis placed much more emphasis on finding cognitive process characteristics universal to all disorders, while Aaron Beck tried to differentiate different pathological conditions based on the content of cognitive processes.

An interesting psychotherapist who significantly developed and complemented the methods of cognitive therapy is Donald Meichenbaum, who, in his works, sought to draw on the ideas of L.S. Vygotsky and A.R. Luria. He created a specific method of self-instructions based on the use of inner dialogue to balance behavioral reactions. He applied this method to reshape the behavior of children with hyperactive and impulsive behaviors. In his research, he attempted to teach schizophrenic patients to engage in a "healthy conversation" by modifying their cognitive patterns. The initial stages of this process involved a symbol-digit test and the Porteus Maze Test of non-verbal intelligence. Patients gradually learned to use self-regulating statements in their everyday lives. As one set of skills was consolidated, new exercises were introduced, such as proverb tests and interviews. Meichenbaum taught his patients to first evaluate their behavior on a specific scale and then, if the assessment was unsatisfactory, instruct themselves to achieve the desired comfortable behavior.

The somatic direction in psychotherapy originated with one of Sigmund Freud's disciples, Wilhelm Reich, who initially worked using traditional

Freudian concepts of the psychoanalytic process and later began developing his own theoretical and practical concepts for conducting psychotherapy.

Wilhelm Reich's theory of muscular armor has become one of the fundamental concepts in most branches of body-oriented psychotherapy. Reich viewed any neurotic process and its associated defense mechanisms, such as repression, suppression, and denial, as a complex of muscular tensions existing within the body. These tensions are caused by emotions, states, experiences, and desires that have been suppressed at various stages of the patient's life. The therapist's goal in this case was to gradually release this tension, aiming to form a balanced, or, as Reich called it, genital personality. The emphasis on genitality was largely connected to Reich's belief that sexual suppression is the key process leading to neurosis. However, Reich also considered seven zones in the human body that, to varying degrees, can block the expression of different emotions and states through their tension.

Later on, Reich began developing various new concepts, such as the theory of orgone energy existing in the human body, which, in theoretical terms, closely resembled Anton Mesmer's concept of magnetic fluid transmitted from the mesmerist to the patient for the purpose of healing.

Reich even designed specific devices intended to accumulate and transmit this energy to patients. However, such an invention was not recognized within the scientific community.

Wilhelm Reich's personality, like many of his inventions, is ambiguous. Nevertheless, it is clear that his works made a significant contribution to the development of psychotherapy in general and its body-oriented forms in particular.

Numerous direct and indirect disciples of Wilhelm Reich continued the development of his theoretical concepts and practical methods. Among the most well-known are Franz Alexander, the creator of psychosomatic psychoanalysis, as well as Alexander Lowen, the founder of bioenergetic analysis, Marion Rosen, the founder of the Rosen Method, and Ida Rolf, the creator of Rolfing.

In addition to Wilhelm Reich, an interesting method of body physiotherapy and psychotherapy was developed by physicist and judo practitioner Moshe Feldenkrais. His method initially originated as an attempt at self-physiotherapy when, after refusing surgery on his injured knee, he began independently developing rehabilitation techniques and conscious movement. After some time, he started sharing his discoveries with colleagues and others, conducting lectures and training courses related to the topic of rehabilitation. His restorative practice allowed him to return to judo training at the Budokwai dojo in London. Over time, his method found its place both in clinical physio-rehabilitation and body-oriented psychotherapy.

The Feldenkrais Method provides a unique opportunity to work with the muscular framework of the human body in a special way. Feldenkrais discovered that by working with slow movements and minimal physical intervention on the body and its specific segments, tensions hidden within the body can be quickly and effectively released, subsequently revealing the emotions existing behind the muscular framework. Some exercises of the method can be performed as dynamic individual exercises, while others require the practitioner to work directly with the patient.

At first glance, it may seem that the method is not capable of bringing anything exceptional to the transformative dynamics of the mind and body. However, the effectiveness of the method can indeed be remarkable, and brief manipulation of the patient's body can serve as a catalyst for personality change. It is unlikely, however, that this method can fully replace the psychotherapeutic process; rather, it can serve as an excellent complement and instrumental foundation for transformative body practices.

Each body therapy method possesses its own unique qualities and characteristics, but ultimately, they utilize similar principles that allow for the exploration of various facets of a person's mental and physical potential.

Psychodrama and Pharmaceutical, Psychedelic Therapies

The starting point for drama therapy in psychotherapy can be traced back to the beginning of the 20th century when, independent of other psychotherapeutic traditions, the psychologist, psychiatrist, and sociologist Jacob Moreno created an original method of psychotherapy based on the theatrical context. This context provides an opportunity to integrate multi-level communication into the practice of psychotherapy, implying a deeper level of self-communication, more precisely, with different parts of one's own personality. It enables the ability to establish a specific type of contact with various group participants in a form that is not accessible in ordinary social communication, allowing the expression of emotions that are usually not fully conveyed. It facilitates a dissociated, detached understanding of the current life context and enables a higher level of awareness.

Additionally, as the creator of the method, Jacob Moreno stated, "to encounter the world in both its social and cosmic meanings." Presumably, by the term "cosmic meaning," Moreno meant the attainment of changes in personality at more abstract and global levels that can transform a person's identity, rather than just a specific pattern of reaction.

Moreno named his therapy method "psychodrama," which translates literally as "the action of the soul." The key distinction between psychodrama and other methods was that it was not a typical conversational form of psychotherapy. The essential aspect of the transformative therapeutic process was the observed or performed action.The psychodramatic format of work, in many ways, became an opposition to other therapeutic methods of that time and formed a matrix of therapeutic interaction of an entirely different type. Based on this matrix, similar forms of psychotherapy were subsequently developed, relying on a dramatic mode of work. According to Moreno, the most similar types of psychotherapy to psychodrama are Virginia Satir's "family sculpture" and Bert Hellinger's "family constellations," which may significantly differ in their theoretical and practical foundations. These methods should not be classified as imitative since their literal adoption was either incomplete or absent altogether. For example, Virginia Satir, whom some call the "Mother of Family Therapy," initially used the dramatic context to enact various emotional situations in a family undergoing therapy. In cases where a family member was absent, she would simply involve another group participant to obtain a more comprehensive and dramatic picture. During group psychotherapeutic dramatic interactions, Satir focused less on spontaneity and improvisation. More often, she authoritatively established fixed positions for each participant in the therapeutic enactment and determined the speech constructs that one participant had to express to another. Occasionally, during the process, she would begin explaining the fundamental dynamics of the present moment and the specific changes that might be necessary for the psychotherapeutic changes to take effect. In the vast majority of cases, Satir utilized her dramatic method to resolve family conflicts.

Family constellations, developed by German psychotherapist Bert Hellinger, are essentially a synthesis of Jacob Moreno's psychodrama, Virginia Satir's "family sculpture," Arthur Janov's primal therapy, Milton Erickson's hypnotherapy, Kurt Lewin's group dynamics, Rupert Sheldrake's morphic field concepts, and more. In this case, we can observe the relative integrative nature of the method, but despite the various forms of theoretical and practical borrowing, the actual approach differs radically from its predecessors in many ways. The therapeutic "play" itself, in the vast majority of cases, relies on a subtle sensitivity to the roles played by the "representatives" or actors involved. Based on the information derived from the movement and sensations of the actors, the psychotherapist employs various therapeutic techniques. Sometimes, the approach can be highly directive, with the therapist dictating most of the changes according to certain principles. In other cases, the dynamics of the dramatic constellation within the group itself can serve as a model for non-directive psychotherapeutic work.The pharmaceutical vector encompasses the methodology of pharmacological treatment for various neurotic and psychotic disorders in modern medicine. Different medications are used to address a multitude of psychiatric symptoms. The full development of pharmacotherapy, which enabled the creation of various therapeutic drugs, occurred only in the mid-20th century. Prior to the 1950s, in medical practice for the treatment of mentally ill individuals and the alleviation of various neurotic and psychotic disorders, various plant-based preparations were predominantly used, such as opiates, cocaine, belladonna, and henbane. Non-plant substances such as bromides, internal calcium administration, lithium salts, antihistamines, and others were also popular. In the majority of cases, the use of pharmaceutical agents does not cure the underlying mental disorder but helps manage its symptoms and aids in the patient's socialization. Occasionally, an extended period of symptom control can assist the patient in normalizing their internal mental processes. However, it is all too common to witness individuals suffering from certain disorders who are compelled to take these medications for many years, even decades. Unfortunately, the current development of this vector does not allow for the creation of substances that effectively treat the disorder. Nevertheless, despite some negative aspects associated with the use of pharmaceutical agents, countless patients would not be able to lead even remotely normal lives without them. Furthermore, the application of these agents is often the only means to stabilize a patient's condition to a level where other psychotherapeutic methods can be applied.

The psychedelic vector encompasses theories and practical methods focused on the clinical use of substances that alter the patient's state of consciousness.

The post-psychedelic method describes therapeutic approaches that have evolved from psychedelic methods but no longer rely on chemical means to alter the patient's state of consciousness.

Integrative Therapy

This vector in psychotherapy focuses on integrating various fragmented pieces of therapeutic knowledge into a cohesive whole. At times, these fragments may inherently contradict each other at a theoretical level. When we speak of integration, we mean creating a new organized integrity from fragments of other theories and practices. In this case, the quote by martial arts master Bruce Lee, the creator of Jeet Kune Do, is highly applicable: "Absorb what is useful, discard what is not, and add what is uniquely your own."

The creators of Neuro-Linguistic Programming (NLP), Richard Bandler and John Grinder, as well as their colleagues and students, have come closest to embodying such a philosophy. Over the past 40 years, they have actively developed this approach to psychotherapy and transformed it into something greater than just psychotherapy. However, in NLP, the idea of integration was never postulated as an end in itself.

One key advocate of integration in various fields of science, religion, and specifically psychotherapy is Ken Wilber. His ideas have laid the foundation for an integrative theory that can be effectively utilized in an interdisciplinary context.

On the other hand, if we consider the philosophy of an eclectic approach, it implies using various theoretical concepts and practices in psychotherapy without attempting to unify them into a specific, comprehensive system.

Applicability of Psychopathological Profiles

In the "**Psychology and Psychotherapy: Theories and Practices**" series, I will provide a brief analysis of how the method can be applied to patients with various psychopathological profiles. These profiles often impact the effectiveness of a specific therapeutic approach.

It would be inaccurate to claim that specific methods can only be effective with individuals of a particular profile. However, practical experience indicates that certain patient personality traits are more amenable to change when specific methods are utilized.

Understanding the greater or lesser applicability of different psychotherapy vectors can help foster integrative thinking among psychotherapists, without limiting the practice to methods that may only be fully applicable in certain cases.

I will provide an analysis through the prism of eight **psychopathological profiles**:

- **Hysteroid** Profile
- **Paranoid** Profile
- **Psychopathic** Profile
- **Obsessive-Compulsive** Profile
- **Schizoid** Profile
- **Epileptoid** Profile
- **Schizophrenic** Profile
- **Manic-Depressive** Profile

2

Provocative Psychotherapy

In my opinion, the provocative psychotherapy approach is primarily influenced by the works of two American psychiatrists, Frank Farrelly and Milton Erickson.

While Farrelly focused on using sarcasm, humor, and irony when interacting with patients, Erickson's work included a wide range of techniques, not limited to the provocative approach alone, but also incorporating hypnosis. In this chapter, we will explore aspects of Erickson's work and analyze his methods of provoking patients. However, it is important to note that Erickson himself did not refer to his work as provocative. We will extensively delve into the application of Ericksonian hypnotic practices in books from the *Psychology and Psychotherapy: Theories and Practices Series*, specifically the *Hypnotherapy Fundamentals: Complete Guide* dedicated to the use of hypnosis in psychotherapy.

So, let's begin with Frank Farrelly.

Provocative Psychotherapy by Frank Farrelly

This form of psychotherapy originated in the 1960s. Farrelly, a young psychiatrist, initially practiced Carl Rogers' humanistic psychotherapy. However, through his own practice, he gradually developed a unique method that was different from others and formed his own understanding of effective psychotherapeutic work. Farrelly shared an epic story of when he began to have insights regarding the provocative approach. He was treating a married couple, where the husband had strong jealousy and believed his wife was cheating on him. She vehemently denied all accusations.

Farrelly was tasked with conducting a therapy session with the woman at her home, attempting to uncover the truth about their relationship. If she was not lying, then her husband could be diagnosed with paranoia. Frank went to the patient's home, conducted the therapy session, and noted that she behaved somewhat strangely. Her face reflected surprise and mild anxiety, and she answered questions directly. Eventually, she confessed that she had indeed been unfaithful. Frank didn't fully grasp what he was doing differently in his work that made the woman reveal what she hadn't said before.

Inspired, he returned to work, visited the restroom, and discovered that his white shirt was sticking out of his fly. It seemed that this unintentional criterion caused significant confusion for his patient and somehow made her more cooperative. He shared this incident with his colleagues, sparking hearty laughter. This incident allowed Frank to realize how creating confusion in psychotherapeutic work can influence a patient's behavior. This case was like the apple falling on Newton's head, leading to the understanding of the force of gravity.

Subsequently, he began experimenting with his ideas with different patients. In the first ten years of his practice, he worked extensively in a psychiatric clinic with psychotic patients, who often became the targets of his provocative experiments. Frank said that one day he entered the room with a group of schizophrenics who were busy on the floor.

He walked up to them and started teasing and making faces at them. They glanced at each other and began whispering anxiously, "Who let this mentally ill guy in here?" Undeterred, Frank continued to tease them. The schizophrenics asked him, "Who the hell are you?" Frank pointed to his badge, which displayed his psychiatrist credentials, and replied, "I'm a psychiatrist, and the fact that I have this identification means I'll leave the clinic today and go home, but it seems like you guys will stay here!"

In order to fully comment on Farrelli's work and explain the influence of his provocative method on patients' consciousness, it is worth digressing and commenting on some other topics.

Since Farrelli considered himself the father of humor in psychotherapy and, in my opinion, rightfully so, let us pay attention to the etymology of the word "humor" and trace its relationship to earlier times. Let us start with ancient Greece. It is from there that the word "humor" itself originated. In ancient Greece, thanks to Hippocrates, who is rightfully considered the "father of medicine," the doctrine of human temperament emerged. According to Hippocrates, a person's behavior is directly related to the balance of four bodily fluids that, in his opinion, circulate in the body - blood, yellow bile, black bile, and phlegm. Cholerics have an excess of yellow bile, which makes them impulsive. Phlegmatics have an excess of phlegm, which makes them calm and sluggish. Sanguines have an excess of blood, which makes them active and cheerful. Melancholics have an excess of black bile, which makes them sad and fearful.

In ancient Greek medicine, a person's state was described by the balance of these four bodily fluids and was called "humor." It was the proper balance of these fluids - the proper "humor" - that determined a person's health and well-being.

Different descriptions of the sense of humor can be found among various philosophers and thinkers of different eras. Let us mention some of them. For example, the Scottish philosopher D. Hume, in his essay, described a structural-logical process that can constitute a sense of humor. He referred to it as "the result of observing two or more illogical, incongruous, or absurd parts or circumstances considered to be united in one complex object or group."

In his book "The World as Will and Representation," A. Schopenhauer wrote that the two non-coinciding elements from which humor arises are a concept assimilated by us and a real object that "is conceived in this concept."

One of the first articles dedicated to humor in psychotherapy was found in Sigmund Freud's works. He named it "Humor and Its Relation to the Unconscious'' and published it in 1905. He hypothesized that humor is closely related to processes occurring in our unconscious. Like dreams, humor allows us to actualize those aspects of the unconscious that may be suppressed by the superego. Freud also divided humor into three categories, which he referred to as "joking," "comic," and "imitative." Humor creates a certain framework within which what is forbidden to express in other contexts and is prohibited by a person's superego can become acceptable and ecologically sound. Our aggressive and sexual tendencies, placed in a humorous context, can automatically be interpreted as socially acceptable.

Freud considered humor a specific "detour" through which our excessive psychic energy can be directed. According to Freud, humor is formally one of the sublimation processes of the psyche and a defense mechanism.

The English sociologist M. Malkay argues that humor serves to maintain social order by creating a special environment for expressing the contradictions that individuals encounter during socialization and active interaction with others. Malkay's theory largely coincides with Freud's views.

Evolutionary psychologist Geoffrey Miller, in his book "The Mating Mind", formulates and justifies an interesting theory stating that humor, in the context of natural sexual selection, served as a way to demonstrate intelligence. This makes humor in humans somewhat analogous to a "peacock's tail", indicating the individual's good genes.

To examine the structure of Frank Farrelly's work in more detail, we need to consider the main forms of transmitting humor that he uses in his provocative work. Most of the tools he employs are directly related to satire and are rhetorical figures of speech. These elements include irony, sarcasm, hyperbole, grotesqueness, allegory, and parody. In addition, Farrelly uses jokes, anecdotes, puns, and black humor. Let's describe them in more detail.

- **Irony**, translated from Ancient Greek as "pretense," is a satirical device in which the true meaning is concealed and contradicts the apparent observation. Irony is most often manifested through the contrast between verbal and non-verbal messages. For example, a phrase could be: "Oh yes, now you clearly understand me" (said when the interlocutor makes another mistake in a task). This phrase is spoken with a harsh, aggressive, or contemptuous tone. Farrelly is a master of playing with irony. For instance, when a patient tells him that they are going to achieve something, Farrelly asks, "Who?! You?!"—and does so with a manner and voice that clearly indicates his strong doubts about their ability to succeed in any way.

- **Sarcasm**, translated from Ancient Greek as "tearing of flesh," is one of the satirical techniques and is interpreted as a caustic mockery, the highest degree of irony, reinforced by an immediate intention to express the implied meaning. Sarcasm differs from irony in that it contains an expression of the highest degree of disapproval and even hatred. A brilliant example of sarcasm is Albert Einstein's phrase: "Two things are infinite: the universe and human stupidity. Of course, I'm not so sure about the universe." A notable example of sarcasm in Frank Farrelly's practice is the case of a woman who complained to him about not having enough energy to finish her dissertation. Frank began looking at her slight plumpness and pointed out why she didn't need to rush and could stay in place, gaining fat. He commented that men love fat women because they are faithful wives, and furthermore, they have a range of advantages, such as providing warmth in winter and shade in summer with their layers of fat.

- **Hyperbole** is a stylistic figure of explicit and intentional exaggeration aimed at emphasizing a specific meaning. Simple examples of hyperbole include phrases like "I've heard it a million times," "We've known each other for a hundred years," "Fast as lightning," and so on. Farrelly often uses hyperbole to exaggerate or diminish certain qualities of the patient's personality or behavior. Naturally, the use of hyperbole in provocative therapy goes hand in hand with irony and sarcasm.

- **Grotesque**, translated from French as "bizarre" or "comic," is a variety of artistic imagery that focuses on the bizarre and contrasting combination of the real and the fantastic, the comic and the horrible, the sublime and the grotesque, etc. A splendid example of literary grotesqueness is Hofmannn's novella "Little Zaches, nicknamed Zinnober." A direct example of the psychotherapeutic use of the grotesque by Frank Farrelly is the case he described when he had to start working with a very obese woman who underwent extensive physiological and psychological rehabilitation and weighed over 150 kilograms. When she entered the office, Farrelly said, "Hey, who let this Zeppelin dirigible in here?" The patient was initially embarrassed but then laughed and happily began working with the therapist. She had become so accustomed to people carefully trying to conceal their attitude toward her excessive weight that the grotesque honesty of the psychotherapist simply shifted her perspective.

- **Allegory**, translated from Ancient Greek as "metaphor," is a representation of an idea or concept through comparison with a specific artistic image or dialogue. It is often used in poetry, fables, and morality tales. Examples of allegories include "The world is a dove," "Fidelity is a dog," "Death is a skull," and so on. A vivid example of allegory in provocative therapy is the case of Frank Farrelly working with a young man who wanted to be a good leader. Frank took hold of his cheeks and began comparing him to a cherub, telling him that with such a charming and attractive appearance, he didn't need to worry about social achievements.

- **Parody**, a term consisting of two Ancient Greek words, "para" and "dia," translates as "beside, against" and "song," respectively. It involves creating a comic effect through intentional and deliberate imitation of certain traits of personality or behavior. The first notable example of parody in literature is the ancient work called "Batrachomyomachia" or "The Battle of Frogs and Mice," which parodies the style of Homer's "Iliad."

- **Joke** is a phrase or text that possesses humorous content. It may employ various rhetorical figures of speech and usually has a climax. Referring to various jokes by Farrelly, let's mention one remarkable example. By provoking a patient and pointing out their "worn-out" appearance, he commented, "Your eyes look like little holes in the snow, as if someone peed on it!"

- **Anecdote**, translated from Greek as "unpublished," is a brief narrative or retelling of an interesting incident. Anecdotes typically involve an unusual resolution intended to evoke laughter. In this case, we would like to provide an example from the work of therapist Stephen Gilligan, who often uses provocative elements in his therapy and seminars. We witnessed the following situation during the fourth day of a six-day generative trance training program led by Gilligan. Towards the end of the day, Stephen decided to liven up the audience a bit and said, "I would like to tell you an anecdote, but I'm not sure if you're mature enough for it." It's worth noting that there were over 250 therapists in the audience. All the program participants shouted back, "Stephen, we're listening!" He agreed to continue and shared the following anecdote: "Once upon a time, a cucumber, a mushroom, and a penis met at a bar. The cucumber started complaining that people pick and slice him, drizzle him with oil, and eat him. The mushroom complained that, in addition to everything else, he gets fried and cut into small pieces. When it was the penis's turn, he revealed that he usually faces an even more brutal fate. They put a plastic bag over him, stuff him into a red cave, and repeatedly slam his head against the ceiling until he throws up!" Half of the audience burst into uproarious laughter, while the other part froze in silent shock due to the unexpected semantic range of the anecdote. In our observation, the use of such provocative elements in education significantly enhances the quality of material assimilation and, when properly employed, can greatly enhance the effectiveness of both therapy and learning in general.

- **Pun**: A rhetorical and literary device that uses different meanings of a word or different words and phrases in the same context.

- **Dark humor** often uses cynicism to ridicule death, diseases, traumas, pathologies, and other grim subjects that people usually don't like to joke about. It can employ irony, sarcasm, and other rhetorical figures of speech, but in a much harsher manner. The term itself originated in French and was popularized by André Breton, who compiled the "Anthology of Black Humor" in 1939. In Frank Farrelly's practice, we observed several instances where he compared patients to the well-known patient Helen Keller, who was blind, deaf, and mute. In other cases, Frank would directly comment on the patient's symptom as fatal, leading to worse consequences, and attribute it to poor heredity, suggesting that psychotherapy alone cannot yield positive results.

- **Oxymoron**, translated from ancient Greek as "witty foolishness," is a figure of speech that combines contradictory concepts, creating a combination of incongruity. Examples may include "joyful sadness," "living dead," "dead souls," and so on.

Farrelly Factors

Frank Farrelly conducted various seminars worldwide dedicated to the provocative psychotherapy method for about 50 years. His students often asked Frank how reproducible his psychotherapy method was. Frank usually liked to joke and said that he believed only 400 million people were capable of provocative psychotherapy. He also enjoyed sharing a story about one of his seminars in Germany, where a German attendee asked him about the main personal characteristic necessary to effectively conduct provocative psychotherapy. Frank replied, "Write it down!" All of his German students eagerly reached for their pens, ready to jot down the "secret knowledge" from Frank Farrelly. To their surprise, he said, "To be a truly good provocative psychotherapist, you need to be born Irish!" As we can see from his responses, Farrelly not only practiced provocative forms of psychotherapy but also had a provocative communication style in general.

Some of Farrelly's students from the Netherlands—Jaap Hollander, Graham Davies, and René Dubois—modeled his behavior during provocative psychotherapeutic work. Based on their modeling, they identified key rules, strategies, and patterns that they believed were most characteristic of his behavior in the psychotherapy process. In total, they came up with seven categories that encompassed 39 behavioral elements.

Categories

1. Regular therapist behavior. This refers to what the therapist consistently does during the psychotherapeutic process.
2. Cause-and-effect behavior. These are specific, fixed reactions of the therapist to certain patient actions.
3. Alternative means of provocation. These are specific forms of behavior that the therapist uses intermittently, rather than consistently.
4. Reactions to patient comments about problems.
5. Reactions to patient comments about self-esteem.
6. Internal processes accompanying Frank Farrelli during provocative work sessions.
7. Strategic actions.

Regular Therapist Behavior

Physical contact support: During psychotherapeutic sessions, Farrelli often touches the patient. This can involve touching their hands, patting their shoulders, wiping the patient's tears (symbolically or actually, if present), and touching and holding the patient's chin. Overall, Frank frequently enters the patient's personal space. If the patient avoids these touches, he repeats them after a while.

Use of different intonations: Depending on the patient and the topic being discussed, Farrelli's intonation can vary significantly. The following types of intonations can be observed:

- ***Playful***: This tone of voice is often used to start an interview. For example, Frank jokingly refers to a patient named Alexander as "the emperor" and asks what his specific problem is.
- ***Hypnotic***: With this tone of voice, Farrelli starts stating various therapeutic truths.
- ***Pretend-upset***: Farrelli may use this tone of voice when he notices that what he is doing or saying is disliked. Other applications of this type of voice are also possible.
- ***Pompous***: We have noticed that Farrelli tends to use a pompous tone of voice when commenting on his grandiose and absurd ideas about the patient's future.
- ***Condescending***: This tone of voice is often used when the patient's shortcomings come into focus.

Use of nonverbal mirroring: Quite often, during work with a patient, Frank mimics their postures, gestures, tone, intonation, and other nonverbal signals. As far as we could ascertain, he does not do this intentionally. This phenomenon seems to occur naturally during communication. In cases where intentional mirroring of nonverbal communication does occur, it takes on a mocking and parodic character.

Use of anecdotes, jokes, and comedic stories: Depending on the patient and their case, Farrelli may share anecdotal stories that are relevant to the situation. An interesting aspect is Frank's feedback regarding how he accumulates jokes for therapy. When reading a book, he highlights particularly interesting and humorous moments. If he hears a good joke in real life or in a video, he envisions how that joke can be applicable during a provocative therapy session with a patient.

Complete focus on the patient: Farrelli strives to ignore other stimuli unrelated to the work. He may also speak firmly to the patient, emphasizing that while he is working with them, they should be focused on him. If someone in the audience disturbs him, he can authoritatively request silence. Sometimes, the demand for silence in the audience can take on a provocative character. For instance, we have seen Frank speak sternly to a participant in the group who was disrupting the silence, warning that if they didn't calm down, he would approach and sit on their face!

Lack of actual assistance to the patient: It implies that a provocative psychotherapist should not give the patient serious advice on how to be or what to do. Here, we must emphasize the non-directive quality of their work. Behind the strange, sarcastic, grotesque, and foolish advice lies the intention to push the patient towards independent decision-making and conclusions. In this sense, Frank Farrelly's style of work can be quite similar to Milton Erickson's approach.

Lack of a clear plan for working with the patient: A provocative psychotherapist does not have a clear idea of where they want to lead the patient. There is no clear plan or goal. Actions are intuitive and oriented towards verbal and nonverbal feedback from the patient. If the therapist's behavior indicates that they do have some plan, it often has an absurd connotation.

Easy distraction from the topic and absurd focus of attention: Farrelly often switches from one topic to another, ignoring the completion of the previous one. He frequently elaborates on absurd and insignificant details. He may indifferently comment on what the patient considers important and, conversely, discuss as highly significant what the patient deems irrelevant. There may be examples where, in the middle or towards the end of a session, Frank clarifies with the patient what exactly their problem is.

Provocation of desired behavior: The term "provocare" translates from Latin as "revealing, eliciting." However, this "challenge" of behavior in provocative psychotherapy takes on a non-directive and quite often an inversive form. Behind the teasing lies the intention to evoke self-confidence; behind sarcastic remarks about flaws lies the desire to discover energy to eliminate them; and behind irony regarding certain personality traits lies the intention to create self-awareness in the specific personal context of the patient, and so on. Here, one can recall a phrase from Goethe's work spoken by Mephistopheles: "I am part of that power which eternally wills evil and eternally works good."

Causal-dependent Behavior

Eliciting emotions in the patient: Farrelly believes that one of the main goals of provocative therapy is to evoke various emotions in the patient. The spectrum of emotions can be very diverse, including joy, anger, sadness, embarrassment, and so on. Throughout the therapy, Farrelly explores the patient's reactions to various topics. If the reaction is strong, he continues to comment on the topic; if it is weak, he may start looking for other points to focus attention on. Farrelly has a specific list of main topics that are frequently used in provocative therapy, such as male-female relationships, sex, politics, religion, and others. Each patient may have their own vulnerable areas that need to be discovered during the therapeutic process.

Acting contrary to the patient's wishes: If a patient insists on one thing, do the opposite. If they want the topic of discussion to be changed, keep it unchanged. If they want the therapist to stop, it becomes an excellent command to continue doing what the therapist is currently doing.

Noting and commenting on strong nonverbal reactions from the patient: Farrelly observes strong nonverbal reactions from the patient, may exaggerate their description, and asks the patient if they understand what is happening to them at the moment.

Detailing information: When a patient utters abstract and vague phrases, Farrelly asks them to clarify and provide a more detailed description. Sometimes, for the purpose of obtaining detailed information from the patient, Farrelly uses a provocative trick. Instead of asking for clarification, he starts uttering presumed possible details himself. However, he does it provocatively and absurdly, which the patient often disagrees with and responds to by providing the actual necessary information.

The use of trance work: Sometimes, during the interaction with a psychotherapist, the patient may enter a light trance state and appear "suspended." Farrelly takes advantage of these moments to utter certain therapeutic truths, such as "Deep down, you must know," "We know that there is some solution," "There are things you can truly change," and so on. Thus, he often employs cliché phrases that hold inherent truth and are difficult to resist due to their statements of obvious facts. In this pattern, conventional provocation is not employed; only resourceful statements are used.

Serious and non-provocative approach to significant traumas: When Farrelly hears patients' stories about the loss of loved ones or severe illnesses, he immediately adopts a serious tone and occasionally expresses condolences. If the death of a loved one or a serious illness is the main theme of therapy, his approach becomes gentle and delicate. Farrelly avoids using harsh and rigid provocations regarding these topics.

Mirroring incongruent messages: When a patient conveys an incongruent message, verbally stating that something is important while non-verbally indicating the opposite, Farrelly responds by demonstrating similar behavior. For instance, if a patient speaks with a lethargic and apathetic tone, emphasizing the significance of something, Farrelly responds in a similar intonation, acknowledging that it is indeed very important.

Alternative means of provocation

Interrupting and cutting off the patient: Farrelly frequently employs this pattern. Sometimes he interrupts the patient right at the beginning of their reasoning or simply doesn't allow them to finish their sentence. Rarely does he grant the patient the opportunity to speak at length. The underlying philosophy of this pattern is that in the practice of provocation, politeness and etiquette should not be observed.

Parodying and mimicking the patient: Farrelly exaggerates certain types of patient behavior, mimicking them in a comedic manner. At times, the mimicry may even transition into a small theatrical performance for a solo actor.

Demonstrating how the patient's behavior can influence others: This pattern is naturally executed in an exaggerated, comedic manner. If the patient behaves aggressively, Farrelly may pretend to be frightened and ask them not to hit him, shielding his face with his hands as a protective gesture. In the case of excessive sexual behavior exhibited by a female patient, he may play the role of a man struggling to restrain his sexual urges, and so on.

Incorrect and unexpected interpretations of the patient's behavior and reactions: The more absurd and strange these interpretations are, the better. Sometimes the comments may have no relevance to the actual topic at hand. In other cases, Farrelly may propose something diametrically opposed to the real situation.

Strange, unconvincing, and foolish attempts to refute the patient's comments about any achievements: Farrelly starts presenting various strange arguments to support the notion that success is not truly success. He may suggest that it could lead to negative consequences or simply be greatly exaggerated. All refutations are often illogical and far-fetched.

Discrediting the patient's belief in the positive feedback they receive from others in response to their behavior: Farrelly may begin listing peculiar reasons why this is not the case and why the patient needs to change their perspective on the current state of affairs.

Asking the patient to repeat strong statements: If a patient makes any statement about themselves or life, Farrelli may pretend not to understand or misunderstand, thereby provoking them to repeat the phrase.

Dramatization and exaggeration of fantasies, fabrications, and inventions: To illustrate his point, Farrelli doesn't just tell a story; he turns it into a small, one-actor theater. During the performance, he may associate with various characters from history and speak from the perspective of each character.

Reactions to patients comments about problems

Encouragement of problem behavior: Farrelli focuses his attention on the various real shortcomings of the patient and tries to persuade them to maintain and preserve these shortcomings. For example, if Farrelli learns that the patient is living off other people who help them, he starts convincing the patient that they are engaging in very advantageous behavior and that they should choose friends who allow them to take advantage.

Offering surrealistic solutions: Farrelli constantly suggests strange, absurd, and surrealistic solutions to current problems and tasks. As he comments on these solutions, he often proposes problematic and environmentally unfriendly types of behavior and reactions. If the patient starts resisting, Farrelli continues to insist on his proposal and sometimes tries to present it as the only possible option.

Offering absurd interpretations: This point is very similar to the previous one. However, in this case, various strange interpretations of what is happening, what has happened, and what may happen to the patient are offered rather than solutions.

Minimizing the magnitude of the problem compared to other more favorable life factors: Farrelli may provide comments regarding areas of the patient's life where things are going well and begin to persuade them that nothing needs to be changed because of that. The comparisons are often absurd and come across as silly.

Reactions to the patient's comments about self-esteem

Exaggeration and caricature of negative self-esteem in one's state or behavior: If the patient tells Farrelli that things may not be going exactly as they would like, he may start proving to them that they are already at rock bottom with no way out. Naturally, absurd interpretations are used to support his opinion.

Exaggeration and caricature of negative perceptions of one's appearance: This pattern is almost a replica of the previous one, but the focus shifts to the perception of one's body and overall appearance.

Exaggeration of existing cultural stereotypes: Farrelli particularly enjoys playing on the exaggeration of stereotypical cultural perceptions of male and female images. He may use exaggerations of religious, cultural, and political stereotypes.

Internal processes accompanying Frank Farrelli during provocative therapy sessions

Entering a resourceful humorous state: This state allows for tuning into the desired provocative wave in communication and generating the necessary psychotherapeutic interventions.

Perceiving the patient as a close friend and maintaining warm feelings towards them: No matter how harsh the sarcasm coming from the provocative psychotherapist towards the patient may be, it should stem from a friendly attitude and acceptance.

Engaging internal mentors: During the session, one can imagine what people whom they consider their mentors in various aspects of life would say about the patient. A good frame that creates the necessary state for implementing this pattern could be a question to oneself: "What would one of my acquaintances say about this person?" and so on.

Visualizing internal monitors: Farrelli, during his interaction with the patient, can visualize various monitors next to him that offer different ways of communicating with the patient and different options for guiding provocative work.

Strategic actions

Shifting responsibility for events from the patient to circumstances and vice versa: If the patient blames themselves for something, start reproaching the world, society, other people, and circumstances. If they start blaming others, lay all the blame on them. Naturally, this is done in a tragicomic and absurd manner.

Taking one side in a conflict the patient comments on: It is possible to support both the patient's side and the opposing side. The provocative psychotherapist begins to favor the side whose defense can evoke more emotions and protest reactions from the patient. A very good example could be an existing conflict between the patient's parents.

Demanding the patient entertain the psychotherapist: Farrelli often emphasized in his seminars that "the patient's main task is to entertain the psychotherapist!"

Exhibiting behavior wilder and more absurd than the patient's: For instance, when Farrelli worked with an eight-year-old child who burped in his presence, he started burping even louder and more intensely.

Archetypal Foundation of Provocative Work - Trickster and the Sacred Fool Myths

Studying Frank Farrelli's work reveals that his method of therapy is, in many ways, a fascinating "underbelly" of many other forms of psychotherapy, particularly humanistic therapy, in which Farrelli began his career as a psychotherapist. Provocative therapy demonstrates how many beliefs prevalent in the psychotherapeutic context, when turned upside down, can produce not only a good but even a better effect. This may give rise to the humorous belief that the competence of a provocative therapist is a form of competent incompetence in conducting the psychotherapeutic process.

Here, we are reminded of Mephistopheles' line from Goethe's work: "I am part of that power which eternally wills evil and eternally works good." This quote indeed aligns well with the philosophy of provocative work, although it requires some additional clarifications. Farrelli commented in his seminars that he perceives provocative therapy as a type of exorcism, where the patient's neurosis is "expelled" through mockery and teasing. Farrelli expressed his belief that "the devil does not tolerate mockery of himself." He also emphasized that it is the symptom itself that is being ridiculed, not the patient. And indeed, a person who can afford to joke about their symptoms is at least halfway towards recovery.

Farrelli also introduced an interesting metaphor into his work, referring to provocative therapy as a form of "devil's advocate" work. In this case, we see not literal mockery but rather the therapist adopting a role where they comically begin to defend the symptom to the patient, persuading them to preserve and keep it. The foundation of this approach lies primarily in the intentional incongruence of the message, where part of the verbal message clearly reflects the defense of the symptom, while non-verbal bodily and auditory messages reflect the comedy and grotesque nature of the message. Not to mention that the verbal rational arguments themselves are often quite absurd. Thus, the psychotherapist begins to reveal and mock the shadowy, unconscious aspects of the patient's personality through their behavior.

The projection of the shadow from the depths of the unconscious onto the therapist's behavior leads to the initiation of possible psychodynamic processes. After all, a symptom exists and remains invulnerable only when its key meaning pattern is deeply hidden in the unconscious. In this case, a good metaphor can be the fairy tale character Koschei the Immortal, whose death is hidden in an egg that is far away from him. Additionally, by exploring Farrelli's work, we can find a profound underlying intention—to turn everything inside out. If a person wants to get rid of a particular behavior, persuade them to maintain the same pattern. If a person praises their own merits, convince them that they are not particularly significant. If a person believes they are guilty of something, start convincing them of the correctness of their opinion, but do it in a tragicomic manner.

In Paul Radin's book with commentaries by Carl Jung and Karl Kerényi, a very interesting mythological character belonging to the mythology of the Winnebago Indians is described, whose behavior somewhat resembles the philosophy of provocative work. This deity is called the Trickster. Radin's book dedicated to the Trickster presents a large number of myths about him. These myths are quite strange, and their plots may be incomprehensible to the Western mentality. However, if we read a certain number of these myths, we will discover a very interesting meta-meaning that permeates them.

Paul Radin

In various myths, the Trickster appears in different forms. In one myth, he is a man, in another, a woman; in one, he is a hero, in another, a criminal; in one, he saves someone from death, while in another, he becomes a killer. This list can go on, but the essence remains the same. The Trickster embodies philosophical notions of non-duality, which are characteristic not only of Native American Indians but also of Indian sages.

In the ancient Indian treatise "Bhagavad Gita", it is mentioned that the person who attains a state of non-dual mind is saved. The state of non-duality is the simultaneous perception of opposites as parts of a whole, which allows a person to perceive the world in its true form. We believe that it was Hindu concepts of non-duality, or teachings closely related to these concepts, that influenced Carl Jung in creating his idea of the existence of the archetype of the Self in personal and collective unconsciousness.

Carl Jung

In one of his books, Carl Jung provides a direct definition of this archetype, stating that "the Self is the union of opposites." True opposites can be perceived as masculine and feminine, light and dark, manifest and hidden, and so on. Each individual opposition can be embodied in a separate archetype, which itself may consist of individual opposites.

In Jungian psychology, the Trickster archetype is often perceived as a variation of the Wise Old Man archetype. In my opinion, it also has a more abstract nature and serves as a kind of meta-archetype, representing the transformation of one archetype into its diametrical opposite. Jung called the process of transitioning from one thing to its diametrically opposite enantiodromia, which he considered a key vector of natural transformation in the individual's personality.

We believe that the process of enantiodromia is an integral part of the

Trickster's archetypal function, both as a mythological figure and as an abstract process. There is a belief that the Trickster archetype finds its embodiment in various gods or heroes in different mythological structures and exists in almost every cultural tradition. All the embodied figures convey the key qualities inherent in the Trickster archetype.

Most often, the image of the Trickster hero embodies demonic and comedic traits, possessing the qualities of a trickster and prankster. It can be a god, a human, or an anthropomorphic animal. In the process of solving the challenges that arise during the development of the myth, the Trickster violates various rules of a certain property and eventually finds a distinctive solution to the existing challenge.

At this moment, an analogy arises with the provocative form of psychotherapy, which violates numerous rules existing in other psychotherapeutic methods and often generates solutions that are so original that they can be awe-inspiring. In my opinion, in the process of interacting with the patient on a deep level, a provocative psychotherapist associates with the archetype of the Trickster and its transformative psychic energy, capable of introducing new original solutions.

An interesting parallel to the image of the Trickster in Winnebago Indian mythology is represented by the thunder deity Heyoka in Sioux-Dakota myths. He is the patron of hunting. Heyoka embodies the paradoxical nature of the Trickster's image and all the processes and phenomena inherent in it. There are mythological descriptions that depict a joyful Heyoka as crying heavily, while when he is saddened, he laughs. Heat affects him as if it were cold, and vice versa.

Once again, we can draw a cross-reference to the provocative nature of the work, which, according to Farrell, unlike other methods of psychotherapy, does not fight against the resistance of the patient but instead creates it, with the aim of using the energy of this resistance to transform the symptom.

The Sioux people believe that after thunder, the world begins to renew itself, and it is appropriate to welcome it with joy. People who assume the role of Heyoka in the tribe are often referred to as clowns or madmen because they perform acts that are contrary to what is natural and expected. Once again, we can recognize Farrell's behavior in these descriptions. Indeed, his behavior is often perceived by people as clowning and a manifestation of madness. However, this is not the only role he can assume within the context of psychotherapeutic practice.

Dr. Walker, an American anthropologist, describes the ceremony dedicated to Heyoka as follows: "When someone seeks a vision and sees lightning or Thunderbird, such a person must subsequently mimic Heyoka through clowning and absurdity in words and actions. The special action he must perform is to snatch meat from a boiling pot with bare hands and offer it to someone."

Let's provide examples of how the Trickster archetype is embodied in various other mythological figures:

- Little St. Martin in Basque mythology
- Loki and Odin in Germanic and Scandinavian mythology
- Hephaestus, Hermes, and Odysseus in Ancient Greek mythology
- Azazel in Levantine mythology
- Baron Samedi and Papa Legba in Voodoo mythology
- Reynard the Fox from Dutch folklore
- Ivan the Fool from Russian folklore
- Nasreddin Hodja, from the folklore of Central Asia and other countries;
- Uncle Tompa from Tibetan folklore
- Puss in Boots from French folklore
- Sun Wukong, the Monkey King, from Chinese mythology
- Kitsune, Susano-o, and Kappa in Japanese mythology
- Iktomi Heyoka in Lakota mythology
- Amaguk in Inuit mythology
- Anansi the Spider among West African peoples;
- Hare among Bantu ethnic groups
- Tjank or Tokoloshe among the Zulu people;
- Set in Ancient Egypt
- Figaro from the folklore of the Spanish people;

- Br'er Rabbit from US folklore
- Hershele Ostropoler from Jewish folklore
- Coyote (Huehuecoyotl) in Aztec mythology.

In my opinion, these mythological and cultural figures, to varying degrees, reflect the meanings contained within the Trickster archetype and can be perceived as symbolic prototypes of provocative forms of psychotherapeutic work.

The stories of these characters can also be used as metaphors in teaching provocative therapy. This form of education is highly significant as it focuses on the perception of information primarily through the activity of the right hemisphere of the brain, which processes the perceived world through abstract symbols, unlike the left hemisphere, which prefers clear and detailed information. It is the activity of the right hemisphere that is capable of creating a sense of flow during the practice of provocative therapy, where therapeutic interventions arise easily and naturally, closely connected to verbal and non-verbal messages coming from the patient to the psychotherapist. In my opinion, this sense of flow becomes accessible only when the psychotherapist grasps the abstract core of the work itself, which can be understood by studying myths, legends, and folklore related to various manifestations of the Trickster archetype.

Provocative Group Psychotherapy

At times, Farrelly demonstrated examples of his work with a group during his seminars. The technique of provocative therapy itself did not undergo significant changes, but certain elements of this applied practice are worth noting.

In our view, a group for this form of therapy should be limited in terms of the number of participants, with an optimal range of 4–8 individuals. And based on our practice, it's closer to 4 rather than 8. A smaller number of people, less than 4, does not create the full effect of group psychotherapy, where each patient can create multiple transferences onto their peers. A larger number, more than 8 individuals, is undesirable as the provocative approach relies heavily on the intensive work of the psychotherapist, and their attention simply won't be sufficient for all participants, or they will be spread too thin to create the necessary therapeutic effect. The optimal duration for the group session is 45–90 minutes. With an increased number of participants, it is better to slightly extend the time.

Initially, the therapist starts by introducing various minor provocations to the group participants while carefully observing their non-verbal reactions. It is quite possible that a provocation directed at one participant elicits a strong response from another. General phrases aimed at provoking the entire group may also be uttered. At times, the therapist may spontaneously switch from one patient to another. After working with one patient, they may receive feedback on the topic being addressed and then switch to another topic. Let us formulate the key rules of group provocative therapy.

Rules of Group Provocative Therapy

1. Therapist takes on the majority of the activity.
2. Therapist constantly switches from one patient to another.
3. The amount of time dedicated to each patient can vary significantly, ranging from a brief phrase to a dialogue lasting up to 5 minutes.
4. Provocations should ideally engage not only the targeted patient but also others. The aim is to create interventions that can provoke multiple individuals or even the entire group simultaneously.
5. It is possible to intertwine the meanings of conversations with different patients logically and provocatively. Some patients can be used as instruments to provoke others.
6. Strive to allocate approximately equal time to each patient.
7. Capture the sense of flow and act intuitively, shifting from one person to another.

During one of his seminars, Farrelly shared that he had previously applied group provocative therapy to working with groups of criminal psychopaths in prison. One participant in such a group once told Frank that he was cool. Frank asked him, "What makes you say that?" The prisoner replied that he behaved terribly in their presence but was sincere in his communication and did not burden them with lofty "humanistic crap."

Provocative Coaching

Farrelly commented on how his student from the Netherlands, Jaap Hollander, along with some colleagues, organized an educational program specifically dedicated to provocative coaching work. Frank himself did not differentiate between regular provocative psychotherapy and coaching practice, stating, "To me, they are one and the same." Nevertheless, if we specifically consider the philosophy of coaching, which is primarily focused on assisting in achieving future goals rather than therapeutic exploration of the past, there are certain changes in provocative work that, in my opinion, should be taken into account. The following focal points should become the focus areas for provocative work in coaching.

Provocative Attention Foci for Coaching

1. **Future orientation**: The provocative therapist directs the vector of provocation more toward future events.
2. **Working with the inferiority complex**: This focus emphasizes the deliberate creation of an inferiority complex that can serve as energy for goal attainment.
3. **Coach as "devil's advocate"**: This focus guides the therapist's efforts to present all the advantages and benefits that can be gained if the patient abandons their goal.
4. **Provocative metaphors of achievement**: The therapist employs various absurd metaphors of goal attainment. For example, the therapist might say to the patient, "Simpleton Ivan started by lying on the stove. Maybe you should find one and lie on it for a while too?"

5. **Multiple false goals**: Operating within this focus, the therapist begins to suggest numerous minor, insignificant additional goals to divert the patient's attention. Naturally, this is done in a comedic manner to make it appear as theatrical absurdity to the patient.

Provocative Drama

In the course of our practice, we have developed a highly interesting way of applying provocative work within a group setting, which, to the best of our knowledge, Farrelly has never used in his practice. The essence and philosophy of provocative work itself remain unchanged. However, different group members can participate in the actual dramatic representation of verbal provocation for the purpose of provoking reactions. Initially, the therapist may work in the usual provocative style. However, as the context of the symptom is understood, they begin to model the situation itself through the use of substitutes playing different roles. The therapist directs the scene, providing instructions on where each performer should stand, what posture to assume, and what to comment on. If necessary, the therapist may ask the patient to improvise within the given thematic context. Sometimes, the patient themselves can also actively participate in the provocative drama. Therefore, provocative work incorporates structural and technical elements from other forms of dramatic psychotherapy, such as Jacob Moreno's psychodrama and Virginia Satir's "family sculpture."

Advantages of this approach include

1. Visualizing the role within the problematic context.
2. The ability to more intensely associate and dissociate while reenacting the problematic context.
3. Dramatization with the help of group participants can greatly emphasize the comedic aspect of the work, leading to stronger emotions.
4. Active involvement of other group members in the psychotherapy

process.

We have been testing this form of therapeutic work since 2014. During seminars on provocative psychotherapy, we demonstrate provocative drama as an instrumental variation of Frank Farrelly's conventional therapeutic techniques.

Provocative Methods in Milton Erickson's Practice

Milton Erickson never used the term "provocative" to describe his methods. He is more widely known for his mastery of hypnotherapy. However, with most of his patients, he worked not through hypnosis but by applying various verbal techniques in psychotherapy, some of which embody key principles of provocative work. Erickson did not focus much on humor in psychotherapy, but occasionally used it very effectively. Like hypnosis, Erickson's humor was also highly non-directive. The essence of Erickson's various forms of work is very similar to Farrelly's approach, but the methodology may differ.

Milton Erickson

Erickson, like Farrelly, spent a considerable amount of time working in a psychiatric clinic with severely mentally ill individuals. Establishing rapport and trust with them was not always easy. However, despite this, Erickson was a master at adapting to patients, even those with severe disorders. After emotionally connecting with the patient, Erickson would then begin to provoke the desired behavior through his own actions. Erickson's therapy strategy can be described in three main points, which he applied in the vast majority of his cases.

1. Accession.
2. Leading.
3. Utilization.

Accession

At this level, the therapist begins to mimic specific verbal and non-verbal forms of the patient's behavior. This can include posture, movement, voice volume, intonation, and timbre. Connection can be established based on a person's values, beliefs, motivational patterns, action algorithms, and behavioral strategies. The therapist determines which aspect of behavior needs adjustment depending on the patient and symptoms.

Leading

Once the psychotherapist has "connected" with the patient, there is a need for them to stay in rapport with the patient at the level of mirroring their behavior. Depending on the requirements, this can range from mirroring the patient's non-verbal communication for 5–10 minutes to deeply mirroring various behavior algorithms and strategies over the course of several months. During the leading phase, the therapist is able to guide the patient's movements. The patient becomes receptive to certain recommendations from the therapist that align with their internal world. This is not yet the moment of healing, but rather a step in the direction of it.

Utilization

This stage involves the therapist carrying out a specific action or actions that reflectively exaggerate the patient's behavior while continuing to adapt and lead them. This action leads the patient to insight and sometimes catharsis. Here are a few examples of Erickson's work that incorporate these three main principles of his practice and, in my opinion, embody the fundamental principles of provocative psychotherapeutic work.

Leslie Cameron-Bendler Case

Leslie was a very attractive girl who was accustomed to interacting with men using the language of female flirtation. Some people in her circle even called her a "flirt machine." She began attending Erickson's seminars with her friends when he was already in his seventies. During one of these seminars, she decided to test her flirting skills on Erickson and see what would happen.

Erickson noticed Leslie's flirtation and decided to "adjust" her a bit. He paused his lecture, looked intently at her, and then exclaimed, "Young lady! You must be out of your mind and in need of a psychiatrist!" He then took his left hand and lifted his right hand, which didn't work due to a long-standing illness, before letting it fall back down onto his knee. He then looked at Leslie again and said, "Even my hand doesn't get up!" Other group members laughed, Leslie blushed, and she no longer attempted to flirt with him. As one of her friends put it, she changed a bit after that, ceasing to turn almost any interaction with different men into a flirting game.

In this case, we witness Erickson's symbolic micro-adjustment through verbal pattern interruption when he exclaimed that she might need a psychiatrist, rapid pacing when he manipulated his hand, and a splendid utilization of the phrase that even his hand wouldn't lift. This serves as an excellent example of concentrated provocative work using irony and sarcasm in a nondirective manner.

Case of Jesus from the Clinic

At the clinic where Erickson worked, he was assigned to supervise a patient with schizophrenic symptoms who believed he was Jesus. Erickson pondered for a while on how to best interact with the patient, and once he had a plan, he began implementing his strategy. He went to the patient's room and asked, "Are you Jesus?" The patient replied, "Yes, of course! I am He, without a doubt!" To this, Erickson countered, "There is a carpentry job near the clinic; they are building a new wing. Are you willing to help?" The patient answered, "Certainly, I want to help people because I am a carpenter too!"

Afterward, Erickson requested, "Look, I know you're Jesus; there's no doubt about that, but other people you'll be working with may not be ready to acknowledge that. To avoid distressing them, please refer to yourself by the name and surname stated in your passport. By doing this, you'll spare them any worry." The patient thought for a while and agreed with Erickson not to reveal his "true" identity.

For the next six months, he diligently worked at the construction site, gaining a reputation as a good and helpful worker. He refrained from calling himself Jesus in front of others, which brought joy to everyone. However, in conversations with Erickson, he still considered himself as such.

After six months, the psychiatrists decided to hold a consultation to talk with the patient and observe the progression of his symptoms. They were even considering discharging him from the clinic as he had displayed excellent behavior for a prolonged period. The day before the consultation, Erickson once again asked the patient not to confess to the psychiatrists that he was indeed Jesus, so that they would release him, allowing him to freely travel the world and do good deeds.

The patient followed Erickson's advice, successfully engaged in a conversation with the psychiatrists, and was subsequently discharged. He later moved to another city, formed a community of people helping others in difficult situations, gained respect and authority within the group, and actively and successfully engaged in social volunteering. Every year on Christmas, he sent Erickson a card with greetings and a lot of gratitude for the help he had received. At the end of the letter, his real name was always written, followed by the initials J.C. (Jesus Christ).

In this case, Erickson primarily focused his attention on accessing and leading the patient. Utilization, manifested in pushing the patient to not acknowledge to other psychiatrists that he still considers himself to be Jesus, does not differ significantly from the subsequent steps. Although, to a large extent, something exaggerated in this case was simply unnecessary. It is worth noting that this work reflects the anti-psychiatric philosophy, which suggests that it is not necessary to cure the patient. It is sufficient to socially adapt them and ensure their well-being, and, as in this case, what they think of themselves and how they want to be called is irrelevant.

In my opinion, the key to constructive changes in the patient was the prolonged guidance of the patient himself. It was through this pattern that Erickson managed to "provoke" the necessary behavior. Although this form of provocation differs significantly from Farrelly's work, it demonstrates an interesting form of interaction, somewhat resembling the "devil's advocate" game of Farrelly. Erickson truly began "defending" the patient's symptom, but did so not to eliminate it but rather to place it in a more favorable social context.

Case of an Aggressive Girl

A 12-year-old girl with aggressive behavior was kept in a clinic. She would attack psychiatrists and nurses at the clinic, latching onto their hair and attempting to pull it out as soon as she had the chance. She also made attempts to tear their clothes, and when alone in her room, would rip apart the sheets and pillows.

Erickson spent some time developing a strategy for interacting with the patient. To do this, he sought the support of the clinic director and obtained permission to break some items in the girl's room for therapeutic purposes. He wanted to tear apart all the intact sheets and pillows in the room and then break the radiator off the wall.

To accomplish the latter, he asked for the heating to be turned off in her room and arranged for a nurse to stage a scene in front of the girl. When everything was prepared, he entered the girl's room. She sat on the bed, snarling angrily, ready to attack him. Erickson grabbed the items lying on the neighboring bed and vigorously and maliciously tore them apart near the girl.

He tore apart a sheet, a towel, and a pillow, emptying them of all feathers and scattering them around the room. The girl looked at him with surprise and concern. Then Erickson invited her to join him in tearing everything around them apart. She willingly joined in this total act of psychotherapeutic vandalism. When they were done with the items, Erickson asked her to help him break the radiator off the wall. They struggled with the radiator for some time until the girl gave up and it fell to the floor with a crash.

Finally, Erickson invited her to take a walk down the clinic corridor and left the room. The girl followed him hesitantly. There, they were met by a nurse, with whom Erickson had arranged to stage something in front of the girl. He ran toward the nurse, screaming angrily, then grabbed her sleeve, pulled it forcefully, and tore it off. The nurse let out a demonstrative scream. At that moment, something changed in the girl. She looked at Erickson in indignation and said, "Dr. Erickson, are you sure you can do that?"

In this case, we can see that Erickson's provocation was successful due to the strong amplification of the patient's behavior.

A splendid example of provoking the desired behavior can be seen in Erickson's work with one of his daughters. His five-year-old daughter had a habit of constantly biting her nails and could not get rid of it. No persuasions or comments from others worked.

Erickson decided to talk to her and said that for a big girl like her, it was essential to bite her nails, and one could say that nail-biting was currently her most important responsibility. Therefore, she needed to bite them regularly, every day, according to a strict schedule, precisely 15 minutes in the morning, afternoon, and evening.

At first, his daughter started following the recommendation and diligently did it for the next two weeks, but then she stopped following the schedule and stopped biting her nails.

This gentle provocation worked by reframing the context. Erickson shifted the pathological behavior into a different frame and significantly raised its significance. Erickson knew that it was easier for a little girl to get rid of what she had to do than what she wanted to do.

Understanding this method of provocation can significantly expand the technical arsenal proposed by Frank Farrelly.

Although Erickson did not always use literal humor in his therapy, he still regarded the use of anecdotes as one of the possible ways to deliver therapeutic information to the patient.

Jeffrey Zeig writes in his book "Milton Erickson Training Seminars" that the use of anecdotes in psychotherapy can have several significant advantages.

1. Anecdotes are not threatening and do not contain threats.
2. Anecdotes provide the patient with an opportunity for enjoyment.
3. Anecdotes stimulate independent behavior since understanding and comprehending their meaning requires the individual to do so independently and make decisions based on this realization.
4. Anecdotes can be used to work with patient resistance. For example, an anecdote may contain a metaphor for action or hint at a specific meaning.
5. Anecdotes are applicable for controlling the communicative framework of relationships.
6. Anecdotes can shape a model of behavior in consciousness.
7. Anecdotes are a suggestive tool. Their use can create hypnotic confusion, thereby increasing the patient's sensitivity to hypnotic suggestion.
8. Through anecdotes, we can more easily remember the context of communication and the key meanings associated with it.

We observe a more systematic approach to studying the influence of anecdotes on the process of psychotherapy and its effectiveness.

For example, Zeig may have commented on Erickson's behavior in the following way: "Erickson had the ability to play with your attention and his own. He constantly joked, telling his stories. He intended to make you laugh and engage you in the game."

In this case, we should emphasize that for Erickson, the therapeutic process was largely associated with a state of playfulness, of which humor was an integral part. However, Erickson's humor was very subtle and veiled compared to the directive forms of irony and sarcasm characteristic of Farrelly. In my opinion, by studying the work of these two therapists, one can gain an understanding of a comprehensive approach in the practice of provocative psychotherapy, integrating both directive and non-directive methods of work. It should also be noted that Erickson was a master of creating provocative traps for patients, which he could build endlessly, unlike Farrelly, who focused on one-on-one conversations with the patient or in the presence of a group of other patients.

Pathopsychological Profiles and Provocative Therapy

Hysteroid Profile

Based on our observations, hysteroid patients respond remarkably well to the influence of provocative therapeutic methods. Typically, their reactions are strong and intense. While hysteroid patients may play along with the therapist to some extent, it does not alter the essence or quality of the work. The main challenge in working with patients of this profile is navigating the traps of their excessively strong emotional reactions, which a provocative psychotherapist may inadvertently trigger. What may appear to be a powerful and intense emotion on the surface may merely be an expression of the patient's need for attention, especially in the context of group-format provocative therapy.

Paranoid Profile

It is worth noting that individuals with paranoid traits often struggle with understanding irony, sarcasm, and humor directed at them. They frequently fail to grasp the use of irony, and if they do, they begin to speculate about the therapist's motives. The favorite projections of paranoid individuals include perceiving the therapist as incompetent or making unwarranted sexual advances if the patient is of the opposite sex.

While these characteristics do not pose obstacles to provocative therapy per se, it is advisable to consider the specific nature of the patient's character and moderate the level of provocation to avoid going overboard. Initially, it is preferable to engage in a gentle approach to allow the patient to become accustomed to the therapist's communication style. More significant provocations are better introduced closer to the second half of the session.

For paranoid patients, it is highly recommended to describe the rules of provocative therapy and what the therapist intends to do in relation to the patient. Without understanding the framework of the therapeutic work, the patient may fail to perceive it as therapeutic. One of the most effective forms of provocation for patients of this profile is the "devil's advocate" technique, in which the therapist methodically, diligently, and absurdly tries to convince the paranoid individual to maintain their symptoms. Mockery and teasing aimed at this profile yield rather mediocre results.

Psychopathic Profile

Despite Frank Farrelly's claim of working with murderers and rapists in prisons, he did not provide a detailed description of what he specifically did with them. Only a few comments indicate that psychopaths appreciated his more straightforward approach. In our view, this information is too limited to generalize, as we have not personally worked with murderers and rapists in prisons using provocative psychotherapy.

However, we have encountered individuals with psychopathic personalities who are more socially adaptive, on several occasions. It is important to note that psychopathic individuals rarely seek therapy voluntarily because they believe everything is already fine with them. Sometimes, situations arise when a psychopathic person comes to therapy claiming that everything is fine, but according to their acquaintances, they should see a therapist. Such individuals do not tend to continue therapy sessions.

The psychopath's inability to experience guilt and shame makes them challenging subjects for provocative therapy. Being in a passive position, being controlled, having therapy conducted on them, or being provoked contradicts their predatory nature. In our work with psychopaths, we found that their psychological essence responds weakly to provocative work. Although the results may vary depending on the individual, we frequently receive consistent feedback from individuals of this profile that provocations simply do not affect them, even when they are highly sophisticated.

We do not analyze the long-term effects of provocative therapy with psychopathic personalities since they usually do not stay in therapy for an extended period and are inclined to downplay any impact the therapist may have on them. In the short-term form of work, the therapeutic effect we observed was minimal. However, similar weak effects of verbal psychotherapy are observed in all other schools of psychotherapy. We have not found any examples of any psychotherapy approach claiming to successfully correct psychopathy in any form.

Obsessive-Compulsive Profile

According to my observations, this profile responds excellently to the influence of provocative therapy, and various techniques can be effective. The "devil's advocate" technique and harsh mockery of symptoms can be particularly beneficial. I have not encountered strong resistance or rejection of this form of therapy from patients.

Schizoid Profile

When working with this personality profile, it is necessary to dose the provocative therapeutic "poison." This is because behind the coldness and lack of emotions of the schizoid individual often lies a very sensitive and vulnerable person. During the therapeutic process, it is important to take note of the level of irony and sarcasm that the patient can tolerate.

Schizoid individuals are narcissistic and extremely sensitive to any jokes directed at themselves. This should be taken into account in order to achieve a therapeutic effect and not simply provoke and further close off the patient. If the patient's narcissism is too pronounced, the optimal approach would be to focus on the "devil's advocate" technique, in which the therapist absurdly attempts to support the symptom and convince the patient to maintain it. Provocative psychotherapy has proven to be highly effective in working with patients of this profile.

Epileptoid Profile

Epileptoid patients generally respond well to provocative work and do not exhibit strong resistance to it. The intensity of provocation may need to be adjusted based on the individual. However, most of these patients tolerate moderate and high levels of provocation quite well.

The main challenge may arise when working with epilepsy patients with low levels of intelligence. They often fail to understand mild irony and may take offense at harsh sarcasm, rarely benefiting from such provocation.

Schizophrenic Profile

Farrelly repeatedly described and commented on the excellent effects of provocative work on schizophrenic patients. It can temporarily bring them to a relatively normal state. Similar effects have been observed not only in schizophrenic patients but also in individuals with a schizoid accent in their personalities. Absurdity, irony, and sarcasm directed at individuals with this profile can effectively balance and regulate their behavior.

Manic-Depressive Profile

Patients with this profile generally respond well to provocative therapy. However, their reactions can significantly vary depending on the phase of manic-depressive dynamic they are in.

During the manic phase, patients may excessively engage in a comedic and humorous context of therapy, losing their serious approach to the process. It is preferable to avoid this situation, as it can sharply reduce the effectiveness of therapy. The patient should be aware of what they are engaging in. Otherwise, the therapy's effectiveness will decline.

Ideally, meeting the patient during the interphase, where neither manic nor depressive states dominate, is excellent. In the depressive phase, there may be difficulties with normal reactions to the therapist's jokes. During this period, the patient's sense of humor may temporarily diminish.

However, In my opinion, this is not a contraindication for provocative therapeutic work.

3

Humanistic Psychotherapy

Humanistic psychology and psychotherapy construct their theories and practices based on the fundamental belief that humans are unique, holistic systems with a vast spectrum of untapped possibilities waiting to be discovered.

The humanistic vector in psychotherapy emerged largely as an opposition to psychoanalysis and behaviorism, which dominated the psychotherapeutic market in America by the 1950s. Moreover, during this period, a significant humanistic movement unfolded in various spheres of life in the United States, gaining momentum in the 1960s and 1970s.

Hippies advocating for freedom of sexual expression, drug use, and opposition to warfare, as well as the feminist movement fighting for women's rights, the acceptance of homosexuality, and so on, all became part of this movement. The era was characterized by total democratization and humanization.

Humanistic psychology and psychotherapy attempt to maintain their focus on studying and nurturing the positive aspects of an individual's personality, thereby contrasting with psychoanalysis, which primarily delves into unconscious complexes and personal traumas.

In addition to a particular form of psychotherapy, humanistic philosophy also gave rise to humanistic pedagogy, which advocates for education based on empathy and the support of students rather than rigid authoritarian coercion.

The following beliefs, which shape therapeutic work, are postulated in humanistic psychology and psychotherapy:

1. **Principle of Holism**: A person is a holistic system and cannot be viewed as a collection of separate organs or psychological processes.
2. **Key Points of Attention**: These include the creative force, freedom of will, and spontaneity in a person's thinking and behavior.
3. **Responsibility to the World**: Understanding that every action and its consequences entail individual responsibility helps foster a more mature stance toward the world.
4. **Principle of Respect and Acceptance**: Tolerance plays a crucial role in this principle, allowing for the acceptance of diversity in the world and in individuals by approaching them with respect.
5. **Principle of Self-Actualization**: Self-actualization is perceived as the primary driving force of personal growth. It postulates that individuals are inherently good, neutral, and oriented toward the future.
6. **Principle of Being in the Here and Now**: Embracing the present moment allows for a genuine understanding of oneself and life. Resisting this notion leads to dwelling on the past or anticipating the future, causing individuals to live more in fantasies than in reality.

There are numerous scholars who have contributed to the development of humanistic theories and practices. Let us list some of them and then examine each one in more detail: Abraham Maslow, Carl Rogers, Elias Porter, James Bugental, Frederick Perls, Charlotte Bühler, Everett Shostrom, Hans-Werner Gessmann, and Erich Fromm, among others.

Abraham Maslow and Self-Actualization

Abraham Maslow (1908–1970) was an American psychologist and a key figure who greatly influenced the development of humanistic psychology and psychotherapy. He was born in New York to Samuel Maslow and Rosa Shilovskaya, who emigrated from the Kiev region in the early 20th century. He was the eldest of seven children. In his childhood, he suffered greatly from anti-Semitism due to his Jewish nationality. He wrote about his perplexity regarding how he managed to maintain his mental well-being despite everything he went through.

Abraham Maslow

Maslow became acquainted with psychology through Edward Bradford Titchener, who was teaching at Cornell University at the time. Abraham Maslow studied behaviorism, a popular school of psychology at the time, in America. He attended the University of Wisconsin, where he obtained a doctorate in psychology in 1934. In the same year, he began working as a research assistant for behaviorist Thorndike. He deeply studied the works of one of the founders of behaviorism, John Watson. Overall, during the early period of his scientific career, he was also influenced by Clark Hull, Norman Cameron, William Sheldon, and Harry Harlow.

His mentor for his doctoral dissertation was Harry Harlow. His research focused on dominance and sexuality in primates. However, over time, Maslow's scientific orientation towards behaviorism began to fade, and he became interested in other theories. In 1937, he accepted a position as a professor at Brooklyn College, where he worked for the next 14 years. During his years at Brooklyn and Columbia Universities, he met and collaborated professionally with Fromm, Kofoed, Wertheimer, Horney, Sullivan, Benedict, Horkheimer, Cardiner, Adler, Goldstein, and Ansbacher.

At Brooklyn College, he met scientists with whom he started to develop the concepts of humanistic psychology and self-actualizing personality. Regarding this, Maslow wrote: "My research on self-actualization was not planned as research and did not begin as research. It began as an attempt by a young, thinking person to understand two extraordinary teachers whom he loved and admired. These two individuals were Max Wertheimer and Ruth Benedict." Max Wertheimer was the founder of Gestalt psychology, which became another major theoretical foundation in the field of psychology. Ruth Benedict was an anthropologist who represented ethnopsychology in American anthropology.

In 1943, Maslow published two articles describing his key ideas that had formed at that time. These articles were "The Dynamics of Personality Organization" and "The Theory of Personality Motivation." In the preface to the book "Towards a Psychology of Being", Maslow identifies his ideas about the humanistic psychology he created as follows: "If I had to express in one phrase what humanistic psychology means to me, I would say it is the integration of Goldstein (and the Gestalt school of psychology as a whole) with Freud (and various psychodynamic theories) under the aegis of the scientific spirit of my mentors at the University of Wisconsin."

The humanistic ideas that Maslow developed in the 1940s faced strong resistance from his colleagues, most of whom were proponents of psychoanalysis or behaviorism. It was only after becoming the first dean of the psychology department at Brandeis University in 1951 that his ideas gradually began to form a coherent theoretical foundation, and his works caught the attention of colleagues. In 1967, he was elected president of the

American Psychological Association. Maslow passed away in 1970 from a heart attack.

One of the key theoretical and practical concepts that Maslow developed throughout his professional career was the idea of self-actualization. However, it should be noted that Maslow borrowed the term itself from his teacher, the Gestalt psychologist Kurt Goldstein. It was Goldstein who first introduced the term "self-actualization" into the scientific context, although as a neurophysiologist, he understood it somewhat differently from how Maslow later understood it.

Goldstein understood self-actualization as a "special tension that enables further organized activity of the organism." In his theoretical explorations, Goldstein claimed that a person can postpone the satisfaction of their lower needs, such as sleep, sex, and food, if there are other motives that determine it. It was formally because of this that Goldstein was the first to initiate the study of meta-motivation, although he did not use this term to refer to motivation that conditions other motivation.

Maslow's definition of "self-actualization" is as follows: "The full use of talents, abilities, capacities, and the like as a process of self-realization of human potential." Maslow also writes: "I imagine the self-actualizing person not as an ordinary person to whom something has been added but as an ordinary person from whom nothing has been taken away." Furthermore, he comments that the "average person is a human being with suppressed and repressed abilities and talents."

According to Maslow, in order to study the limits of human potential, one must focus on the best representatives of humanity. He makes an analogy, stating, "To find out how fast people can run, you need to study the best athletes and runners, and it would be meaningless to take an average sample from the population of a city."

Prior to Maslow, much of the personality theory developed by various psychologists focused on the examination of pathological forms of behavior. For example, Freud constructed his understanding of the human psyche by studying neurotic patients rather than successful and strong individuals in society.

In this sense, Maslow's ideas were quite revolutionary and later spawned numerous followers studying the structure of excellence. Richard Bandler and John Grinder, for instance, began engaging in this endeavor in the 1970s when they created neuro-linguistic programming (NLP), which subsequently became identified in NLP's core beliefs as the "science and art of studying an individual's subjective experience."

In my opinion, behavior modeling in NLP has become a worthy continuation and embodiment of Maslow's theories. However, this information is not widely disseminated within NLP circles and training programs, with Michael Hall being an exception. After 2000, he began mentioning Maslow's contribution to the development of personality modeling in neuro-linguistic programming and neuro-semantics in his training programs.

Maslow embarked on his "modeling" of self-actualizing personalities as he perceived them. He included 18 individuals in his list of people to study, with nine of them being historical figures and the other nine being his contemporaries. He modeled personalities such as Abraham Lincoln, Albert Einstein, Eleanor Roosevelt, Jane Addams, Aldous Huxley, Baruch Spinoza, and others.

It is worth noting that Maslow rather assembled a collection of well-known individuals who corresponded to his notions of successful and "enlightened" self-actualization. In doing so, he ignored many "dark" geniuses in various fields of science and individuals who, on the one hand, achieved global fame and personal self-actualization but, at the same time, did not meet several criteria of Maslow's conception of self-actualization. As a result, Maslow's ideas about the qualities of a self-actualized person became somewhat idealized.

In his book "The Farther Reaches of Human Nature," Maslow presents his main reflections on self-actualization and describes, in his opinion, the paths through which individuals can self-actualize.

Maslow also comments that self-actualization is:

- The complete experience of one's life

- Taking responsibility for one's actions
- Existing in reality, not just potentially
- Developing the ability to make better life choices
- Experiencing peak moments in life.

Maslow also emphasized that part of self-actualization could involve the presence of a transcendent spiritual experience, not only among priests, poets, musicians, and teachers but also among businessmen and politicians.

Also, in his works, Maslow uses the term "synergy," which was first introduced by Ruth Benedict. Maslow describes the process of synergy as a state where the success of others becomes the basis for individual satisfaction.

Maslow introduces the term "plateau experience." In some sense, this term is similar to the concept of a peak experience but has some differences. Maslow understood the plateau experience as living at a high level of enlightenment or awakening, accepting the sharpness and precision of the beauty of things without unnecessary noise.

Maslow perceived the defense mechanisms of the psyche as certain barriers to personal development. In addition to the existing types of defense mechanisms, he added two of his own:

1. **Desacralization**: Deprivation of meta-meanings and meta-motivations in an individual's personality.
2. **The Ion Complex**: Resistance to uncovering one's true potential.

Maslow considered himself a Freudian, behaviorist, and humanist. He referred to the humanistic movement in psychology as the "third force" that should integrate the knowledge accumulated before it and transform it qualitatively. Maslow also spoke about the possibility of developing a "fourth force" in psychology, which, in his opinion, should be the psychology of transcendence. It is worth noting that he partly influenced the development of transpersonal psychology, which actively evolved in the 1960s and 1970s.

In his research, Maslow selected individuals who not only had the ability to perceive facts but also had the skill to discern the essential, valuable, and worthwhile aspects that could be used as objects for imitation by all of humanity.

During the study of self-actualizing individuals, Maslow asked the following questions:

- What interests them?
- What do they love?
- What motivates them?
- What do they fight for?
- What is valuable to them?

He also questioned the choice of self-actualizing individuals for his research:

- How do people make good choices?
- Where do such individuals come from?
- How do they grow?
- How do they learn this?
- What can hinder making good choices?
- What can assist in making good choices?

Maslow emphasized that the choices made by self-actualizing individuals would differ significantly from the choices made by deviants, psychopaths, sadists, masochists, and the like. Understanding the differences between these two groups can make a substantial contribution to psychology and psychotherapy.

Maslow believed that humanistic psychology is inherently anti-authoritarian and compared it to Chinese Daoist philosophy, particularly the works of Laozi, which are permeated with humanism and a non-directive philosophy of relating to the world. In Maslow's view, being

Daoist in relationships means understanding the person rather than instructing them.

Maslow wrote about seven types of needs, the hierarchy of which became known as "Maslow's hierarchy of needs." Let's describe it in more detail.

Maslow's Hierarchy of Needs

1. **Physiological needs:** This refers to the need for food, water, sex, and sleep.
2. **Safety needs:** The ability to protect oneself and not experience fear regarding one's survival.
3. **Belongingness and love needs:** The desire for others to perceive the individual as part of their "tribe." This motivation is reminiscent of Alfred Adler's concept of social interest.
4. **Esteem needs:** At this level of motivation, there is a desire not only to belong to a group but also to occupy a favorable hierarchical position within it. A wide range of social achievement needs are formed, which are oriented towards social status. This level of motivation bears similarities to Carl Jung's archetype of the "persona."
5. **Cognitive needs:** This is where the desire to explore the world emerges and is not driven by hierarchy or social benefits. The key focus becomes interest in knowledge, study, research, and understanding. This level of motivation shares many similarities with Jungian psychology's concept of the "self."
6. **Aesthetic needs:** The need to harmonize one's life and fill it with beauty, grace, and various creative expressions.
7. **Self-actualization needs.**

According to Maslow, the transition to the next type of motivation occurs when the previous one is at least partially satisfied. As lower needs are gradually fulfilled, the need for higher ones begins to emerge.

However, despite its elegance and popularity, Maslow's pyramid has not been validated through experimental research (Hall and Nougaim, 1968;

Lawler and Suttle, 1972). Validating Maslow's pyramid is challenging due to the abstract criteria of satisfaction at each level of motivation.

Furthermore, Maslow's belief that the satisfaction of each level is directly related to a person's age further complicates matters. For example, according to Maslow, full satisfaction with lower levels of motivation occurs during childhood and adolescence, while higher levels can only be fully satisfied after the age of 50.

It is also worth noting that Maslow believed that self-actualization could be achieved by no more than 2% of individuals. Considering that Maslow did not conduct any empirical research, his models and the percentages attributed to them should be regarded as mere assumptions.

Carl Rogers and Humanistic Psychotherapy

The best way to understand an individual is to see the world through their eyes. Carl Rogers was born in Oak Park, Illinois, USA, in 1902. Rogers was the fourth of six children. He described his childhood as having a strict, religious, and moral atmosphere. He considered his parents to be good and loving people but deeply immersed in religious dogmas.

Carl Rogers

During his childhood, he was quite lonely and had almost no friends outside of his family, so he spent most of his time reading various books.

After completing school, he wanted to become a farmer, so he chose agriculture as his main subject of study at the University of Wisconsin. However, during his second year, he began actively studying religion and the intricacies of religious activities, aspiring to become a pastor in the future. In 1922, he traveled to Beijing for a conference of the World Student Christian Federation, where he stayed for six months. After the trip, he began to have significant doubts about his religious beliefs.

Subsequently, he enrolled in a seminary, but after some time, he became disillusioned with religious institutions. At the end of his second year of studies, he decided to change the direction of his career and pursue psychology. Later, he became an atheist.

Carl Rogers entered the Teachers College at Columbia University, where he studied educational and clinical psychology. In 1928, he obtained a master's degree in psychology, and in 1931, he earned a doctorate in clinical psychology. From 1931 onwards, he actively engaged in working with delinquent and underprivileged children.

From 1935 to 1940, he lectured at the University of Rochester and wrote the book "Clinical Treatment of Problem Children" in 1939, based on his experience working with troubled children.

In 1940, Rogers returned to Columbia University, where he gradually began to develop his humanistic ideas. In 1942, he published the book "Counseling and Psychotherapy." In 1945, he started working at the University of Chicago, where he was offered a position as a professor and director of the university's counseling center.

In 1946, in collaboration with John L. Wallen, he wrote a work entitled "Counseling with Returned Servicemen," which examined the specific application of the client-centered approach to the problems faced by servicemen returning from combat zones.

In this work, the authors explore the peculiarities of applying a client-centered approach to the problems faced by servicemen returning from combat zones.

In 1951, he completed his next book, "Client-Centered Therapy: Its Current Practice, Implications, and Theory," in which he fully articulated his views on the method of psychotherapy. In large part, his client-centered approach was influenced by Neo-Freudianism, particularly the works of Otto Rank. One of Otto Rank's students, Jessie Taft, had a particularly strong influence on him. In 1954, Rogers published the book "Psychotherapy and Personality Change." In 1956, Rogers became the first president of the American Academy of Psychotherapists. In 1957, he returned to the University of Wisconsin, where he began participating in a major research program aimed at treating schizophrenic patients with psychotherapy at the State Psychiatric Hospital. However, after some time, his approach to treatment proved to be less successful than expected, with only minimal positive changes observed in the patients.

He continued to work at the University of Wisconsin from 1957 to 1963. In 1961, Rogers published his new book, "On Becoming a Person." It is worth noting that Carl Rogers and Abraham Maslow were the main pioneers in humanistic psychology, which began to flourish in the 1960s.

In 1964, Rogers transitioned to a research position at the Western Behavioral Sciences Institute in La Jolla, California. Four years later, in the same city, he moved to work at the Center for Studies of the Person.

In 1969, Rogers published the book "Freedom to Learn," dedicated to the topic of client-centered education. In it, he elaborated on how this type of learning could be implemented and its advantages compared to orthodox forms of education.

Between 1974 and 1984, Rogers, together with his daughter Natalie Rogers and psychologists Maria Bowen, Maureen O'Hara, and John Wood, conducted a series of training programs in various countries worldwide. In addition to the United States, they taught the client-centered approach developed by Rogers in Brazil and Japan, focusing on cross-cultural communication, personal growth, and self-improvement.

In his later years, Rogers made attempts to apply his theories to various situations of political oppression and national conflicts. He traveled the world, spreading the ideas of humanism.

In 1985, Rogers visited the Soviet Union, delivering lectures and seminars on his therapeutic approach. He was amazed that his work was well-known to a large number of Russians.

In 1987, Carl Rogers broke his hip. The surgery was successful, but the following night his pancreas stopped functioning, and he passed away a few days later from a heart attack. Carl Rogers' person-centered therapy brought a new understanding of the process of relationships and their transformation. This approach finds wide application in both psychotherapy and educational activities. The foundation of Rogers' theory is based on the "phenomenal field" theory of personality developed by Combs and Snell in 1949. Throughout his life, Carl Rogers wrote 16 books and numerous articles.

Carl Rogers' theories were based on 19 assumptions. Let's list them and try to provide some commentary:

1. All individuals are part of a constantly changing world that creates a stream of events. Each person is the center of this world. This belief emphasizes the uniqueness of each individual and directs the process of psychotherapy toward understanding their depth rather than trying to fit them into a specific, fixed template. While this belief is somewhat idealistic, it allows for the exploration of new forms of interaction with the client. On the other hand, a template-based perception of symptoms will inevitably face the problem of a mismatch between therapy tools and the patient's personality.
2. We react to the world based on our perception of it. What we perceive is what we consider reality. Korzybski said in 1933, "The map is not the territory." In other words, reality is not exactly how we perceive it. As seen from Rogers' perspective, the map does become the territory to some extent. However, this can lead to a philosophical debate. It is worth noting that both positions can offer interesting focal points for attention. Rogers' perspective emphasizes the importance of individuality, while Korzybski's position provides

a broader perspective that the world is somewhat larger than how we imagine and perceive it.

3. The organism reacts to the phenomenological field as a whole. In this case, we see Rogers forming holistic beliefs about the integrity of the mind and body, as well as their various parts. The therapist's focus becomes the consideration of the organism's and individual's wholeness.
4. The world we perceive eventually becomes a part of our ego. In this case, Rogers points to the continuous process of experiential integration that takes place in our consciousness. This belief may resemble the phrase, "We become what we think."
5. Contact with the environment and evaluative interaction with it form the individual's self-structure. Through this process, we develop the framework of our values and beliefs. Understanding how an individual interacts with the environment allows us to assess their personality characteristics and anticipate the particularities of their future life path.
6. The organism has three basic tendencies throughout its life. These tendencies are to actualize its inherent potential, to maintain the accumulated and achieved positions, and to improve through the accumulation of experience as much as possible. This idea by Rogers aligns closely with Maslow's concept of self-actualized individuals. It is also worth noting that this belief enables the therapist to see the explicit and implicit potential in the client's personality, rather than focusing solely on pathological manifestations. This naturally opens up new possibilities in therapeutic practice.
7. The best way to understand an individual is to see the world through their eyes. Associative experiences of another person's inner world truly provide a tremendous amount of new experience that is inaccessible from the usual position of perception and the processes of thinking and inference. This belief is inherent in many renowned psychotherapists and psychotherapy systems. Some leave this belief at the philosophical level, while others create specific practices to

facilitate their own or the patient's ability to re-experience the emotions of another individual. Dramatic methods in psychotherapy or similar approaches are particularly effective for these purposes, where the patient intentionally takes on the role of another person and tries to feel and experience them as they are. Examples of such methods include Jacob Moreno's psychodrama, Virginia Satir's "family sculpture," Frederick Perls' gestalt therapy, Bert Hellinger's family constellations, and so on.

8. All behavior is primarily goal-directed and driven by the organism's attempts to satisfy its needs. This belief allows for the recognition of the existence of deep layers of personality that determine specific behaviors. In this case, Rogers significantly expands the old reductionist behavioral approach, which states that psychology should exclusively study observable behavior. Understanding the external and internal creates a holistic picture of perception and understanding of reality.
9. Emotions in the human psyche accompany behavior aimed at satisfying needs and are connected to determining the significance of certain actions or reactions. They are an integral psychological mechanism that contributes to the maintenance or improvement of the organism's functioning. The ability to express emotions correctly and appropriately is an inherent adaptive mechanism of the human psyche.
10. Part of an individual's values are derived directly from their experience of interacting with the world, while another part may simply be borrowed from other people, thereby distorting the adequacy of reality perception. The ability of an individual to integrate into their behavior those values that are derived directly from their experience is an integral part of personal growth. The work of a psychotherapist can significantly assist the patient in this process.
11. Experiences and the knowledge acquired by an individual: **a**) undergo symbolization, during which the experience is consolidated within the person; **b**) are ignored if something incompatible with the experience is perceived; **c**) undergo a series of distortions during symbolization

due to various incompatibilities with the experience. One of the main barriers to personal evolution is the application of old perceptual filters to any new experience. Only by expanding one's worldview can a person find answers to questions that have not yet been discovered.

12. Most forms and modes of behavior that an individual may exhibit in their life are directly related to themselves. This self is, to some extent, an abstract core of the personality, encompassing various variations of possible actions.
13. Sometimes a person's behavior may be caused by organic experiences and needs that have not been symbolized. Such behavior is likely to be incompatible with the individual's personality structure and, in a way, does not "belong" to them. It is worth noting that it does not "belong" because it has not yet acquired a form that can be integrated into the structure of the Self.
14. Psychological adaptation occurs when the sensory and visceral experiences of the organism are assimilated or can be assimilated at the symbolic level, in accordance with the person's self-concept. Fragments of experience may require different lengths of time for assimilation and may demand varying degrees of effort. The more similar the block of experience obtained is to the experience regularly received by the individual, the faster and easier its assimilation will be. Experience that significantly deviates from the structure will trigger various conflicts within it. Resolving such conflicts may lead to partial or complete restructuring of the individual's self.
15. Psychological maladaptation occurs when the individual's organism begins to deny the conscious significance of sensory and visceral experiences that are symbolized and are unable to integrate into the gestalt of the self. This situation can generate persistent or potential tension and anxiety. This anxiety signals the passage of a crisis stage in an individual's existence. Depending on the specificity of the individual, the duration and quality of this period can significantly vary. However, at some point in everyone's life, crises of different intensities occur. The emergence of certain symptoms

in an individual is directly related to such an adaptive crisis. In this case, a psychotherapist can assist the patient in resolving the crisis. Therapeutic conversation, in particular, can provide a unique opportunity for that. Rogers believed that the therapist's task in this case was to support the patient in their movement toward resolving the crisis stage of life.

16. Experiences that do not align with the structure of the individual's self can be perceived as a threat and trigger aggression. The more rigidly organized the individual is, the more likely it is that such a situation may occur. Such rigidity in the structure of the self often takes the form of internalized values from parents or other close individuals. Abandoning limiting beliefs can significantly transform and change a person, affecting many aspects of their life. This aggressive reaction is one of the existing defense mechanisms of the individual, and it manifests in different degrees among different people and social groups. Radical transformation of the self-structure is perceived by consciousness as an experience somewhat similar to death. Throughout their development, individuals can learn to endure such transformations, but it often requires time.
17. In conditions primarily associated with the absence of threats to the individual's structure, experiences that are incompatible with it can be perceived more accurately and explored with the goal of assimilation. Undoubtedly, a positive attitude towards an experience can give individuals the opportunity to fully perceive it. Such an attitude towards the patient can create excellent conditions for seeing and understanding the essence of the existing problem and interacting with it accurately.
18. When individuals successfully create a comprehensive and integrated picture from their perceived sensory and visceral experiences, their ability to perceive and understand others significantly increases. Creating such a comprehensive picture often requires time and effort. The psychotherapeutic context is an excellent catalyst and facilitator of such integrative processes.

19. As individuals deeply comprehend and accept their own structures, they begin to replace the system of values based on introjections with a system of values oriented toward their own experience. Metaphorically, this process can be likened to the digestion and assimilation of food in the gastrointestinal tract. The maturation of the adult ego is directly related to the ability to rely on one's own experience. A person who is guided by externally imposed convictions without understanding their meaning is, to a greater extent, a child, regardless of their social status, income level, or self-esteem.

Carl Rogers had very similar ideas to Abraham Maslow about individuals who deeply actualize their potential. Maslow referred to such individuals as self-actualizing, while Rogers called them fully functioning. In his works, Rogers listed the key characteristics of a fully functioning person, which we will present here along with comments.

1. **Growing openness to experience:** As the individual's capacity to cope with anxiety related to experiences that differ from the structure of the self actualizes, their confidence in overcoming diverse obstacles and dealing with life's challenges increases. A person opens up to new experiences when they are ready. This readiness is determined by the level of self-integrity and the depth of its integration. The more congruent the different parts of the self are with each other, the more the individual's ability to gain new experiences is actualized. Openness to experience also emphasizes the level of maturity in an individual's personality. Although maturity itself is not one-dimensional and unequivocal, different parts of the personality mature at different times and at different rates. This is similar to the diversity of different types of intelligence, which number more than 20. Individuality cannot develop simultaneously in all types of intelligence; there will be more of certain qualities and significantly fewer of others. As with openness to experience, growth follows a similar pattern. Openness to experience always has a direction but

simultaneously serves as a kind of meta-frame that predefines an individual's capacity for assimilating new experiences and integrating them.

2. **Existential way of life:** The richness of each moment of existence, in which individuality is manifested, and the self-esteem of the personality derive from personal experience and are independent of numerous social introductions. This naturally leads a person to states such as excitement, courage, adaptability, tolerance, spontaneity, and gentleness and implies a foundation of trust. As Rogers said, "to partially open one's spirit to the experience that comes here and now and to discover what structure it has, an existential way of life entails deep awareness of the individual and the integrity and integration of their self-structures. Many of the qualities described in this section bear a striking resemblance to those of an enlightened individual in the East. Similar descriptions can be found in Buddhism, Hinduism, Taoism, and so on.
3. **Increased self-trust:** A person begins to trust their thoughts, decisions, and judgments more without losing touch with reality. A personal sense of good and evil arises. The need for external guidance diminishes. A person who trusts themselves is capable of much more effectively understanding and transforming the world through their actual interaction with it. However, this self-trust is not blind; it is based on logic, sound thinking, and personal experience. It is not the self-trust of a madman or fanatic. It is the self-trust of an adult who clearly acknowledges who they are, where they are, and in which direction they are going. To achieve this state, a person must go through the experience of life's challenges, analyze them, and deeply integrate them. Sometimes a person can do this on their own, while other times they may need someone who can support them in this process. If one person helps another in this, the significance lies not in direct teaching but rather in pushing the person to find their own answers within themselves.
4. **The ability to make free choices:** This ability is formed during the

growth and maturation of the personality. The individual begins to realize that most of the barriers they create for themselves are related to human reasoning. Therefore, the freedom to make choices primarily depends on the state of mind of a mature individual. This maturity is directly related to the ability to be responsible for one's behavior. Responsibility makes freedom a mature experience.

5. **Manifestation of the creative aspect of personality:** The ability to express the creative potential of one's personality is directly related to a sense of personal freedom. Creativity can liberate a person from dogma and allow them to live life in a unique way. It reveals the true creativity of the individual's personality, the very creativity that enables personal identification to become more integrated and resilient. It is also worth noting that true creativity begins to manifest in an individual as they gradually shed the need to conform to various socially nonconstructive frameworks and accumulate experience.
6. **Reliability and constructiveness of personality:** A person who is aware of the needs inherent within them can maintain a balance between those needs and harmonize one need with another. For example, aggression can be balanced by kindness, callousness by empathy, and detachment by acceptance. The ability to find balance among different potentials determines the reliability and constructive functioning of an individual in society. However, at times, to achieve such balance, one needs to gain an understanding of what it means to exist within various polarities. This process requires time, and some individuals may need their entire lifetime for it.
7. **A rich and meaningful life:** A person begins to live their life with maximum concentration. All the emotions inherent in human life, both positive and negative, become more intense and vivid. Rogers believed that such a life was not for the faint-hearted. It entails personal growth and expansion, acquiring greater and greater possibilities. Living such a life requires tremendous courage.

Initially, Rogers referred to his psychotherapy system as "nondirective therapy." Later, he began to call it "client-centered therapy." He believed that the theoretical and philosophical foundation of his method could be applied in various life contexts and serve as a philosophy for an individual's life journey to some extent.

Working on the theory of client-centered learning, Rogers put forward five hypotheses regarding the educational process.

1. A person cannot directly teach another; they can only facilitate the other's learning.
2. A person truly grasps things that are directly related to maintaining and enhancing the structure of their individual self.
3. Assimilated experiences that will be involved in changing the structure of the self can be denied and distorted.
4. The structure and organization of the self seem to become more rigid under threat and weaken boundaries once these threats begin to recede.
5. The most effective educational situation is one in which:
   a) the threat to the learner is minimized; and
   b) a differentiated perception of the field is facilitated.

Rogerian Rhetoric

The humanistic approach found its reflection in the rhetorical field. In 1970, Richard Young, Alton L. Becker, and Kenneth Pike published the book "Rhetoric: Discovery and Change." This book actively applied the philosophy of the Rogerian approach as a specific alternative to the foundations of Aristotelian rhetoric. The key to Rogerian rhetoric lies in the process of recognizing and understanding one's opposition rather than engaging in direct confrontation with it.

Person-Centered Politics

By the end of his life, Rogers came to the conclusion that the ideas he actively advocated and implemented in psychotherapy and education could be effectively used in a political context to address pressing societal challenges in this domain. The central aspect of Rogers' philosophy in this context is shifting the focus of political life from a series of constant wars to the creation of dialogue between opposing sides. Such a dialogue can foster mutual respect and lead to various forms of conflict resolution, transforming it into a more constructive form of social interaction. In the last ten years of his life, Rogers actively participated in fostering constructive dialogue among different politicians, both in the United States and beyond.

Elias Porter and the Emergence of the Nondirective Approach in Psychotherapy

Elias Hall Porter (1914–1987) was an American psychologist whose work significantly contributed to the formation and development of Carl Rogers' client-centered therapy. In the 1930s, he was a student of Calvin S. Hall and Robert Lipman. In his work, Porter described experiments with rats that confirmed that rat learning in a maze can occur even without the presence of a formal reward. He defended his master's thesis in 1938 at the University of Oregon. In 1941, he completed his doctoral dissertation at Ohio State University. Porter's dissertation formally became the first empirical study to document the effectiveness of the nondirective approach in counseling.

Elias Porter

At the University of Chicago, he was a colleague of Carl Rogers, Thomas Gordon, Abraham Maslow, and Will Schutz. Porter's primary contribution to psychology was his development of the nondirective approach in counseling, the theory of understanding relationships, and various psychometric tests.

Porter's collaboration with the RAND Corporation resulted in two noteworthy publications. The first was an essay called "The Spindle Parable," and the second was his book "Developing the Work Force," published in 1964. This book was one of the first to consider the organization of a social system as a holistic organism. In these works, the nature of human behavior was directly examined and studied in the context of the organizational system to which it belonged. This theme was another innovative contribution by Porter to psychology.

Regarding Porter's contribution to psychometric testing, it is worth mentioning that his early research, conducted in collaboration with Rogers, aimed to measure the level of directive or nondirective behavior of therapists in their work. Porter's test, which measured personal closeness criteria, confirmed the existence of four unproductive orientations, according to Erich Fromm.

Theory of Consciousness About Relationships

This theory represents an intriguing combination of various forms of psychological thinking. It incorporates the concepts of:

1. Edward Tolman's behaviorism,
2. Kurt Lewin's empiricism,
3. Carl Rogers' client-centered psychotherapy,
4. Erich Fromm's and Karen Horney's theories of personality.

The theory is based on four premises, which we will examine in more detail.

1. **Human behavior is driven by motivation:** Through the study of Fromm's, Rogers', and Maslow's theories, Porter concludes that the primary motive behind the behavior of the vast majority of individuals is the desire to feel worthy and the pursuit of various means of achieving self-esteem through life interactions. Porter also believed that self-esteem and self-actualization were the primary drivers of personality development.
2. **Motivation for change arises from conflict:** Porter posits the idea that when individuals have the freedom to pursue various pleasures, it becomes monotonous and predictable. On the other hand, during conflicts or confrontations, changes occur in the motivational sphere, intertwined with different values and beliefs, which manifest in various forms of behavior. Porter suggests that individuals predictably and consistently change their motivation. This sequence includes three stages: the first stage involves caring for oneself, one's own problem, and another person; the second stage involves caring for oneself and one's own problem; and the third stage involves caring solely for oneself. Porter further asserts that the key motive in conflict is the preservation of one's integrity and self-esteem.
3. **Personality weakness is an exaggerated strength:** Porter adopts Fromm's idea that the strength of personality can become its weak-

ness and presents the concept of ineffective behavior driven by positive motivation.

4. **Clarity and authenticity enhance the quality of self-exploration:** Porter proposes the concept that the clearer the conception of personality in personality theory and the closer it aligns with how an individual experiences themselves, the more effective it can be as a means of self-knowledge. Porter believes that psychometric testing should emphasize practical application rather than diagnostic and prognostic capabilities. He also hypothesizes that personality filters influence perception and condition it.

James Bugental and the Search for Authenticity

James Frederick Thomas Bugental (1915–2008) was born in Fort Wayne, Indiana. During his childhood, he lived in various places, including Ohio, Illinois, Michigan, and California. In the 1930s, he enrolled in university, where he studied psychology.

James Bugental

Bugental was a well-known psychotherapist who actively worked on the theory and practice of existential-humanistic psychotherapy. He obtained his doctoral degree from Ohio University and became a member of the American Psychological Association in 1955. He served as a professor at Saybrook Institute, an honorary lecturer at Stanford University, and an honorary professor at the Institute of Humanistic Studies. Additionally, he held the position of president of the California Psychological Association.

In his book "The Search for Authenticity," he formulated the fundamental postulates of humanistic psychology. Let us enumerate them and provide comments.

1. **The human individual cannot be reduced to the sum of its parts:** This holistic concept can be found in the works of many authors dedicated to humanistic philosophy. Consciousness, mind, body, human behavior, emotions, and sensations together form a cohesive system. Through the interaction of these elements, the system generates new qualities and properties that may not exist individually. Therefore, reducing the whole to the sum of its components is unwarranted reductionism, simplifying the multitude of meanings inherent in being human.

2. **Each person is inherently unique:** Every individual has the capacity to unfold their uniqueness through the process of socialization. However, socialization can lead to the suppression of one's uniqueness, causing individuals to follow paths significantly divergent from their profound essence, which allows for self-realization and self-actualization. Therefore, the search for and realization of uniqueness present a significant challenge for individuals. It can be considered one of the primary existential challenges of life. By effectively realizing their true potential, individuals can deeply connect with reality and apprehend it in all its splendor. In the therapeutic process, the therapist can assist in unveiling the patient's uniqueness, facilitating its emergence into the world.

3. **Human consciousness includes self-awareness in the context of other human individuals:** A human being is inseparable from the society in which they exist. Personal growth and development occur in relation to the people around them, other living beings, and the world as a whole. Self-awareness emerges through contact with the environment. However, it is essential to understand that the quality, quantity, appropriateness, direction, purpose, and other aspects of contact matter. Therefore, self-awareness in the context of others poses a challenge for individuals—a task that they continuously address throughout their lives. Depending on their success in resolving this task, we can observe individuals at various stages of personal evolution.

4. **Every person has a choice about how to live and is capable of taking responsibility for their actions:** However, the ability to make choices and bear responsibility is the realm of the adult ego. It requires courage to perceive the world as it is and to let go of illusions about it and oneself. In doing so, a person is able to notice in the world the opportunities that can bring real growth and the unfolding of their potential. A person with a childish ego merely plays with a microscopic version of reality that they create in their mind. This microscopic version of reality is safer as long as there is someone who takes responsibility for the person. And a person can become so accustomed to this state that they become unable to understand and conceive of something greater and more powerful. However, life presents various challenges to a person and stimulates them to grow and develop. The sooner a person grasps this impulse from the world, the more their life becomes a journey that brings joy and enthusiasm.

5. **Human beings possess their own intentions in life and are in search of meaning, value, and creativity:** A person who is capable of setting life intentions and realizing them is able to truly unfold their potential

> in life. The search for various meanings that weave into our lives can provide the support that helps us withstand the most difficult circumstances, restore ourselves after a challenging period in life, and find a new direction in personal growth and self-improvement. The ability to appreciate the world allows us to experience joy from being in it. And, naturally, the creativity of an individual signifies that they are capable not only of taking from the world but also of giving something of value to others. This creates a sense of inner wholeness and a feeling of connection and unity with the world.

Bugental believed that what we call intensive psychotherapy is actually an accelerated educational process aimed at achieving maturity. According to him, the psychotherapist is a figure capable of accelerating this process, moving the patient forward from a standstill, and through therapeutic conversation, creating optimal opportunities for the realization of their personal potential.

He also believed that the most powerful influence capable of changing the human personality is love for another person.

Bugental spoke of being truly alive as being condemned to constant growth and infinite change. It also means finding one's identity in this ever-changing process and understanding that fire will eventually destroy any stable structures we try to build. He also gave a beautiful metaphor for the human personality, saying that we consist of a flame and its dance—the dance of our lives.

Frederick Perls and Gestalt Therapy

Frederick Perls (1893–1970) was a German-American psychiatrist and psychoanalyst. Born in Berlin, Germany, Perls initially aspired to pursue a legal education but later changed his path and became a medical student. He served in World War I and, upon his return, resumed his medical studies. He specialized in neuropsychiatry and became an assistant to Kurt Goldstein, who was working with soldiers affected by cranial and brain injuries. During his studies, Perls developed a keen interest in psychoanalytic theories. In 1927, he became a participant in Wilhelm Reich's seminar in Vienna.

Frederick Perls

The character analysis conducted by Wilhelm Reich significantly influenced the formation of Frederick Perls' psychotherapeutic thinking. In 1930, Perls underwent a course of psychoanalysis with Reich in Berlin. That same year, Frederick Perls married Laura Posner and became the father of two children. In 1933, as the Nazi regime gained power and began persecuting Jews, Perls and his family relocated to the Netherlands and then, a year later, to South Africa, where he established a psychoanalytic institute. In 1936, Perls had his first encounter with Sigmund Freud. However, Freud showed no enthusiasm for engaging with him. This encounter left Perls deeply disappointed and significantly shaped his future theoretical and practical direction. Consequently, Perls abandoned the practice of psychoanalysis and developed his own therapeutic approach, which he named Gestalt therapy.

The foundational ideas of Gestalt therapy were developed in the 1940s and 1950s by Frederick Perls, his wife Laura Perls, and Paul Goodman.

Gestalt therapy can be considered a form of revision of psychoanalysis, although it would be more accurate to describe it as a near-complete transformation with extensive influences from Eastern philosophy, psychodrama, Gestalt psychology, existential psychology, and more.

Together with Paul Goodman and Ralph Hefferline, Perls authored the book "Gestalt Therapy: Excitement and Growth in the Human Personality."

Gestalt therapy gradually gained popularity, leading to the formation of Gestalt groups in various cities across America by the end of the 1950s. In the 1960s, Gestalt therapy started gaining recognition in Europe.

Initially, Perls' method of Gestalt therapy did not aim to analyze the patient's unconscious content. Instead, Perls emphasized the importance of focusing on the present moment and attaining awareness through it. According to Perls, a therapist practicing Gestalt therapy assists the patient in developing mindfulness skills that can be effectively applied outside the therapy context. Another goal of Gestalt therapy is to strengthen the patient's sense of a cohesive self-image. This sense of wholeness is often achieved by re-experiencing various fragments of the patient's own experiences. Perls incorporated practical tools from Jacob Moreno's psychodrama to facilitate this process. For instance, the empty chair technique, which is utilized as a form of monodrama in psychodrama, may be employed. In this technique, the therapist may ask the patient to imagine the figure of their father sitting on an empty chair beside them and express specific phrases directed towards their relationship with him. After the patient conveys various messages to the represented father, the therapist may inquire about the patient's experiences and provide further guidance for exploration and understanding.

In 1952, after moving to New York, Frederick Perls, together with a group of colleagues, founded the New York Gestalt Institute. The group of co-founders included Laura Perls, Paul Goodman, Isidor Fromm, Elliot Shapiro, Richard Kitzler, and Paul Weiss.

Gestalt therapy gradually gained popularity. By the end of the 1950s, Gestalt groups were being established in many cities across America. By the 1960s, Gestalt therapy had begun to gain popularity in Europe.

The method of Gestalt therapy developed by Perls was not intended, according to his plan, for analyzing the content of the patient's unconscious. Perls' focus was on the present moment and the awareness that the patient could achieve by concentrating on it. According to Perls, a psychotherapist practicing Gestalt therapy helps the patient develop mindfulness skills that the patient can then effectively apply outside the context of psychotherapy.

Another goal of Gestalt therapy is to strengthen the patient's conscious sense of wholeness as an individual. This acquisition of wholeness often occurs through the associated reliving of various fragments of one's experience. To effectively carry out such an action, Perls borrowed some practical tools from Jacob Moreno's psychodrama. For example, the empty chair technique, which is used as a form of monodrama in psychodrama, is a way of playing the role of one actor. For instance, when a patient needs to resolve certain emotional issues with their father, a Gestalt therapist may ask the patient to imagine the figure of the father on the adjacent empty chair and express specific phrases towards him that relate to the context of their relationship.

After the patient expresses various messages to the represented father, the therapist may ask the patient to switch to the empty chair where the represented father is and symbolically take on his role. Subsequently, in the role of the father, the patient voices specific thoughts that emerged in this state. The therapist can thus move the patient from one role to another until some therapeutic outcome is achieved. Symbolic integration of the experience projected onto this figure occurs during the process of living out the role of another person. The process of dialogue between different roles serves a similar function.

If this technique is performed correctly, the patient can not only shift their focus on the situation but also radically change their attitude towards it. In the process of changing one's attitude, insights, vivid verbal and non-verbal signals indicating that the patient has reached a new level of understanding, and catharsis, intense purifying emotional reliving that allows expressing previously blocked emotions, can be observed.

Perls spoke about the concept of contact as a form of interaction between a person and someone other than themselves. Contact is also a way of selecting a figure from the perceived flow of information, thereby transforming the rest into the background. The terms "figure" and "background" were borrowed by Perls from the theories of Gestalt psychology, which developed certain ideas about the process of perception. However, despite the similarity of some terms and the very name "Gestalt," which can be translated from German as wholeness or form, Gestalt psychology theories and Perls theories have very little in common.

The failed encounter between Perls and Freud resulted not only in his departure from the basic theories of psychoanalysis but also in a certain intolerance towards excessive theorizing and the construction of various discrete scientific models. This gave rise to the legend that Perls could even say that he hadn't read a single book on Gestalt psychology. Most likely, this was a provocation on his part, but unfortunately, many followers of Gestalt psychotherapy might believe it.

The concept of contact, according to Perls, is divided into five main phases, each endowed with different meanings:

1. **Resting state**: Consciousness is in equilibrium; new connections are not yet planned or created. The resting state implies that the motivation for establishing new contact has not yet been actualized due to various reasons.
2. **Pre-contact**: A specific figure in the perceptual field is highlighted. Attention is focused on it, and actions that can be taken in relation to it begin to be planned. Anticipation of the outcome is possible. Various emotional states may arise, related to both the anticipation of contact and the anticipation of the final contact result.
3. **Contacting**: Direct engagement with a new object in the surrounding world. It involves applying old behavioral patterns that were used in response to stimuli or exploring new ways of interacting with the object for various reasons.
4. **Full final contact**: Bringing the contact to a logical goal that may have

existed prior to the contact or was formed during the contact. The final contact implies completing the gestalt, that is, carrying out a specific action or a series of specific actions that serve as markers of contact completion.

5. **Post-contact (assimilation)**: The assimilation of past accumulated experience and its arrangement in consciousness. The quality of the contact is evaluated and compared with other contacts that have occurred in the person's experience. The states experienced by an individual during the post-contact phase are closely related to how the final contact was completed. If the completion is successful, the states will have a positive character. However, if the final contact was not completed in the right way, frustration or other negative emotions may arise during the post-contact phase. Planning for correcting mistakes made during the last contact is also possible during this phase. The anticipation of improving future contacts is also possible.

In gestalt therapy, personality is regarded as the process of interaction between an individual and the surrounding environment, and it is divided into three key elements.

1. **Id** represents the combination of emotional processes and sexual drives.
2. **Persona** encompasses specific memory processes and recollection, which fixate individual characteristics within one's consciousness.
3. **Ego** is the part of personality that makes various life decisions when the need arises.

In my opinion, this division was made as a specific form of reworking the concept of personality division in traditional psychoanalysis, which differentiates the human personality into the superego, ego, and id.

Gestalt therapy has also significantly reworked and transformed the understanding of resistance, which may manifest in the patient during the therapeutic process. An essential distinction is that, according to gestalt therapists, resistance is a form of interaction between the organism and the surrounding environment that is effective at certain stages of personality development and existence. However, due to certain circumstances, it emerges in an inappropriate context and does not pertain to the necessary individuals.

Despite gestalt therapy's focus on the "here and now" state, working with the past and the future can still be conducted. For instance, one of the renowned gestalt therapists, Claudio Naranjo, coined a special term for this purpose, called "presentification," which signifies considering the past or future in the context of the present. A practical embodiment of this idea involves representing the past or future as if it were happening in the present and employing a dramatic method to enact the situation. It is worth noting, however, that Naranjo's theoretical and practical contributions are not universally applied and endorsed by all schools of gestalt therapy.

In my opinion, it is worth adding that Naranjo's ideas clearly reflect the realization that without certain concepts rejected by Perls, therapy becomes less effective. Nevertheless, in order to avoid constructing a separate form of psychotherapy, Naranjo attempted to create a "loophole" to explain and mark the past and future in a way that aligns with the fundamental principles of gestalt therapy.

Frederick Perls discussed the concept of defense mechanisms in the psyche in his works, largely influenced by Sigmund Freud's psychoanalysis. Freudian and Neo-Freudian theories extensively explore various defense mechanisms of the psyche. Perls incorporated only four of them in his practice:

a) projection, b) introjection, c) fusion, and d) retroflection. Later, Gestalt psychotherapy added another defense mechanism to this list—deflection. Let us provide commentary on each defense mechanism individually.

1. **Projection:** In the process of activating the defense mechanism of projection, specific qualities, properties, emotions, and other psychological processes of an individual begin to be ascribed to external objects. Simultaneously, the individual often resists

acknowledging these projected aspects within themselves. It is inherent for individuals to project their negative qualities and properties, although positive qualities can also be subject to projection. This projection often occurs with a temporal delay. For example, a person may possess certain qualities and properties they appreciate at the age of 20. However, as the years pass, they change and lose those qualities. Subsequently, this person may unconsciously project their positive qualities onto certain individuals without even realizing it. It is crucial to understand that projection is almost always an unconscious process oriented towards discarding something deemed unacceptable in the current life situation for various reasons. Awareness of the process of projection can lead to insight—a comprehension and conscious realization of what truly occurs in one's consciousness. If individuals are genuinely honest with themselves, such awareness can result in significant transformations in their psychological and behavioral spheres.

2. **Introjection:** In the process of activating the defense mechanism of introjection, an individual begins to perceive certain external values, qualities, peculiarities, and characteristics of others as part of their own personality. This acceptance is non-judgmental and uncritical. Introjection is predominantly observed in children, who, through this defense mechanism, form the foundation of their personalities. Excessive reliance on this defense mechanism in adulthood indicates a reluctance to let go of the childlike ego and certain illusions associated with it. The presence of the introjection defense mechanism implies the individual's unwillingness to take responsibility for certain aspects of their life. It reflects an infantile position where internal comfort is achieved by avoiding the analysis of information that could inform life choices. Individuals who employ the defense mechanism of introjection consciously or unconsciously identify with specific personalities (or multiple personalities) that become transmitters of specific ideas, qualities, states, and more. What

emanates from these personalities is often immune to criticism and remains unanalyzed. The manifestation of this defense mechanism is frequently encountered among adherents of various religious organizations, although other social contexts can also provoke its usage. The process of transitioning from the childlike ego to adulthood entails a gradual abandonment of this defense mechanism. In this case, the phrase from Buddhism spoken by Gautama Buddha to his disciples suits perfectly: "Do not believe in my words, test them through your own experience." This phrase splendidly illustrates the conviction that guides the rejection of the defense mechanism of introjection, implying personal and even spiritual growth during this process of abandonment.

3. **Fusion:** The defense mechanism of fusion, also known as confluence, involves the unconscious process of perceiving oneself and another person (or a group of people) as parts of a single entity, something indivisible. A person exhibiting the defense mechanism of fusion does not see or feel the difference between their "self" and the "self" of another person. Thus, the illusion of greater security can be achieved. Often, fusion occurs among various family members or the entire family as a whole. Sometimes fusion can be mutual, and sometimes it can be one-sided. Mutual fusion, for example, can be observed between a mother and a child or between lovers or spouses. Sometimes mutual fusion can be observed between two friends. The process of one-sided fusion can occur between an individual and someone they idolize, an object of imitation, admiration, and so on.

4. **Retroflexion:** This defense mechanism directs certain emotional processes that, for various reasons, cannot be expressed, back onto the individual. In one way or another, retroflexion arises from an inner prohibition that blocks the expression of a particular emotion or behavior. As a result, the energy of the emotion begins to transform into one symptom or another. Retroflexion most often blocks the

expression of aggressive feelings. A simple example could be a situation where someone angers someone else, but due to moral reasons or social context, they cannot fully respond to the person who is the stimulus eliciting the emotion.

5. **Deflection:** This defense mechanism manifests itself in the avoidance of direct contact with the interlocutor. Direct contact is replaced with surrogate behavior, such as inappropriate humor, describing insignificant details of certain situations, or deviating from the topic of conversation. By actualizing this defense mechanism, a person does everything possible to avoid full emotional contact with another person or group of people to whom the individual belongs.

In the context of therapy, Perls proposed a specific self-suggestion text that, in the author's opinion, can help individuals experience and cope with various offenses and problems in relationships. He called this text the "Gestalt Prayer." The text is as follows: "*I do my thing, and you do your thing. I am not in this world to live up to your expectations, and you are not in this world to live up to mine. You are you, and I am I. If, by chance, we find each other, it's beautiful. If not, it can't be helped.*"

This "prayer" reflects Perls' philosophy of a harmonious personality as one that is capable of relying on oneself, one's values, behavior, resources, and so on.

In many ways, for Perls, the ability to rely on oneself was associated with his concept of being in the "here and now," which he consistently advocated as the optimal state for a harmonious individual. He borrowed the idea of this state from Zen Buddhism. It is worth noting that Perls was an atheist and could not embrace the idea of worshiping a deity. When he encountered Buddhism, he was attracted to the ideas inherent in this religious context. However, he discovered that Buddhism also had rituals of worship, which did not appeal to him. Consequently, his interest in this religion soon waned. Nevertheless, the ideas he gleaned from studying this spiritual tradition continued to live in his mind and manifested in the therapy practice he taught.

Some critics of Gestalt therapy have repeatedly emphasized that it is not a fully scientific method of psychotherapy, as many of its practices are overtly borrowed from various spiritual traditions. Moreover, these borrowings lack depth, having not been thoroughly filtered through the rational, Western perspective that is not entirely devoted to religious practice.

However, Gestalt therapy is not limited to borrowing solely from Eastern religions. Despite Perl's "conflict" with many other concepts inherent in his approach, they can be seen as the flip side of Freud's beliefs about the process of psychotherapy and the patient's personality. For example, Freud considered the patient's ability to analyze their behavior and intellectually understand the analytical interventions provided by the analyst as one of the important values in the patient's personality.Perls, on the other hand, perceived any tendency of the patient to engage in intellectual analysis as a form of resistance, hindering the expression of emotions and effective psychotherapy. He referred to individuals who excessively analyzed themselves, others, and the world as "paper people" and sometimes criticized patients who displayed such behavior. To our knowledge, this sometimes led to his refusal to work with certain patients. By reviewing old video recordings of Perls' work, one can observe that he paid great attention to catharsis in his therapeutic practice with patients. He sought to discover other repressed and suppressed emotions within the patient and encouraged their full expression. This demonstrates the significant influence of Wilhelm Reich's theory and therapy practices on his work. At the core of his practice, he was much closer to Reich than Freud, although he did not place as much emphasis on sexuality as Reich and Freud did. His focus more often lay in the search for unexpressed anger, hatred, and resentment towards others in general and the patient's parents in particular.

It is worth noting an interesting characteristic. Despite his antipathy towards Freud and his fundamental theories, Perls maintained an emotionally detached position from psychoanalysis during his work. This is evident in video recordings of his sessions, where he not only neutrally commented on the patient and gave them instructions but also constantly smoked tobacco, which was also a favorite of Sigmund Freud's.

It may be interesting to note that the creators of Gestalt therapy believed for a long time that their work was purely practical and could not be confined to specific theoretical frameworks. Perls even humorously referred to theorizing as "elephant dung." We suspect that this derogatory attitude towards the very natural human process of theorizing was a specific response to Perls' resentment towards Freud, who was a master at constructing elegant theories in the field of psychotherapy. Based on this fact and many others, we can speculate that Perls' deep-seated grudge against Freud largely laid the foundation for the development of Gestalt therapy. It is worth noting that Freud had numerous conflicts with his students, and he generally treated well those who adhered to the foundations of his theory and practice. However, the dissenters were often persecuted. A vivid example of this was the relationship between Sigmund Freud and Alfred Adler.

However, despite the negative attitude towards theorizing, certain theories were eventually needed. At least for the purpose of more effectively teaching gestalt therapy to other psychotherapists. This task was primarily taken up by Perls' colleague, Paul Goodman, who provided most of the definitions for concepts in gestalt therapy in his works. Perls' works were rather sparse in this form. Another interesting and somewhat amusing concept in gestalt therapy was the classification of people into "top dogs" and "underdogs," created by Perls. The "top dog" is a person who enjoys lecturing, moralizing, and presenting themselves as all-knowing and all-seeing. Such a person always assumes they are right by default, while others are assumed to be wrong. Individuals of this type feel that they don't need anyone, that they can handle everything independently, and that the people around them are less competent than they are. The "underdog" is a fawning sycophant, polite and praising the interlocutor, often admitting their own wrongness and downplaying their merits and achievements. This person believes that without servility and compliance, they are not needed by anyone and are unlikely to succeed in important life matters. These two personality profiles represent specific extremes that some individuals tend to immerse themselves in. Understanding the specificity of these profiles can help identify the appropriate points of focus in therapeutic work. Additionally, awareness of this model can be a useful tool for tracking one's neurotic unconscious reactions and behavior patterns.

In gestalt therapy, an original method of working with dreams was proposed. In contrast to the psychoanalytic approach, the gestalt therapist does not provide any interpretations of the symbols and images that manifest in patients' dreams. The therapist assists the interpretation to emerge within the patient's own consciousness. This is done by directing the patient to sequentially associate themselves with all the key elements of the dream. Let's provide an example from our practice. One of our students, during a lecture on gestalt therapy, shared a dream that she did not understand. She dreamt that she was walking through a market and encountered a male vendor selling a basket of apples. She approached him, looked into the basket, and saw snakes wriggling beneath the apples. We asked the student to first associate herself with the man from the dream and comment on how she felt, in what specific ways her states were changing, and whether any particular meanings arose during this process. We then repeated the same with other dream images: the basket, the apples, and the snakes. After re-experiencing the images, the patient remained silent in puzzlement for a while, but then, a few moments later, she exclaimed that she understood the meaning of the dream. She hypothesized that the man in the dream was evidently a projection of her real-life partner, and the basket with apples and snakes symbolized their complicated relationship, which, on the surface, seemed fine and pleasant but, upon closer examination, revealed aspects that one would prefer not to notice.

Charlotte Bühler and the Course of Human Life

Charlotte Bühler (1893–1974) was a psychologist, a doctor of philosophy, and an expert in child psychology. At birth, she had the surname Mahalovski and was born in Berlin. She studied social and natural sciences at the universities of Berlin and Freiburg. In 1915, she moved to Munich, where she began writing her dissertation. In Munich in 1916, she attended lectures by Oswald Külpe, where she met her future husband. In 1918, she defended her dissertation and obtained a doctorate in philosophy. Initially, Bühler's scientific research was dedicated to the psychology of thinking. She then actively started addressing issues in child and adolescent psychology. Later on, she became a renowned specialist in child development and youth psychology. Bühler's studies in child psychology ultimately led her to develop ideas about the phases of personality development. One of her extensively published works was the book "The Mental Life of the Adolescent." Bühler directed various projects involving precise observation methods for early personality development processes.

Charlotte Bühler

In 1933, Bühler published the book "The Life Course of a Human Being as a Psychological Problem," based on numerous experiments she conducted on this subject. It is worth noting that this work remained foundational for the study of the life cycle for several decades.

Due to the persecution of Jews in Germany during the 1930s, she first moved to Oslo, Norway, with her husband and then emigrated to the United States in 1940. In 1942, she assumed the position of chief psychologist at the central hospital in Minneapolis. Bühler later obtained full U.S. citizenship and relocated to Los Angeles, California, where she became the chief psychologist at the county hospital. She was also known for her private practice in Beverly Hills. Additionally, she collaborated with various humanistic psychologists and psychotherapists, such as Abraham Maslow and Carl Rogers. Together with them, Bühler led the Association for Humanistic Psychology.

Charlotte Bühler studied philosophy in Germany and was a student of Edmund Husserl, from whom she acquired a significant number of philosophical beliefs about the world and human beings.

Bühler examined the biographies of individuals belonging to different social circles, including intellectuals, military personnel, entrepreneurs, farmers, workers, and others. Based on her scientific and research endeavors, she formulated a conception of the multifaceted life course of a human being. During the process of studying biographies, she analyzed three key aspects:

1. The external aspect of life that can be objectively evaluated.
2. The creative aspect of an individual's life, if present.
3. Specific changes in the individual's inner world regarding self-perception and overall life.

In the book "The Life Course of a Human Being," co-authored with Fritz Massarik, Charlotte Bühler described five temporal phases of a person's life course.

1. **First phase**: Up to 16–20 years of age. Within the context of this developmental phase, individuals demonstrate a relatively low level of self-awareness and self-determination.
2. **Second phase**: From 16–20 to 25–30 years of age. During this period, individuals are in the process of searching for suitable activities and a companion for life.
3. **Third phase**: After 30 years of age. In this phase, individuals often achieve full self-determination, finding meaning in life and their place within it, both in the work context and in personal relationships.
4. **Fourth phase**: The phase of an aging individual. During this phase, the primary physiological processes of the body begin to decline, and individuals often conclude their professional journey.
5. **Fifth phase**: After 65–70 years of age. In this phase, individuals tend to live more in the past through memories, thoughts, and conversations about what has and hasn't been accomplished in life. Time is often spent in a purposeless existence.

While examining numerous biographies of different individuals, Bühler found a wealth of information for contemplation on topics such as human perceptions of destiny, death, and the meaning of life. These themes were among the least explored in the context of scientific psychology at the time. For Bühler, the life course is primarily the result of the self-development of the human spirit.

Bühler considered individual psychological development through the lens of life outcomes and the realization of an individual's inner essence. She also believed that the life course is a process of the formation of goal structures within the personality.

Bühler posited that the primary driving force of human personality is intention, and she also spoke of the idea of the intentional core of personality and developed this theory through the prism of genetic concepts.

In Bühler's view, the intentional core of personality is a spiritual formation that is inherent in a person from the beginning and only changes in its diverse manifestations as the personality develops. The process of upbringing can distort the intentional core of personality, thereby causing various symptoms. It is the self, the "Selbst," that embodies the purposefulness and intentionality of the individual, aimed at the realization of their best potentials, which Bühler referred to as "existence."

She believed that the self-realization of a person is only possible when the individual's orientation is towards the future. It is worth noting that the orientation of the individual towards the future was characteristic of humanistic psychology and shared by many psychologists and psychotherapists who supported the beliefs of this school. She also noted that the completeness of the self-realization process is directly related to the individual's ability to set not just any goals but specifically those goals that correspond to the potential of their inner essence. Bühler referred to this ability as the self-determination of personality. According to her, a person whose life is filled with various meanings and goals is genuinely healthy. Accordingly, the key function of the therapist is to create favorable conditions for the formation of meaning and goals within the client. In her opinion, psychotherapy is capable of assisting a person in their self-awareness.

It is worth noting that Bühler's concept of self-realization was closely aligned with Abraham Maslow's ideas of self-actualization. In 1940, Charlotte Bühler formulated the idea of the existence of four basic tendencies in personality.

1. **First tendency**: The striving for the satisfaction of basic life necessities, such as the need for food, a comfortable place to sleep, etc.
2. **Second tendency**: Adaptation to various conditions of the surrounding environment.
3. **Third tendency**: Creative expansion aimed at acquiring new knowledge and experience and the broadening of various forms of life activities.
4. **Fourth tendency**: The establishment of internal order and the creation of specific ways to organize and rank acquired experiences. This can involve keeping a diary, writing an autobiography, memoirs,

etc. Additionally, this tendency relates to the process of self-esteem formation in relation to one's life achievements.

The different combinations of these tendencies can determine the path that an individual will take towards self-realization.

In Bühler's model of tendencies, we also observe some similarities to Abraham Maslow's theories, particularly his hierarchy of motivation.

Everett Schostrom and the Concept of Manipulative Personality

Everett Leo Schostrom (1921–1992) was an American psychologist and psychotherapist born in Rockford, Illinois. Schostrom completed his studies at Stanford University and obtained a Ph.D. in 1950. He became a proponent of humanistic psychology and was one of Abraham Maslow's students. Schostrom developed the Personal Orientation Inventory (POI), a questionnaire dedicated to the concept of self-actualization of personality created by Abraham Maslow.

Everett Schostrom

In his book "Therapeutic Psychology," Schostrom raises the question of whether the notion of an eclectic style in psychotherapy, which involves borrowing from different psychotherapeutic systems, has garnered a positive reputation. At times, therapists who attempt to practice eclecticism superficially assimilate various psychotherapeutic schools.

Schostrom comments on the understanding of the terms psychotherapy and counseling, stating that if there is a semantic difference between these terms, it constitutes an intricate problem. Schostrom also reports, "Approximately half of the courses approved by the American Psychological Association do not make an academic distinction between clinical and counseling specializations."

Schostrom describes the relationship between therapeutic psychology and various contexts in which it can be applied to a greater or lesser extent. These include school psychology, social welfare, psychiatry, pastoral counseling, counseling psychology, and clinical psychology.

Schostrom provides insights regarding the theoretical foundation of psychotherapy, stating that theory primarily helps explain the emerging dynamics between the therapist and the patient and enables the prediction of probable events that may occur during this interaction with a certain level of confidence. Additionally, the theoretical foundation allows for the logical integration of various concepts, ideas, and experiential elements that arise in the practice of psychotherapy. Therefore, theory serves as an excellent foundation for practical work.

In the context of the therapist's personal development, Schostrom unveils inspiring ideas, stating that during the practice of psychotherapy, the therapist should rely on their own beliefs and largely practice their unique form of therapy. Schostrom further comments that Freud was not a Freudian, Jung was not a Jungian, and Rogers was not a Rogerian. Each of these renowned therapists relied to a great extent on the theory and practice of their teachers but developed their own distinctive style during their professional development. Hence, it can be said that there are no right or wrong methods of work. There are methods that have emerged through practice and methods that have been borrowed from the practices of other therapists.Schostrom presents intriguing perspectives on individuals with various life problems, portraying them as manipulators who relate to themselves, other people, and the world in general as inanimate objects. The object of manipulation becomes an object in itself. Schostrom's goal in psychotherapy was to transform the manipulator's personality into an actualizing personality—someone who perceives themselves, others, and the world as animated entities. In this case, it is important to note that Schostrom's conceptualization of manipulative individuals largely overlaps with individuals with psychopathic and schizoid accentuations. A psychopath tends to relate to others as inanimate objects, while a schizoid may sometimes perceive themselves as objects. Therefore, the manipulator archetype created by Everett Schostrom represents a collective image encompassing various psychopathological profiles.

By the way, Shostrom allows himself generalizations like "modern man is a manipulator," which creates additional specific meanings for this term, indicating that, in Shostrom's opinion, modern culture can cultivate a materialistic attitude towards the world. This default transforms a person into a neurotic, separating them from their emotionally significant sphere.

Shostrom writes that as a result of endless manipulation, modern man has almost completely lost the ability to express himself directly and straightforwardly, becoming an anxious automaton living in the past and the future but not in the present. Shostrom believed that modern individuals may talk a lot about their feelings but rarely experience them on a deep level.

Shostrom was also convinced that the opposite of a manipulator, a self-actualizing person, is capable of trusting their feelings and intuition at a profound level. They allow themselves to have desires, make mistakes, provide sincere help to others, and express constructive aggression. According to Shostrom, the first and primary characteristic of a manipulator is the concealment of their true feelings in relationships. He states that a manipulator is similar to a poker player who constantly tries to hide a weak card. He also believes that a manipulator avoids the risk of being emotionally involved in a social situation and avoids any emotional disturbances.

Shostrom identifies eight types of manipulators, four of whom are oppressors and four are oppressed. Conditionally, the oppressors can be referred to as the dark side of manipulation, while the oppressed represent the light side. However, one should not think that dark manipulation is stronger or more cunning than light manipulation. By studying the profiles, you can discover that each type of manipulator is cunning in its own way and capable of making the lives of those around them uncomfortable through direct or indirect methods.

It is worth noting that a person can combine several types of manipulation in their behavior. Quite often, a person belonging to a certain profile will instinctively seek out another person who is their opposite. If finding an opposite is difficult, there may be attempts to transform into their opposite.

The enactment of two opposing roles allows them both to unfold different potentials. Based on the interaction models of opposing manipulative personalities, we often witness the development of plots in various books and films where the protagonist stands against the antagonist, but formally, each of them belongs to different types of manipulators. For example, "the judge" against "the defender" or "the hooligan" against "the good guy."

Oppressive Manipulators

1. **Judge:** This type of manipulator is a pronounced critic and skeptic. They strive to find faults in others and thoroughly dissect them once they are discovered. They can be very tedious in their communication, criticizing and moralizing others. They try to identify something to criticize, even when there is technically nothing to criticize. Excessive self-importance often makes them insensitive to feedback from others. Such individuals tend to be judgmental, distrustful, resentful, and vindictive.
2. **Bully:** This personality actively expresses an aggressive stance. They often display cruelty towards others, and their preferred method of

controlling people involves various threats. They enjoy tormenting and making others' lives unbearable. Having someone oppressed nearby is the norm for the "bully," and their absence causes them distress. The "bully" likes to provoke others, even in the absence of a formal reason for aggression. Once someone falls into their trap, the "bully" enthusiastically engages in their game.

3. **Calculator:** This individual constantly seeks to calculate and control everything. They deceive, confuse, and strive to outwit others. They exhibit excessive meticulousness toward others, even when it is unnecessary or unwarranted. They use calculation as a means to control those around them, which gives them a sense of superiority and dominance. For this person, calculation is also a way to express aggressive feelings.
4. **Dictator:** This manipulator seeks to demonstrate power and dominance over others, disregarding their opinions and judgments by referring to authorities. They constantly emphasize their own authority, highlighting their titles and status. They enjoy talking about how others are inferior to them. They exhibit dominance more directly and authoritatively, ignoring hints and other ways of conveying information. They meticulously maintain the image of a tyrant and despot, striving to oppress others verbally and non-verbally. Even slight resistance infuriates them.

Misguided Manipulators

1. **Defender:** This individual is the antithesis of a "judge." They fervently demonstrate help, support, and protection towards others, often to an excessive extent. By excessively indulging others, they hinder their ability to develop independence. They frequently involve themselves in the affairs of others rather than tending to their own. They often assume the role of an unconditional guardian. Living with the conviction that others cannot cope with life's challenges without their assistance, support, and guardianship, they actively seek out

individuals who would require their help and support. If they fail to find such individuals, they experience strong frustration. They often strive to do much more for others than is truly necessary. It is worth noting that the defender's assistance can often lead to highly negative consequences for those whom they care for. They do not enjoy being around individuals who are capable of taking care of themselves. They can be quite intrusive in their eagerness to offer help, and if their desire to support is rejected, they become deeply offended and lament that despite their goodwill, they are met with hostility. Sometimes, they even provoke situations in which people may need their help. They frequently believe that their actions bring exceptional benefits to their surroundings. They do not welcome criticism directed at them. They rarely accept constructive criticism from their environment, and even if they manage to comprehend that their actions are untimely and inappropriate, the effect of these explanations is short-lived. After some time, consciously or unconsciously, they revert to their previous behavioral patterns.

2. **Admirable Guy:** This individual excessively demonstrates kindness, caring, and attentiveness. They can overwhelm others with their goodness. They are the antithesis of "hooligans" and often emerge victorious in confrontations with such individuals. They strive with all their might to shape an excessively positive image of themselves in their surroundings. They consider themselves morally righteous and highly virtuous. They frequently systematize and practice some form of spiritual or moral philosophy, which they attempt to incorporate into every action. Unlike the defender, the admirable guy is not intrusive, but through their kindness and positivity, they attempt to win over those around them and make it difficult for others to refuse their requests. And indeed, they often succeed. It is nearly impossible to provoke this admirable guy into a negative or aggressive reaction. Even if someone offends them in some way, they demonstratively forgive them. They enjoy making the act of forgiveness a public matter. They love recounting stories to others about how caring and

attentive they have been in various life situations.

3. **Clinger:** This personality type is the complete opposite of a "calculator" and seeks to emphasize their dependence, drawing attention to it from others. They constantly search for individuals who can take care of them. Through their behavior, they create the impression of someone easily fooled. They demonstrate obvious or illusory helplessness and an inability to cope with the difficulties of the world. They directly or indirectly convey to others that they cannot undertake anything without assistance. They exhibit profound infantilism. They strive to find someone who can organize their own lives and themselves. They are skilled at social games that involve inducing guilt in others if they refuse to help. They enjoy being lectured and guided, but rarely use the information they receive to become independent. They often unconsciously engage in actions that worsen their own situation, providing them with sufficient resources for manipulating others through pity. They can be particularly dangerous for individuals who possess empathy for others.
4. **Doormat:** This individual is the typical victim of a "dictator" and is largely their antithesis. They demonstrate sensitivity and vulnerability. They are often passive and silent, meekly accepting the hardships of their lives. They maintain a position that suggests they are likely unable to change their life circumstances. They provide multiple justifications for their real or illusory helplessness. Verbally and nonverbally, they provoke others to perceive them as someone who can be exploited. They frequently refuse, consciously or unconsciously, to make any changes in their lives. They attribute their refusal to others, the situation, the world, certain qualities of their personality, or their physical body that, in their opinion, cannot be altered. They enjoy engaging in conversations where they discuss the various burdens of life with those around them. The doormat believes that everything good belongs to the past, while the future appears bleak and burdensome. Attempts to persuade them otherwise often end in vain. Facts that could potentially change their perspective are usually

ignored or overlooked.

Shostrom believes that every person carries within them a range of manipulative potential, which is actualized in different individuals at different times and for various reasons in life. Through group therapy and the interaction among its participants, one can learn to recognize various forms of manipulation inherent in both oneself and other group members.

Regarding the reasons for the desire to manipulate others, Shostrom agrees with Frederick Perls' position. Perls believed that such a need arises as a result of an internal conflict between a person's desire to be free and independent from others and their desire for others to take responsibility for their lives and care for them.

Shostrom highlights Erich Fromm's perspective on the desire to manipulate others. According to Fromm, the root of manipulation lies in a person's inability to love and accept themselves as they are. As a result, individuals may adopt manipulative roles, seeking a surrogate for love. However, the manipulator is left with only an illusion, constantly needing to prove to themselves and others that they deserve something good. Regardless of their efforts, what they receive remains a mere illusion that they may cling to throughout their lives. The deep-seated desire for power over others serves as a means for manipulators to ensure that love and others' sympathies toward them never run out.

Examining the early stages of personality development, we observe that an infant's cry when a particular need is not met is a form of manipulation toward the maternal figure—an attempt to draw attention, love, and care. As children grow, they begin to discover ways to gain the sympathy of their parents or others in their environment. When a child is uncertain about receiving certain sympathies, they may take specific actions to guarantee that they will, at least in some form, receive love. This process reveals the social mechanisms underlying the formation of manipulative qualities in one's personality, closely intertwined with the people in their environment. Behind the manipulative quality of a person lies pain and suffering, resulting from the non-acceptance of oneself by others as they are. Thus, manipulation becomes a way for individuals to solve various life tasks.

However, manipulation often becomes a temporary cover-up rather than a means to alleviate inner pain. For example, when a young child realizes that their parents do not punish them when they deceive them, they may start using lies in many situations. In such cases, we witness how the environment and upbringing, to some extent, can reinforce the manipulative behavior inherent in an individual. In the process of psychotherapeutic work, the aim is to uncover this pattern, make it conscious, and attempt to teach the person to act differently.

Shostrom also discusses the viewpoints of Jay Haley, Eric Berne, and William Glasser regarding the formation of manipulative behavioral styles. Jay Haley, while working with patients suffering from schizophrenia, discovered that they fear emotional closeness with others, striving to avoid it and prevent its emergence, which shapes their manipulative style of behavior.

Eric Berne suggested that people engage in various social games, manipulating others, when they fear intimacy and want to avoid it, as well as to control their emotions to some extent.

William Glasser proposed the hypothesis that the key motivation for manipulative behavior is the fear of deep involvement in relationships with others.

Shostrom also presents Albert Ellis's opinion, who believed that manipulative behavior may arise in the early stages of a person's personality development when the individual forms certain false conclusions about life and what constitutes appropriate behavior. As a result, a person may begin to believe that correct behavior is one that is approved by everyone. In an attempt to please everyone, individuals start manipulating others in one way or another.

Hans-Werner Gessmann and Humanistic Psychodrama

Hans-Werner Gessmann was born in Germany in 1950. He is a German psychologist, psychotherapist, doctor of psychological sciences, and professor of clinical psychology and psychotherapy. He is known as the creator of humanistic psychodrama.

Hans-Werner Gessmann

In 1973, Gessmann founded the Bergenhausen Psychotherapeutic Institute in Duisburg. During its operation, the institute has trained over 1,500 psychotherapists.

Since 2008, Gessmann has been actively collaborating with colleagues from Russia and teaching clinical psychology at Kostroma State University. He is a professor of general psychology and developmental psychology at the Moscow State Social Academy.

Since 2012, he has been an invited professor of systemic family psychotherapy at the Moscow State Psychological and Pedagogical University.

Throughout his productive professional career, Gessmann has published over 56 monographs and 160 articles.

Hans-Werner Gessmann states that psychodrama was included among the methods of humanistic psychology by Hilarión Petzold in 1980. According to Petzold, psychodrama can be considered one of the oldest methods of humanistic psychotherapy. Gessmann also points out that psychodrama in Germany has undergone significant additions and revisions. The first transformations of psychodrama were carried out by Heike Straub, a student of Moreno, who supplemented psychodrama with group dynamic methods. Gessmann comments that psychodramatic methods are increasingly being used in the context of applying psychoanalytic concepts. This has been done by psychotherapists such as Adolf Friedmann, Serge Lebovici, Didier Anzieu, Baskin, Widlöcher, and others. Erdmann and Henne noted a significant similarity between the theoretical concepts of psychodrama and the analytical psychology of Carl Jung. Followers of Alfred Adler, such as Ansbacher, Ackermann, Corsini, and Dreikurs, actively applied psychodramatic methods outside the theories of Jacob Moreno.

In the 1940s, Czander and Lipitt developed behavioral role-playing games based on Jacob Moreno's intervention and sociometric practices. These practices were used to train desired behavior. Lazarus began combining cognitive-behavioral therapy with role-playing in his practice. It is also worth noting that since 1969, Petzold has been integrating psychodrama with behavioral therapy. He called his method "bihe-viodrama." One of Jacob Moreno's well-known students, Ann Anselin Schützenberger, combined the theories of Sigmund Freud, Jacob Moreno, and Carl Rogers. It was she who made attempts to create an integrative psychodramatic therapy, elegantly combining the theory and practice of other psychotherapeutic approaches.

Since the early 1980s, Gessmann has been developing the ideas of humanistic psychodrama. He turned to Jacob Moreno's original ideas and synthesized them with new knowledge gained through therapeutic practice. According to Gessmann, the concept of personal responsibility for one's own life and society, of which the individual is a part, occupies a central position.

He explains that the achievement of self-realization goals for an individual is carried out within a group and with the help of the group. Gessmann believes that humanistic psychodrama, which actively integrates the values and beliefs of humanistic therapy, creates excellent conditions for learning and transformation. At the same time, the responsibility for change is given to the client participating in psychotherapy.

It should be noted that such an approach in the context of psychotherapeutic treatment is often a double-edged sword. On the one hand, it encourages the patient's personal growth, development, and formation of an adult ego. On the other hand, it elegantly shifts the responsibility away from the psychotherapist, which in some cases can lead to undesirable consequences. However, it is important to remember that the ideas of humanistic psychology and psychotherapy are highly idealized. Therapists who practice these methods sometimes choose not to acknowledge the "dark side", reveling in beautiful yet utopian notions of the therapeutic process.

Gessmann writes that during participation in humanistic psychodrama, the client learns that they are the ones making choices and are capable of consciously making decisions and taking responsibility. In therapy, the client can also choose the goal of the work and the scope of the psychodramatic action. The construction of the play scene occurs with the involvement of the psychotherapist, who helps the client focus on the truly important moments of the process.

In the warm-up stage preceding the therapeutic process, clients can approach setting the goal of the therapeutic work more consciously and understand which feelings truly require processing. After the warm-up phase, the client with whom the therapeutic work will take place is determined, followed by the selection of the protagonist, who will play the main role in the process. Depending on the need, other participants who will play roles are also chosen. The role of the auxiliaries is not pure improvisation within the context of their assigned role. They should try to adopt the client's subjective world of representations and reflect them in their performance, shaping their behavior through the lens of the client's perspective on the situation.

During the actual therapeutic action, it is desirable for the protagonist to have a sense of having fully realized the theme of their request. The dramatic session can provide the client with an opportunity to structure and comprehend their existing experience on a deep level, form ideas that can be used to change their current life situation. Through the externalization of their experience and the role-playing of the auxiliaries, a profound therapeutic effect can be achieved, allowing the client to depart from old worldviews and acquire new ones that are more suitable, constructive, and ecologically sound regarding themselves and the world.

At the end of the work, group sharing is essential, where group members share the peculiarities of their experience gained during the process.

Through participation in psychodramatic sessions, the more frequently group members take on various roles, the more they can become aware of their ability to understand other people, empathize with them, and delve into the deep essence of meaning existing within the personalities of others.

Gessmann emphasizes that the primary intention of humanistic psychodrama is to contribute to the independent development of the individuals participating in the psychotherapeutic group. He also indicates that all methods of this form of therapy are subordinate to this goal. Within the context of the humanistic psychodrama method, there is a belief, which clearly originates from the humanistic tradition in psychotherapy, that human beings have a natural need for growth and self-realization. This need can be utilized in the therapeutic process as a deep motivation for transformation and constructive changes. Like in humanistic psychology, humanistic drama assumes the presence of creative and innovative potential in individuals concerning personal development and interaction with others and the world as a whole. It is also mentioned that the tendencies towards self-actualization are fundamental driving forces within an organism, actively seeking realization in the external world and fostering the development of various human abilities.

Gessmann emphasizes that self-awareness and self-realization are essential aspects of the therapeutic process in humanistic psychodrama. If the client can achieve a balance between personal and social satisfaction, they are capable of attaining complete fulfillment, self-respect, and fully accepting themselves.

It is postulated that all mental processes occurring within an individual have a purpose and positive intention and are important to some extent. The search for meaning and emotional satisfaction becomes a significant motivation in the process of group psychodramatic work. This search becomes a therapeutic exploration in which new patterns of behavior are sought. These patterns can greatly improve the individual's relationships with their social environment, as the real experience of dramatic work allows for a deeper understanding of the alignment of behavior with the context and provides comprehensive feedback from other participants in the interaction. Based on this experience, the worldview of each group participant can significantly expand.

During the process of working with the humanistic psychodrama method, the psychotherapist's focus shifts from any specific mental disorder to the client's worldview, with which the therapeutic work is conducted. Through a thorough exploration of the client's worldview, it is possible to understand how its individual elements align, to a greater or lesser extent, with the social context in which the client exists. Respectful acceptance of the client's inner world provides an opportunity for more effective change and directs development in the desired direction. The client is viewed as a unity and integration of mind, body, soul, spirit, and the social group to which they belong. This holistic perception enables not only the alteration of specific elements but also the transformation of the entire system to which the individual belongs. In this theoretical and practical aspect, we observe the orientation of humanistic psychodrama towards a holistic approach in therapeutic work. It also aligns with theories of systemic family therapy, where the family to which the individual belongs and other social groups they are related to constitute the primary focus of therapeutic work. Humanistic psychodrama is open to incorporating methods from other forms of therapeutic processes. However, it should be noted that this approach is not primarily oriented towards an analytical process, in which the therapist authoritatively provides comments on the patient's experience. Instead, the focus is on group interaction, which facilitates the development of insight and catharsis in the patient.

In humanistic psychodrama, influences from gestalt therapy can be observed. For example, the principle of "here and now" is postulated, suggesting that individuals should concentrate their attention not on memories of past events or potential future occurrences, but on the sensations and emotions that arise within them at the present moment.

There are several significant principles borrowed from Carl Rogers' humanistic therapy that are crucial in humanistic psychodrama:

1. **Empathy**: The ability to sympathize and empathize with others, considering their feelings and needs. Orienting one's actions in accordance with the needs of the group to which the individual belongs.
2. **Respect**: Accepting the differences that exist between an individual's personality and the personalities of others involved in the group to which they belong. Respecting another person provides an opportunity to deeply understand them, expanding not only one's worldview but also enabling effective interaction with others.
3. **Congruence**: Consistency in the communication of one's personality. This primarily refers to the alignment between verbal and non-verbal aspects of behavior, as well as the alignment between what a person thinks, says, and does. The level of congruence within a person allows for an understanding of the specific neurotic processes that are characteristic of them. It can be said that the concept of a holistic and non-neurotic individual is largely synonymous with the concept of a congruent person.

In the therapeutic process, the therapist seeks to avoid a clear hierarchy between themselves and the patient. Thus, the therapist merges with the group, allowing participants to be natural in their behavioral and emotional expressions. Congruence in the therapist's communication is of great significance, as it can serve as a model of self-expression for other group members.

Erich Fromm and Humanistic Psychoanalysis

Erich Seligmann Fromm was born into a family of Orthodox Jews in Frankfurt-on-Main. His mother, Rosa Fromm, was the daughter of a rabbi, and his father, Naftali Fromm, was not only the son of a rabbi but also a grandson. After completing school in 1918, Erich enrolled at Heidelberg University, where he actively studied psychology, philosophy, and sociology. His mentor was Alfred Weber, under whose guidance he defended his dissertation in 1922. Fromm studied psychoanalysis at the Berlin Psychoanalytic Institute, where notable figures such as Wilhelm Reich, Max Eitingon, and Sandor Rado taught. It was at this institute that Fromm became acquainted with Karen Horney. He began his psychoanalytic practice in 1925. At the age of 26, Fromm left Judaism and became a Christian. In his future works, he will devote considerable attention to the human spiritual experience. After the Nazis came to power in Germany, Fromm moved to New York, where he started working as a professor at Columbia University. In 1946, Fromm became a co-founder of the William Alanson White Institute of Psychiatry.

In 1950, Fromm relocated to Mexico, where he began teaching at the National Autonomous University of Mexico. He worked there until 1965. From 1957 to 1961, Erich Fromm also taught at Michigan State University and, from 1962 onward, at New York University. In 1974, he moved to Muralto, Switzerland. After a series of heart attacks, Fromm passed away in his home in 1980.

Erich Fromm

Fromm is well-known as one of the creators of the neo-Freudian and Freud-Marxist schools of thought. He examined various psychoanalytic concepts and made efforts to find practical applications for them in life. Fromm believed that psychoanalysis had not provided sufficient understanding of how individuals should live to experience well-being, what methods of child-rearing would be more successful, and what value systems should be instilled in people to improve their quality of life. Fromm attempted to shift the focus of psychoanalysis from behavior motivated by biological factors to cultural motives generated through the process of human upbringing and social interaction, which predetermined the development of neurotic personality mechanisms in individuals. Fromm commented, "Human nature—human passions and anxieties—are a product of culture." Fromm offered an intriguing interpretation of the classical Freudian concept of the Oedipus complex. He argued that Freud had misunderstood the myth of Oedipus, overlooking several important factors. For instance, Freud based his interpretation on Sophocles' tragedy "Oedipus Rex," neglecting the other two parts of the trilogy: "Oedipus at Colonus" and "Antigone." Fromm explained that his understanding of the Oedipus myth primarily focused on it as a model of a child's reaction to parental authority, involving specific emotions and behaviors associated with the desire for freedom from it.

Fromm believed that as individuals develop and socialize, they experience a need for the integration of acquired experiences. The striving for the unity of diverse experiences can lead individuals to desire to create and be part of idealistic systems. The existence of various religious systems serves as a vivid example of this phenomenon. Fromm claimed that every person requires a specific system of life orientations, a set of beliefs and values, and a particular object of devotion. This is why we can observe the existence of religious systems throughout human history.

Fromm stated that Freud's great discovery was extending the method of attaining truth within the context of psychotherapy. He provided specific tools through which this truth could be grasped. Freud discovered that individuals are capable of dispelling illusions by consciously penetrating their own psychic structure.

According to Fromm, critical and creative thinking in individuals carries a liberating function due to their negative attitude towards thinking illusions. Fromm discusses the concept of the "social filter" existing in the context of the spirit of the time. Through this "social filter," only certain ideas and interpretations of personal experiences can penetrate people's minds. Fromm argues that this "social filter" not only determines the logic of thinking but also the content of philosophical systems. What is unthinkable for a person is often impossible to express verbally since language may not possess the necessary words for such experiences. Fromm's concept of the "social filter" closely aligns with linguist Noam Chomsky's ideas of the "map" and the "territory," as exemplified by Chomsky's famous phrase "The map is not the territory," suggesting that the way we interpret the world is not the same as the interpreted world. Fromm's concept of the "social filter" and Chomsky's concept of the "map" share many similarities, as the map of the world largely serves as the filter that allows one thing into our consciousness while discarding another.

Fromm comments that in the context of the "social filters" of his time, Freud developed theoretical and practical concepts. Fromm believes that for Freud, these filters were theories of bourgeois materialism and an authoritarian-patriarchal stance. The dogma of bourgeois materialism was adopted by Freud from one of his teachers, the physician and physiologist Ernst von Brücke. Freud was a student of von Brücke, and his theories greatly influenced Freud. Some of von Brücke's theories, in particular, led Freud to the idea of psychodynamics, which forms the basis of most of his work. Fromm writes that during Freud's development of psychoanalysis, little was known about how hormones influence and condition human psychological life. However, sexuality and its manifestations were practically the only phenomena where the connection between the psychological and the physical was relatively well known.

According to Fromm, Freud's authoritarian-patriarchal stance was also very strong. As an example, Fromm cites Freud's reaction to a statement made by John Stuart Mill, whom Freud respected. Mill expressed his views on the equality of men and women. In one of his letters, Freud wrote, "In this matter, Mill is completely insane." Naturally, we can find traces of Freud's authoritarian-patriarchal stance in many of his theories. One of the most typical examples is his concept of "penis envy," which is unconsciously attributed to many women.

In his work "The Dogma of Christ," Fromm states that Freud managed to remove the differences between individual and social psychology, demonstrating the special interdependence between what happens in the psychological and social spheres. As a result, these two spheres cannot be considered separately. Fromm also comments that society plays a dual role for the individual: one that is frustrating and one that is satisfying. Various social restrictions that impose certain boundaries on individuals' needs can produce neurotic states, but at the same time, the satisfying role of society can also create neurotic states. The proper balance of these roles can lead to a state of equilibrium.

Regarding religion, Fromm writes in this work that the purpose of religion in society is to prevent psychological independence from the people, to intellectually intimidate them, and to induce a state of infantilism in which it becomes easier to submit to authority. On the other hand, religion provides people with a certain level of satisfaction, making life tolerable enough for them not to desire rebellion.

In the article "Credo," Erich Fromm discusses that, in his opinion, the primary choice a person can make is between life and death. Every action of an individual implies this choice. Fromm comments that there are numerous factors that can influence a person's choice. These factors include psychological constitution, the specificities of the social environment, one's family, friends, and so on. Regardless of these factors, Fromm believes that the main task of an individual is to expand the scope of their destiny, strengthening that which leads to life as opposed to that which leads to death. Individuals who predominantly orient their lives and actions toward processes associated with creation, birth, and creativity are referred to as "biophiles" by Fromm. On the other hand, those who are primarily driven by desires for destruction, annihilation, killing, and elimination are called "necrophiles." Fromm's concept of biophile and necrophile profiles represents the true polarity that provides an understanding of the spectrum of personal qualities.

In the same work, Fromm states that he knows of two paths that can be considered good choices. The first path is following moral values and adhering to clear rules in life. However, Fromm warns that maintaining the integrity of this path is quite challenging. On the other hand, he sees the path as one of developing a sense of goodness and performing good deeds that contribute to the happiness of others. Fromm also suggests that if a person fails to choose life and development, they inevitably become destroyers and turn into "living corpses." Fromm believed that both good and evil are hidden within every individual, simply in different proportions. The family and society surrounding an individual have a significant influence on their choices in life. It is within this context that the framework of a person's values and beliefs is formed. Therefore, Fromm believed that society and its structure were key factors in shaping one's personality.

Expanding on the theme of necrophilic personality, Fromm writes the work "The Anatomy of Human Destructiveness", in which he examines Adolf Hitler as a vivid representative of this profile. In this article, he offers his psychoanalytic analysis of Adolf Hitler's parents, Alois and Klara Hitler, who, according to Fromm, greatly influenced the formation of Adolf's necrophilic character. In the analysis, he highlights the selfishness, coldness, and authoritarianism of his father, who loved wine and women, and the patience, submissiveness, and excessive love of his mother. Fromm argues that Klara's excessive love for her son shaped his strongly pronounced narcissistic character and a sense of his exceptional personality. Fromm also points out that Hitler was a clear representative of the Oedipus complex. That is, he was strongly attached to his mother and harbored resentment towards his father. It is worth noting that his father, Alois Hitler, did not subject him to physical punishment. Instead, they often argued, and his father would reprimand him for certain actions. Fromm offers a profound analysis of Adolf's childhood, adolescence, and youth. When Hitler was 14 years old, his father passed away. He easily coped with the death of his parent and even perceived it as liberation from a tyrant. Interestingly, he himself became a similar tyrant for the world in the future, and the world breathed a sigh of relief when Adolf Hitler died. Here we observe a psychoanalytic tendency to symbolically repeat the path of the father, despite strong conscious resistance. Fromm also comments that Hitler not only lacked interest in school subjects but showed no interest in anything and made no effort. Additionally, Fromm adds that Hitler was excessively lazy, and his life energy was constantly in a state of tension.

In the work "Zen Buddhism and Psychoanalysis," Fromm writes that both Zen Buddhism and psychoanalysis share the desire for human well-being through the study of human nature. While psychoanalysis, as a product of Western thought, is a method of psychotherapy, Zen Buddhism is a philosophy and practice aimed at the "enlightenment" of the individual. At the same time, Fromm comments that Zen Buddhism is increasingly gaining interest among psychoanalysts. According to Fromm, the philosophies of Buddhism, Zen Buddhism, and Taoism structurally resemble psychoanalysis. These philosophical systems aim not to worship a monotheistic deity but are primarily focused on the spiritual development of the individual through self-analysis and various trance practices.

Fromm believed that the emergence of psychoanalysis is a clear confirmation of the existence of a spiritual crisis in Western culture at that time. Psychoanalysis provides specific theoretical and practical recommendations for overcoming this crisis and becomes, to some extent, a surrogate, replacing religious practices. Although psychoanalysis is rooted in scientists who possessed rationalistic and materialistic value systems, it finds resonance in the minds of many people in the scientific community.

Fromm comments on one of Freud's beliefs that "where there was **Id**, there shall be **Ego**," meaning that conscious control eventually emerges from unconscious aggressive and sexual feelings and behaviors. According to Freud, in order to feel well, a person must strive to free themselves from the burden of unconscious processes in the psyche. But Freud did not simply postulate the significance and importance of self-control. This idea existed in various philosophical and religious currents before him. Fromm believes that Freud offered a practical method through which conscious control over unconscious processes could be achieved. Freud wrote, "An analyst who seeks to be a model for the patient in certain situations and plays the role of a mentor must have a certain superiority over the patient." In this conviction, we can see a manifestation of Freud's authoritarian position.

Fromm points out that psychoanalysis, aligns with Zen Buddhism in the idea that knowledge transforms a person. Freud believed that every time a person gains self-knowledge, they undergo transformation. In Buddhism, Zen Buddhism, and Taoism, we can find numerous ideas that are similar to this postulate. For example, Buddhism teaches that one of the key sources of human suffering is ignorance, and by eliminating ignorance, one can progress on the path of spiritual development. Another significant aspect of psychoanalysis that aligns Freud's theories with Zen Buddhism is that Freud never regarded conscious rational processes in the psyche as the key and determining factors of human behavior. Freud considered the unconscious, which is vastly greater in comparison to the conscious realm, as the key element of the psychic process. The method of free association aimed to unveil the veil of unconscious processes and, through this action, make other elements of unconscious experience conscious.

Fromm understands well-being as the state of complete maturity in an individual's personality. And maturity, in this case, is not only understood as the ability to critically comprehend reality. Fromm compares the state of maturity to what Heidegger meant by "letting things be what they are in reality." An analogy to this state can be found in the words of Gautama Buddha, who said that "suffering is the non-acceptance of what is." To a large extent, psychoanalysis provides individuals with the opportunity for gradual acceptance of the reality of the unconscious world and, consequently, the world that surrounds them. Well-being can be achieved by overcoming alienation from the external world. According to Fromm, well-being is the full realization of one's inner potential, the "awakening" of the individual, and a rejection of orientation towards average social values. Additionally, according to Fromm, well-being can be achieved through the acquisition of the ability to express the creative aspect of one's personality, enabling the harmonious realization of the diverse potential of the unconscious. In these beliefs of Fromm, the humanistic philosophy and ideas of Abraham Maslow and Carl Rogers are clearly reflected.

Pathopsychological Profiles and Humanistic Therapy

Hysteroid Profile

Representatives of the hysteroid profile respond very well to humanistic forms of therapy. Complete acceptance and respect, with the therapist's attention solely focused on the patient and their needs, create an even stronger therapeutic effect without criticism or moralizing. However, excessive indulgence of the conscious and unconscious needs of the hysteroid personality does not always lead to constructive results. Unfortunately, just like absolute power, absolute indulgence corrupts absolutely. In this case, it is worth noting that the approaches of different psychotherapists may vary. Humanistic ideas can take on various forms in practical therapeutic work.

In my opinion, if a therapist practicing a humanistic style of psychotherapy can deliver acceptance to the patient correctly and in moderation, it can create a magnificent therapeutic effect. Conversely, when this is not achieved, we may observe the hysteroid patient using the humanistic therapist as an ideal spectator of their tragicomic theater.

Paranoid Profile

A gentle acceptance of the humanistic approach can be a true balm for the soul of a paranoid individual. In my opinion, this form of therapeutic work is one of the most optimal when dealing with paranoid personalities, at least in the initial stages of psychotherapy.

The gentle, accepting style helps navigate the "sharp edges" of the paranoid person's personality, thus gradually establishing rapport, even in cases where it is difficult to achieve. However, it should not be deluded that a patient whose paranoid personality has developed over many years will instantly "melt" from the "warmth" of the humanistic approach. There is a high probability that some patients will suspect the gentle therapist of insincerity. The display of emotional warmth may be perceived as a form of manipulation.

The paranoid client may project that the therapist is overly accepting, either because they want the patient to stay longer and bring in more money or, in the case of a therapist and patient of opposite genders, because it may generate suspicions of the therapist's sexual interests toward the patient.

It is essential to remember that the paranoid individual's worldview consists of seeing others as people who want something from them, who can cause them harm, exploit them, or manipulate them in various ways. The humanistic form of communication may feel foreign to the paranoid individual and be perceived as unnatural.

Therefore, when working with such patients, the level of "humanism" should be strictly dosed to avoid provoking rejection due to excessively accepting forms of communication.

Psychopathic Profile

For psychopathic individuals, the humanistic form of therapy is often perceived as a sign of weakness on the part of the psychotherapist. For a psychopath, personal weakness and polite acceptance can be almost synonymous. The psychopath divides the world into predators and prey, and naturally, this division will occur in their relationship with the therapist. We should note an interesting observation. The psychopathic personality remains interested in therapy only if they can continue projecting the image of the victim onto the psychotherapist. Once the psychopath is convinced that the therapist is not easily manipulated, they will leave therapy and often not return. Additionally, the psychopath does not require emotional acceptance from the person onto whom they project the victim role. They feel good as long as the idea persists in their minds that they control their interlocutor and can harm them as needed. Therefore, we assert that the humanistic form of therapy can be constructive when working with psychopathic personalities only when combined with other forms of therapeutic work. However, even with a combined style of psychotherapeutic work with a psychopath, it is not often possible to achieve any constructive results.

Obsessive-Compulsive Profile

When working with patients who have an obsessive-compulsive personality profile, humanistic therapy can be quite effective, provided that the therapist chooses the right approach. Based on our observations, the instrumental "core" of the method is more significant in working with individuals with OCP than the overall philosophical approach. We also believe that combining the humanistic approach with other forms of therapeutic work, such as hypnotic practices or systemic family therapy techniques, yields good results when working with patients of this profile.

Schizoid Profile For schizoid individuals, we consider the humanistic approach to be one of the most effective. Although on a conscious level, the schizoid may appear emotionally cold and detached, deep within their consciousness, they yearn for warm emotional contact. If another person provides them with warm emotional communication, disregarding the sometimes unbearable behavior of the schizoid, it can gradually reveal their emotional potential. Humanistic therapy is particularly beneficial in the long term when working with schizoid personalities. In such cases, profound positive personal transformations in the patient can sometimes be observed.

Epileptoid Profile

For individuals with an epileptoid profile, the humanistic approach can yield decent but not excessively profound results. Deep trance involvement in therapeutic work or the manifestation of active motor behavior is crucial for epileptoid individuals. A good, receptive humanistic conversation establishes an excellent foundation for such a patient but often does not trigger deep psychodynamic processes. We recommend combining the humanistic approach with hypnotic and body-oriented forms of therapy. In my opinion, this combination of therapeutic interventions is most likely to achieve the highest effectiveness in working with the patient.

Schizophrenic Profile

When working with patients with a schizophrenic profile, humanistic forms of psychotherapy take on a certain flavor of Ronald Laing's anti-psychiatric philosophy and other like-minded thinkers. The primary key to therapy for schizophrenics is considered to be complete and unconditional acceptance of them as they are. Naturally, the anti-psychiatric movement questions the validity and adequacy of disease criteria, transforming the schizophrenic into a specific, unique individual. Humanistic work, on the other hand, allows the patient to experience a greater sense of acceptance. It is worth noting that humanistic therapy can yield constructive results in patients with mild schizophrenic profiles since schizophrenia is not an internally divided reality. To some extent, when a reality is divided by someone, it ceases to be schizophrenic. However, when working with individuals who have a more pronounced schizophrenic accent or with fully diagnosed schizophrenic patients, pure humanistic therapy is of limited applicability without the parallel use of other therapeutic methods.

Manic-Depressive Profile

When working with individuals with a manic-depressive profile, the humanistic approach can provide a solid foundation for communication with the patient, but often it will not yield satisfactory results without the use of additional therapeutic methods. However, in general, representatives of this profile tend to perceive this style of work normally and adequately. Decent results in working with manic-depressive patients can be achieved by combining the humanistic approach with body-oriented forms of psychotherapy.

4

Somatic Psychotherapy

In psychotherapy, Wilhelm Reich (1897–1957), an Austrian psychologist and one of Sigmund Freud's followers, can be considered to some extent the "father" of the somatic vector. Reich developed ideas about the abolition of repressive morality and sought to address the need for comprehensive sexual education among the general public.

During the process of psychoanalysis with his patients, Wilhelm Reich began to pay attention to the fact that their products of repression and suppression could manifest as fixed tensions in the body. He later referred to this as muscular armor, which is formed by a certain number of muscular contractions. Each muscular contraction represents a specific emotion that, for various reasons, was not expressed and released. Similarly, in certain areas of the muscular armor, blocked sexual impulses can be suppressed. Reich distinguished seven levels of muscular armor:

1. **Eyes:** In this segment of the muscular armor, the emotion of sadness is usually suppressed. The release of tension in this segment can be achieved through clockwise and counterclockwise eye movements, as well as strong squeezing and releasing of the eyelids.

2. **Oral:** This section often conceals repressed anger, which "sleeps" in the jaw and lip muscles. Simulating chewing movements or theatrical

grimacing can help release this emotion.

3. **Neck and tongue:** In this segment, emotions of anger, sadness, and disgust may be hidden. Everything that one wanted to express but remained unspoken seems to be dormant in this somatic segment. The release of emotions in this segment is possible through imitation of various forms of screams, groans, grunts, and retching movements.

4. **Chest:** This segment encompasses the entire arms, chest muscles, shoulders, shoulder blades, and the broadest muscles of the back. Joy, anger, fear, and sadness are concealed in this segment. There are several ways to release the emotions "asleep" in the chest segment, including different techniques of intense breathing, striking, gripping, tearing, and pressing.

5. **Diaphragm:** In this segment, the suppression of anger, dislike, and disgust occurs. The emotional release of this segment is achieved through the simulation of vomiting accompanied by deep breathing.

6. **Abdomen:** This segment hides anger, fear, and disgust. Emotional release in this segment is achieved through deep abdominal breathing, massaging, tickling, and pressing.

7. **Pelvis and abdomen:** This segment contains the suppression of excitement, anger, pleasure, and fear. Ways to release the energy trapped in this segment can include muscle tension and relaxation in the pelvis, pelvic rocking movements, various kicks with the legs, and stomping on the floor.

One particularly interesting theory of Reich's was his concept of a universal life energy, which he called "orgone energy." Reich believed that the disruption of the flow of this energy within the human body stimulates the emergence of various physical and psychological disorders.

Reich's ideas about orgone energy in many ways resembled Anton Mesmer's concept of magnetic fluid, which he believed could be transmitted from the physician to the patient and thus heal them. Naturally, both Mesmer's magnetic fluid and Reich's "orgone energy" were not accepted by the scientific community.

To demonstrate the existence of orgone energy, Wilhelm Reich began constructing "orgone accumulators." These were boxes with walls made of alternating layers of metal and dielectric material. According to Reich's belief, this arrangement allowed orgone energy to accumulate within them. After the energy accumulated in the orgone accumulator, the patient was placed inside, where the orgone energy was supposed to impact them in some way. Unfortunately, Reich did not experimentally test the effectiveness of his creation. He did not conduct tests with a control group or attempt to determine the influence of the placebo effect on patients undergoing his orgone therapy.

Wilhelm Reich

As reported by Reich, he was able to detect and measure the presence of ethereal orgone energy using a modified Geiger counter. Reich categorized orgone energy into positive orgone (POR) and deadly orgone (DOR). He claimed to have even healed various forms of cancer by having patients sit in orgone accumulators for a certain period of time. According to Reich, out of 15 cancer patients considered hopeless, six were saved, and five extended their lives by half a year.

This form of therapy practiced by Wilhelm Reich with his patients greatly contributed to the deep antipathy towards him among many members of the psychoanalytic community. Reich began to be persecuted for his unscientific practices with patients. During the court hearing for his case, he passionately defended his position, resulting in a two-year prison sentence for contempt of court. He later died of a heart attack while in prison. His works were confiscated and burned, which was highly unusual for the late 1950s in America.

However, despite Wilhelm Reich's controversial and unscientific theories, orgone therapy continues to exist to this day. In 1986, a group of scientists at the University of Marburg in Germany published the results of their research, in which they tested the influence of the orgone apparatus on subjects. They published their research data, stating that a 30-minute stay in the orgone accumulator can elicit a sequential positive psychophysiological effect that cannot be observed in subjects inside a box lined only with fiberglass.

One engineer from the USSR, Sergei Kolokoltsev, studied Reich's works for a long time and based on his drawings, created his own orgone apparatus. He sought like-minded individuals with his Reichian stance and published in various journals. In February 1991, the Spanish journal "News of Science and Technology" mentioned his work, referring to the apparatus he created as the "Reich-Kolokoltsev accumulator." In June 1991, a clinic equipped with two orgone energy accumulators created by Kolokoltsev was opened in Moscow, in paid clinic No. 5. According to comments from authors of articles dedicated to orgone therapy in Moscow, the therapeutic results of sitting in orgone apparatuses were consistently positive.

It is quite difficult for us to evaluate this information since the potential effectiveness of orgone apparatuses at a theoretical level strongly contradicts the laws of established physics. Therefore, we must be aware that at the moment, orgone Reichian theories can be considered more of an esoteric practice than a physical form of psychotherapy. Additionally, Kolokoltsev's apparatus was not subjected to placebo testing, which could likely have played a role in the process of therapy involving orgone energy.

Many of Reich's theoretical and practical findings were highly disputed and unscientific. However, it was Reich who shifted the focus of therapy onto the patient's body, and this action ultimately led to the widespread development of body-oriented therapy in the works of numerous psychotherapists.

Birth Trauma and Methods of Somatic Psychotherapy

The concept of birth trauma was introduced by one of Sigmund Freud's close disciples, the psychoanalyst Otto Rank (1884–1939). Rank explored the subject of dream analysis and attempted to correlate the material obtained with various myths and legends among different peoples in the world. In his book "The Trauma of Birth and Its Significance for Psychoanalysis," he examines the process of childbirth as a traumatizing experience that predisposes the development of neurotic and psychotic processes in individuals at a later age. Interestingly, Otto Rank formally became the first psychoanalyst without a medical education. In the early 1920s, Rank expressed a series of concepts that led to a complete break with his teacher, Sigmund Freud. Rank was one of the first to attempt to apply psychoanalysis to the study of poetry, religion, and art. In his work "The Myth of the Birth of the Hero," he deeply and meaningfully presents an example of his analysis of various mythological stories and legends, attempting to synthesize their details into a coherent representation, thus approaching the ideas of archetypes and the collective unconscious described in the works of Carl Jung.

Rank believed that birth trauma became the foundational basis for the emergence of anxiety processes and various types of fears in an individual's future. Rank presents his idea that, on an unconscious level, a person seeks to restore the original state in which they existed in the maternal womb.

However, the body simultaneously remembers all the "horrors" of birth, which should produce an unconscious conflict between the desire to return and the desire never to repeat the experience undergone during the process of coming into the world.

In his psychoanalytic theories, Rank created the notion that the process of psychotherapy, in a sense, guides the patient toward a metaphorical rebirth, as the unconscious representation of healing and birth can be synonymous.

Otto Rank

The psychoanalyst assumes the role of the patient's spiritual father. In this sense, psychoanalysis itself acquires the profound purpose of assisting the patient in overcoming unresolved birth trauma.

When considering the theme of rebirth in psychotherapy, it is necessary to mention three main schools that have had the most significant influence on theoretical and practical research within this subject. These are Stanislav Grof's holotropic breathwork methods, in which the author emphasizes not only the perinatal experience, which can be activated in the patient's consciousness due to hyperventilation, but also the exploration of transpersonal aspects of the unconscious. Leonard Orr's method, similar to

Stanislav Grof's, utilizes hyperventilation to facilitate the re-experiencing of the intrauterine state and the birth process.

Orr used hot lamps to recreate the temperature at which a child relives the process of development in the womb and its emergence from it. Much less known in psychotherapeutic circles is the school of the English psychotherapist F. Lake, who applied hyperventilation similarly to Grof and Orr in the process of psychotherapeutic work. Lake is also the author of a theory that describes the reasons for a child's reaction to the stress experienced during birth. The fourth school practicing the technique of rebirthing developed within the framework of the somatic therapy school—David Boadella's biodanza. The development was carried out by two psychotherapists in the course of their clinical practice, namely L. Marches and L. Olars.

Leonard Orr

Grof, as one of the pioneers of transpersonal psychology and the study of altered states of consciousness, made a significant contribution to the development of understandings of the experience a child undergoes. It is thanks to Stanislav Grof that the world of psychotherapy has gained magnificent practical methods for resolving birth trauma. In the 1950s, while still a young psychiatrist, Stanislav Grof actively studied the experiences patients had when taking LSD-25 during psychotherapy sessions in clinical settings. Grof conducted thousands of psychedelic sessions with his patients, and a significant portion of the feedback he received after therapy sessions depicted experiences of being in the prenatal state and the process of birth. Based on his observations, Stanislav Grof developed models of four basic perinatal matrices, the imprints of the experiences that every individual undergoes during their time in the womb and emergence from it.

The first basic perinatal matrix (BPM-**1**), according to Stanislav Grof, encompasses the impression of being in the maternal womb from the moment of conception until the placental separation and the onset of the first contractions. The infant perceives this segment as a certain form of "oceanic bliss," a sense of connection and unity with something greater, merging with it. Provided there is a benign emotional flow during pregnancy, the imprinting has an exclusively positive character. However, if the mother experiences emotional trauma or physical injuries, the child's unconscious mind records and imprints this experience into the perinatal matrix.

The second perinatal matrix (BPM-**2**) contains sensory information about the experience of placental separation, the first contractions, and the mother's emotional state accompanying this process. The child perceives this experience as a form of torment, where the main emphasis lies on feelings of hopelessness and the inability to resist the immense force directed towards the infant.

The third perinatal matrix (BPM-**3**) records the experience of passing through the birth canal. At this stage, the child already senses that something is happening. The feeling of hopelessness gives way to a sense of struggle. Depending on the speed and complexity of the birth, the negative aspect of imprinting this matrix can vary significantly.

The fourth perinatal matrix (BPM-**4**) captures the experience of being outside the mother's womb during the first five hours. The dominant emotions in this matrix are feelings of liberation, completion, and overcoming obstacles. There is a sense that the old world has vanished while the new one is just beginning to take shape.

Holistic Pulsation Massage

Tovi Browning, an Israeli specialist in osteopathy and reflexology, has made interesting advancements in somatic psychotherapy. She has developed the method of holistic pulsation massage, which essentially serves as a preventive system for various physical ailments, a therapeutic approach that can be used in psychotherapy, and naturally, a method of rehabilitation following physical traumas. This method has been influenced by gestalt psychotherapy, Alexander Lowen's bioenergetic analysis, and the works of David Boadella, the creator of the bodynamics method.

Since ancient times, body rocking has been used in shamanic and later religious practices as a means of altering consciousness, inducing trance states, and facilitating psychological transformation. Body rocking is inherent in young children and is often observed before falling asleep or upon awakening. Such rocking is commonly accompanied by a sense of pleasure, and attempts to interrupt this movement elicit negative emotions in children. In manual therapy practice, specific forms of rocking were first utilized by Dr. Trager. His method was based on the idea that rocking the patient's arms, legs, and torso in specific directions could rapidly reduce pathological muscle tension and alleviate pain responses. Curtis Turchin compiled Dr. Trager's developments into a more cohesive system and named this form of work "pulsation." Tovi Browning further refined this method, introducing several modifications. She described her findings in the 1992 book "Gentle Miracles: Holistic Pulsing" and later in "The Power of Softness: Holistic Pulsing" (1999).

This method is based on three levels: the level involving techniques of conventional body massage, the level of osteopathy and manual therapy, and the level where psychotherapeutic work takes place. Due to the gentle nature of most of the techniques employed, this method can be applied to individuals of various ages, ranging from young children to the elderly. The principle of "non-violence" embedded within the technical repertoire of this method enables its successful application in postoperative recovery periods. During the massage process, the patient can remain mobile and maintain activity. The therapeutic dialogue with the patient, which holds psychotherapeutic significance, plays a significant role in the massage session. Vibrational and rocking movements, rubbing, stretching, and unfolding form the foundation of the method's toolkit. The method encompasses seven principles for executing the technique.

1. **Universal Movement:** The work should create movement throughout the patient's entire body.

2. **Expansion and Lengthening:** This principle allows for the release of emotions held within the body.

3. **Connection:** The work extends through massaging the boundaries and adjacent areas, as well as through the patient's awareness of differences in reactions across different body regions.

4. **Mutuality:** Contact in the session is established through the hands and encompasses a specific psychological attitude of empathy and compassion.

5. **Absence of Coercion:** This principle emphasizes the absence of directiveness in therapeutic work and the ability to adapt to the patient's body responses.

6. **Healing, Not Fixing:** The work occurs not with any singular block in the body but with the entire body simultaneously. This reflects the holistic approach of the method.

7. **Self-Healing:** The therapist teaches the patient to find their natural

body balance.

The method includes three primary components, clearly drawn from the philosophy of humanistic forms of psychotherapy. These components are awareness, the ability to be present in the "here and now"; acceptance, the ability to embrace one's own feelings and the feelings of others, to acknowledge differing perspectives, and ultimately, to accept reality as it is; and responsibility, the ability to remain realistic, recognize the boundaries of one's own responsibility, understand that the main resources for changing one's life lie within oneself, and grasp the fact that the individual is ultimately responsible for their unfolding within the context of their life.

Tovi Browning

I find Tovi Browning's assertion that every muscular block harbors a resource for healing, and that each block should be approached with love, acceptance, and respect, to be highly valuable.

Moshe Feldenkrais Method

The founder of the Moshe Feldenkrais Method (1904–1984) was born in the city of Slavuta, Ukraine. He received a Zionist education at home and acquired some knowledge of Hebrew. In 1918, he embarked on a six-month pilgrimage to Palestine. In 1925, he began working as a cartographer in the British Survey Department. It was during this period that he started practicing jiu-jitsu. In 1925, while participating in a football match, he sustained a knee injury. Conventional methods of physical rehabilitation proved ineffective, prompting him to develop his own therapeutic technique, which would later evolve into a distinct method of practice.

In 1930, he enrolled in an engineering college in France and, from 1933, worked as a scientific collaborator at the Radium Institute under the guidance of Frédéric Joliot-Curie. In 1933, Feldenkrais encountered Jigoro Kano, the founder of judo, and began studying his style of combat. He achieved a first-degree black belt in judo in 1936, followed by a second-degree black belt in 1938. In 1940, he worked with Paul Langevin, conducting research in the fields of magnetism and ultrasound.

In 1942, he published a manual on unarmed combat, "Practical Unarmed Combat." His developed method of rehabilitation aided his own recovery from a re-injured knee during his judo practice. In 1949, he published his first book on his rehabilitation method and relocated to Israel, where he actively promoted his method. He continued teaching his method of rehabilitation until his passing in 1984.

Moshe Feldenkrais

The main feature of the method is the cultivation of mindfulness regarding the changes that occur within an individual during the process of therapeutic somatic work. The exercises in the method are highly diverse, conducted in various body positions, and target different muscle groups and muscle complexes.

Two primary forms of work are practiced within the context of the method. The first is individual work, in which the therapist directly engages with the patient's body. This work is typically performed on a massage table or on the floor with a mat and is known as "functional integration." The second form of work is presented in the format of group sessions, where the facilitator demonstrates movements and their specific execution, and the participants replicate them. This form of work is referred to as "awareness through movement."

Feldenkrais emphasizes that individuals base their actions on their self-image, which is shaped by three factors:

- The innate biological constitution of the individual
- Upbringing and the social environment in which the individual grew up
- The process of self-education and reevaluation of personal and collec-

tive experiences

Feldenkrais asserted that the first two factors lie beyond conscious control, unlike self-education, which serves as the primary method of self-transformation. He also believed that these three factors determine an individual's major successes and failures in all social spheres.

Furthermore, he stated that the inclination to identify oneself with a social mask, aimed at displaying success or failure, can lead to a disconnection from one's deeper needs and personal fulfillment. In many ways, Feldenkrais's ideas about the conflict between the social mask and internal needs are similar to Carl Jung's theories of archetypal masks and the Self. The dynamics of the latter predetermine the state of the individual. It is difficult to determine whether Feldenkrais adopted this idea from Jung or independently developed a theory that bears many similarities. However, he undoubtedly manifested it qualitatively on a practical level.

Feldenkrais devoted significant attention to the theory and practice of cultivating optimal bodily habits that restore natural grace to the body, fostering a balanced and harmonious perception of one's self-image. Many exercises in his methodology revolve around seeking more comfortable positions while standing, sitting, and lying down. One particular exercise that promotes balance and targeted body work is referred to as "manipulon." In contemporary Feldenkrais training programs, students delve into the study of over 90 different "manipulons" over a span of three years.

Within the Feldenkrais system, several guiding principles have emerged. Let us outline some of them.

In the Feldenkrais Method, certain principles of work are currently distinguished. Let's highlight some of them.

1. **Questioning system:** The work within this method is primarily based on the questions posed by the therapist to the patient rather than the answers provided. It also teaches the individual to find their own answers rather than relying on pre-established corrective programs.

2. **Discerning differences:** The ability to perceive and register differences is crucial in the learning process, as it allows us to become aware of our progress and direction.

3. **Slower is faster:** Slow execution of movements enables a deeper understanding and awareness of the psychological and physiological processes occurring in the body.

4. **Less is more:** The power of precision. By reducing the number of movements and minimizing their amplitude, we can more effectively reach the key microscopic action that creates the most efficient change.

5. **Simplicity and ease:** During the learning process, attention is focused on simple and understandable differences in the patient's reactions. This principle contradicts the societal belief that "no pain, no gain."

6. **Variation of speed:** Preference is given to slow movements in exercises, emphasizing their nuances, the clarity of transitions, constituent parts, differentiation, development, patterns, and obstacles that may arise during interaction.

7. **Differentiation**: f**ragmenting "embedded" patterns:** In therapeutic and educational interactions, the aim is to differentiate and fragment motor patterns that are not yet fully under conscious control.

8. **Learning from one side to the other:** This principle refers to the mutual learning between the right and left sides of the body and, more broadly, the right and left hemispheres of the brain. If one part of the body is unable to correctly perform a certain motor pattern, the other part can serve as a model for imitation, facilitating and expediting the learning process.

9. **Diversity and variability:** Introducing variety into a bodily pattern potentially expands an individual's level of awareness and improves movement control.

10. **Quality of movement:** The primary criterion for movement quality in the Feldenkrais Method is accuracy.

11. **Auxiliary movements:** These movements are performed to assist the primary motor pattern being worked on. Sometimes, a series of auxiliary movements can significantly enhance the movement that is the focus of attention in the work.

12. **Moving in a different direction:** When faced with resistance in a motor pattern, instead of continuing to move in the same direction and applying more pressure, we start trying to perform the movement in a direction that can facilitate further progress. After some time, we can return to the main area of resistance and determine the changes that occurred after continuing the movement in alternative directions.

13. **Unfamiliar movements:** Any unfamiliar movements can contribute to an increased level of awareness by breaking up routine and automated patterns.

14. **Minimal movements:** This criterion speaks to the tendency to seek optimal ways of action and self-organization. Paying attention to minimal changes teaches the patient precision.

15. **Learning to become one's best teacher:** When we constantly orient ourselves to societal templates and fail to find recognition of our individuality, we generate tension in our bodies. By not rigidly adhering to a template during the instruction process for performing a new exercise, we allow the patient to learn from themselves and identify what works best for them and what doesn't.

16. **Awareness:** This criterion implies directing our activity towards overall coordination and seeking a balance between self-attention and attention to others in the present moment.

17. **Imagination:** This principle highlights the need, in certain cases, to mentally rehearse the desired movement in order to initiate the process of change at a more intense and profound level.

18. **Attitude towards the environment:** This criterion emphasizes the importance of the interconnection between the experiential changes occurring during the process and the surrounding environment, the world.

19. **Self-referencing:** Here we observe a criterion that highlights the significance of maintaining a constant connection between cognitive processes and the changes that take place during therapeutic learning and subsequently outside of it.

20. **Patterns, differences, questions:** In this case, we mention the interrelationship of various mind-body systems: physiological, neurological, emotional, and cognitive. When we observe any changes occurring in one system, we begin to explore how these changes manifest in the functioning of other systems, both individually and collectively.

21. **Grounding, precision, simplicity:** Feldenkrais practitioners strive not to impose their limiting beliefs on the patient, using the simplest and down-to-earth terms in communication, remaining reality-oriented, and aiming to be highly precise in their work with the patient.

Although the International Feldenkrais Federation now states that this method is neither a medical practice nor a massage practice or any other form of bodywork, in some countries, the method is associated with body-oriented therapy.

Thomas Hanna's Method

One of Moshe Feldenkrais's best-known students was Thomas Hanna (1928–1990), an American. Thomas earned a doctoral degree in philosophy and religion in 1958 and then worked at several universities in America, France, Germany, and Belgium. In 1965, he became the dean of the Department of Philosophy at the University of Florida. In the early 1970s, Hanna became acquainted with Moshe Feldenkrais, deeply embracing his philosophy and unique somatic practice. In 1975, he organized the first training program in the United States for Feldenkrais's method. This collaboration continued until 1977.

During his practice of the method, Hanna began to modify and introduce a range of theoretical and practical innovations. Particularly, Hanna arrived at the idea that all events in a person's life lead to the formation of specific patterns in their body. He maintained the key principles of the Feldenkrais method in his work. He named his method "Somatic Education according to the Hanna Method" or "Hanna Somatics." In addition to the foundational teachings of his mentor, Feldenkrais, Hanna incorporated theories developed through research on the physiological consequences of stress conducted by Hans Selye, as well as somatic development and maturation by A.F. Fraser.

Hanna discusses residual somatic memory, which remains after traumas and stresses, and how a therapist can utilize the brain's ability to relearn—neuroplasticity—to address this residual memory and correct the distorted body image at both the psychological and physiological levels. He introduces the term "sensory-motor amnesia" (SMA) to explain this process. According to Hanna, performing various exercises during practice promotes the integration of motor and sensory areas of the brain, leading to a clearer and fuller perception of body image. Naturally, through practice, muscular blocks are released, overall body coordination and muscular control improve, and posture and gait are corrected.

Hanna tragically died in a car accident in 1990.

Thomas Hanna

Many practitioners perceive Hanna Somatics as a variation of the Feldenkrais method.

Rosen Method

One of the most intriguing methods of body-oriented therapy is the Rosen Method, created by American physiotherapist Marion Rosen (1914–2012). Marion was born in Germany into a Jewish family and was the fourth child. During Marion Rosen's training in Germany, one of her teachers was Lucy Heyer, a student of Elsa Gindler, who developed numerous breathing and relaxation techniques for working with patients' bodies during her professional practice. Lucy Heyer's husband, Gustav Heyer, was a student and associate of Carl Jung.

Gustav's patients simultaneously underwent bodywork and relaxation sessions conducted by his wife, Lucy, and her student, Marion. The combination of verbal methods with somatic work greatly influenced the future philosophy of the method that Marion Rosen would create. Before World War II, at the age of 23, Marion Rosen decided to permanently leave Germany and move to the United States. It is worth mentioning that an American psychoanalyst, Karen Horney, helped Marion obtain a visa to the United States. Initially, Marion went to Sweden to complete her studies. However, when she received her visa and was about to embark on a ship across the Atlantic to America, the Germans occupied Norway. They inspected all ships leaving ports in search of Jews, who were then disembarked and sent to concentration camps. Therefore, Marion chose a different route to America—via Russia, then Japan, and from there to California. She settled in Berkeley. In 1944, Marion underwent training in physiotherapy and rehabilitation at the Mayo Clinic.

Marion Rosen

For several decades, Marion actively practiced a combination of verbal psychotherapy methods and active somatic work, establishing herself as an excellent specialist in this field. It was only in the early 1970s that Marion began taking her first students, and in 1980, she started conducting the first training programs based on the philosophy and practical aspects of her method. She later held seminars dedicated to her method in many European countries. Marion passed away in Berkeley, California, in 2012, at the age of 98.

Bioenergetic Analysis by Alexander Lowen

One of the highly recognized and popular methods of body-oriented psychotherapy is "bioenergetic analysis" developed by Alexander Lowen (1910–2008), one of Wilhelm Reich's disciples.

Lowen was born into a Russian immigrant family in New York in 1910. He initially pursued a legal education but later became acquainted with Wilhelm Reich, whose work intrigued him, leading him to study Reich's character analysis method.

Alexander Lowen

Lowen's personal struggles served as a significant motivation for his exploration of psychotherapy. He wrote the following about his work: "In 1938, I realized that my life was empty and experienced depression. I understood that my depression was connected to a lack of excitement in my body and a lack of adequate physical activity. Upon returning from work, I started performing exercises daily. The exercises yielded the desired results and helped me realize that I wanted to be more in my body than in my head."

During the autumn of 1939, Lowen would come to the park after work and, sitting in the sun, document these exercises. He became engrossed in the exploration of consciousness and the body, recognizing the profound disconnection between his consciousness and body within his own personality.

It was during this period that Lowen became a student of Reich's character analysis courses. As Lowen later commented, he found numerous answers to his pressing questions within Reich's theories. He stated, "I became fascinated with working with the body primarily because I had always been involved in sports and physical activity and knew that it made me feel good. Additionally, I had a host of sexual problems. Instead of resolving them, I became engrossed in Reich's perspectives, which, unlike other therapists, genuinely addressed sexual issues."

In 1942, Lowen began his personal therapy with Reich. Three years later, he completed therapy with Reich and ventured into conducting his own independent practice.

After practicing independently for a while, Lowen met another one of Reich's students, John Pierrakos, with whom he began a fruitful collaboration. It was with Pierrakos that Lowen commenced the development of fundamental body practices and exercises for his therapeutic method—bioenergetic analysis. This method, at the time, was considered innovative and original, combining traditional psychoanalytic processes with various exercises aimed at working with the patient's body. In his practice, Lowen drew significantly from Sigmund Freud's idea that internal conflict arising in a person's consciousness manifests as fixed tension in the body. This belief was actively expanded upon by Wilhelm Reich. Lowen paid considerable attention to reintegrating the patient's ability to experience pleasure and enjoyment, emphasizing that traditional social aspirations, such as money, power, and success, cannot fully provide these states within the individual's body.

In 1951, Lowen received his medical degree from the University of Geneva.

Lowen derived many ideas for his method from ancient Chinese metaphysics, which discussed the circulation of "qi" energy within the human body. He referred to this energy as bioenergy in his works. However, due to borrowing terminology and certain methods from Chinese non-traditional medicine and philosophy, some therapists began to perceive Lowen's method as unscientific and discredited. It should be noted that Lowen appears to have been deeply kinesthetic, predominantly forming internal representations of the perceived world through ordinary bodily and motor sensations. In this case, it is particularly important to consider that the vast majority of psychotherapists constructed their therapeutic theories through the prism of their own psychological profiles and often regarded freedom of self-expression through their dominant sensations as the primary criterion for therapeutic effectiveness. Individuals who live through bodily sensations rarely prioritize the development of a comprehensive theoretical framework for their innovative ideas, which may lead to their ideas being perceived as pseudoscientific and rejected by a portion of the scientific community.

In 1958, Lowen published his first book, "The Language of the Body," which, in the spirit of Reichian ideas, explored the psychotherapeutic issue of the relationship between consciousness and the body.

Alexander Lowen placed special emphasis on the energy of the human body and described it as a "bioelectric ocean" based on chemical and energetic exchange. His technique is largely based on Reichian breathing techniques and other methods of emotional expression. Lowen used various body positions as tension amplifiers that could lead to deeper relaxation of the body and the release of underlying emotions.

To express emotions such as anger, rage, and indignation, Lowen employed striking techniques. By allowing the patient to strike a soft object with their hand or foot, he provided an opportunity for the emotions to be fully expressed. Sometimes, he used a stick, suggesting that the patient strike the soft object with it. Lowen began testing this technique on his own by hanging a punching bag in the basement of his house. Through working with the punching bag, he explored how striking techniques could lead to the release of blocked emotions. Subsequently, he incorporated this practice into his psychotherapeutic approach, encouraging patients to express their pent-up emotions through strikes.

Here is an interesting example from our practice that vividly illustrates the effectiveness of therapeutic "striking" work:

The patient was a 34-year-old man who experienced regular, aggressive paranoid delusions for many years. When he was in a romantic relationship with a woman, he would start having paranoid fantasies about her possible infidelity when she was away from home. He would then rush to find her, confront her with a scandal, and bring her home, often culminating in sexual intercourse. This pattern repeated itself with various women.

While working with this patient, we discovered a case from his youth that, in my opinion, served as the basis for his neurotic behavioral pattern.As the patient described, when he was 17 years old, he was dating his first girlfriend. After a walk together, when they went their separate ways, he suddenly felt the urge to follow her and see where she was going. After some time, he saw her in a park area, already near another young man, engaged in kissing. The enraged young man rushed towards them. However, his opponent turned out to be much bigger and stronger. He stopped the young man by simply placing his hand on his head and keeping him at a distance. There was no actual fight, and the patient's aggressive energy remained unexpressed. In our view, this event eventually led to the deep-seated need for repeatedly reenacting the traumatizing episode, where the primary goal appeared to be the full expression of repressed feelings of aggression and resentment. We believed that simple analytical awareness might not be sufficient when working with him, so we incorporated Alexander Lowen's striking method of bodywork. To release the blocked emotion, we used a small karate pad that was worn on the hand and could withstand strikes of varying intensity.

We asked the patient to visualize the face of the young man his girlfriend was kissing on the surface of the pad and start striking it. The force of the emotions and strikes was simply phenomenal. It was challenging for us to hold the pad in our hands. It is worth noting that the patient had no combat training. After the release of emotions, the patient's muscular tension significantly relaxed. He felt much better. Over the next few months of therapy, he did not report any paranoid urges. We are unaware of the patient's subsequent progress.

Based on our experience, often one or a few sessions of therapeutic striking techniques are sufficient to allow the full release of blocked emotional energy residing in the body, thereby significantly improving the patient's quality of life.

Striking techniques can also be performed with the feet. For example, Lowen suggests lying on the floor and kicking the air with the feet 100 times with each leg. In addition to striking techniques, one can engage their voice for a powerful expression of emotions. Start screaming and loudly utter the necessary words to fully express the anger and indignation residing in the conscious and body.

During the grounding exercise, the patient is asked to place their hands on the floor, slightly spread their legs, and straighten them, feeling vibrations in their knees. Lowen's followers explain that this position largely facilitates a sense of safety. In the yogic tradition, this exercise closely resembles the posture of "padahastasana," where the hands are placed under the feet with palms facing upwards. According to yogis, this asana stretches the spinal column and alleviates pain, fatigue, and tension.

Lowen also suggested an exercise involving a chair or other support for the hands at the back, in which the patient, holding onto the support, slowly squats until the heels start to lift and then returns to the original position. In his opinion, this exercise can provide an impulse for the actualization of emotional energy dormant in the soles and legs as a whole.

Additionally, Lowen often proposed the half-bridge pose as an exercise, which, in his view, could activate the expression of various suppressed emotions. In the Indian yogic tradition, this pose is known as "setu bandhasana," and it is believed to have a beneficial effect on multiple organs of the body.

Like Stanislav Grof, Alexander Lowen employed deep breathing techniques in his practice, suggesting that patients lie on the floor and begin to breathe intensively for 5-7 minutes, allowing various pent-up emotions to emerge. Unlike Lowen, Grof conducted much longer breathing sessions for his patients, lasting 30-90 minutes, placing special emphasis on this technique, during which patients would spontaneously start pounding the floor with their hands and feet, screaming, and assuming the half-bridge pose, naturally expressing repressed emotions.

For many years, Lowen conducted seminars on his psychotherapeutic method at the Esalen Institute in California, as well as in other cities in America, Europe, and even Japan. Although he mostly lived and worked in New Canaan, Connecticut.

Like Wilhelm Reich, Alexander Lowen actively explored issues of sexuality in the psychotherapeutic context, developing many of his ideas, methods, and practices. Like Marion Rosen, Alexander Lowen actively combined verbal methods of work, mainly psychoanalytic, with active somatic work.

Lowen explains the origin of tension in the body as a result of an internal conflict between the "pleasure principle" and reality, which imposes prohibitions and restrictions on the desire for pleasure. In this case, we see a nearly complete replication of Sigmund Freud's concepts describing the conflict between the superego and the id, the moral and animal aspects of personality. Essentially, Lowen interprets the culture in which an individual lives as the primary cause of neurotic and psychotic personality disorders.

During the process of releasing muscular blocks while working with a psychotherapist, clients most often experience subsequent results as a demonstration of new ways of behaving in their previous social context and during conflicts. Specifically, they change their attitude towards themselves and the world and begin to feel much better, both mentally and physically.

Lowen develops his own conception of character, which significantly differs from orthodox psychology. In his understanding, character is a specific way and style of behavior through which a person learns to control their desire for pleasure. Naturally, character finds its representation in the form of various types of tension. Lowen identifies five primary characters and five fundamental rights of the individual, which, in his opinion, are formed during childhood. The violation of a specific right leads to the formation of a particular character.

The rights of the individual identified by Lowen are as follows:

1. The right to be, live, and exist.
2. The right to satisfy one's needs.
3. The right to be independent, separate, and autonomous.
4. The right to be independent, separate, and autonomous, but with resistance to the world.
5. The right to have desires and move towards fulfilling those desires.

Next, we present the five characters distinguished by Lowen in his works:

1. Schizoid character.
2. Oral character.
3. Psychopathic character.
4. Masochistic character.
5. Rigid character.

Schizoid character arises as a result of a violation of the right to live. It develops due to the emotional rejection of the infant at the very beginning of life, with the mother often being held responsible for this. Subsequently, this leads to a fear of establishing contacts with the external world, an inability to experience full pleasure from the world, and self-destructive tendencies in behavior. Lowen believed that tension in individuals with a schizoid character arises at the base of the skull, although it is more accurate to say that the tension arises throughout the body, almost entirely separating the brain from the body.

If we were to provide a comment regarding this character, formally, Lowen adopted the model of the schizoid personality type, identified by Eugen Bleuler back in 1907, and developed it in the context of somatic work.

Oral character is formed as a result of a violation of the right to satisfy one's needs. It arises due to a reduction or complete cessation of satisfying significant needs for a certain period, such as prolonged waiting for food intake or prolonged separation from the maternal figure. There is a hypothesis that this character type often forms in individuals who were fed according to a specific schedule in infancy, following the recommendations of pediatricians. To a large extent, this character type is characterized by a lack of independence in the individual. Lowen describes a person with an oral character excellently: "What the oral type perceives as love, others perceive as a demanding request to love them." Lowen believed that the main behavioral criteria defining an oral character are dependence, intrusiveness, talkativeness, a desire to attract attention, strong oral habits such as smoking, constantly drinking something, and a constant need to eat something.

Lowen's oral character closely resembles the hysteric, demonstrative personality type studied in traditional psychiatry.

Psychopathic character type is formed as a result of a violation of the right to be independent, separate, and autonomous. According to Lowen, it develops between the ages of two and four through contact with the parent of the opposite sex, often due to emotional and/or physical violence. The individual believes that they have been betrayed by the parent of the opposite sex. Those with this type of character are egocentric and narcissistic, disregarding the needs of others, frequently lying, and lacking feelings of guilt and shame. They have little trust in almost anyone and tend to be skeptical in their thinking.

In many ways, this character type is analogous to the contemporary psychiatric concept of a psychopathic personality disorder.

Masochistic character is formed as a result of a violation of the right to be independent, separate, and autonomous, but with the application of resistance to the world. It develops through overprotection and excessive control from the maternal figure between the ages of one and three. The dominant feelings experienced by individuals with this character type are guilt and shame. Control of behavior is manifested as a means to avoid shame and guilt. They fear genuine freedom in relationships and may either have a strong inclination toward overeating or, conversely, be highly ascetic in their eating habits. Lowen provides an excellent description of the masochistic character: "A chronic subjective sense of suffering, which objectively manifests as a tendency to complain, a chronic inclination to harm oneself and engage in self-flagellation (moral masochism), as well as an obsessive desire to torment other people."

The closest psychiatric profile to the masochistic character may be the epileptoid character, but this correspondence is only partial and not definitive. In many cases, we assume that individuals who are subject to maternal hypercontrol in early and late childhood often exhibit epileptoid personality traits in adulthood.

Rigid character is formed as a result of a violation of the right to have desires and move toward fulfilling those desires. It develops between the ages of four and six through interactions with the same-sex parent. In their thinking and behavioral reactions, they rely on a specific experience of injustice received during childhood, manifested by the parent's actions, and harbor anger towards them, constantly resenting their wrongdoings. The expression of individuality in their personality is blocked. They constantly strive for perfection, both consciously and unconsciously, in an attempt to establish themselves as good in all aspects before their parent. They are excessively pedantic and consider any imbalance in relationships as an injustice, whether it involves receiving more or less than others. This character type fears making concessions in various forms of relationships, perceiving it as a sign of weakness.

From our experience, we note that this character type is not necessarily a result of trauma stemming from the parent of the opposite sex, but rather from the paternal figure.

In psychiatric interpretation, this type is closely related to obsessive-compulsive disorder. Some traits may resemble schizoid disorder.

Throughout his life, Alexander Lowen wrote 14 books that have been translated into many languages. The main ideas permeating his work are the ability to listen to one's body, express one's emotions, and live in harmony with the world and oneself.

In 2006, Lowen suffered a stroke, and he passed away on October 28, 2008.

Rolfing by Ida Rolf

Ida Pauline Rolf began developing her method of body therapy in the 1960s to rehabilitate World War II veterans who sought her help, often having lost faith in traditional medicine and searching for alternative treatment methods that could alleviate their suffering. Dr. Rolf, a doctor of biochemistry and a researcher in the fields of manual therapy, anthropology, Indian yoga, and homeopathic practice, was also a follower of Wilhelm Reich's ideas, which she successfully incorporated into her practice. At the age of 24, she defended her doctoral dissertation and was awarded a degree in psychology and biochemistry. She engaged in teaching activities at the Rockefeller Institute in the Department of Biochemistry.

Ida Rolf

The name that Ida Rolf gave her method changed from time to time. Throughout her practice, she used various names for her method. The following names should be mentioned: "postural relaxation," "structural integration," and "deep massage."

Essentially, Rolfing was created to free individuals from the stress patterns residing within their bodies. Similar to the Feldenkrais method, Rolfing places great emphasis on the idea of body awareness, improving various ways of moving, standing, sitting, and lying down. Through bodily changes, it seeks a path to personal transformation.

However, unlike similar methods like Rolfing, Ida Rolf more often attributed the blocking of bodily self-expression and the formation of body armor to physical rather than psychological stressors. This significantly diverged from Wilhelm Reich's vegetotherapy ideas, thus more strongly predisposing her method toward physiological aspects.

Ida Rolf largely embraced a holistic approach to the human body, considering each organ and part as part of a unified functional system.One of her important beliefs was that therapists should work with the entire body, not attempting to "fix" only a specific part. Echoes of the holistic worldview can also be found in the conviction that damage to one area of the body can lead to the distorted functioning of other body parts. An interesting observation by the method's author was that a body correctly performing its functions eventually assumes a vertical position that requires no significant energy expenditure. It is difficult to determine where Ida Rolf derived such a belief, but it is possible to trace a connection or borrowing of elements from bodywork in Chinese culture, as has previously occurred with Alexander Lowen. Chinese practices such as tai chi and qigong specifically emphasize the practice of "standing like a tree," which, according to the Chinese, can bestow strength and health upon individuals. The fundamental toolset of Rolfing consists of deep massage techniques applied to various parts of the body, utilizing the therapist's elbows and the joints of their fingers. In contrast to the gentle and non-invasive Feldenkrais method, the process of Rolfing can be very intense and painful for the patient. Strong manipulation is employed when deep holding patterns are identified. In this regard, we can observe a manifestation of a more coarse and directive orientation of the method, which, it should be noted, is not necessarily synonymous with ineffectiveness. In our understanding, an integrative approach to working with the body should encompass various tools that may, at times, differ radically from one another.

Due to its almost complete disregard for the psychological aspect of somatic work, in my opinion, Rolfing is more effective when combined with another method that takes into account internal psychological processes.

In practical work, Rolfing therapy is conducted as a sequence of 10 sessions, with each session focusing on different parts of the body. Special attention is given to muscle blocks in the pelvic area. Let's examine in detail the functional content of each session.

- During the first stage, the work encompasses the entire body, with particular emphasis on the chest, abdomen, and thighs.
- The second stage involves focusing on the feet, ankles, and their movement.
- The third stage directs attention towards stretching the muscles of the sides and those between the pelvis and chest.
- The fourth, fifth, and sixth stages concentrate on different parts of the pelvis, its overall functional mobility, and the release of muscular tensions residing within.
- At the seventh stage of the process, the focus shifts to the patient's neck, head, and face.
- The eighth, ninth, and tenth stages of the sessions aim to achieve overall body integration by incorporating all the changes attained in the preceding levels.

Ida Rolf paid great attention to promoting the elongation and smoothing of muscular fascia, which are the connective tissue sheaths that unite bones, muscles, and organs as a whole. She considered this to be an essential aspect of the therapeutic process. She believed that if a person is mentally and physically healthy, the fascia will not remain in a deformed state. Ida Rolf wrote, "A person is an energy field, just as the Earth with its outer force shell is also an energy field."

The release of muscle blocks and tensions can often indirectly provide a powerful impulse for personal growth and development.

Authentic Movement by Mary Whitehouse

This method entails expressive improvisation that allows participants to freely engage with their bodies and integrate their holistic image into their consciousness.

Mary Starks Whitehouse (1911–1979) was a disciple of renowned professional dancers Martha Graham and Mary Wigman. Later, Whitehouse, intrigued by the philosophy of Carl Jung, became a psychotherapist and started incorporating expressive dance movements as a therapeutic method in her work with psychiatric clients. Whitehouse sought to manifest Carl Jung's concept of "active imagination" in the practice of dance, creating an intriguing experimental approach to psychotherapeutic work.

Mary Whitehouse

During the practice of authentic movement, participants begin in a comfortable position with their eyes closed, waiting for any impulse to arise within their bodies, which gradually unfolds into actual movement. People freely move within the space, exploring the material of the unconscious that freely expresses itself through movement. According to Whitehouse, the primary goal is to establish an internal connection with authentic intuitive movement, which can fully unfold the diverse spectrum of human consciousness. The participant, who engages in the movement, becomes a witness to the expression of emotions without relying on intellectualization and projection as defense mechanisms.

Exercises within this method can be performed by an individual participant, in pairs, or in a full group format, where the intuitive movement facilitates mutual contact among the different group members.

The term "authentic movement" was coined by Whitehouse's follower, Janet Adler, who significantly expanded the method's conceptual toolkit.

This method extends beyond the boundaries of conventional psychotherapeutic application and is often used in the form of embodied meditation, aimed at unlocking the inner potential of the human personality.

Authentic Movement and "5 Rhythms"

An intriguing variation of authentic movement introduced by Whitehouse is the practice of meditation and self-exploration through the "5 Rhythms," created by Gabrielle Roth in the 1960s.

This practice aims to bring the mind to a state of calmness and balance, allowing the body to freely express itself within the context of specific rhythms that resonate throughout the therapeutic meditative process. The practice incorporates a unique shamanic essence. In various cultures, the spontaneous movement of a shaman during rituals is a significant tool for inducing trance states and establishing a connection with the spiritual realm. There is a noticeable influence from Eastern philosophy, which gained particular popularity in America during the 1960s and 1970s. It is worth mentioning that the "5 Rhythms" practice has also been influenced by various methods of psychotherapy.

Gabrielle Roth

At the core of this form of work, which, according to Gabrielle Roth, is more of a spiritual practice than psychotherapy, lies the idea that everything around us is energy that moves in waves and rhythms.

During the practice itself, the facilitator sets a specific mood for the group through certain phrases they speak and the accompanying music, which is carefully selected to match the mood of each rhythm. The rhythms are played in a fixed sequence and bear the following names:

1. **Flow:** The melodic accompaniment possesses a spherical, flowing, trance-like effect, initiating self-expression.

2. **Staccato:** The rhythm is more rigid, powerful, and strong, lifting energy from the depths of the body.

3. **Chaos:** The melody is more spontaneous and chaotic, evoking sensations of irrationality in consciousness.

4. **Lyrical:** The sound is melodic, subtle, and reminiscent of classical compositions.

5. **Stillness:** The accompanying soundtrack creates a calming, soothing atmosphere, inducing a sense of safety.

Usually, the practice of all five rhythms takes approximately 45 to 90 minutes, with each rhythm receiving 10 to 20 minutes of dedicated time. During extended seminars focusing on this method, which can last up to ten days, participants deeply explore the different rhythms in theory and practice.

Trager Approach

The founder of the Trager Approach, Milton Trager, was an athlete, dancer, and bodybuilder. During his sports practice, he became interested in psychotherapy and later obtained a medical degree in Mexico. He then completed a two-year residency in the field of psychiatry. The main idea that Trager developed in his practice was the interconnection between the processes occurring in the mind and the body of a person. In this, we see his orientation towards a holistic approach in general medical practice and specifically in psychotherapy. Trager applied his original somatic method to work with complex conditions such as post-polio syndrome, Parkinson's disease, and various other neuromuscular disorders.

Milton Trager

Practitioners of the Trager Approach claim that the approach itself and its technical repertoire are capable of releasing deeply ingrained patterns of mental and physical tension, rigidity, and restriction, unlocking the muscular armor, and bringing about a state of profound balance and equilibrium in the mind and body.

In the context of the approach, the practice begins with entering a meditative state, which Trager referred to as "hook-up." After that, the practitioner smoothly and gradually manipulates the patient's body through touch and active and passive movements. No forceful or painful movements are applied. Curiosity, playfulness, and effortlessness are key attitudes in the process of practicing the approach and guiding and shaping the work. Specific exercises, which Trager called "mentastics," are also employed, requiring the patient's attention and concentration.

Biosynthesis of David Boadella

David Boadella, the creator of this psychotherapeutic approach, based his theoretical and practical investigations on the ideas of English psychoanalyst and researcher F. Mott, who built his theories on the assumption of the dependence of human behavior on emotional intrauterine experiences.

F. Mott claimed that the emotions experienced by an individual during the period of their mother's pregnancy significantly influence not only the individual's mental and behavioral activities but also the physiological functioning of various organs in the human body. The theoretical and practical foundation for biosynthesis largely draws from Wilhelm Reich's theories, which have influenced the development of numerous other body-oriented methods of psychotherapy. Boadella also integrates the theory of rational relationships and extensive data from embryology into his practice.

David Boadella

From the Reichian theory, Boadella derived the idea that a person's personality manifests itself on three levels:

1. The level of defense, which finds representation in the form of a social mask,
2. The level of negative, painful emotions such as hatred, anger, anxiety, and others
3. The level of positive feelings that constitute the core of one's personality. These feelings can include joy, happiness, love, empathy,

acceptance, and more.

When a threat to the core level arises, the defense level and negative, painful emotions can be activated.

The primary goal of biosynthesis is the integration of cognitive, emotional, and physiological processes and finding balance between them. Great attention is given to the abstract ideas of deep personal growth that can occur through somatic work. This naturally imbues the method with a strong philosophical foundation, setting it apart from many other methods that primarily aim to relieve patients of muscular blocks and restrictions.

The therapeutic process in the approach is based on three fundamental principles:

1. **Grounding principle:** Which aims to achieve a state of relaxation and overall equilibrium, enabling individuals to manage their internal psychological processes and maintain an effective connection with their surrounding reality. On a physical level, this is embodied in the search for a balance between physical tension, movement, and a selected fixed posture of the body. It corresponds to the level of the embryonic mesoderm, the middle germ layer, which serves as the basis for the formation of the circulatory system, bones, and muscles of the body.

2. **Centering principle:** In the context of this principle, the focus shifts to the internal organs of the human body. The practical focus involves working with emotional states and the respiratory system. This process balances the rhythms of energy flow inherent in the body's metabolism and the functioning of the nervous system. It also allows individuals to accumulate positive emotions more effectively and release accumulated negative emotions stored within numerous somatic blocks. Breathing techniques are used, stimulating awareness and the body on multiple levels and enabling the concentration of resources within oneself. It corresponds to the

level of the embryonic endoderm, the inner germ layer, from which the respiratory and digestive organs develop.

3. **Visioning principle:** This principle is oriented towards creating connections between different channels of communication by seeking correspondences between feelings, speech, and gaze during motor activity. The integrity of self-expression becomes a significant criterion for the effectiveness of the psychotherapeutic process. It corresponds to the level of the embryonic ectoderm, the outer germ layer, from which the skin, nervous system, sensory organs, and brain arise.

During the work, all three main principles are sequentially applied to improve and enhance the effective interaction of the psychological and physical aspects on various levels.

Biodynamic Psychology and Psychotherapy by Gerda Boysen

Gerda Boysen was born in Bergen, Norway, in 1922. Her interest in psychotherapy and psychoanalysis arose in 1947 when she read Wilhelm Reich's book. Subsequently, she underwent vegeto-analysis with one of Wilhelm Reich's disciples, Ola Raknes. Gerda then began studying psychology in Oslo and also qualified as a physiotherapist.

Gerda Boysen

In Wilhelm Reich's concepts, she was particularly drawn to the idea of the interconnection between repressed emotions and existing muscular suppression in the body. She wrote her book "Uber den Korper die Seele heilen," in which she described the development of her own method of body psychotherapy based on the ideas of Wilhelm Reich, Carl Jung, and Sigmund Freud. She named her method "Biodynamic Psychology and Psychotherapy."

In 1969, Gerda Boysen moved to London and established the International Educational and Methodological Institute to further develop her method. She became the first woman in Europe to create her own psychotherapeutic institute. Boysen's books on biodynamics have been translated into multiple languages.

Boysen notes that the process of stress release is closely related to the processes occurring in the digestive system. She concludes that proper massage techniques can allow suppressed feelings, dormant within the muscular armor, to manifest. She also observed an interesting phenomenon: the release of emotional constriction is often accompanied by noises from the intestines, similar to those that occur during digestion. She named these noises "psychoperistalsis."

Boysen frequently used a stethoscope to monitor psychoperistalsis in her patients during the psychotherapeutic process. An intriguing fact is that she learned to differentiate between different types of psychoperistaltic sounds and draw specific conclusions about the patient's unconscious processes based on them. According to Boysen, if psychoperistaltic activity was greatest at the end of a session, it was considered a good criterion for the quality of psychotherapeutic work.

It is worth noting that biodynamic massage can be practiced independently of full biodynamic therapy as a relaxation and muscle release technique.

After specific material from the unconscious is raised through massage techniques, it undergoes the necessary analytical processing, which facilitates deeper processes of awareness and understanding of internal conflicts.

Hakomi Method by Ron Kurtz

This form of body psychotherapy was developed by Ron Kurtz in the 1970s. The method integrates psychology, systems theory, various body-oriented psychotherapy techniques, and Eastern philosophy. The Hakomi Method is based on five key principles:

- Mindfulness
- Non-violence
- Organicity
- Unity
- Holism of body and mind

Some followers of the Hakomi method add two additional principles:

- Truth
- Mutability

The Hakomi Method helps individuals recognize the patterns of functioning within themselves as a self-organizing system, composed of experiences, values, beliefs, motivations, emotions, cognitive processes, images, etc. The method directs the patient's attention to reevaluating values and beliefs that can contribute to constructive changes.

Ron Kurtz

The method itself comprises six main stages that a therapist goes through when working with a patient:

1. **Establishing a healing relationship:** At this level, empathetic connections are established between the therapist and the patient, forming the foundation of the healing process. It involves the practice of "loving presence" aimed at creating an empathetic effect.

2. **Cultivating mindfulness:** At this level, the therapist assists the patient in becoming aware of how their experience is organized and helps them focus on it.

3. **Eliciting experience:** Within this context, the therapist begins to help the patient engage with various components of their experience and structural elements of their personality, such as memories, emotions, values, beliefs, etc. This process is called "mindfulness-based experiment", which includes different body-oriented and verbal methods designed to access pre-existing experiences that

require processing in a safe manner.

4. **Processing:** This level is necessary for accessing the deeper emotions and memories that underlie the symptoms. If the patient is ready to go deeper, the therapist facilitates this process. As different values and beliefs associated with the experience emerge, they are attended to and analyzed.

5. **Transformation:** After re-experiencing and analyzing the material, the patient begins to recognize potential new healing experiences and becomes open to them.

6. **Integration:** At this level, the therapist and patient work together to establish a connection between the new healing experience gained through psychotherapy and the patient's real life.

Throughout the psychotherapy process, various practices are utilized, such as "contact and tracking," "probing," "taking over," "resistance containment," and many others. These practices aim to develop greater sensitivity and awareness, both within and beyond psychotherapeutic practice.

Technique of Frederick Alexander

Frederick Alexander (1869–1955) was an Australian theatre actor known for his performances in Shakespearean plays. During his public performances, he experienced significant voice loss and had to seek different methods of professional rehabilitation. Through self-experimentation, Alexander acquired the ability to inhibit unnecessary contractions in his neck and head movements. He discovered the substantial influence of these patterns on the quality of speech. Over time, he realized that by practicing body exercises, he had completely resolved his voice problem.

Frederick Alexander

Alexander's practice is primarily based on somatic re-education, with a primary focus on a person's posture and movement. The author believed that habits of holding the body in uncomfortable positions could significantly affect cognitive processes, self-awareness, and the physical health of an individual. Although the literal focus of the practice is the patient's body, Alexander considered his method primarily directed toward working with the mind.

American philosopher John Dewey utilized Alexander's technique to address headaches, back pain, and vision impairment, yielding significant results. Renowned American psychologist and researcher Aldous Huxley took lessons in the technique from Alexander and held his work in high regard. In his work "The Art of Seeing," Huxley comments on his views regarding this technique. Additionally, the method of Alexander influenced the work of Frederick Perls, the founder of Gestalt psychotherapy, who considered Alexander one of the inspirations for his therapeutic practice. Another practitioner of Alexander's method was Moshe Feldenkrais, although it is difficult to determine the extent of their collaboration.

Followers of Alexander's technique claim that it can address various physiological processes in the body, enabling the restoration of lost potential and the healing of individual parts. In 2015, diagnostic data emerged confirming that Alexander's technique can significantly reduce back and neck pain and aid in the rehabilitation of Parkinson's disease.

The process of Alexander's approach largely relies on awareness of action, which is a necessary criterion for constructive therapeutic changes. Modeling bodily behavior through the therapist during various natural processes such as walking, standing, sitting, and lying down is an essential tool for identifying issues that can be addressed through therapy. It is also important to understand that changes in each patient often begin with different habits. In practice, the semi-supine position is utilized as a means of relaxation and redirecting accumulated muscular tension. This position is referred to as "constructive rest." The "Ah" breathing exercise is used to coordinate free breathing and reproduce different sounds. The fundamental values emphasized in the implementation of the method are freedom, efficiency, and patience. As with many other body-oriented methods of psychotherapy, excessive effort, restrictive conclusions, and judgments are undesirable.

Alexander's technique finds application in vocal training in music schools. Practitioners of this method comment that it allows for a balanced use and control of airflow, significantly improving various vocal skills. The Alexander technique is also commonly applied in actor training. Practicing actors acknowledge that the technique enables a substantial reduction in stage fright and enhances improvisational abilities.

Furthermore, instructors of the method indicate that some people employ its tools for personal growth and development in various other domains of human activity. Typically, the exploration within the framework of the method involves around 10 to 40 sessions, lasting approximately 30 minutes each.

Alexander wrote four books dedicated to his method.

Psychosomatic Medicine

Psychosomatic medicine is not merely a physically oriented form of therapy; rather, it explores the close relationship between the psychological and the physical primarily on an analytical level. The concept of the mind-body connection permeates ancient philosophy, and echoes of this idea can be found in Ancient Greece, Hinduism, and Taoist philosophy. For example, Plato wrote, "The greatest mistake in treating diseases is that there are physicians for the body and physicians for the soul, although the two cannot be separated... Where the whole body is sick, the parts cannot be healthy."

The interconnection of mind and body can be found in many Indian Vedic and Yogic treatises. For instance, in India, it is believed that one of the paths to achieving control of the mind, known as rajayoga, involves the practice of physical exercises, namely hatha yoga. However, the yogic notions of mind control extend far beyond the realm of mental health and are more appropriately associated with spiritual practice, one of which manifestations is the health of the mind and body.

Numerous body-oriented psychotherapists draw inspiration from various ideas and practices of rajayoga for their psychotherapeutic methods. One prominent example of such borrowing is Stanislav Grof's technique of holotropic breathing, which originates from the breathing techniques (pranayama) used as a means of achieving the state of rajayoga. In pranayama, this specific breathing technique is called "bhastrika."

Descriptions of the interdependence of emotional processes and the states of different organs can be found in the treatises of Chinese Taoists.

- Diseases of the heart, small intestine, tongue, and blood vessels are associated with hatred, while healing is manifested through love.
- Diseases of the liver, gallbladder, eyes, and tendons are connected to the emotion of anger, and healing lies in kindness.
- Diseases of the kidneys, bladder, ears, and bones are linked to fear, and healing is found in courage.
- Diseases of the spleen, stomach, mouth, and muscles are associated with worry and anxiety, and healing lies in tranquility and serenity.
- Diseases of the lungs, large intestine, nose, and skin are connected to sadness, and healing is attained through courage.

A considerable number of psychosomatic medicine practitioners turn to the works of ancient Chinese philosophers in search of inspiration and new ideas for their practice. The term "psychosomatics" was first used by the physician Johann Christian Heinroth. As a branch of psychotherapy, psychosomatics began to actively develop in the first half of the 20th century thanks to the works of F. Alexander, F. Dunbar, D. Smith, and many others.

Sigmund Freud expressed the idea of the interrelationship between psychological and physical processes but never actively developed this theme. He often equated them with hysterical symptoms, primarily dealing with conditions such as allergy, asthma, phantom pregnancy, and the like. He did not analyze more serious illnesses. To a large extent, he attributed the manifestation of these hysterical psychosomatic symptoms to the operation of defense mechanisms of repression and denial, which led to the somatization of unexpressed psychic energy.

Johann Christian Heinroth

The theoretical and practical developments of the psychosomatic discipline, along with its integrative philosophy, often diverge from the classical conceptions of medicine as a whole and psychiatry in particular regarding existing symptoms. However, it is worth noting that contemporary classifications of mental disorders are making attempts to integrate psychosomatic perspectives. This is already being done in certain sections of the DSM-5 and ICD-11. Additionally, the Research Domain Criteria (RDoC) project, developed by the National Institute of Mental Health in the United States, deserves mention. As stated by the project coordinators, "RDoC aims to create a new taxonomy of mental disorders through the integration of findings from the fields of genetics, neurobiology, and behavioral sciences." Bruce Cuthbert serves as the coordinator of this project.

Franz Alexander

One of the founders of this field was Franz Gabriel Alexander (1891–1964), an American physician and psychoanalyst of Hungarian origin who studied in Berlin. In 1919, after completing his medical education, he became a student at the Berlin Psychoanalytic Institute and a member of Karl Abraham's psychoanalytic group. In 1932, he was appointed director of the Chicago Psychoanalytic Institute, which he led until 1956. During his tenure at the institute, he actively collaborated with the psychoanalyst Karen Horney. Alexander criticized some of Freud's concepts, particularly the theory of libido, and sought to support the emerging ideas of his colleagues.

Franz Alexander was not the sole innovator in the development of psychosomatic concepts and the holistic approach in medicine. These theories existed before him. However, Alexander succeeded in accurately synthesizing the existing information and significantly expanding upon it.

The key idea of his work is the integration of somatic methods in medicine, such as pharmacology, dietetics, and surgery, with psychological and psychoanalytic approaches to assistance and support. Alexander believed that physiological illnesses have causes that are not solely physical but also have a psychological origin, relating to human experience in particular.

Formally, he began applying methods of classical psychoanalysis, originally developed for the treatment of neurotic disorders, to somatic conditions and achieved unique results. Franz Alexander saw the lifestyle adopted by a patient in accordance with their psychological profile as an intermediate link between the individual's psychological profile and the illness. Consequently, he emphasized that, depending on the individual's lifestyle, we can observe the occurrence of the same illness among representatives of different profiles.

In his theory of specific conflicts, Alexander states that the type of somatic illness is directly linked to an unconscious emotional conflict existing within the individual. He also emphasizes that the expression of emotions can greatly influence the functioning of various organs in the body. For example, according to his perspective, elevated blood pressure may arise as a result of repressed anger, and gastrointestinal problems may emerge from frustrations related to dependency tendencies.

It is worth commenting that the idea of the interdependence between emotional processes and the functioning of a specific organ is not pioneering; similar ideas were expressed by Chinese Taoists, whose theories can be traced back thousands of years. Naturally, their theories belong to non-traditional Chinese medicine. It is difficult to ascertain whether Alexander adopted the theories of Chinese Taoists or arrived at similar conclusions independently, but numerous correspondences can be found in their fundamental theses.

In his research, Alexander did not transform theories into unambiguous interpretations of the causes of illnesses but acknowledged the multifactorial nature of their formation. On the one hand, many interpretations of the causes of illnesses described by Alexander can be quite explicit and clear from a theoretical standpoint, such as the influence of anger on arterial pressure. However, some of these interpretations may only be comprehensible to psychoanalysts; for instance, the dependence of constipation on anal-sadistic tendencies within an individual's personality.

Alexander largely supported the theories of psychologist and psychoanalyst Helen Flanders Dunbar (1902–1959) and frequently cited her in his works. Dunbar was born in Chicago, Illinois. Her interest in psychosomatic medicine arose from her own experiences. In childhood, she suffered from rachitic pseudoparalysis, and during her teenage years, doctors diagnosed her with a "metabolic disorder."

She had a strong interest in potential integrative processes not only between psychology and medicine but also between religion and science. Dunbar underwent personal psychoanalysis with psychoanalyst Helen Deutsch and worked as an assistant in the psychiatric clinic of Burghölzli, where Eugen Bleuler and Carl Jung practiced. She engaged in active correspondence with Carl Jung, displaying significant interest in his views on various religious movements.

Dunbar is considered one of the founders of psychosomatic medicine and is even referred to as the "mother of psychosomatics." She founded the American Psychosomatic Society and the journal "Psychosomatic Medicine." She was a student of psychoanalyst Felix Deutsch and applied the ideas of Sigmund Freud and Wilhelm Reich. She advocated for a holistic approach in psychology and medicine.

Dunbar played an important role in the clinical pastoral movement, where various clergy members were given the opportunity to practice in hospitals and acquire a foundation of medical knowledge for a comprehensive understanding of illness.

She proposed an original psychological version of the physical laws of thermodynamics, which she called "emotional thermodynamics."

Her laws are as follows:

- Psychic energy seeks expression through a physical symptom if it cannot be expressed at the behavioral level.
- Problems in personality and unresolved internal conflicts lead to energy leakage and depletion, ultimately resulting in somatic issues.

Dunbar initiated the first large-scale study on psychosomatics, analyzing the psychological and physiological histories of over 1600 patients hospitalized at Columbia Presbyterian Hospital from 1934 to 1938. During this study, she developed her theory of specific personality types. She stated that the psychological profile of a patient suffering from a particular disease, such as ischemic heart disease, would significantly differ from the profiles of patients prone to frequent fractures, for example.

Helen Flanders Dunbar

Empirical verification of Dunbar's personality profiles was not confirmed, but it served as a good starting point for investigating the interplay between mental processes and physical illnesses.

Another creator of psychosomatics and psychosomatic medicine is Jelliffe Smith (1866–1945), an American neurologist, psychiatrist, and psychoanalyst.

Jelliffe Smith

Smith graduated from Brooklyn Polytechnic Institute in 1886 and then from medical college in 1894. His first publication, released in 1890, focused on botanical issues.

Starting in 1896, he became interested in psychology, neurology, and psychiatry, conducting research on the influence of psychological factors on somatic diseases. In 1899, he became the editor of the "Journal of Nervous and Mental Diseases."

In 1907, he met Carl Jung at the International Congress of Psychiatry and Neurology, which led him to revise his critical attitude towards psychoanalytic theory. In collaboration with W. White, he launched the first English-language psychoanalytic journal, the "Psychoanalytic Review," in 1913.

Together with W. White, he published the "Textbook of Neurology and Psychiatry" in 1915, which systematically examined the psychoanalytic approach. In 1918, he published the first practical guide to psychoanalysis, "The Technique of Psychoanalysis."

Most likely, Smith is the pioneer of psychoanalysis, as he was the one who proposed using psychoanalytic techniques for the treatment of somatic diseases. Apart from Jung, he engaged in active correspondence with S.

Freud, E. Jones, O. Rank, E. Bleuler, and E. Kraepelin.

In 1921, he had the opportunity to meet Sigmund Freud. In total, he authored over 400 articles and books on psychology, psychoanalysis, and medicine.

Philosophy of the Continuum Concept

The magnificent theoretical concept deeply applicable in the practice of somatically oriented therapy was introduced by Jean Liedloff in her 1975 book "The Continuum Concept." The central theme of the book revolves around the idea that humans possess a specific set of expectations referred to as the continuum by the author. These expectations were developed throughout human evolution as a means to more effectively satisfy our psychological and physiological needs and enhance our overall adaptive capacity.

According to Liedloff, this accumulated evolutionary experience can be actualized through development. Ignoring certain actions that can actualize this evolutionary experience may lead to a need for compensation and the development of various psychological and social disorders. For young children, such actions can include:

- Immediate placement of the child in the mother's arms after birth.
- Constant carrying of the child and physical contact with other individuals.
- Co-sleeping with parents at an early age.
- Breastfeeding on demand.
- Prompt response by parents or caregivers to urgent bodily signals (anger, crying, whimpering.)
- Acceptance by adults that infants are inherently social and ready for full interaction at their developmental level, both psychologically and physiologically.

According to Liedloff, the greatest harm parents can inflict on their child is doing what the child can do for themselves. This statement holds true for both infants and individuals in adolescence, reaching the stage of personality development.

Throughout our psychotherapeutic practice, we have repeatedly encountered confirmation of Liedloff's "Continuum Concept" philosophy, observing how parents traumatize their children by neglecting the evolutionary aspects of their development in their behavior. Simple overprotection is just the cornerstone of this problem. It's worth noting that these disruptions are not limited to children and can also manifest in adulthood.

One very significant disruption, already observed by many psychotherapists, is the modern trend of husbands being present during their wives' childbirth. Evolutionarily, men were mostly disconnected from the birthing process and did not witness the emergence of the newborn from the womb. This role was primarily fulfilled by women, who acted as midwives. We and our colleagues have recorded a considerable number of cases where men, after witnessing their wives' childbirth, partially or completely lost their sexual attraction to them. In our understanding, the birthing process is considered an archetypal event, and its observation is taboo for men.

Jean Liedloff

Violation of this taboo often leads to an unconscious need to distance oneself from the sexual object. Another violation, in line with the philosophy of the Continuum Concept, is the practice of placing the newborn on the father's chest after a cesarean section. Analyzing such cases, we have found examples of a complete reduction in sexual attraction toward women among men for many years. This reduction occurs not only with their wives but also with other women. It is highly likely that after this process, men undergo a hormonal shift, partly transitioning into a feminine role, with all the consequent effects related to the transformation of hormonal homeostasis. We strongly believe that the production of oxytocin and vasopressin, which are abundantly produced in mothers during physical contact with their child, becomes significantly enhanced, while the production of testosterone, crucial for sexual attraction to women, is likely to decrease or may not arise at all.

The philosophy of the Continuum Concept goes beyond bodily rules and taboos in the interactions between parents and children, as well as between men and women in a sexual relationship. However, the proper hygiene of the correct bodily cycle of contact is, in my opinion, its foundation. It can be perceived as a form of somatically oriented therapy aimed at behavioral correction within the framework of bodily manifestations. A properly adjusted homeostasis of bodily communication between individuals can likely become an essential element in predicting the emergence of neurotic and psychotic processes in an individual's psyche.

Arthur Janov and "Primal Scream" Therapy

It is quite challenging to categorize this form of psychotherapeutic work solely within the somatic vector of psychotherapy. It would be more accurate to say that the main focus of this methodology is the artificial induction of catharsis and the exploration of intense emotions through a specific ascetic process, combined with verbal work with the psychotherapist. Nevertheless, this form of work incorporates a significant number of concepts related to the somatic vector, which is why we include it in this chapter.

Arthur Janov was born in Los Angeles in 1924 to Russian-Jewish immigrant parents. He studied at the University of California, Los Angeles, where he obtained a master's degree in social work. He then earned a Ph.D. from Claremont University, defending his dissertation on "Exploring the Differences in the Polarity of Jewish Identity" in 1960.

Initially trained in psychoanalysis and practicing it, Arthur Janov later modified and transformed his approach during his practice, eventually creating his own therapy called "Primal Scream." In his technique, he integrated a multitude of theoretical aspects and practical elements from Wilhelm Reich's work, one of the most significant figures in the development of somatically oriented forms of psychotherapy.

During his work, Janov discovered that in early childhood, around the age of three or four, a person experiences a primary emotional trauma directly related to contact with parents or parental figures. This trauma arises from the rejection of the natural expressions of the developing personality. According to Janov, the experience of rejection and primary emotional pain during this period is completely suppressed and amnesicized by individuals, eventually becoming the foundation for all neurotic processes that develop later in life. Janov hypothesized that by immersing the patient in the period of primary trauma formation and triggering a cathartic release of the contained emotional pain, it would be possible to dismantle the foundation upon which the "neurotic structure" is built.

Janov describes a case involving one of his students, Danny Wilson, who spontaneously entered a re-experiencing of the primary trauma during group psychotherapy. Wilson told Janov about an incident he witnessed at a theater where a man named Ortiz performed in front of an audience wrapped in swaddling clothes and sucking milk through a tube. During his performance, he loudly exclaimed, "Mom! Dad! Mom! Dad!" At the end of his act, he vomited the contents of his stomach into a plastic bag.

Listening to Wilson's feedback about his reactions to this performance, Janov, as an experiment, asked him to intentionally scream, "Mom! Dad!" At first, Wilson resisted, but after some time, he followed the therapist's recommendation and fell to the floor, emitting loud, incoherent sounds and writhing as if in agony. He involuntarily continued shouting the psychotherapeutic mantra, "Mom! Dad!" After a while, Wilson let out a soul-piercing scream and, as his seizure came to an end, said, "I did it! I don't know exactly what, but I can feel!"

Arthur Janov

Janov admitted that this particular case left him perplexed for several months. It was a puzzling experience for him as he had never witnessed anything like it before. The session with Wilson was recorded on video, allowing Janov to review this therapeutic experience multiple times. But according to his comments, it did not provide him with any conclusive insights.

After some time, Yanov managed to recreate a similar process with another patient whom he named Gary Hilgard. Gary spoke about his parents who constantly argued and ruined his life. Yanov decided to try with him what had caused intense re-experiencing of childhood trauma in Danny Wilson: shouting loudly, "Mom! Dad!" At first, Gary also refused to perform the therapist's exercise but eventually complied with the recommendation. Yanov discovered that this phrase began to trigger intense breathing and palpitations in Hilgard. After a while, Hilgard began to writhe and convulse and then let out a powerful scream. Everything was repeated almost exactly.

When Gary regained consciousness, he commented that he had experienced a large number of different insights and illuminations about himself and his life. Life seemed to have formed from scattered fragments into a coherent picture.

Analyzing these two cases, Yanov began to come to the conclusion that he had discovered something important. He tried to repeat this technique of calling for mother and father with other patients and, as he writes, encountered similar results again and again.

Thanks to observing such therapy scenes, Yanov began to form his own understanding of primary pain as a deep emotional imprint that could be found in the consciousness of any neurotic.When the technique of the "primary scream" was fully developed, it consisted of two main stages. In the first stage, the patient underwent a three-week isolation in a hotel room without contact with the outside world, except for communication with the psychotherapist who came and spoke with the patient for three hours every day. The patient was not allowed to read, watch TV, or use the phone. If necessary, the amount of food consumed and the duration of sleep were reduced. The use of any substances that alter the state of consciousness was prohibited. Due to this form of isolation, the level of mental and physical tension experienced by the patient constantly increased, leading to sharp regressive shifts in perception back to childhood sometime around the end of the second week. Various traumatic childhood experiences manifested. Sometimes this shift occurred spontaneously, while other times the psychotherapist helped the patient by guiding them into childhood through various questions. Sooner or later, the greatest regression occurred, during which the patient began to re-experience the primary traumatic experience. The psychotherapist acted as a sitter and observer and, if necessary, assisted the patient in expressing their emotions during the process.

The second part of the therapy involved regular participation in group psychotherapy sessions with other patients who had completed the three-week individual course of the primary scream. This part could last up to ten months. During the group work, participants actively shared and discussed their experiences of therapeutic isolation, seeking ways to integrate this experience into their everyday lives. Quite often, during the group therapy sessions, many participants spontaneously regressed into the experience of primary trauma, re-experiencing emotions that had not been fully expressed during the first part of the psychotherapy.

Yanov comments that there were cases where almost the entire group could regress into a regressive state, exhibiting various emotions.

Arthur Yanov wrote that patients who completed the full course of his psychotherapy reported significant changes in their behavior. At a deep level, the tension in the patient's muscular armor changed. The person became much more relaxed and calm. There was often no longer a need for nicotine, alcohol, or various narcotic drugs. Yanov also discovered that transformations occurred in the patients' sexual lives. Their sexuality became balanced. Excessive neurotic sexual needs decreased, while the depth and quality of their sexual experiences significantly increased.

Many well-known personalities underwent "primary scream" therapy, which significantly increased its popularity. John Lennon, Yoko Ono, Steve Jobs, and others went through it. However, as we know, none of them completed this form of psychotherapeutic work to the end.

Pathopsychological Profiles and Somatic Psychotherapy

Hysteroid Profile

According to our observations, patients with a hysteroid profile do not particularly favor body-oriented psychotherapy. It does not evoke enthusiasm in them. However, any therapeutic work that focuses on the hysteroid individuals themselves will be accepted in some form. It is worth noting that pure hysteroids, without the presence of other profiles, rarely engage in any form of physical exercise in general. If they do engage in physical activity, it is usually done to impress others. In my opinion, various practices of body-oriented psychotherapy can be applied to hysteroids, but significant results should not be expected.

Paranoid Profile

Individuals with a paranoid profile predominantly live in their heads rather than their bodies, resulting in a buildup of muscular tension. Similar to hysteroids, paranoids are not inclined towards engaging in sports or physical exercises. Therefore, it should not be expected that body-oriented therapeutic exercises will be easily accepted. Until trust in their body sensations is at least partially restored, the effectiveness of body-oriented therapy exercises will be relatively low. However, we believe that in combination with cognitive, psychoanalytic, or other forms of psychotherapy, certain body practices can be appropriate. Nevertheless, pure bodywork with individuals of the paranoid profile does not hold much significance, in my opinion.

Psychopathic Profile

Psychopathic personalities do not struggle with expressing negative or sexual feelings. They frequently engage in various forms of sports activities but have almost lost their ability for empathy and compassion. When we introduced different breathing techniques to patients with this profile, they often accessed emotions of pain and suffering that psychopaths carefully guard within themselves. As soon as this level of emotional exploration was reached, psychopaths most often requested that the technique be suspended, complaining of dreadful emotional states.

Many times, after intense emotional experiences, they discontinued psychotherapy altogether. It is important to understand that in other forms of psychotherapy, once the real products of suppression are accessed in psychopathic individuals, the situation is almost the same. This escape from the therapy context occurs for various conscious reasons.

At times, while working with psychopathic personalities using breathing techniques, we initially witnessed the profound disclosure of transpersonal aspects of their consciousness. However, once the patients entered the realm of their actual negative personal experiences, they frequently discontinued therapy or simply refused to engage in body-oriented techniques.

It should be noted that psychopaths, as they do not lose their connection to their bodies, are often hypersexual and may consume large amounts of alcohol and drugs. They can easily tolerate high dosages. In contrast to patients with other profiles, they more easily control their dependencies and often fail to recognize the reasons why they should eliminate them.

Generally speaking, the effectiveness of body-oriented psychotherapy with psychopathic personalities is extremely low or does not yield any constructive results.

Obsessive-Compulsive Profile

Individuals with an obsessive-compulsive profile may react differently to body practices. Some patients perceive the therapist's actions easily and experience significant therapeutic effects relatively quickly. However, resistance to these practices during the initial stages of therapy is commonly observed. Moreover, this resistance is primarily of an unconscious nature. On a conscious level, patients frequently express a desire to collaborate.

For patients suffering from OCD, such unconscious resistance is related to emotional alienation from the paternal figure. If the therapeutic process effectively addresses the topic of parental relationships, the quality of body-oriented therapeutic interventions can greatly increase.

Schizoid Profile

Individuals with schizoid personalities have significant issues with embodiment. They often do not engage in any physical exercises and may be skeptical about them. Based on our experience, attempts to involve schizoid individuals in physical psychotherapeutic practices almost never lead to anything. Sometimes they try to perform some exercises, but more often than not, they do them sparingly and rarely complete them. At times, the experience of bodily-oriented practice can simply frighten them, causing a lack of desire to return to it. However, the therapy itself is usually not discontinued. Instead, cognitive and analytical methods are preferred, allowing them to feel more comfortable. In our observations, it can be attempted to involve schizoid patients in physical therapeutic practices as a complement to other forms of therapeutic work. However, if they encounter significant difficulties in performing them, it is better to temporarily step aside and engage in something else.

Epiloeploid Profile

Individuals with epileptoid personality have a strong connection with their bodies. When engaging in various body-oriented practices, they experience intense emotional reactions. It is relatively easy and fast to access suppressed traumatic feelings. In my opinion, personalities with epileptoid traits are among the most receptive to bodywork. However, body therapy for them still needs to be accompanied by basic analytical processing and cognitive correction.

Schizophrenic Profile

Working with individuals with a schizophrenic profile requires an extremely delicate and gentle approach to body-oriented work. During physical practices, there is a significant risk of a temporary exacerbation of symptoms or the emergence of new ones. Moreover, this exacerbation or symptom occurrence often does not represent a complete release of suppressed emotions. Strong emotions in schizophrenic individuals mainly arise from unresolved internal conflicts. Bodywork may simply highlight these conflicts, but it is often incapable of resolving them. Therefore, we would argue that working with patients of this profile using body-oriented psychotherapy should be done very cautiously or ignored altogether. Sometimes the ability to perform certain body practices by patients with this profile can be an excellent criterion for positive progress. However, the foundation for the work will still rely on methods from other schools of psychotherapy. In this case, body therapy acts more as an assistant.

Manic-Depressive Profile

Individuals with manic-depressive personality profiles can be highly responsive to body-oriented psychotherapeutic methods. A significant portion of their emotional dynamics is linked to deep processes of suppressing traumatic experiences, especially those related to the time spent in the mother's womb and the birthing process. When working with MDP patients, we have often discovered that their birth experiences were problematic and difficult. The process of the infant's emergence from the womb was frequently hindered, and there were sometimes significant traumas in attempts to extract them. Techniques of body therapy can facilitate revisiting and reliving these traumatic experiences, allowing for emotional cleansing. Although, at times, it may be necessary to employ tools from other forms of therapy to facilitate regression into the past, hypnotic methods can be particularly useful in these cases.

5

Existential Psychotherapy

The roots of existential psychotherapy can be traced back to ancient philosophers, as evidenced by the dialogues Socrates had with people. Socrates' students—Antisthenes, Plato, Crito, Aristippus, and others—followed his style of conversation.

In the philosophical school of the Stoics, we can see a number of ideas that can be considered elements of existential philosophy. More modern philosophers such as Nietzsche, Schopenhauer, Hegel, and others largely anticipated the formation of existential philosophy as a separate direction of perceiving reality, based on which existential psychotherapy later began to take shape.

Conditionally, we will consider the Danish philosopher and writer Søren Kierkegaard (1813–1855) as a starting point in existential philosophy, whose works would later have a significant influence on various philosophers, scholars, and other thinkers. Naturally, Kierkegaard's works do not yet contain anything directly related to psychotherapy, but the key direction of thought of this philosopher will become the foundation, or even the abstract core, for the work of a number of psychotherapists.

Kierkegaard was born in Copenhagen into the wealthy merchant Peter Kierkegaard's family. He graduated from the theological faculty of the University of Copenhagen in 1840. His dissertation was devoted to the examination of the theme of irony in ancient Greek authors. The title of his dissertation was "On the Concept of Irony, with Constant Reference to Socrates."

Søren Kierkegaard

In his works, he criticized the way of life of many Christians who wanted to be spiritual people and prosper socially. Kierkegaard saw this as a form of spiritual burnout in Christian philosophy.

He believed that one can only comprehend Christ through paradox, thus making a qualitative leap in one's spiritual development.

Kierkegaard's ideas about the knowledge of the higher spiritual principle through paradoxical thought processes align his philosophy with some schools of Hindu philosophy, such as the teachings of Advaita Vedanta by Shankaracharya. Kierkegaard's paradoxical nature is similar to the concept of non-dual perception of the world, which is considered a significant achievement in spiritual practice in many Hindu religious schools. The Bhagavad Gita mentions that one who has achieved non-dual perception of the world is saved.

Kierkegaard sees the main purpose of human existence as the absolute freedom of the individual and the potential freedom of choice. In my opinion, Kierkegaard once again aligns with the philosophy of some schools of Hinduism, which consider liberation from the cycle of samsara as the goal of existence. In Shaivism and Krishnaism, this is moksha. In Buddhism, it is nirvana.

According to Kierkegaard, there are three stages of existence that a person goes through on the path to God.

Kierkegaard's Three Stages of Existence:

1. **Aesthetic:** This stage is characterized by living through the experiences of individual moments in life. At this stage, there is no analysis of the past or introspection that would allow the individual to avoid any previous mistakes. On the other hand, the individual does not attempt to plan the future clearly.
2. **Ethical:** At this stage, the person is capable of taking responsibility for their past and caring for their future.
3. **Religious:** In the religious stage, a person lives with a sense of eternity.

Partly, Kierkegaard's model of the phases of human existence bears resemblance to Freud's model of the structure of the personality. The aesthetic phase of life, characterized by immediate, earthly concerns, resembles the "id," which seeks to satisfy instincts as quickly as possible. The ethical phase, which allows the individual to engage in more meaningful social activity, is reminiscent of the concept of the "ego." And the religious stage bears resemblance to the "superego."

Naturally, such similarities are highly conditional and relative; however, we are inclined to believe that on a deep abstract level, Freud and Kierkegaard operated with closely related units of meaning.

Regarding Freud and Kierkegaard, we can recall a comment made by Karl Jaspers, one of the founders of existential philosophy and a continuator of Kierkegaard's legacy. In his book "General Psychopathology," Jaspers wrote that Freud characterized the nature of human instincts as animalistic, while Kierkegaard restored the spiritual dimension to human life. In this case, we observe a certain opposition between Freud's and Kierkegaard's theories.

However, it should be noted that Kierkegaard was not a practicing therapist but rather a secluded thinker, whereas Freud was primarily oriented toward literal medical work, dealing with various patient symptoms such as sexuality, aggressiveness, anxiety, and so on. As a result, Freud was significantly more focused on the materialistic aspect of human personality.

By considering Kierkegaard's and Freud's theories as complementary, one can significantly broaden their understanding of the world of the psyche.

Kierkegaard's political views were characterized by strongly expressed monarchical radicalism. He believed that the democratic form of societal organization was a "portrait of damnation."

Kierkegaard died of tuberculosis during a flu epidemic.

Another founder of existentialist philosophy, Martin Heidegger, incidentally claimed to have no relation to this philosophical movement.

Nevertheless, historians of philosophy consider Kierkegaard, Heidegger, and Jaspers to be among the most significant figures in existential philosophy. Therefore, let us dedicate some attention to Heidegger.

Martin Heidegger

Martin Heidegger (1889–1976) was born in Messkirch, Germany, into a modest Catholic family. His father, Friedrich, was a craftsman, and his mother, Johanna Kempf, was a peasant. It is worth adding that Heidegger's father held a lower clerical position in the Church of St. Martin, which is likely why he named his son after the saint. The religious orientation of his father significantly influenced the destiny of Heidegger, leading him to decide to enter the Jesuit monastery in 1909 to become a monk. However, a heart condition prevented him from taking this step. Due to his heart disease and the accompanying neurasthenia, in 1914, during his military conscription, he was deemed only partially fit for service and was not involved in combat during World War I, serving instead as a rear-guard auxiliary.

After abandoning his monastic career in 1909, Martin enrolled in the Theological Faculty at the University of Freiburg. In 1911, he transferred to the Philosophy Faculty, where he studied until 1915. During his studies in the Philosophy Faculty, he defended two dissertations: one in 1913 on the topic of "The Doctrine of Judgment in Psychologism" and another in 1915 on "Duns Scotus's Doctrine of Categories and Meaning." In 1917, he married his student Elfride Petri, and in 1919, their son Jörg was born. From 1922 on, Heidegger worked at the University of Marburg, where he gained wide recognition.In 1928, he assumed the chairmanship of the department previously led by his mentor, Edmund Husserl. It is worth noting that Heidegger was considered one of the most talented students of Husserl and was involved in editing various works, such as "Lectures on the Phenomenology of Inner Time-Consciousness," "Formal and Transcendental Logic," "Cartesian Meditations," and so on. In 1933, after the Nazis came to power, Heidegger became the rector of the University of Freiburg, joined the NSDAP (National Socialist German Workers' Party), and engaged in active political activities, incorporating Nazi rhetoric into his speeches. Due to Heidegger's proximity to the Nazi party, friendly relations between him and Jaspers broke down. It is interesting to consider Heidegger's psychodynamics and view his joining the Nazi party as a kind of rebellion against his mentor and predecessor, Husserl, who was Jewish and whom he did not attend the funeral of in 1938. In 1945, following the fall of the Nazi regime, Heidegger was convicted and found guilty of consciously supporting the Nazi regime, leading to his suspension from teaching at the university until 1951. In 1947, Heidegger published his "Letter on Humanism," in which he described the main differences between his views on existentialism and humanism. One of Heidegger's fundamental works, "Being and Time," was first published in 1927 and is dedicated to his mentor, Husserl. In this work, Heidegger revolutionizes the understanding of ontological problems, providing a detailed description of the philosophical interconnection between being and time. According to Heidegger, being is time itself, and it becomes intelligible only on the horizon of time. Heidegger's approach to the concept of being is a result of analyzing what we truly are—the analysis of the existent.

Heidegger introduces the term Dasein into philosophical discourse, which can be interpreted as "being-here" or "being-in-the-world." There are numerous other interpretations of this term, as its literal translation is nearly impossible. In an everyday sense, the term Dasein can be understood as "existence" or "being."

According to Heidegger, Dasein is the being that is capable of questioning being itself. It is through awareness of the existential structure of Dasein that a person is able to find meaning in their existence. While a being is defined by the question "What is being?" being itself, according to Heidegger, is determined by the question "What does it mean for something to exist?"In contrast to his teacher Husserl, who believed that philosophy should involve the description of experience, Heidegger argued that experience already takes place in the world and in the being of humans. In many ways, when observing the opinions regarding this postulate, we see not so much a contradiction as an attempt to describe the subject from different perspectives. The fact that being already exists in experience does not mean that a philosopher cannot describe it. Heidegger insists that the question of the concept of being and its meaning must be posed in philosophy, explaining that being itself is not a being. He then begins to explain the term "being," stating that everything we talk about, have in mind, or relate to is considered to be a being. Heidegger believes that being can be defined by its existence without an explicit conception of its meaning.

Intentionality, as understood by Husserl as the notion of consciousness being directed towards something, transformed in Heidegger's philosophy into the concept of "care", which became the foundation of his philosophical conception.

According to Heidegger, the structure of human existence is essentially characterized by "care," which represents the unity of three elements:

- **Being-in-the-world**: This refers to the fundamental mode of human existence, where individuals are inherently connected and embedded within their environment, actively engaged with the world around them.
- **Projection-into-the-future**: It signifies the forward-reaching aspect of human existence, where individuals are constantly oriented towards possibilities and potentialities, always striving and projecting themselves towards future goals and aspirations.
- **Being-within-the-worldly-entities**: This concept highlights the interconnectedness of human existence with the entities present within the world. It emphasizes the mutual influence and coexistence between humans and the entities they encounter, acknowledging the significance of relationality and engagement with inner-worldly beings.

We have presented only some of Heidegger's concepts to outline the direction of his philosophical thought. The materials written by Heidegger are often presented in highly abstract language, and he consistently operates with abstract concepts. The practical application of his concepts is not explicitly indicated, so a person who decides to embody Heidegger's philosophy in their life will have to embark on a lengthy journey of comprehension and understanding of his works. Among psychotherapists, there was one person who attempted to transform Heidegger's philosophy of being into a form of existential psychotherapy. This individual is the Swiss psychiatrist, psychologist, and one of the founders of existential psychology, Medard Boss, whom we will discuss in more detail later on.

Jean-Paul Sartre

Another existential philosopher who cannot be overlooked in the realm of existential psychotherapy is the French philosopher Jean-Paul Sartre (1905–1988). Although he did not have a therapeutic practice of his own, he made attempts to creatively reinterpret Freudian teachings in his works.

Sartre was born in Paris to Jean-Baptiste Sartre, an officer in the French Navy, and Anne-Marie Schweitzer. His father passed away before he turned two years old, so he was raised in the home of his maternal grandfather, Karl Schweitzer, and his uncle, Albert Schweitzer, a renowned German-French philosopher, physician, and missionary. Jean-Paul was the only child in the family. He received his education at the Lycée La Rochelle and the Higher Normal School, where he defended his dissertation in philosophy. Subsequently, Sartre underwent an internship at the French Institute in Berlin. From 1929 to 1944, he taught philosophy at various universities in France, including Paris, Lyon, and Le Havre. Afterward, he decided to dedicate himself exclusively to literary work. In 1938, Sartre published his novel "Nausea," which brought him fame. He also created a series of socio-philosophical, psychological, and historical biographies of famous writers. He published philosophical works such as "Transcendence of the Ego" (1936), "Imagination" (1936), "Sketch for a Theory of the Emotions" (1939), "The Imaginary" (1940), and so on. One of Sartre's most fundamental works is his 1943 book "Being and Nothingness," in which he expresses the necessity for the development of existential psychoanalysis.

During the German occupation, Sartre organized an underground group called "Socialism and Freedom."

In his philosophical and political views, Sartre was, to a great extent, a revolutionary and a rebel, which led him to actively support the Cuban Revolution in 1959. He met with Che Guevara and engaged in various discussions with him. He also actively participated in anti-war protests during the Vietnam and Korean Wars. He demanded Algerian independence, which resulted in ultra-rightist radicals throwing a bomb at his house.

In 1968, Sartre became a participant and, to some extent, a symbol of the French Revolution. Interestingly, when the raging students seized the Sorbonne, they allowed only Sartre to enter.

Sartre passed away from lung cancer. More than 25,000 people attended his funeral.

Jean-Paul Sartre

Sartre believed that a person is driven by visions of perfection, which he referred to as "ens causa sui." He also regarded phenomenology as one of the achievements of modern philosophy, as it helped eliminate the dualism that presumed a hidden nature in existence. According to Sartre, phenomenology, to some extent, dissolved the "illusion of the world behind the scenes." He believed that the social role a person plays is equivalent to human existence, regardless of its specific nature. The division of people into racial identities and classes is a form of self-deception, in his view. He emphasized that a person cannot be reduced to their social role, which is merely a superficial shell. This shell is often clung to tenaciously by individuals. Sartre concluded that overcoming self-deception requires realizing that existence and self-projection are distinct and uncontrollable. The understanding of one's existential being is manifested when a person begins to focus on what they fundamentally are rather than the superficial social roles they are involved in.

Nonetheless, Sartre believed that to become an "authentic being," one must maintain a balance between their existence and the relevant social roles in their life. Sartre had an interesting perspective on human relationships, suggesting that people are drawn to each other not due to some genuine attraction but because through another person, an individual can perceive themselves.

One of the criticisms Sartre leveled against Freud was that Freud undeservedly distanced himself from contemplating the future, primarily focusing on understanding the patient's past and their childhood development. As a result, Sartre's philosophy emphasizes both the past and the future of the human individual, forming a more comprehensive view of the person.

In contrast to Freud, Sartre posited that consciousness, which constitutes the essence of human existence, plays a pivotal role in a person's life rather than various unconscious processes that Freud postulated as leading and predetermining a person's life. Sartre commented that "existential analysis rejects the postulate of the unconscious; for it, the psychic fact coincides with consciousness." It is also worth noting that Sartre saw a greater division within the psyche between fundamental consciousness and unreflected consciousness, avoiding the traditional Freudian division of consciousness into the conscious and unconscious.

Sartre agreed with the notions in classical psychoanalysis that a child's relationships with other people and the surrounding objects contain manifestations of sexuality but refused to attribute any sexual significance to these relationships and objects in his understanding.

According to Sartre's perspective, every action of a person should be perceived as a projection of oneself towards possibilities. He agreed with psychoanalysts that there is meaning behind every action. At the same time, he rejected reducing this meaning to a simple consideration of the individual's past actions.

Carl Jaspers

One of the key representatives of the existential approach in psychotherapy is psychiatrist, psychologist, and philosopher Carl Jaspers (1883–1969), who made a significant contribution to the theoretical profiling of mental disorders and the methodology of their treatment.

Carl Jaspers was born in Germany in Oldenburg. His father was a lawyer and banker, and his mother was a peasant. Initially, Jaspers followed in his father's footsteps and began studying law at the University of Heidelberg and later at the University of Munich. However, by 1902, he had decided to change the direction of his studies and start pursuing medicine. By 1908, he had completed his medical studies at the University of Heidelberg, obtaining a medical degree in 1909. Jaspers then embarked on his career and worked at the psychiatric clinic in Heidelberg from 1909 to 1915. Through his work, he came to the conclusion that the theory and practice in the field of psychiatry were unsatisfactory. Subsequently, he actively worked to improve the methodology of psychiatric approaches to patient treatment.

Carl Jaspers

In 1913, Jaspers defended his doctoral dissertation, which was later published under the title "General Psychopathology" and went on to be reprinted numerous times. After defending his dissertation, he became a lecturer at the University of Heidelberg and never returned to regular clinical practice. Instead, he dedicated himself to research and various theoretical investigations related to psychiatric, psychological, and philosophical topics. In 1921, Jaspers became a professor at the University of Heidelberg, where he interacted with renowned scholars such as Max Weber, Georg Lukács, Georg Simmel, Emil Lask, and Ernst Bloch.

Martin Heidegger had a significant influence on Carl Jaspers. Formally, Jaspers and Heidegger are considered the founders of existentialism in the history of philosophy. However, significant disagreements arose between these two scholars because Heidegger aligned himself with the fascists. Jaspers' wife was a baptized Jew named Gertrud Mayer, and due to this fact and many others, Jaspers could not accept Heidegger's position. Jaspers and Heidegger severed their relationship, and by 1933, Jaspers asserted that he had nothing in common with Heidegger's thoughts and actions. As we understand it, such a statement could have a direct connection to their friendship being broken. Naturally, Jaspers' anti-Nazi position made him a target of political persecution, and from 1937 to 1945, he constantly lived under the threat of arrest, although he managed to avoid this fate.

After the war, he was counted among the intellectual elite of Germany who had no connections with the Nazis, which made him a significant figure in German society at that time.

During the early stages of his career, while working with patients, Jaspers not only studied their formal biographical data but also paid great attention to how the patients themselves related to their symptoms. This method later became known as the biographical approach and became common in both psychiatric and psychotherapeutic work.

Jaspers expressed an interesting idea, commenting that in the process of studying the symptoms of a mentally ill person, greater emphasis should be placed on the form of symptom manifestation rather than its specific content. This shift in focus from the content of the symptom to its form found profound realization in the theoretical and practical methods of neuro-linguistic programming, which emphasize the structure of a person's experience rather than its meaningful and content-related components.

Jaspers introduced his specific distinction in understanding the term "delusion" as a symptom of a mental disorder. He distinguished between primary, or autochthonous, delusion, the cause of which cannot be determined, and secondary delusion, where the causes of its emergence can be clearly traced.

In his work dedicated to nostalgia, Jaspers analyzes various pathological manifestations of this phenomenon. He examines the manifestation of nostalgia among the indigenous people of South America, who may go without eating, starve, and endure many hardships in the jungles. However, at the same time, they become ill and die when provided with regular food, being disconnected from their natural habitat. Jaspers cites the notes of Froer about the people of the Orah tribe in Madagascar who become melancholic when temporarily leaving their homes.

Jaspers also presents the observations of the Frenchman Delaporte, who witnessed manifestations of nostalgia among the peoples of Siberia. He describes how an epidemic of nostalgia broke out among soldiers in Philipville in 1745–1746. Many of them died, and the remaining soldiers were forced to return to their homeland.

Furthermore, Jaspers establishes a specific nosological classification of nostalgia, dividing it into the following elements:

1. **Primary nostalgia:** It arises in healthy individuals without any underlying medical conditions.

2. **Secondary nostalgia:** It develops as a result of other illnesses or conditions.

3. **Psychological nostalgia:** It pertains to nostalgia primarily affecting the psychological aspects of an individual.

4. **Somatic nostalgia:** It refers to nostalgia that manifests predominantly in somatic or bodily symptoms.

5. **Complex nostalgia:** It denotes nostalgia characterized by multiple and intertwined factors, such as psychological and somatic components.

6. **Hidden nostalgia:** It represents nostalgia that remains concealed or unrecognized, often existing at an unconscious level.

7. **Simulated nostalgia:** It describes nostalgia that is feigned or simulated by an individual, without genuine underlying sentiments.

When discussing delusional jealousy, Jaspers presents the psychiatric understanding of this symptom as well as his own unique interpretation of the subject matter. He identifies the following types of jealousy:

1. **Psychological jealousy:** It encompasses jealousy that arises from emotional or psychological factors.

2. **Baseless jealousy:** It refers to pathological jealousy without a rational or adequate cause.

3. **Manic jealousy:** It involves a state where an individual perceives infidelity everywhere and lacks critical judgment regarding their thoughts and actions.

4. **Delusional jealousy:** It denotes jealousy accompanied by fixed false beliefs (delusions).

In the case of delusional jealousy, the patient may start experiencing illusory distortions of reality. This means that their consciousness begins to distort perception by adding and "drawing" things that were not originally there. Illusions, on the other hand, only involve distortions of perception. However, delusional jealousy can sometimes develop into full-fledged hallucinations, where the patient perceives things that do not exist at all. Particularly interesting is when illusions and hallucinations of a sexual nature become prominent in delusional jealousy. Patients may be haunted by complete hallucinations of how their partner is betraying them.

These hallucinations are characteristic of the schizophrenic process in the patient's personality. Paranoid experiences can occur during and after sleep in patients with jealousy delusions. The patient may feel that when they were asleep, someone lay next to them, and that sedatives were given to prevent them from sensing that someone came to their sexual partner. Various hallucinations of memory may also arise. Jaspers confesses that the true cause of delusional jealousy remains a mystery to him.

Jaspers mentions that, according to certain authors, delusional jealousy is directly related to certain physiological processes in the human body. For example, the psycho-physical functioning of the genital apparatus and specific periods in women's lives. Regarding the first point, Jaspers quotes comments by Richard von Krafft-Ebing, who observed various manifestations of delusional jealousy in alcoholics. Krafft-Ebing mentioned that unsatisfactory coitus and the preservation of libido can become significant grounds for the emergence of delusional jealousy in individuals suffering from alcoholism. As for the second point, Krafft-Ebing considered the fact that, in some women, paranoid processes in their psyche intensify during the premenopausal and menopausal periods of their lives. The lactation period, menstruation, and senile jealousy are also mentioned.

Jaspers devoted significant attention to the symptoms of illusions and hallucinations in his patients. He believed that hallucinations could arise as a coherent, interconnected line of experiences united by a common meaning. In other words, a hallucinatory experience does not necessarily have to be fragmented and meaningless. Certain experiences become a connecting link that manifests in the patient's consciousness not only as hallucinations and illusions but can also be imbued with profound meaning. Jaspers also mentions that these experiences require separate investigation.

According to Jaspers, studying the diversity of the hallucinatory process in patients can help us observe and understand the interconnections that arise between symptoms. Consequently, we can gain a better understanding of the symptom itself and begin to treat it more effectively.

Jaspers also comments on Köhler's experiments involving the creation of various illusions of perception in healthy individuals. For example, subjective experiences of visual phenomena can be perceived as objective under certain conditions. The interplay of light and shadow can be perceived as a real object. The judgments that arise in consciousness can form coherent units of meaning from such illusions. By exploring this aspect of hallucinations and illusions, Jaspers attempts to understand the psychopathological process in the patient's consciousness, analyzing it through the prism of the natural processes of perception inherent to our mental apparatus.

Regarding philosophy, Jaspers believed that it is an inseparable heritage of humanity, and its main tasks are the elevation of human beings and assistance in attaining freedom and independence. He stated that philosophy needs constant improvement to achieve its goals. Jaspers considered philosophy itself not to be a complete scientific discipline, although science is a helper to philosophy. A highly significant term in Jaspers' works is "existence," which he understood as the source of thought and action within the individual. In many ways, we can observe a correspondence between the term "existence" and the ancient philosophers' notions of the human soul.

Medard Boss

Medard Boss (1903–1990), a Swiss psychiatrist and psychologist, was born in the city of St. Gallen. In his youth, he aspired to become an artist, but his father insisted that he choose a different career path, citing the relatively low financial prospects of being an artist. Boss underwent training in Paris and Vienna, where he met Sigmund Freud and became his patient. It is worth noting that Boss's father opposed his therapy with Freud, but the son disregarded his objections and underwent 30 sessions of psychoanalysis with Freud within a year. Interestingly, during the course of his psychoanalysis with Freud, Boss experienced financial difficulties and paid Freud with money that was meant for his own sustenance. To prevent Boss from starving, Freud would return a portion of the money to him.

In 1928, Boss obtained a medical degree from the University of Zurich. Like Carl Jung, he collaborated with Eugen Bleuler, who became his mentor in the field of psychiatry. Boss assisted Bleuler at the Burghölzli clinic for four years. Boss also studied psychoanalysis under Ernst Jones, Otto Fenichel, Karen Horney, Kurt Goldstein, Wilhelm Reich, and Hans Ben-Eschenburg. In the late 1930s, two significant encounters greatly influenced Boss's professional trajectory. Firstly, he met Carl Jung and subsequently attended his seminars for over a decade. Secondly, he met Ludwig Binswanger, who instilled in Boss an appreciation for Martin Heidegger. Boss met Heidegger in 1946, and this encounter allowed him to solidify his theories of Daseinsanalysis, leading to the publication of several books, including "The Meaning and Content of Sexual Perversions" (1949), "Dream Analysis" (1953), "Introduction to Psychosomatic Medicine" (1954), and "Psychoanalysis and Daseinsanalysis" (1957). Boss continued to maintain correspondence with Heidegger for the next 25 years until Heidegger's death. Boss frequently invited Heidegger to Switzerland to familiarize psychiatrists and psychoanalysts with his ideas. He also attempted to involve Carl Jung in Heidegger's philosophical concepts, but Jung declined, considering Heidegger's works to be "incomprehensible."

Medard Boss

Although Boss's interest in Daseinsanalysis was associated with Binswanger's work, he approached certain interpretations of Heidegger's philosophy critically. Boss believed that Heidegger's existential analysis did not allow for viewing neurotic individuals as having their own world projects, as Binswanger suggested. He maintained that the essential structure of a person could be defined through the prism of their potential modes of being. Thus, it can be said that the Daseinsanalysis of Binswanger and Boss differs significantly in both theoretical and practical aspects. However, both authors considered a reevaluation of psychoanalysis in an existential dimension to be necessary.

In addition to studying under well-known mentors, Medard Boss also had the unique experience of living and working in India for an extended period, from which he drew significant inspiration from its culture. He made two six-month trips to India, studying Hindi at the Jung Institute. In 1971, he published his seminal work, "Foundations of Medicine," in which he attempted to examine the intersection of medicine and psychology.

Medard Boss's personality is intriguing in that he proposed one of the first working models of existential psychotherapy. He believed that throughout their lives, individuals constantly "unfold" their existence. Everything that manifests in a person's behavior and consciousness must have its reasons. In the pursuit of understanding these reasons, individuals may seek to grasp the finite boundaries of reality. Boss emphasized the inseparability of the individual and the world, or "being-in-the-world." He perceived his variation of Dasein analysis as a revealing or illuminating analysis that allows what is in darkness to come into the light. During therapy, the analyst assists the patient in attaining their fundamental "illumination" or enlightenment and openness to the world and others.

Boss wrote that humanity can be likened to a radiance born from a multitude of rays, each expressing an individual person. According to Boss, humans have "spiritual luminosity" in this regard. He considered the defense mechanisms of the psyche to be products of one's unwillingness to illuminate certain aspects of one's life. In the context of psychopathology, this corresponds to the choice of "life-in-darkness." Individuals who suffer from various neurotic and psychotic disorders are, in his view, constrained by specific boundaries of their world perception, and the process of mental illness serves as an illustration of the patients' inability to surpass those limits. The rigid frameworks instilled in individuals from early childhood in a social context can become insurmountable barriers to the manifestation of their true existence and existential potential.

Boss's concept of "attunement" is particularly interesting for reflection. For example, anger automatically tunes us to hostile behavior, a hostile attitude, hostile people, and so on. Boss believed that we are always illuminating the world to some degree; it's just that sometimes we illuminate certain aspects more prominently while others receive less illumination, or we engage in this illumination with different shades.

Boss posited that openness should serve as the foundation and cornerstone of psychotherapy. The patient's ability to perceive things as they are should be the primary criterion for their recovery.

This state, according to Heidegger, is called Gelassenheit, which refers to a state of being able to accept everything that happens around us as given. It is worth mentioning that the term used by Heidegger was drawn from medieval mystics and reinterpreted in his own way. An interesting similarity can be seen in Buddhist philosophy and Gautama Buddha's phrase: "Suffering is the non-acceptance of what is." In my opinion, the concepts of Heidegger and Boss reflect wisdom that has existed in philosophy and religion for a very long time.

Boss writes that, thanks to Heidegger's influence, he developed the idea of a new approach to psychopathology and its understanding. Boss believed that, based on Heidegger's views, the following disease patterns could be identified:

1. Diseases that arise as a result of damage to the human being's bodily manifestation of human existence.
2. Diseases caused by the impairment of the manifestation of "being-in-space" and "being-in-time" as elements of "being-in-the-world."
3. Diseases caused by the disruption of "attunement-to-being."

4. Diseases caused by impairment in the fulfillment of the fundamental characteristics of "openness-of-being" and the freedom of Dasein.

Boss believed that in the process of therapy, the psychotherapist should help the patient establish a connection with their inner "child" and guide them in re-experiencing the path of maturation, paying attention to the personal resources that, for various reasons, were not engaged. He believed that the neurotic individual retains the childlike ego within themselves but loses the openness to the world that allows for the adequate expression of this ego. Through Dasein analysis, patients can free themselves from various behavioral and cognitive stereotypes and uncover a sense of existence that can provide freedom of choice, the ability to make the right decisions in life, and the responsibility for them, which are key characteristics of an adult, non-neurotic personality. An interesting feature of Boss's Dasein analysis was its reorientation of the key question in psychoanalysis from "why?" to "why not?", which allows the patient to approach a state of acceptance of what happens to them in life.

Boss deeply integrated working with dreams into his practice. However, unlike Freudian and Jungian analysts, he did not analyze dreams but focused on uncovering meaning during the therapeutic process. He believed that dreams vividly illustrate how we "illuminate" our lives, or in Freudian terms, what we repress in them.

Boss's existential therapy and its philosophy contribute to the understanding and practice of the boundaries of poetry, metaphorical language, and abstractness. A therapist who is immersed in this approach can convey abstract moods to the patient during conversations and thus introduce new dimensions of understanding.

Boss was highly critical of the concept of the unconscious, which was a key element in classical Freudianism. Although Boss directly worked with the unconscious in his practice, he could not accept Freud's interpretation of it. He even believed that the term "unconscious" should be excluded from the vocabulary of psychopathology. He also believed that the narrow horizons of personal perception prevent unconscious processes from becoming conscious, and this narrowness is not synonymous with psychic unconsciousness. Expanding the horizons of perception can be achieved through existential work with the patient. The patient's "Dasein" can indicate what existential care can contribute to. Boss adopted the term "care" from Heidegger, where it was considered a comprehensive concept encompassing various emotions and forms of human-world relationships.

Boss had his own opinion on the phenomenon of transference, as originally presented by Freud. He believed that the neurotic individual does not transfer their feelings towards their father or mother onto the psychotherapist. Rather than what may be perceived as transference, Boss commented on a consequence of the patient's inability to transcend infantile forms of experiences and actions.

Boss viewed the patient's resistance during psychotherapy as a form of their refusal to acknowledge their own uniqueness and their inclination towards social comfort, the desire to be accepted within a group. Therefore, Boss could perceive the acceptance of psychoanalytic interpretation by the patient as resistance itself. In our view, this interpretation can significantly enhance and complement the qualitative understanding of the patient's resistance during psychotherapy.

It is also worth noting that while in Freudian concepts the key conflict in the individual lies in the opposition between morality and instinct, in Boss's philosophy, this conflict can be reduced to a confrontation with the desire to embrace one's hidden potential in consciousness and reject it due to motives of social comfort and stereotypy.

The primary focus of Boss's existential therapy was to assist the patient in uncovering their potential and making it more open to the world.

Ludwig Binswanger

Ludwig Binswanger (1881–1966), one of the founders of existential psychotherapy, was born in the city of Kreuzlingen, Switzerland. Ludwig's father was the founder of the private sanatorium "Bellevue" in Kreuzlingen, and his uncle was a professor of psychiatry at the University of Jena.

After reaching adulthood, Ludwig pursued medical studies at the University of Zurich, where he obtained his medical degree in 1907 and defended his dissertation on "The Psychogalvanic Reflex Phenomenon" under the guidance of Carl Jung. He also studied in Lausanne and Heidelberg.

From 1906 onwards, he began working at the Burghölzli Clinic, affiliated with the University of Zurich.

Ludwig Binswanger

In 1910, Binswanger was elected president of the psychoanalytic society.

In the context of his professional activities, Binswanger had the opportunity to interact with various medical luminaries of the time, such as Sigmund Freud, Carl Jung, Eugen Bleuler, and others. In 1907, Binswanger and Jung participated in a meeting of Viennese psychoanalysts. Warm relations were established between Binswanger and Freud. Their correspondence consisted of more than a hundred letters. Binswanger also acted as an intermediary between Freud and Jung when their relationship deteriorated in 1912. It is worth noting that Binswanger and Freud remained friends until Freud's death in 1939.

In 1936, Binswanger wrote a work dedicated to Freud's 80th birthday. It was titled "Freud and His Concept of Man in the Light of Anthropology" and mainly commented on how Freud's theories and psychoanalysis greatly simplify and narrow down the understanding of the reality of the human world. Freud responded very warmly in his letter, explaining the following: "I have always lived only on the ground floor and in the basement of the house. You claim that by changing the point of view, a person can see the upper floor, which accommodates such distinguished guests as religion, art, and so on. You are not alone in your views; most educated representatives of homo natura believe in this. In this regard, you are a conservative, and I am a revolutionary. If I had another lifetime for work, then without a doubt, I could find a place for these noble guests in my little underground house." Thus, one can conclude that if Freud were alive, his theories would sooner or later have approached concepts close to existential philosophy.

Ludwig Binswanger attached great importance to his ideas about "the consideration of the human spirit" in his works. He believed that the inability of some patients to achieve insight in the context of psychotherapy could be perceived as a result of their inability to elevate themselves to the level of "spiritual communication" with the psychoanalyst. Binswanger shared his ideas with Freud in 1927, to which he received the response, "Yes, the spirit is everything." Binswanger could hardly believe his ears. After all, Freud's theories were very materialistic. But Freud continued his sentence, saying, "Humanity has always known that it possesses spirit. I had to show it that there are also instincts." It is also worth noting that Freud simply considered Binswanger to be a delicate person who, in the process of his professional development, maintained adequacy in his relationship with his teacher.

His work is influenced by philosophers such as Edmund Husserl, Martin Heidegger, and Martin Buber, whose works largely shaped the development of Binswanger's existential professional trajectory. The main period of Binswanger's professional activity was spent as the chief physician of the sanatorium in Kreuzlingen from 1911 to 1956. In 1942, Binswanger published his book "Basic Forms and Knowledge of Human Existence," in which he began to describe his ideas related to existential therapy.

Thanks to the precedence of this work, Binswanger can rightfully be considered the first scholar to attempt to introduce existentialist ideas into psychotherapy. In his work, Binswanger attempted to qualitatively combine the fundamental concepts of Sigmund Freud's theory and practice of psychoanalysis with the philosophical ideas of Martin Heidegger and his existential analysis. Binswanger tried to apply Heidegger's theories, which largely considered human existence at the ontological level, to the phenomenological level. That is, not in relation to the human individual in general but directly to the specific person, the patient with some symptom who is in need of help.

Binswanger understood life as a unified and concrete phenomenon, encompassing the entirety of time, both past and present, and the future. This unity, referred to as "being-here," Binswanger named Dasein. According to him, in existential psychotherapy, the treatment of symptoms should not be disconnected from a deep and abstract understanding of them. Understanding, in Binswanger's conception, is directly linked to the ability to approach the object of understanding using its language to apprehend the personal structures of the human being based on their own terms rather than the observer's experience. Binswanger comments that understanding an object is a form of participation in its existence until the object reveals its true essence.

He views various psychiatric symptoms in patients as a form of "narrowing" the world in which the existence of the individual's personality unfolds. He also believes that symptoms in an individual are formed as a result of the transformation of the essential structure of Dasein. In his opinion, the absence of existential freedom in a person can give rise to a wide spectrum of symptoms, both neurotic and psychotic. It is important to note that symptoms, whether purely physical or social, are closely connected to an individual's sense of existential freedom. A person who has lost connection with their abstract core becomes obsessed with external ideas unrelated to the depths of consciousness, which naturally leads to burnout from various perspectives. The illnesses themselves are merely the cornerstone. Even worse for an individual can be the absence of understanding that the symptom exists—that symptom that distorts the structure of the individual's personality and is not oriented towards understanding its existential foundation. According to Binswanger, the degree to which the freedom of Dasein is subordinated to the power of something else is the primary Dasein-analytical criterion of mental illness.

In his method of existential therapy, Binswanger introduces the term "world-project," which represents a comprehensive re-experiencing of "being-in-the-world" and unity in the ways of its actualization. He believed that the life of every living being is such a world project that finds its embodiment through modes of expression and action. Binswanger highlights some key points regarding the understanding of the term "world-project."

1. Each world-project is exceptional and unique and can be grasped through conscious interpretation and study.
2. It serves as an existential a priori for the human personality.
3. The individual begins to recognize oneself within the immediate boundaries of their world-project, compare different individual world-projects, and perform an existentially oriented structural analysis of oneself.

The way in which a person exists in the world is the immediate content of their own world-project. Binswanger believed that the key function of his existential analysis was to restore the person's freedom by overcoming their detachment from the future and various distortions that may occur in their "enclosed" world-project.

In his works, Binswanger approached the concept of the unconscious somewhat differently than Freud did in his classical psychoanalysis. Binswanger commented that, in the context of his therapeutic work, he could not do without focusing on the unconscious processes within the patient's psyche. However, at the same time, he stated that, through his practice, he came to the understanding that it is incorrect to view the conscious and unconscious as opposing forms.

Binswanger introduces the term "extravagant ideal," which can be used by an individual as a specific form of masking a life position. He believed that these "extravagant ideals" of individuals often do not correspond to their actual life position, thereby creating insurmountable obstacles in the individual's life and on the path of their existence. Binswanger posited that the presence of an "extravagant ideal" in a person can confine them within the framework of a single life project, significantly limiting their possibilities. Furthermore, he had the notion that the schizophrenic process can only be deeply understood if it is initially interpreted as an existential mode of extravagance.

According to Binswanger, the goal of existential therapy is to guide the patient back from their "extravagance" to the coherence of their experiential existence and to open up new possibilities and conditions for the development of a fully integrated and authentic personality.

Viktor Frankl

Viktor Emil Frankl (1905–1997), an Austrian psychiatrist, psychologist, and neurologist, was the founder of logotherapy and one of the key figures in the field of existential therapy. He was born in Vienna into a Jewish family of civil servants. From a young age, Frankl showed an interest in psychology and even wrote his graduation thesis on the psychology of philosophical thinking while studying at the gymnasium. He also became interested in psychoanalytic ideas during his youth and corresponded with Sigmund Freud. Upon Freud's recommendation, Frankl's work was published in the International Journal of Psychoanalysis. He later joined Alfred Adler's Society for Individual Psychology and published in the International Journal of Individual Psychology but left the society in 1927 due to disagreements. After completing his gymnasium education, Frankl entered the University of Vienna, where he studied psychiatry and neurology.

During the early stages of Frankl's career, Sigmund Freud and Alfred Adler were the key figures who influenced his professional thinking.

However, as his professional development progressed, he deviated from their theoretical and practical prescriptions to a large extent.

In 1928, Frankl founded a counseling center in Vienna and became its head for the following several years. In 1933, he conducted research on the "neurosis of unemployment." One of the primary focuses of Frankl's attention in psychology became the theme of depressive personality disorders and suicide, exploring their characteristics and specificity. From 1932 to 1937, Frankl worked with a large number of female patients suffering from suicidal tendencies in a pavilion he led called the "suicide pavilion" (selbstmörderpavillon). Over 30,000 women became his patients there. At that time, Frankl did not yet realize that he would end up in a German concentration camp, which in some ways resembled both a pavilion of killings and suicides. We can infer that the skills Frankl acquired while working with thousands of suicidal patients greatly aided him in the concentration camp, helping him and other prisoners survive.

In 1942, Viktor Frankl, his wife Tilly Grosser, whom he married in 1941, and his parents were deported to a concentration camp, where Frankl, along with physician Karl Fleischmann, organized secret psychological support for the prisoners. They were assisted in their work by a fellow inmate and doctor, Dr. Wolff, who actively used autogenic training in his practice.

Viktor Frankl

Unfortunately, Wolff died in the concentration camp from pulmonary tuberculosis. In his work at the camp, Frankl paid great attention to preventing suicidal tendencies among the prisoners, and his years of experience dealing with this symptom greatly aided him in this task. Sadly, almost all of Frankl's relatives died in the camp. His wife was killed in Bergen-Belsen; his father died in Theresienstadt from pulmonary edema; and his mother was killed in Auschwitz. Among his family members, only his sister survived, as she managed to emigrate to Australia. In 1945, Frankl was liberated from the concentration camp by American troops. Gradually, he began to recover from the stress he endured, and in 1946, he became the head of the Vienna Neurological Clinic, where he continued to work until 1972. In 1947, Frankl married his second wife, Eleonora Katarina Schwindt. Their daughter, Gabrielle, followed in her father's footsteps and became a child psychologist. In total, Frankl wrote 32 books and received 29 honorary doctorates.

In his book "Psychotherapy and Existentialism," Frankl mentions that in the early 1930s, he introduced the term "existential analysis" as a variant name for his method of "logotherapy," which he developed in the 1920s. He also writes that when the Americans translated his term "existential analysis," it became "existential therapy," which was already used by

Ludwig Binswanger and later by Medard Boss in their Dasein analysis. Due to the fact that too many authors began using the term "existential therapy" in different meanings, Frankl decided to use the term "logotherapy" to avoid terminological confusion.

Frankl believed that logotherapy could surpass existential analysis by encompassing more than just an analysis of existence. Logotherapy is concerned not only with existence but also with the meanings with which a person endows that existence. According to Frankl, logotherapy is not merely an analysis but a comprehensive therapy.

The fundamental position of logotherapy is that it is based on a clear philosophy of life. More specifically, it is based on three fundamental assumptions that are links in one chain. These are:

1. **Freedom of will:** This freedom is part of a person's immediate experiential data. There are various psychological, physiological, and social conditions that are difficult to overcome by nature. However, a person retains the freedom to take a particular position in relation to conditions that are difficult or impossible to change. A person is free to change what may seem insurmountable in terms of meaning.

2. **Will to meaning:** According to Frankl, the will to meaning is something that guides the will to pleasure in Freud or the will to power in Adler. For Frankl, pleasure and power are derived from the meaning with which they are endowed. Frankl also emphasizes that he speaks more about the will to meaning than the need for meaning or attraction to it.

3. **Meaning of life:** In this assumption, the meaning itself becomes the immediate subject of consideration. In the context of undergoing logotherapy, a person has the opportunity to expand their field of vision through specific interactions with meanings and their transformation. Additionally, through participation in logotherapy, a person can come to the realization that their life is filled not only with

> the meanings of their actions but also with various feelings, specific interactions with truth, goodness, and beauty that exist in the world and in other people, and their unique qualities.

Frankl believed that a person's life is ordered by their orientation to meaning. Meanings predetermine the direction of movement in life. A person's values and beliefs are determining factors in their life path, and transforming them can significantly influence the quality of human life.

Orientation to meaning exerts a multidimensional and multifactorial influence on human life, predetermining the course of various mental processes at different levels of generalization. In the context of their life, a person feels inclined to manifest and actualize the meanings inherent within them in their activities, creative products, communication, spirituality, and art. According to Frankl, the quest for meaning in life is not some secondary mental process or "secondary rationalization" of instincts, but the primary motivating force in the realization of personal potential.

The absence of a meaningful life, Frankl called it the "existential vacuum." It is a specific frustrating state when meaningfulness has not been fully defined because, for some reason, it is incorrectly formed in the individual's personality or something has happened in the individual's experience that has caused them to lose old meanings and not yet acquire new ones. In a sense, the presence of an existential vacuum creates the foundation for the development of various neurotic and psychotic processes in an individual's personality.

Meanings possess a certain attracting force, just as the gravitational force of the Sun holds the Earth in its orbit. Without "meaningful gravity," a person is deprived of a certain strength that unifies fragmented experiences and the personality into wholeness. On the other hand, the absence of an existential vacuum and the presence of profound meanings in one's personality that determine a person's state and actions can serve as protection against various challenges, problems, and stresses that will inevitably occur in a person's life. A person who possesses a powerful core, even if they fall, will be capable of standing up and performing what they did before significantly better. To some extent, the life story of Victor Frankl himself is a vivid confirmation of this.

Frankl believed that life could be meaningfully understood in three distinct ways:

1. By what we contribute to life through our creative activities. This involves actively engaging in acts of creation, whether it be through artistic expression, professional endeavors, or personal relationships.
2. By what we receive from the world, utilizing the various available resources and goods that life offers us. This includes deriving satisfaction and fulfillment from the experiences, relationships, and material possessions that come our way.
3. By our stance toward fate, which may be unchangeable for various reasons. This pertains to our attitude and position in relation to the circumstances and events that unfold in our lives, even if we cannot alter or control them directly.

Frankl's perspective highlights the multifaceted nature of finding meaning and purpose in life, emphasizing the roles of creativity, engagement, appreciation, and acceptance in our existential experience.

According to Frankl, the meaning of life should not coincide with existence; it should be ahead of it, setting the pace. Frankl believed that guilt from the past and potential death in the future were the two main threatening factors in a person's life. Since both the first and second are inevitable, the only thing that can truly help a person in this regard is humility. However, this humility is not something passive and sacrificial; Frankl believed that it is only in the face of guilt that it makes sense to strive for improvement, and it is only in the face of death that it makes sense to act. The humility that Frankl spoke of provides the strength for development, accepting life's challenges, and resolving situations that initially may have seemed insurmountable.

Additionally, Frankl believed that reconciliation and consolation were significant tasks of psychotherapy. A person needs to reconcile with the finiteness of their being. In this sense, according to Frankl, the function of psychotherapy can be similar to the function of religion. However, closeness in this sense should not imply literal merging, as the goal of therapy is the patient's well-being, while the goal of religion is the salvation of a person in various forms.

Naturally, a psychotherapist should not determine the meaning of life for the patient. They must find their own meaning of existence. The psychotherapist can simply provide some support on this path.

Rollo May

Rollo May (1909–1994), a renowned American psychologist and psychotherapist, was born in Ada, Ohio. The name given to him at birth was Ris, which he later changed to Rollo. He was the second child of Earl Taitt May and Mollie Bauton May. Rollo's older sister suffered from schizophrenia, and his parents were poorly educated and paid little attention to their children.

After completing high school, Rollo enrolled in the Michigan State College of Agriculture and Applied Science. During his college years, Rollo became one of the organizers of a journal that criticized government policies. As a result, the college administration decided to expel him. In 1930, after his expulsion, he enrolled at Oberlin College, where he earned a bachelor's degree and specialized in English language, Greek literature, and history.

After graduating from college, Rollo moved to Thessaloniki, Greece, where he engaged in teaching activities. In 1933, due to his parents' divorce, he returned to the United States and later entered the Union Theological Seminary in New York, where he obtained a doctoral degree in theology for his work under the guidance of the philosopher Paul Tillich.

Rollo's first wife was Florence de Fries, with whom he had twin daughters. However, pastoral work did not inspire Rollo much, and he decided to further his education. He received training at the William Alanson White Institute of Psychiatry, Psychoanalysis, and Psychology. May explored the role of a consulting psychologist and started working at the City College of New York, where he became acquainted with Harry Stack Sullivan, one of its founders and a renowned American psychotherapist.

In 1946, he opened his own private practice, and in 1948, he became a faculty member at the White Institute, where he had received his training, continuing to work there until 1974. In 1949, he earned a Ph.D. in clinical psychology. In the 1950s, May became fully convinced of his existential views and became one of the most prominent popularizers of existential philosophy and psychotherapy in America and the world. From 1950 to 1969, he was considered one of the intellectual leaders of the humanistic movement in psychology, along with Maslow and Rogers. However, he later distanced himself from this school because it had deviated significantly from existential philosophy.

Rollo May

Rollo went through several divorces and remarriages. In 1971, he married his second wife, Ingrid Schull, and in 1989, he married his third wife, Georgia Lee Mill Johnson. May passed away at the age of 85 in Tiburon,

California, due to chronic heart failure.

May believed that the existential approach was closely related to the thinking of William James, who emphasized the immediacy of experience and the unity of thought and action.

This was significant for one of the fundamental figures in existential philosophy, Kierkegaard, who wrote: "For the individual, only that which is embodied in action is true." May comments that considering the existential approach in psychotherapy as a return to 19th-century philosophical psychology is incorrect. He believes that the existential approach is an attempt to understand human experience through the knowledge underlying our science as well as the nature of the individuals who undergo it. The existential approach emphasizes the focus on the individual's existence, and this emphasis is manifested in the fixation on human existence as it directly manifests itself.

May mentions that the term "existence" itself emerged from ex-sistere, which can be translated as "to manifest." So, the goal of the approach is precisely the manifestation of the deeper layers of the psyche, awareness of which can lead a person to a fuller level of existence. The existential approach does not exclude the possibility that other methods of psychotherapy can effectively help in treating individuals, but in reality, understanding another person without this approach can be difficult. According to May, it is precisely the existential approach that allows for understanding and realizing the deepest layers of human consciousness.

However, in May's opinion, the existential approach is more of a specific approach to the study of human existence than a school of psychotherapy. In May's view, the existential approach is not a system of therapy but rather a specific orientation towards psychotherapy that can be effectively applied to various therapeutic methods, giving them additional meaning and flavor.

Delving deeper into the subject, May writes that without the use of existential concepts such as "being" and "non-being," it can be quite challenging to understand the most fundamental psychological mechanisms such as transference, resistance, and defense mechanisms of the psyche, among others. May points out that, in his opinion, the connection between consciousness and survival instincts is greatly exaggerated. He draws attention to the philosophical positions of Nietzsche and Kierkegaard, who believed that the human individual is a being that creates various values throughout life, which are subsequently embodied in their existence.

May believes that the "being" of a human personality can be defined as an individually unique pattern of possibilities, which will only partially coincide with the patterns of possibilities of other individuals. However, complete coincidence is neither necessary nor possible. The non-coincidence of such patterns is part of the natural course of life, which there is no need to resist.

Rollo May mentions an interesting idea from Abraham Maslow: "It is extremely important for psychologists that existentialists can provide psychology with the philosophical foundations it currently lacks." And indeed, existential psychotherapy serves as a bridge between psychotherapy and philosophy, opening up the possibility for therapists to practically utilize various philosophical constructs. One of the most applicable for this purpose has been the philosophy of existentialism. However, if we expand the boundaries and move to a higher level of generalization, we can discover that we are not talking about the specific beliefs of certain philosophers but about how to connect human action in society with their "being-in-the-world." And if a philosophy other than existentialism proves suitable for this, it would only be a benefit and support for therapy.

May believes that the existential approach is neither purely rationalistic nor anti-rationalistic, but rather a combination of both. May defines existentialism as emphasizing the concepts of identity, uniqueness, and self-experience as essential conditions of human nature, as well as the science and philosophy of human nature. According to May, the existential approach can reveal certain rigid limitations of an analytical and conceptual perspective, creating a new therapeutic map for describing "reality" that can be a powerful aid in assisting patients.

Rollo May believed that within a person's personality, there are potentially five levels of power that they can use in their life in one way or another.

These are:

1. **Power to live:** This power is not a literal manifestation of good or evil; it is primary to them but is not a neutral force. If this power is not realized for any reason, it can lead to various neurotic and psychotic disorders in the individual. The extreme manifestation of powerlessness is death.

2. **Power of self-affirmation:** May argued that every living being has a need not only to exist but also to affirm themselves in life in one way or another. This becomes particularly relevant when we specifically talk about humans. This self-affirmation enables a sense of self-respect, without which normal functioning becomes quite challenging.

3. **Defense of one's "self":** Self-affirmation eventually encounters a certain form of resistance in the world, which requires us to exert additional efforts to achieve success. This power is characterized by greater intensity and external reference in its manifestation compared to the power of self-affirmation.

4. **Power of aggression:** This power comes into play when the opportunity to defend one's "self" is blocked. If a person is deprived of the ability to express their aggressive tendencies for an extended period, it can eventually lead to neurotic and psychotic disorders, as well as uncontrolled use of violent behavior.

5. **Power of violence:** This power comes into actualization when ordinary aggression does not contribute to transforming the situation. It represents a form of last resort—the utmost measure that a human individual can resort to. Unlike other levels of power, where rational cognitive processes and the ability to rely on values and beliefs remain inherent to a person, in this case, external stimuli can lead to an immediate transition to uncontrolled violence without any reflection.

Rollo May believed that all these five forces are ontological legacies within the human personality, meaning they are genetically embedded.

In his book "The Discovery of Being," May writes that existential analysts create a definition with three specific modes of the world, defined by its aspects that can characterize existence within each individual. These are:

1. **Umwelt:** This mode refers to the world around a person, more specifically, their biological component. It is a world of finitude and determinism, where an individual can exist without even being self-aware. It is the world in which a person is "thrown" from birth and compelled to seek survival strategies.

2. **Mitwelt:** This mode represents the world of beings belonging to the same species, sharing common values, and so on. It is the world of interpersonal relationships with all the intricacies of social communication, its problems, and solutions that an individual encounters on their life path.

3. **Eigenwelt:** The third mode points to the world within the person themselves, their internal psychological experiences, where the true "self" of the human individual exists. It is the world of self-awareness. This mode likely exists only in human beings.

It is worth noting that people simultaneously live in all three of these modes. They relate to these three worlds. However, the focus of attention and the levels of conscious engagement in each world can vary among individuals. May argues that the reality of existence in the world becomes lost if the emphasis is placed solely on one mode, excluding the others. He also comments that, according to Binswanger, Freud, in his psychoanalysis, dealt with Umwelt by analyzing instincts and drives. Sullivan, on the other hand, primarily addressed Mitwelt, emphasizing the dominant role of social relationships and various social factors in shaping personality in society. Psychotherapists such as Binswanger, Boss, and Frankl deal more with Eigenwelt, the mode that helps in realizing the process of "being-in-the-world," revealing the abstract nature of the self for deep self-awareness.

In his book "Power and Innocence," May extensively analyzes the causes of violence in human behavior, stating that the cause lies not in possessing power and authority to some degree, but in the awareness of one's powerlessness, helplessness, and apathy. It is these states that drive a person to manifest aggression, which, in this case, becomes a kind of defense mechanism. On one hand, it provides a temporary sense of security, while on the other hand, it prevents a full understanding of the true reasons for one's helplessness. Acts of violence most often occur in the behavior of individuals who seek to enhance their self-esteem, which may be inadequate for various reasons.

Antonio Meneghetti

Antonio Meneghetti (1936–2013) was an Italian psychologist, philosopher, artist, and founder of the ontopsychological school. He was born in the city of Avesciano. His parents were Pietro Meneghetti and Anna Castellani. Antonio was the first of nine children. At the age of 11, he was sent to a Roman Catholic school for education. Meneghetti became a member of the Franciscan Order of Conventual Friars Minor, where, in addition to studying religion, he engaged in painting and restoring frescoes by Michelangelo, Raphael, Titian, and other artists. From an early age, Meneghetti was a multifaceted individual who studied ancient Greek, Latin, and Aramaic languages. He also devoted great attention to music, playing the piano and organ, and studying Gregorian chant.

In the 1960s, he left the Franciscan Order and became a priest in the settlement of Giovanni near Montereale. During this period, his mother fell ill, and he took care of her as well as his eight underage siblings. Meneghetti was greatly influenced by the works of Edmund Husserl, and after becoming acquainted with them, he began studying psychology, philosophy, and sociology. Throughout his career, Meneghetti defended his doctorate in theology, philosophy, and social sciences, obtained a bachelor's degree in philosophy, and received a librarian diploma from the Vatican. He then studied Freudian psychoanalysis in London, attended lectures by Jacques Lacan in Paris, and met Viktor Frankl and many other renowned psychotherapists. He also studied at the C.G. Jung Institute in Zurich.

Antonio Meneghetti

In the 1970s, Meneghetti conducted courses on psychology, including "Fundamentals of Pastoral Psychology," "Client-Centered Therapy of Rogers," and "Ontopsychology." In 1972, he opened the Center for Ontopsychological Therapy in Rome. In the same year, Meneghetti left the Catholic Church, and in 1973, he ceased teaching to fully devote himself to psychotherapy. Meneghetti was married to Loretta Lorezini, and they had two daughters. In addition to his therapeutic activities, Meneghetti became the founder of various conferences dedicated to ontopsychology and authored numerous books on the subject. Some of his best-known works include "Ontopsychology of the Human Being," "Clinical Ontopsychology," "Ontopsychological Pedagogy," "The Wise Man and the Art of Life," "Image and the Unconscious," and others. Overall, Meneghetti authored more than 50 books published in various languages. He was honored with numerous awards, prizes, and honorary titles.

Antonio Meneghetti passed away in Brazil.

The term "Ontopsychology" that Meneghetti used was likely borrowed from the well-known American transpersonal psychotherapist, Anthony Sutich, who proposed this name for the field of knowledge that lies on the border between humanistic and existential psychology.

Meneghetti defined ontopsychology as the psychology of being in a human being, the science of manifestation, and the specificity of existence in relation to human existence.

Meneghetti believed that the unconscious of an individual manifests itself at the level of organized psychic energy, which logical consciousness ignores, thus causing the full potential of the psyche to remain in the unconscious realm.

Following a holistic philosophy that implies the interconnectedness of psychological and physical processes, Meneghetti comments that intrapsychic conflicts can transcend to other levels and transform into physical symptoms. He believes that if the body is healthy, it likely indicates good mental health as well. Therefore, in his view, illness is not only a medical problem but also a moral-psychological issue.

Antonio Meneghetti considered temperament to be the product of the biological influence of both parents during prenatal development. In the early stages of life, an individual actively absorbs information from reality and becomes conditioned by it. However, once the individual's organism acquires a fixed vector of movement and development, they gain the ability to choose the environment in which they feel comfortable existing.

While the environment initially determines a person's behavior, later on, they can influence the environment based on the skills and knowledge they acquire throughout their lives. If a child becomes accustomed to never being denied anything during their upbringing, it can give rise to a sense of absolute superiority and strong selfishness.

Meneghetti observes that, in his opinion, the difference between a neurotic and a mature personality lies in the fact that a mature person fights their battles independently, while a neurotic experiences uncertainty and anxiety because they depend on themselves and their "partner" in their unconscious mind, with whom they constantly engage in an inner conversation about the need or the uselessness of starting an action.

In this case, Meneghetti, presumably metaphorically, refers to certain forms of psychic fragmentation that prevent a person from making the right decision—the same fragmentation that can be characteristic of the schizophrenic process in particular. Meneghetti emphasizes that a neurotic is often conditioned by their unconscious mother, who becomes, in a way, an imposed partner for them, from whom they cannot detach for various reasons.

Meneghetti discusses specific causes that can predispose an individual to the neurotic process. These causes include:

1. Innate heightened levels of personal needs in the early stages of life manifest initially as increased sensitivity and later as significant intellectual abilities.
2. A state of frustration with the maternal figure, which can distort the foundation of the child's personal balance.
3. An excessive need for unconditional primacy, often reflecting impulses of infantile superiority.
4. A psychological inclination to rely on others, especially parental figures, which fully develops by the age of six and subsequently tends to transfer onto other individuals in different contexts. If this tendency is not timely overcome, individuals may encounter significant adaptation problems in society during their maturation.
5. Fear of separation from the figure upon which an individual relies during their developmental process can induce profound distortions within their personality.

Meneghetti believes that the first two causes are synchronous and primary, while the remaining three are specifying factors. Furthermore, he comments that neurotic and psychotic processes largely stem from the refusal to individually utilize the instinctual dynamics of one's personality.

Meneghetti then presents specific approaches to addressing neurotic and psychotic problems. He highlights the following possibilities:

1. Placing the individual in a therapeutic environment for several months.
2. Temporarily depriving the patient of excessive maternal care and presence, as the symptoms that exist within the patient can quickly return to their previous state once they have been worked through. The individual needs to experience their own self-sufficiency.
3. Engaging in a transformative process with the patient at the level of their values and beliefs, leading to a shift in the ethical paradigm of their life.
4. Observing and monitoring the manifestation of various neurotic and psychotic symptoms.
5. Involving the patient directly in various forms of individual and group psychotherapy.

Each of these interventions plays a crucial role in the therapeutic journey towards resolving neurotic and psychotic issues, promoting self-awareness, and facilitating personal growth. The combination of a therapeutic environment, introspection, and active participation in psychotherapy can foster the necessary changes within the individual, enabling them to navigate their psychological challenges and achieve a more balanced and fulfilling life.

Meneghetti devotes significant attention to discussing the phenomenology of latent schizophrenia, which can encompass the following behavioral forms:

1. Regular manifestation of introverted erotism, characterized by a desire for possession. Introverted erotism remains blocked and cannot be expressed outwardly. This nonvital erotism generates internal conflicts within the individual, leading to profound personality

distortions.

2. Excessive subjectivism of the individual, hindering objective behavior and the manifestation of the self in society.
3. The personal need for possession, particularly of objects and people. The inability to let go of attachments can trigger severe internal conflicts within an individual. According to Meneghetti, egocentrism centered on strong attachment is a characteristic of schizophrenia.
4. Blocked associative processes. During upbringing, specific types of thinking and associative processes may be criticized by parental figures, causing the child to receive love with a taste of coercion.
5. Inability to engage in symbolization. Schizophrenic individuals experience difficulties in their metaphorical perception of the world's images. A mentally healthy individual can symbolize perceived images, whereas a schizophrenic person lacks access to this mode of integration. Such individuals interpret figurative meanings as literal.
6. Engaging in dialectical processes solely from within oneself. The challenge lies in connecting with the schizophrenic's inner world and comprehending it. Their internal dialectic may be elusive, leading them to exist in a world that only they can truly understand.
7. Failure to grasp the intentionality of symbols. A schizophrenic may be unable to perceive and understand the relationship between a specific aspect of reality and its verbal expression.
8. High susceptibility to obsession. The schizophrenic seeks to find a place within another person and usurp it. They resist change due to intense fear.
9. Suffering from loneliness. It is challenging to share the schizophrenic's world because there are no individuals who can resonate with their wavelength.

By examining these various aspects, Meneghetti provides valuable insights into the latent forms of schizophrenia, shedding light on the complex psychological processes and challenges faced by individuals with this condition.

Meneghetti concludes that any form of neurosis or psychosis represents a specific fracture within an individual's inner self, resulting in a diminished capacity to mediate the external world in relation to their individuality.

He writes about the "energetic" core of personality, which he discovered in every person during his practice. This core possesses its own mind and manifests itself in all mental and physical processes of the organism. Meneghetti named this core "In-se," which, when translated from Latin, means "to be within." It can be understood as the "center of being." Meneghetti believed that In-se is the ultimate point from which human individuation begins. In-se is a certain principle that decides in favor of existence or non-existence, being or non-being. In-se is the core and center of the existing wholeness of a human being. In many ways, Meneghetti's concept of In-se resembles Carl Gustav Jung's concept of the self, although the authors may differ in their interpretations of the details of their concepts. Jung's interpretations contain more alchemical elements, while Meneghetti's definition clearly reflects existential philosophy.

Meneghetti indicates that within the individual's unconscious, there exists a formation he calls the "deviation monitor." He explains that this part of the personality has a specific structure that censors and distorts projections of reality.

Meneghetti identifies the following spheres of the human being as a whole:

1. In-se.
2. The natural manifestation of life according to the intuition of In-se within its ecosystem.
3. The deviation monitor or distorting grid.
4. Life impulses manifesting themselves as complexes.
5. The conscious, logical "Self."

Only the last sphere is consciously apprehended, while all others belong to the realm of the unconscious.

By discerning and examining these spheres, Meneghetti delves into the intricacies of the human psyche, providing valuable insights into the complex interplay between conscious and unconscious aspects of the self.

Meneghetti provides his commentary on three types of morality that exist within the individual and human nature:

1. **Natural morality:** This morality is inherent in the primary intention of life and can be considered a form of biological morality.

2. **Traditional morality:** This morality is part of the culturally psychological stereotype of the individual, which determines the behavior of the individual within a group or the entire group as a whole.

3. **Legal morality:** This morality is fixed in written form and is the product of a group agreement within a specific community.

According to Meneghetti, the first two types of morality are natural and stem from the depths of human essence, while the third type is characterized by mechanistic qualities. In some aspects, these three types of morality may intersect, but only natural morality embodies the consciousness of existence.

Regarding the human unconscious, Meneghetti points out that it is an energetic quantum of psychic and somatic life that creates the individual. He also emphasizes that the human unconscious is not a center of perversions, chaos, monsters, uncontrolled sexuality, or aggression. Instead, Meneghetti highlights that it is where the human mind concentrates to solve various life tasks and possess the ability to respond promptly. Meneghetti also equates the unconscious with In-se, stating that they correspond to each other.

In Meneghetti's framework, there are three types of existence, each with its own specific interpretation:

1. Metaphysical "Self" or transcendent being.

2. Being as the universal presence of all things.
3. Individual "Self" or being as my presence, existing in the "here and now."

Essentially, Antonio Meneghetti's ontopsychology is a creative reworking of Freudian psychoanalysis, Jacques Lacan's theories, Carl Jung's concepts, and those of other psychotherapists. Significant emphasis is placed on the existential sphere of personality. Simultaneously, Meneghetti actively connects his theoretical constructs with real therapeutic practice.

Irvin Yalom

Irvin Yalom, an American psychiatrist, psychotherapist, medical doctor, and professor at Stanford University, was born in Washington in 1931 to a family of immigrants from the Russian Empire who lived in the territory of present-day Belarus. He grew up in poor, crime-ridden neighborhoods of the city and often faced bullying in school due to his Jewish heritage. Yalom studied at George Washington University, from which he graduated in 1952, and then enrolled in the Boston University School of Medicine, completing his studies in 1956. He completed his internship at Mount Sinai Hospital in New York and at the Phipps Clinic at Johns Hopkins Hospital. Marilyn Yalom became Irvin Yalom's spouse, and together they had four children. Yalom began his career at Stanford University.

Yalom's therapeutic style can be characterized within the humanistic-existential vector of psychotherapy, which is focused on, on the one hand, the respectful acceptance of the patient's personality and, on the other hand, a profound philosophical understanding of the life path that can create a foundation for the therapeutic transformation of the individual.

Irvin Yalom

Irvin commented on his beliefs regarding the necessity of creating a unique therapeutic approach for each patient. Due to the highly individualized nature of each person, applying rigid theoretical and practical templates may result in incompatibility between the method and the patient's personality. When working with a patient, Yalom never has a preconceived plan. The strategy for the appropriate therapeutic intervention arises through direct communication with the patient.

Irvin Yalom writes about the four fundamental themes addressed in existential psychotherapy. These are:

1. **Death:** The awareness of the inevitability of death, the fears and anxieties associated with it, and encounters with various manifestations in life. Contemplations regarding what may await us after death. All these experiences form a fundamental layer of an individual's personality.

2. **Isolation:** This theme is closely related to the sense of social connection within a group. On the one hand, a person needs social interaction and acceptance within a group, but on the other hand, it is within these relationships that a significant number of neurotic

processes can arise. The fear of rejection in a social group, the fear of isolation from society, or conversely, a rigid need for dissociation and detachment due to past emotional traumas, all influence the dynamics of personality development. In addition to the fear of literal isolation, we must emphasize its existential factor, indicating that no matter how close we may be to someone in the world, we remain alone. The more a person senses the existential factor of their isolation, the more they may attempt to compensate for discomfort through various neurotic forms of behavior.

3. **Freedom:** The desire to have the ability to make choices in life, to follow one's own path, and not be dependent on the decisions of others is a key aspect of adult ego development. On the path to achieving personal freedom, individuals encounter various personal challenges. However, the significance of freedom can also carry a certain element of terror for the individual, as true freedom inherently involves accepting full responsibility for one's own life.

4. **Inner Emptiness:** The concept of inner emptiness refers to the existential void within a person, the need to fill life with greater meaning that can bring order and harmony.

Other life problems, to varying degrees, stem from these themes as they are specific derivatives. Solutions adopted at a more abstract level can help define and organize more concrete tasks in an individual's life.

Yalom emphasizes that, unlike psychoanalysis, the existential approach in psychotherapy does not focus on the basic conflicts of the individual related to the suppression of instincts or the internalization of parental figures or significant adults. Instead, it centers around the conflict arising from the individual's confrontation with the realities of existence—the finite factors that are inherent components of human existence.

Irvin Yalom's main books include "Group Psychotherapy: Theory and Practice" (1970), "The Gift of Therapy: An Open Letter to a New Generation of Therapists and Their Patients" (2002), "Existential Psychotherapy" (1980), and others.

Yalom defines existential psychotherapy as a dynamic therapeutic approach that focuses on issues of individual existence. He emphasizes that he has never considered existential psychotherapy as a separate school encompassing a specific set of practices but rather as a way of thinking and a set of values and beliefs that can positively influence the therapeutic process. Although, in reality, Irvin Yalom's method draws heavily on certain psychodynamic principles of Freud and his followers, combined with existential-humanistic philosophy.

Yalom identified eleven basic categories of therapeutic factors in group psychotherapy, which can also be applicable in individual psychotherapeutic work. These factors are as follows:

1. **Instillation of hope:** This factor helps retain the patient in therapy and maintains the intention to work on the symptom. Yalom mentions that many studies show a close relationship between hope for healing and the conviction that it will occur with quality therapy. In this case, Yalom is likely referring to the placebo effect and its use in the context of verbal psychotherapy. Additionally, Yalom seems to mix the concepts of hope and belief, treating them as synonymous, which can lead to some incorrect notions about the placebo effect. To recover, a patient must not simply hope but firmly believe that everything they do can lead to positive outcomes.

2. **Universality:** This refers to the applicability of intervention methods to different patients. This point is particularly relevant in groups where individuals from various psychopathological profiles, age categories, and social strata may gather.

3. **Imparting information:** This category includes specific forms of educating the patient, presenting relevant information related to their personality and symptoms with the aim of their elimination or

reduction. This can involve analytical information directly related to the patient's experience.

4. **Altruism:** In a psychotherapeutic group, patients can learn to transmit positive emotions and states they have acquired to other group members. Altruism develops empathy, which, in turn, provides a sense of complete belonging to the group. It activates profound natural psychotherapeutic processes in individuals undergoing therapy.

5. **Corrective analysis of the influence of the parental family:** The group simulates the family system of each individual, and during participation in group psychotherapy, key nodes of neurotic processes related to family emotional and behavioral situations gradually begin to manifest. When applied correctly, both the therapist and the patients can derive significant benefits from the constructive improvement of the therapeutic process in the group.

6. **Development of socializing techniques:** One of the main triggers for influencing the constructive transformation of the patient during group psychotherapy is social learning. The patient can observe how his social communication skills are realized within the group, and with the support of the therapist and other group members, he gains the opportunity for constructive changes in his personality and behavior.

7. **Imitative behavior:** The patient can largely start imitating the behavior of the psychotherapist and draw a powerful resource for healing from it. Yalom provides an example of the experiments conducted by neobehaviorist Albert Bandura, who was able to cure many patients with snake phobia by simply instructing them to observe the therapist holding a snake in his hands.

8. **Interpersonal influence:** Yalom comments that an individual's mental health is a direct continuation of healthy communication within the group. Therefore, psychotherapeutic assistance is aimed at achieving a specific end result: the better the patient's relationships within the group, the faster they find balance within themselves.

9. **Group cohesion:** The formation of cohesion within the group can be both the goal and a diagnostic criterion of therapy. Disunity indicates unresolved internal conflicts among certain group participants.

10. **Catharsis:** In a therapeutic group, a person has the opportunity not only to release emotions that have been suppressed and repressed but also to improve this process through the group's interactive format. This allows for the integration of the suppressed experiences underlying cathartic emotions more effectively and allows for comprehensive feedback from people who have different opinions regarding the essence of the problem and the emotions being expressed.

11. **Existential factors:** Various complex realizations that can form among members of the therapeutic group during their interactions can provide the opportunity to develop different existential meanings, filling the personal void not only in terms of social acceptance but also at a more global level of understanding the meaning of human existence and personal purpose. To fully embody this factor in practice, certain support from the therapist is usually necessary, who, at certain moments of therapy, could shift the focus of the patients attention to more abstract meanings within the therapeutic context of interaction.

By studying Yalom's works, one can come across a multitude of his reflections on death, isolation, freedom, and the internal emptiness of the individual, based on various situations from his practice and references to the opinions of other psychologists, psychotherapists, psychiatrists, philosophers, and thinkers. Yalom, in his views, remains largely neutral, making it difficult to trace his own opinion on a particular question. He carefully avoids categorization in judgments and sidesteps the "sharp corners" of various conceptions about the psyche and behavior. In my opinion, it is precisely this neutrality of the author that guarantees his success and popularity, since it is much easier for the patient to see a more accurate reflection of their soul in such a psychotherapist.

Pathopsychological Profiles and Existential Psychotherapy

Hysteroid Profile

When working with existential philosophy in the context of psychotherapy, hysteroid patients often have the ability to reveal their personalities in a qualitative and multifaceted manner. What they can discover within themselves may be new and unfamiliar to them. The tendency to mirror the therapist and their philosophical mindset can be highly constructive for hysteroids. With a sufficiently long duration of existential work with patients of this profile, profound and significant changes can be observed, which seemingly cannot dissipate after the completion of therapeutic work.

Paranoid Profile

With paranoid patients, we have often encountered difficulties in their willingness to engage with abstract statements related to the practice of psychotherapy. Paranoids are more often concerned with pragmatic and practical methods of solving life tasks, where clear algorithms with their own rules exist. Sometimes, excessive philosophizing is perceived by paranoid individuals as a deviation from the necessary, correct, and constructive trajectory of personal development. Therefore, in my opinion, the application of existential forms of work with patients of this profile should be done either in a measured manner or in an aesthetic combination with other psychotherapeutic approaches, such as cognitive or hypnotic techniques.

Psychopathic Profile

In my opinion, individuals with psychopathic personalities often struggle to grasp the existential aspect of psychotherapeutic work in a constructive manner. Abstract philosophical concepts are frequently unfamiliar to them, and attempts by therapists to help them understand these concepts rarely yield positive results. In fact, psychopathic individuals often hold a disdainful attitude towards existential thinking, viewing it as impractical and unrelated to the harsh and pragmatic reality in which they live. This reality is characterized by power dynamics between aggressors and victims. Given this, we would not recommend using existential methods of psychotherapy for patients with this personality profile, as they are largely ineffective in addressing their needs.

Obsessive-Compulsive Profile

Patients with this personality profile respond quite well and constructively to the existential form of psychotherapeutic work. Abstract meanings are capable of creating a new foundation of support within them. A new understanding of the world can create the necessary conditions for the formation of essential and meaningful patterns of behavior. In combination with other psychotherapeutic approaches, such as cognitive, behavioral, or hypnotic, the existential form of work with patients of this profile can yield excellent practical results. However, if this therapeutic approach is applied in isolation without the inclusion of additional methods, the emergence of constructive changes in the patient's personality may be somewhat delayed. This is influenced by both the specific characteristics of the patient's personality and how the therapist applies existential practice.

Schizoid Profile

For individuals with a schizoid personality profile, abstract philosophy and existential work can be deeply and constructively perceived. For many schizoid individuals, discussions on existential topics can be beloved even before undergoing therapy.

When one of their favorite conversation topics begins to surface within the context of therapeutic relationships, it can help establish a strong and solid therapeutic alliance with the psychotherapist and lead to relatively quick and positive therapeutic changes. However, at times, an excessive existential approach can provoke schizoid patients into excessive "philosophizing," which can create the illusion of constructive changes. It is important to remember that therapy should provide practical implementation of the changes that the patient acquires theoretically in the behavioral sphere. Without this, therapy outcomes may be perceived as rather conditional. We believe that existential work is one of the best forms of psychotherapeutic interaction with patients with this personality profile.

Epileptoid Profile

Epileptoid patients often exhibit strong religious and philosophical inclinations. It is important to note that profound philosophy serves as a distinct element of their psyche, helping to balance the individual between impulsive behavior, which often violates moral standards, and morality itself. For epileptoids, the philosophy of redemption holds significant value rather than the pursuit of deep meaning in life and death. However, it is important to acknowledge that individual perspectives may vary, although we are primarily discussing the average profile. Thus, based on our observations, engaging in discourse with epileptoids who have a religious inclination can be a solid support. Abstract philosophical conversations unrelated to morality may simply be ignored and fail to generate significant interest. When employing existential methods with individuals of the epileptoid profile, it is crucial to understand the specific nature of this approach and whether it is suitable for them. Otherwise, the level of effectiveness can be quite low.

Schizophrenic Profile

The profile of a person with a schizophrenic personality tends to involve excessive abstract speculation that lacks practical implementation and connection to reality. Some individuals with schizophrenia or schizoid traits may express themselves in a way that resembles profound philosophical statements. On one hand, engaging in existential dialogue with patients who have a schizophrenic profile can help establish a strong therapeutic relationship. On the other hand, in certain cases, these conversations may further fuel the already excessive abstract thinking commonly found in individuals with this profile. In my opinion, the existential approach can be beneficial for patients with this profile, but its effectiveness depends on the experience and skill of the psychotherapist. It is important for the therapist to appropriately balance the amount of existentiality in their work with the patient. Otherwise, therapy may lead to a shared form of madness known as "folie à deux."

Manic-Depressive Profile

Working with patients with the MDP profile can be built upon a specific philosophical foundation that contributes to positive dynamics for the patient and provides insights that can be useful and applicable. However, in my opinion, the existential approach may be insufficiently effective without the utilization of methods from other therapeutic vectors. A notable complement to the existential vector can be found in hypnosis, behavioral therapy, or body-oriented therapy.

6

Dramatic Psychotherapy

The creator of dramatic psychotherapeutic work is Jacob Moreno, a Romanian psychologist, psychiatrist, and sociologist. He is often credited as the pioneer of group psychotherapy, as no other psychiatrists conducted therapeutic activities for groups of patients or published articles on this topic prior to him.

Moreno was born in Bucharest in 1889 to a Sephardic Jewish family from the Ottoman Empire. In 1895, his family moved to Vienna, where he remained after his parents' subsequent move to Berlin in 1905.

Jacob Moreno

Moreno describes a particular mystical experience that occurred when he was 14 years old while standing in front of a statue of Christ in a German town. He writes, "Standing before the statue, I began to understand that I had to make a decision that would determine my entire future. I believe that all people make such a decision in their youth. And then my moment came. I was faced with the question of what I should choose as mine: the entire universe or my family, the lineage from which I came? And I chose the universe—not because my family was worse than other families, but because I wanted to live for something greater, for the world to which every member of my family belongs and where I would like to see them return. My decision meant that all people are my brothers and sisters; all mothers and fathers are my mothers and fathers; all children, regardless of their parents, are my children; and all women are my wives. All the property in this world is my property, and, conversely, everything I have belongs to the whole world."

This experience, apparently, became one of the philosophical foundations of his psychotherapy method and contributed to the formation of the belief that "true psychotherapy can only be the psychotherapy of all humanity."

In 1909, he enrolled at the University of Vienna, where he studied philosophy and medicine.

Moreno writes that in 1912, he met Sigmund Freud only once when, while working at a psychiatric clinic, he attended Freud's lecture on the analysis of telepathic dreams. Moreno and Freud struck up a conversation, and Freud asked Moreno what he was involved in. Moreno replied, "Well, Dr. Freud, I start where you stop. You meet people in an artificial office setting, while I meet them on the street or at their homes in their natural environment. You analyze their dreams, but I try to give them the courage to dream. I teach people how to play God." Moreno noted that Freud looked at him incomprehensibly after his vivid metaphor.

During his education, he decided to pursue a career in psychiatry. In 1913, he began his first psychotherapeutic experiments in collaboration with the physician S. Gruen and the journalist K. Kalber. They created small psychotherapeutic groups for girls, consisting of 8 to 10 participants. The groups met two to three times a week to discuss various problematic situations that arose in their lives.

In 1915–1916, Moreno worked in a refugee camp in Mittenwald, Austria. During this work, he gained an important creative insight that would eventually lead him to the development of sociometry. He discovered that if people were distributed in the barracks according to their race, religion, and political views, it could significantly improve their emotional state and quality of life.

In 1917, he graduated from medical school and became a physician. Moreno writes, "Psychodrama came into being on the 'fool's day,' April 1, 1921, between 7 and 10 in the evening."It was in 1921 that Jacob Levy Moreno began regularly applying his method to address various emotional and behavioral problems. A case described in the history of psychodrama is considered a significant turning point. It involved a man who had decided to end his life through suicide. Working together with his friend Mariana Lornitzo, Moreno decided to conduct a psychodramatic enactment with the man, in which they acted out his fantasies. This work prevented the suicide and further solidified Moreno's belief in the effectiveness of his chosen course of psychotherapeutic work.

Another notable case in the development of psychodrama as a psychotherapeutic method was the "Barbara case," which took place in 1922. Barbara was an actress who often played innocent girls in her theatrical performances. However, when she was alone, she transformed into a true fury, attacking her husband George with her fists and using foul language. Moreno suggested that she play the role of a dirty prostitute in his therapeutic theater who would have a scandal with her pimp and eventually be killed by him. After this enactment, Barbara experienced some changes. Something that wanted to emerge from within her outside of the theater found its place. In subsequent enactments, she occasionally played similar roles as scandalous women, noting that each role helped balance something within her. Another focus of attention became the joint enactment of their domestic quarrels with her husband.

Moreno writes about this: "After a few months, Barbara, George, and I sat together in the theater. They rediscovered themselves and each other, or rather, they discovered themselves and each other for the first time. I analyzed the course of their psychodrama session after session and explained to them how their healing occurred."

There is a popular legend about Moreno and his childhood when he climbed into the basement with a group of neighborhood boys and suggested they play God. It is worth noting that this is a highly peculiar game for young children. Jacob told the others that he would be God, and they would be his angels. The children agreed and constructed "heavens" for him using whatever materials were available. Jacob sat on them, and the other children, acting as angels, ran around him and sang various songs. One boy asked Jacob why he couldn't fly. To meet his comrade's expectations, Jacob attempted to "fly" but ended up falling and breaking his arm. In the future, Moreno will comment on this experience as his first attempt at working with the psychodrama method, jokingly calling it the "therapy of fallen gods."

In 1924, Moreno published a book titled "The Theater of Spontaneity," in which he identified four different types of theater.

1. **Theater of Conflict**: In this theater, conflicts are resolved at the psychological level.
2. **Improvisational Theater**: This level reveals the creative potential of the individual.
3. **Therapeutic Theater**: In this theater, a person plays themselves.
4. **Theater of Creation**: This theater allows individuals to grow and self-actualize.

In 1925, after the death of his father and his arrival in the United States, Jacob took his father's name as his surname and became known to the world as Jacob Levy Moreno. It is also worth noting that in the Hebrew language, the word "Morenu" means "teacher," so there may be several reasons for the name change.

In 1931, Moreno embarked on a research study in Sing Sing prison, where he applied his sociometry as the primary method of investigation. Afterwards, when the work was completed, he presented the research findings at a meeting of the American Psychiatric Association, where he proposed his vision for creating a healthier prison community. It is reported that it was during this meeting that Moreno publicly used the term "group psychotherapy" for the first time.

In 1934, he published his main book on sociometry, "Who Shall Survive?"

In 1936, he established his own psychiatric clinic, "Beacon Hill," which became the source of psychodrama's dissemination worldwide.

In 1937, he began publishing the journal "Sociometry: Journal of Interpersonal Relations."

In 1946, the first volume of his book "Psychodrama" was released.

Starting in 1950, Moreno began traveling to many countries, spreading his method. Through Moreno's work and the efforts of his students, who also disseminated the method in other countries upon his request, psychodrama gained global recognition and application.

In 1974, Moreno passed away.

Jacob Moreno expressed intriguing philosophical thoughts about the idea that the divine act of creation is not complete but continues here and now. He believed that individuals can serve as conduits for the creative work of God through spontaneity in the "here and now" state. Moreno also believed that it is through the manifestation of spontaneity that individuals can "encounter" God. Moreno offers his definition of spontaneity as an adequate response to new conditions or a new response to old conditions. His philosophy is imbued with divine metaphors that he skillfully employs, thus establishing a certain foundation for his method.

In his works, Moreno describes three types of spontaneity in communication:

1. **Transference**: This term, in Moreno's understanding, carries the same meaning as in the theories of Sigmund Freud. It refers to the transfer of one's own feelings and beliefs onto another person.

2. **Empathy**: This manifestation of spontaneity involves refraining from judgments and assumptions and objectively sensing another person as they are.
3. **Tele**: The participation of all communication partners as active subjects in the interaction. It entails mutual acceptance of roles.

A significant part of the psychodramatic method is Moreno's sociometry. Its philosophy states that any person, upon entering a social context, gradually forms a specific matrix of meanings concerning the characteristics of the people around them. Some individuals are perceived more as potential friends; others evoke sexual preferences, and still, others create the impression of people with whom one can interact excellently in a business context. Each such characteristic can be evaluated based on the level of its intensity. A sociometric test can provide invaluable information for understanding the functioning of a group and how to reorganize it to achieve any necessary qualitative changes within it.

One of the key concepts in psychodrama is "role-playing," in which participants portray and explore various facets of emotions and behaviors. Unlike conventional theater, role-playing in psychodrama is not something rehearsed or pre-planned; instead, it arises from the actor's own spontaneity and manifestations.

According to Moreno, the ultimate product of spontaneity is "cultural conserves," which are elements that contribute to the preservation of cultural traditions: language, art, literature, rituals, and so on. In other words, everything that creates a connection with past experiences while also addressing challenges that may arise in the future.

In psychodrama therapy, the term "catharsis" is used, which originated in ancient Greece and meant "an emotionally cleansing experience." The various strong emotions expressed during the process of role-playing possess precisely such a quality and can lead to significant changes in both the cognitive and behavioral domains for the individuals directly expressing them and for those observing the role-playing process.

The facilitator of psychodramatic theater, following theatrical tradition, is referred to as the director and assumes three roles during the process.

1. **Producer**: The performer in this role guides the staging process, fulfills an organizational function, and helps actualize specific elements of the work into reality.
2. **Therapist**: This role assists the patient in working through specific behavioral and emotional patterns and provides necessary support.
3. **Analyst**: The function of this role is the interpretation and analysis of the participants' behavior within the group process. Rational understanding is also a significant part of the psychodramatic therapy process.

The group member who assumes the central role is called the protagonist. Formally, the patient with whom the therapist works is the protagonist in the dramatic play process. However, it is possible for other participants to take on the protagonist's role if the need arises. Participants who play various other roles during the process are referred to as "auxiliary egos." The audience consists of other group members who are not directly involved in the ongoing psychodramatic enactment.

In psychodrama, there are specific phases of the therapy process. The following are distinguished:

1. **Warm-up**: It can be verbal or non-verbal. During this phase, various participants' concerns and themes are explored. A warm-up can also be useful for individuals who may still exhibit resistance to fully engaging in the psychodramatic play.
2. **Psychodramatic action**: This refers to the actual portrayal on stage, which may be chosen by the director based on their own understanding of the necessity and appropriateness of a particular element of the actors' performance. However, the patient themselves can also make choices and propose specific scenes for enactment.
3. **Subsequent discussion**: After the psychodramatic action itself, the protagonist and other group members have the opportunity to share

the peculiarities of their emotional experiences with each other. Such discussions contribute to the integration of acquired experiences at a deeper personal level.

It should be noted that specific methodologies are employed in the psychodramatic process that facilitate participants' self-expression and are integral to the therapeutic process. Let us enumerate some of them.

1. **Monologue**: In a monologue, the protagonist freely expresses their feelings through lines of dialogue. This allows for a deeper awareness of their internal psychological processes through controlled self-expression.
2. **Doubling**: In this practice, another group member begins to mirror the verbal and non-verbal reactions of the protagonist, thereby supporting them and helping them better comprehend their thoughts, emotions, and behavioral responses.
3. **Role reversal**: This practice enables the protagonist to assume a secondary role in the psychodramatic session while another person who previously played the role of an "auxiliary ego" takes on the protagonist's original role. This process can contribute to a more multifaceted understanding of the context and provide an opportunity to see the situation from different perspectives.
4. **Reflection**: This practice is a variation of role reversal. In this case, another person takes on the role of the protagonist and portrays it. The actual protagonist observes the performance of their own role from an outsider's perspective.

Jacob Moreno writes about his understanding of the conscious and unconscious mind: "For the continually creating mind, there would be no division between the conscious and unconscious. The creator is like a runner, for whom the part of the road already run and the upcoming part qualitatively form a unified whole."

Therefore, in the psychology of the creative act, there is no division between the conscious and the unconscious.

Moreno is a great admirer of describing various concrete processes in the psyche using metaphorical language, often with a considerable degree of pathos. As a result, many of his notions about elementary mental processes may be in stark confrontation with the views of other psychologists and psychiatrists.

In his works, Moreno attempts to demonstrate that Stanislavski's works and his method, which postulate key principles of how actors can effectively immerse themselves in a role and perform within it, have no relevance to his ideas about spontaneity. Moreno believes that Stanislavski "reduces the factor of spontaneity to reactivating memories laden with affect. This approach associates improvisation with past experience rather than the present moment."

In this case, we clearly see that Moreno imparts meaning to his notions of spontaneity that separate them from an individual's past experience. From a philosophical standpoint, such a judgment may have value. However, when we discuss the neurophysiology of the brain and the manifestation of spontaneity in a person's personality, we discover that any spontaneous act cannot be detached from an individual's past experience and is generated based on it, or more accurately, through its prism.

In the end, Moreno goes so far as to call Freud and Stanislavski "colleagues," despite their work in different fields. He attributes them collegiality based on their orientation in their activities toward past experience.

Moreno writes about a specific body training that an actor can undergo to achieve relaxation and release their reflexive systems. He discusses specific gymnastic and dance exercises that can cultivate and shape a sense of spontaneity. He also writes about the unresolved issue for actors in the creative process, namely the problem of coordinating the verbal and the physical, as well as excluding from the role performance those actions and gestures that are not directly related to the psychodramatic process.

Virginia Satir and "Family Sculpture"

One of the most popular forms of dramatic work in psychotherapy is Virginia Satir's family therapy. She was born in 1916 on a farm in Wisconsin, USA. At the age of three, she had already learned to read, and by the age of nine, she had read all the books in her school library. She was the oldest of five children in her family.

In her childhood, Virginia often witnessed arguments between her parents, which caused her a great deal of suffering. When she was five years old, she had an appendectomy and had to spend several months in the hospital. It was during this time that her parents were going through a serious conflict and considering divorce. It was then that young Virginia exclaimed that she wanted to be the "judge over her parents." This experience likely influenced her future professional orientation and focus on reconciling various conflicts within patients' families.

Since 1927, Satir has been living in Milwaukee, Wisconsin. She strives to attend as many courses as possible to finish school quickly. She received her high school diploma in 1932 and entered the State Teachers College in Milwaukee. She earned a bachelor's degree in education and then worked as a teacher for several years. She wrote her thesis for a master's degree in psychology in 1943 but defended it only in 1948.

After graduating from university, she began an active psychotherapeutic practice. In the process of working with patients, she started to form her views on the psychotherapeutic process, focusing her attention on the fact that one patient's problems are inseparable from the problems of other family members. Therefore, it is necessary to work with the family as a whole to achieve the desired psychotherapeutic outcomes.

Virginia Satir

In 1955, Virginia worked at a psychiatric institute in Illinois. In her work, she endeavored to spread her philosophy of family focus among her colleagues.

In 1959, she participated in the creation of a research institute in Palo Alto, where she worked until 1966.

In 1962, Virginia received a grant from the NIMH, which allowed her to organize the first training program in family psychotherapy. This is why she is often called the "mother of family psychotherapy."

In 1964, she published her first book, "Conjoint Family Therapy," based on a textbook she wrote for students.

In 1973, Virginia Satir became a professor at the University of Wisconsin and the University of Chicago.

During the period from 1970 to 1980, her work was significantly influenced by the development of neuro-linguistic programming. John Grinder and Richard Bandler considered her one of the founders of NLP. Leslie Cameron-Bandler and Frank Pucelik became her notable students in this form of psychotherapeutic practice.

In 1984, Virginia called on family psychotherapists to shift the focus to nurturing relationships.

In 1987, she visited the USSR.

Satir was married twice but did not have children. Due to a failed pregnancy and its termination, she was unable to become a mother. Later, she adopted two girls. Regarding her unsuccessful family life, Virginia wrote, "I often thought, could I do what I do if I were married? And I realized, No! That's probably my destiny—to travel the world, helping people. Other people have a different fate."

Virginia Satir passed away in 1988.

In 1991, one of the students of John Grinder and Richard Bandler, Steve Andreas, wrote a book dedicated to Virginia Satir's practice. The book was titled "Patterns of Her Magic," in which he summarized the main patterns of her psychotherapeutic practice.

It is worth noting an interesting fact: according to two national American surveys of psychiatrists, psychologists, and social workers, Virginia Satir was recognized as one of the most influential psychotherapists.

Satir's work was permeated with the principles of humanism and humanity. In her work, she constantly strived to sow the seeds of hope. She said, "The family is a microcosm. Knowing how to heal the family, I know how to heal the whole world."

During her therapeutic activities, she often used various group forms of meditation aimed at facilitating necessary therapeutic changes. One of her most famous meditative texts is "I Am Me."

Let's present the text of this meditation:

"I am me. There is no one else in the world like me. Everything that comes from me is genuinely mine. I own everything that is within me. My body, my feelings, my mouth, my voice, all my actions—both for others and for myself. My fantasies, my dreams, my hopes, and my fears all belong to me. All my triumphs and successes, all my failures and mistakes. Since I possess everything within myself, I can understand myself and be friends with myself in all my parts. I know that there are aspects of me that puzzle me and many others that I do not yet know. But as long as I am friendly and loving, I can confidently and hopefully seek solutions to the puzzles and ways to find out more about myself—no matter how I appear or sound, no matter what I say or do. And everything I think and feel at this moment is genuinely me. If later some parts of how I looked, sounded, thought, and felt turn out to be unfitting, I can discard that which is unfitting, keep the rest, and invent something new for that which I discarded. I can see, hear, feel, think, and speak. I have all the tools I need to survive, to be close to others, to be productive, and to find meaning and order in the world of people and things. I own myself, and therefore, I can design myself. I am me, and I am okay."

Virginia Satir proposed a model that classifies individuals based on the stereotypicality of their reactions to stressful conditions. She identified four personal profiles.

1. **Blamer:** If a person belongs to this profile, when faced with a situation they cannot solve or simply a situation that creates significant emotional tension for them, they start displaying strong aggressive emotions towards their surroundings. They begin to shout, accuse, demand, threaten, and so on. Responsibility is often shifted to others.
2. **Mourner:** It is the diametrical opposite of the "blamer." Any stressful, unclear, or threatening situation leads to tears, sobbing, lamenting, and harsh self-blame. They usually take all the blame for the situation upon themselves.
3. **Computer:** This profile avoids strong emotions, carefully restraining and controlling them. They make extensive use of intellectual jargon. The primary reaction to stress is moralizing, lecturing other people about their various actions, citing scientific statistics and other research that can validate the "computer's" righteousness.
4. **Distractor:** A person with this profile constantly redirects their attention to something insignificant and of little importance in stressful situations. The most common emotional reactions are surprise, confusion, and incomprehension. Actions become confused and inconsistent, which, in the overwhelming majority of cases, does not contribute to problem resolution.

Subsequently, Virginia Satir added another profile named the "**Balancer**."

According to the author, individuals with this profile do not exhibit stereotypical reactions like representatives of other profiles. Their actions are constructive and purposeful. Strong emotional reactions are under the volitional control of the individual.

It is important to emphasize that the aforementioned behavioral reactions, characteristic of specific profiles, are activated and intensified specifically in the context of stress and are not simply habitual forms of behavior in society.

As the primary approach to solving family problems, Virginia Satir used a dramatic group form of interaction. In this process, she acted out specific conflict situations that arise within a family and, through restructuring the dramatic session, directed the therapeutic context in the necessary direction. She named this form of therapeutic dramatization "family sculpting" or "family reconstruction." According to Satir, the process itself creates a systemic understanding for patients of the behavioral and emotional processes occurring within the family context.

The technique of "family sculpting" allows for the physical organization of the symbolism of relationships within the family system. Each family member, in the process of therapeutic drama work, can create their own living family portrait by placing their relatives or the people who play their roles in a particular way. The experience of each family member finds its expression in the holistic dramatic picture. When family members witness the structure of communication within the family system, they gain a unique experience of awareness, which can lead to significant changes at the emotional and behavioral levels.

"Sculpting" is not only a means of transforming and changing the family system but also an excellent way to diagnose the characteristics of family communication structure. It provides an opportunity to more qualitatively unify the family and experience the individuality and uniqueness of each member. The psychotherapist, observing the "family sculpture," gains the ability to effectively influence the functioning of the family's specific features if necessary.

To create a complete "family sculpture," it sometimes only requires the participation of three or four people. Absent family members can be represented by other participants or by furniture chosen to symbolize their presence. At times, the therapist's position in the process can be metaphorically characterized as that of an identity "sculptor," and the therapy process itself is referred to as "sculpting," whereby the most balanced image is formed, capable of leading to constructive changes within the family system. Naturally, the changes introduced by the psychotherapist into the "family sculpture" are closely related to the verbal and non-verbal reactions of the family members.

Some therapists who employ Satir's method do not limit themselves solely to "sculpting" but also suggest that participants choose a phrase that could accurately characterize their present position and spatial location.

During the formation of the "family sculpture," the therapist may pose various questions aimed at increasing the family members' awareness of the observed situation. Some example questions include: "How do you feel in your current position in the 'family sculpture'?" "Are you surprised by what you are witnessing now?" "Did you know before that other family members perceive you in this way and not otherwise?" "When you look at the 'family sculpture,' do you perceive it as a reflection of the real situation in the family?" "How would you name the 'family sculpture' that we have created during the psychotherapeutic work?"

The "family sculpture" method can also be used in individual work. In this case, various objects can be symbolically used as substitutes for real people. However, it is worth noting that the group format of the work is preferable as it creates a more objective and accurate picture of the real situation, as well as a strong transformative process for all family members participating in therapy.

Virginia Satir formulated a set of beliefs that, in her opinion, reflect the therapist's position during the therapeutic process. She named these beliefs the "Five Freedoms." Let us consider them:

1. Freedom to see and hear what is here now instead of what could be or should be.

2. Freedom to express what I truly feel and think rather than what others expect.
3. Freedom to be oneself rather than wearing masks.
4. Freedom to ask for what is needed or necessary instead of waiting for permission.
5. Freedom to take responsibility for taking risks instead of acting in old stereotypical ways.

Satir believed that the key determining factor of our behavior is the family in which we grew up and the upbringing provided by our loved ones. She considered the family to be a system that seeks equilibrium in one way or another. The problematic aspects lie in the methods used to create this balance, while the underlying intentions are always pure. She acknowledged that any disruptions in the functioning of the family system give rise to low self-esteem and various forms of defensive behavior, which, in turn, pathologize the communicative context. Satir spoke about how every individual possesses sufficient internal resources to cope with the challenges life presents. She viewed the process of personal transformation as complex, systemic, and subject to specific rules and laws, understanding which enables therapy to be conducted at the highest level of effectiveness.

Upon examining Satir's beliefs, one can observe that many of them were borrowed by the creators of NLP for their practice and subsequently featured as "Presuppositions of NLP."

Bert Hellinger and Family Constellations

Bert Hellinger's family constellations represent a relatively new form of dramatic psychotherapeutic work. Hellinger, a German priest, philosopher, and psychotherapist, was born in Germany in 1925 into a Catholic family. At the age of ten, he studied at a Catholic boarding school affiliated with a monastery. In 1942, he was drafted into the army and fought on the Western Front. In 1945, he was taken as a prisoner of war and held in an Allied camp, but he later escaped and returned to Germany. He studied theology and philosophy at the University of Würzburg.

Bert Hellinger

After Hellinger took his priestly vows in 1952, he was sent to South Africa where he began missionary work among the Zulu tribes. While studying at the University of Pietermaritzburg and the University of South Africa, he earned a Bachelor of Arts degree and specialized as a schoolteacher, which he combined with his priestly activities for the next 16 years of his life in South Africa. He served as the director of a school for the Zulu people and held administrative responsibility for a diocesan area consisting of 150 schools.

Hellinger spent a significant amount of time studying Zulu culture, their language, and participating in various rituals inherent to that culture. It is believed that many of the theoretical and practical insights he acquired from Zulu culture were later incorporated into his psychotherapeutic practice. In particular, it is known that some spiritual rituals of the Zulu people served as prototypes for his family constellations. This understanding suggests that the primary origins of the dramatic psychotherapeutic approach have a deeper and ancient source rather than being borrowed from Jacob Moreno's psychodrama, which is rooted not in shamanic ritual but in theatrical improvisation. However, upon closer examination, similarities can be observed in certain aspects between constellations and psychodrama. Nevertheless, they have very little in common in their theoretical and practical foundations, employing different principles of work and focusing on entirely different aspects.

At a certain stage of his work, Hellinger begins to change his philosophical beliefs and renounces his priesthood. Upon his return to Germany, he marries a woman named Gerda and then moves to Vienna, where he undergoes psychoanalytic training. After completing his training, he joins the Munich Association of Psychoanalysis. In 1973, Hellinger moves to California, USA, to study under the American psychotherapist Arthur Janov and his method of "Primal Scream," which he later practices in Germany. Hellinger recounts that initially he practiced the "Primal Scream" method in its original format, which lasted over nine months. Later, based on his observations, he shortened the course to three months and eventually to four weeks. Ultimately, he concluded that the technique itself could be conducted within a single psychotherapy session.

During a family constellations seminar held in Moscow, Hellinger demonstrated this form of work, which, to a large extent, could be classified as body therapy. He took a seated patient with both hands from both sides and gently pressed her against himself. Then he invited her to try moving forward as if she were crawling through a narrow tunnel. Several assistants began to help her do this, some pulling her from one side while others pushed from the other. After 5—10 minutes, she emerged from Hellinger's "embrace," which had triggered a significant age regression to the moment of birth in her consciousness. The assistants placed her next to the therapist on chairs, and she lay in his arms in a newborn baby state. Afterward, for more than 30 minutes, Hellinger verbally progressed her to her familiar age. In her consciousness, he created a visual metaphor of a staircase, where each step represented the next year of her life. At certain stages, she paused, and tears appeared. At one point, she even experienced vomiting. Hellinger commented on the emergence of various cathartic reactions in the patient's behavior as a reflection and expression of suppressed emotions during different periods of her development.

Hellinger later studied Eric Berne's Transactional Analysis, Neuro-Linguistic Programming (NLP) techniques, and Milton Erickson's hypnosis. From NLP techniques, we can see that Hellinger sometimes provides his patients with basic anchoring techniques. In his execution, the practice of Ericksonian hypnosis became more akin to a form of meditation. The meditations themselves integrate his understanding of the functioning principles of family systems and essentially represent a certain type of directive suggestion, performed in a very gentle form.

In the 1980s, he worked on creating a method of group psychotherapy based on drama. For a long time, this work remained backstage and was not widely discussed. Hellinger shares that he even considered retiring without fully developing his ideas into a comprehensive form of psychotherapeutic work. However, fate had other plans for his creation.

One of Bert Hellinger's students, German psychiatrist Gunthard Weber, in the early 1990s, proposed publishing a series of edited seminars where Hellinger presents the key positions of his method. The book was published in 1993 under the title "Love's Own Truth" and soon became a psychotherapeutic bestseller. Over the next 20 years, Hellinger wrote and published more than 70 books devoted to his therapeutic method. He also conducted training and psychotherapeutic seminars worldwide.

The process of family constellation unfolds in a format similar to Jacob Moreno's psychodrama and Virginia Satir's "family sculpture." A group of people gathers, and one person approaches the psychotherapist and states their request for work. The therapist briefly listens to the request and then selects different individuals from the group to serve as representatives for key figures or processes that need to be represented during the work.

Unlike other dramatic psychotherapeutic methods, the representative either receives minimal information about the role they will play or does not receive any information at all. Participants are then asked to pay attention to bodily sensations and the movements that arise within them. They are encouraged to move where they feel compelled and express the emotions that naturally want to be expressed.

Jacob Moreno's concept of "spontaneity" in this work is interpreted as the "movement of the soul" and relies more heavily on intuitive unconscious processes. The understanding of how role perception occurs draws on Rupert Sheldrake's theory of the morphic field—a unifying psychic space encompassing all living beings that contains necessary information. In Hellinger's perspective, the representative becomes a conduit for the information within this space.

The process of extracting information from the morphic field through the representative's work reflects a phenomenon that is scientifically underexplored. This aspect has subjected the method to numerous criticisms. However, despite this, a large number of psychotherapists have confirmed its effectiveness over many years. This method would not have gained such wide acceptance among the professional psychotherapy community if its key therapeutic aspects were knowingly based on false premises.

The movements of the representatives reflect specific and significant emotional processes existing within the emotional field to which the patient belongs. There can be numerous variations.

Let's describe some of them to highlight the general tendencies of the process.

- The downward movement of the representative reflects a general negative state, sometimes an illness, and sometimes the symbolic need to give a place to the deceased individuals with whom there is a connection.
- Sometimes, if the representative lies down, it indicates that the person whose role they are playing has already passed away or is in poor condition.
- If the representative in the constellations process attempts to leave the room where the group therapy is taking place, it may reflect their unwillingness to live.
- If the representative rotates in place, it may indicate a sense of guilt.
- Continuously looking upward by the representative also signifies a sense of guilt.
- Looking downward by the representative indicates the need to include some deceased person related to the patient's dynamics in the constellation process. In such cases, the therapist selects another person from the group, asks them to lie down in the place where the other representative was looking, and starts experiencing the role.

The representative does not necessarily play the role of a specific person. Roles can reflect emotions, states, abstract processes, and phenomena. Roles can have names such as "Life," "Death," "Fate," "Power," "Illness," "Symptom," "Decision," "Resource," and so on. Different structural elements of the body, organs, and various processes occurring within them can also assume different roles. For example, during the constellation, the therapist may position the patient's representative, a diseased organ, and the illness.

According to Hellinger, the main roles that need to be actualized in the constellation at the beginning of the work should be closely related to the topic of the inquiry. The more secondary roles included in the constellation, the more convoluted and poorly interpretable the dynamics may become.

Therefore, the principle of minimizing the inclusion of roles is employed. Only those elements that are extremely necessary for the manifestation of systemic dynamics are included.

The therapist usually asks the representatives to perform all movements slowly, without haste. They should express verbally what they feel in their bodies, without creating rationalizations. During the enactment of the role, representatives may experience intense emotions directly related to the emotional system of the patient they are working with. Once a participant exits the role, the emotional flow immediately ceases.

While embodying a role, the representative, who knows little or almost nothing about the patient's family, is capable of spontaneously actualizing not only various undifferentiated emotional experiences but also fragments of the patient's family system's past. Sometimes, very old fragments. For example, one of the authors of this text observed how a representative participating in a therapeutic session unexpectedly fell to the floor and started speaking about the sensation of vomiting masses coming out of him and choking on them. After some time, the surprised patient with whom the work was being done commented that this was exactly how his great-grandfather died. Such "reading" phenomena by the representative from the patient's emotional field occur quite often, and therapists sometimes accumulate dozens or hundreds of such stories. Again, despite their astonishing nature, these phenomena cannot yet be fully explained from a scientific paradigm perspective.

Bert Hellinger places significant emphasis on the system of relationships between the patient and their parents. He believes that any non-acceptance, resentment, or negative feelings that a person may transmit towards their parents can manifest as symptoms of varying complexity.

According to Hellinger, many problems in the family system arise due to a disruption of the existing hierarchy within the system. For example, when children look at their parents and begin to criticize their actions, such criticism eventually severs the connection between the child and the parent, depriving the child of the energy they could draw from that relationship.

Depending on the disruption of the connection with one or both parents, the quality of the symptoms can vary significantly. For instance, an emotional disconnection from the father often leads to problems with social integration. According to Hellinger, the figure of the father serves as a guide into the external world for an individual. A person who lacks an emotional connection with the maternal figure often experiences emotional problems associated with an inability to find peace and tranquility. Difficulties in the emotional connection with the mother are frequently the cause of drug and alcohol addiction.

Emotional connection with a parent is seen as the ability to accept what comes from them. However, unfortunately, it is not always easy to accept what comes from parents. Sometimes, it may seem impossible. At times, accepting both parents or one of them can become a lifelong challenge for an individual.

Organizational constellations are an intriguing variation of family constellations, where the focus of the therapist's attention shifts from the family system to the organizational system. This can involve a company, corporation, city, country, and so on. The functioning rules of organizational systems differ little from those of family systems, which is why all therapy methods for families can positively impact the effectiveness of a company's or any other organization's work.

During the process of creating an organizational constellation, substitutes are often selected to represent the company itself, the director, other employees, the problem, or challenge the company faces, and so on.

Let's provide an example of an organizational constellation we observed. The client consults the facilitator about specific financial difficulties experienced by the company, where the client is the director.

The facilitator selects representatives for the work, one of the key roles being that of "secrecy" related to the "symptom." The representative for "secrecy" lies down on the floor and reveals that they are dying in an unpleasant manner. The representative playing the role of money starts following the representative for "secrecy", lying down on the floor.

Subsequently, the facilitator asks the client if they know which deceased person, connected to the company, the financial flow may be following.

The client responds that some time ago, before the financial decline, an unfortunate incident occurred in the company. Next to the company building, there was a small working space where an elderly security guard lived who died in a fire, likely due to excessive alcohol consumption. The company did not provide any support to the guard's family after his death. However, the "conscience" of the organizational system decided differently. The facilitator recommended to the director that they offer financial assistance to the family of the deceased, thereby embodying the positive intention behind the organization's symptom.

Sometimes, structural constellations are considered as a separate form of constellative work. In this form of work, the primary focus of attention is on various elements of the psyche, body, or any other system apart from the family and organizational systems.

For example, in a constellation, a representative of the patient and the organ that troubles them can be placed. Alternatively, a large number of organs can be gathered to observe how they manifest themselves through the behavior of representatives. These can be various elementary mental processes such as intellect, memory, emotions, instincts, attention, perception, will, intention, and so on.

An interesting form of structural constellation can be used for planning and achieving different goals. For instance, representatives can play the roles of elements such as goals, resources, opportunities, information, obstacles, and others. In structural constellations, secrecy can be a crucial element, and its representative can intuitively begin to reveal what is hidden from the attention of both the client and the psychotherapist.

During organizational and structural constellation work, there is often a gradual shift of focus towards the family system of the client. It is because the family system serves as the carrier and prototype of what happens to an individual in other systems they belong to.

The relationships between larger and smaller social systems and their elements can be described through the concept of fractality, introduced in 1975 by the French and American mathematician Benoit Mandelbrot, the creator of fractal geometry. Mandelbrot defined a fractal as a set that possesses the property of self-similarity. That is, the whole has the same shape as one or more of its parts.

For example, the human body can be perceived as an element of the integrity of the family system and fractally reflect the processes occurring within it. This is why we can observe a correlation between relationship problems within families and physical illnesses. Similarly, we can trace the dependence of processes within larger social systems on processes occurring within family systems. For instance, if a large number of family systems belonging to a larger social system encounter similar problems, unresolved family issues will eventually become unresolved problems for the city, country, ethnic group, and so on.

In this case, we see that the family system serves as a kind of fractal link through which we can assess what can potentially happen at other fractal levels, whether larger or smaller, depending on the focus of attention.

At times, Bert Hellinger demonstrated in his work how the constellation process can be applied to very large social systems. For example, one representative plays the role of the ethnic group of Germans, while another represents Jews. In this case, the dynamics relate to more global social processes. Another interesting example is a constellation that Bert Hellinger demonstrated live while in Kyiv in 2010. During this work, he attempted to reconcile the psychic fields at a higher level between the Germans who attacked Ukraine during World War II and the Ukrainians and Russians who defended their country.

According to Hellinger, the processes occurring in large psychic fields constantly and intensely affect the functioning of family systems and the individuals within them.

Bert Hellinger's family constellations have borrowed many ideas from transgenerational psychotherapy, which postulates the inheritance of symptoms from one generation to another. For example, if a person experiences a certain disorder, therapy may focus on events from the personal experiences of the patient's parents, grandparents, or more distant relatives. Hellinger identifies the key relatives with whom a person has a very close psycho-emotional connection. These include the father, mother, grandparents, siblings, paternal and maternal siblings, and sometimes great-grandparents. It does not matter whether a person has had direct contact with them or has never seen them. According to Hellinger's beliefs, family remains family regardless of direct contact. The more significant and profound the events that may have occurred in the lives of certain family members, the greater the influence they can have on the well-being of individuals in subsequent generations.

For instance, Hellinger describes one of his cases in South America involving a young man suffering from schizophrenia. During the therapy process, it was revealed that his ancestors had been slave owners who had treated their slaves cruelly. In the constellation, a representative was chosen to represent the patient, as well as deceased slaves who had served his family. The representative for the patient lowered himself to lie next to the deceased slaves and remained there, expressing empathy for them. As a result, Hellinger believes that the patient's consciousness became fragmented.

Family members do not necessarily have to be blood relatives or sexual partners. They can also be individuals to whom someone from the family has shown great kindness or, conversely, inflicted significant harm.

Any strong influence one person has on another connects their family systems, and this connection can be enduring. It is sometimes referred to as "entanglement." The process of disentangling follows the rule of balance, which vividly demonstrates that everything we give to the world, we intuitively want to receive back. If we have given a lot, we desire to receive an equal amount in return. If we have caused harm, we want to compensate for it. If this does not occur consciously through actions aimed at compensation, a person may unconsciously seek to compensate for the harm through the manifestation of various symptoms on a psychological, physical, or social level. Feelings of guilt and shame, inherent to an individual, are interpreted by Hellinger as feelings of balance. He also believes that such feelings can lead to death through their manifestation in symptoms.

It is crucial to note that feelings of guilt and shame are directly connected to the "conscience" that exists within the social systems to which an individual belongs. For instance, the collective conscience of Muslims allows them to have four wives without experiencing moral qualms about it. However, if Slavic men or women attempt to enter into similar types of social relationships, it is likely to lead to severe personal and emotional burnout. The conscience of a social system, internalized by each individual, sets the boundaries of what is acceptable and unacceptable in behavior and life as a whole. Because the consciences of different social systems can significantly differ, it can lead to conflicts between social systems, where a member of one system may harm members of another social system with a "clear conscience." We can observe numerous examples of such conflicts by exploring human history.

At the organizational level, we can see the manifestation of conscience, for example, in the "survivor syndrome," where only one person survives from a platoon of soldiers, who subsequently may experience profound anguish because they did not share the fate of their fallen comrades. This process of connection with the members of the system to which an individual belongs is called loyalty.

Similarly, family members can be loyal to each other in the manifestation of both positive events in a person's life and the manifestation of symptoms. In such cases, we can witness how, in the next generation, children begin to replicate various significant events from the lives of their ancestors. Loyalty in this case declares, "I am no better than others." Naturally, this process, in the vast majority of cases, has a deep unconscious nature and, when consciously recognized, can be subject to correction and transformation.

An interesting example of correcting this form of transgenerational inheritance is described by NLP trainer Robert Dilts. His mother was diagnosed with stage IV breast cancer and was given a prognosis of approximately six months to live.

Dilts began verbal therapy with her, and some of the techniques he applied were directly related to the concepts of transgenerational psychotherapy. His maternal grandmother and great-grandmother also suffered from and died of cancer. He discovered that his mother held a deep unconscious belief that she was no better than her mother and grandmother, and therefore, she should follow them in illness and death.

Dilts reformed her beliefs in an elegant manner. He asked her to imagine herself first in the role of his grandmother, then as his great-grandmother, and then respond from their perspective about whether they wanted their child to suffer and die like them. She received a definitive answer: "No!" He anchored this state in his mother's consciousness, which apparently became one of the main reasons for her subsequent recovery.

After six months, her stage IV cancer went into complete remission. She lived for another 11 years after her recovery. It is worth noting that this reframing was one of the practices he applied to his mother. He also mentioned that part of her problem was a lack of purpose in life. Specifically, she had already achieved her goals. Her son and daughter were successful and self-actualized; her husband had passed away, and she didn't quite understand why she needed to continue living.

Dilts shared that he helped her form new goals to hold on to her life more firmly.

This story vividly illustrates how family conscience can create symptoms and how psychotherapeutic work can effectively correct such a process that contributes to the onset of illness.

Continuing the topic of schizophrenic disorder mentioned earlier, it is worth adding that Hellinger understands this condition as a manifestation of a specific conflict within the family system to which the patient belongs.

In fact, during his seminars, Hellinger even commented that he perceives schizophrenia not as an illness but as a process of one person in the family taking on the roles of both a killer and a victim. Through his work with patients suffering from schizophrenia using systemic constellations, he consistently observed a similar pattern. Their family systems had at least two roles that could not find reconciliation. Sometimes it could be the role of one killer and multiple victims. It is the simultaneous association with the roles of the killer and the victim that splits consciousness, according to Hellinger's opinion. The killer can come from either the same family or another family system. Ultimately, this does not significantly change the essence of the emotional processes in dynamics. The act of killing another person becomes a fact of their inclusion in the family system. Afterwards, someone will take on the role of the victim in the killer's family, just as someone will take on the role of the killer in the victim's family. This process is complementary.

The process of substitution is formed through empathy with the image introduced into the family system. If members of one system do not want to empathize with the attached role in the current generation, then in subsequent generations, someone will empathize with this image intensely. Sometimes, in constellation therapy for schizophrenia, the symptom can be shifted from a standstill, while other times the patient's association with the killer and victim images may be too strong. In such cases, we observe that, behind this symptom, like many others, lies love. The need within the family system to love what other members do not love. And, of course, this process is unconscious.

The first primary criterion that can somehow change the dynamics is the realization demonstrated in constellation work. The second criterion is the use of interventions that the therapist may recommend to the patient or other representatives. Often, the interventions themselves raise to the conscious level what is hidden in the unconscious through verbalization. In this way, the intervention weakens the symptom itself.processes that create movement in constellation work.

The third criterion may be targeted restructuring—reformulating the constellation process. It should be noted that in the early stages of the development of the family constellation method, Hellinger often performed restructuring. However, over time, he increasingly stopped exerting a rigid influence on the structure of the constellation, thus expressing trust in the systemic unconscious processes that create movement in constellation work.

Because of this, one can attempt to differentiate the technique of constellation work, as well as hypnosis, into directive and non-directive. Literally speaking, therapists practicing Hellinger's family constellations method do not make use of such a division. Nevertheless, in my opinion, such a classification seems to suggest itself.

The process of empathizing with what was previously devoid of empathy can manifest in various symptoms. Let's provide a few examples. The patient is a two-year-old child with sensory aphasia. During the consultation, the child's mother was present and described the situation in detail.

We gathered a detailed family history and discovered the following facts. The child's family—the maternal grandfather and grandmother—have been living in very difficult relationships for a long time but have not divorced. The grandfather has been unfaithful to the grandmother, and she has endured and not left him. Several years before the birth of our patient, the grandfather suffered a stroke, after which he developed severe speech problems. He lost his job and friends and leads a reclusive life, mainly spending time walking, reading, and watching television.

The grandmother does not empathize with him and may even take pleasure in his illness. Their daughter, the patient's mother, loves both her father and mother but has grown accustomed to empathizing with her mother and has shown little empathy toward her father.

In the dynamics of this system, we have discovered that the child sympathizes with the grandfather, whom almost no one sympathizes with. It is in this way that young children can interfere with family dynamics. Every member of the family needs sympathy. If, at the moment, no one sympathizes with a family member, then the next person who enters the family will most likely be the first to show them the necessary sympathy. In many ways, we can see here the embodiment of the rule that children will give space in their lives to what their parents do not want to acknowledge.A similar situation can arise when considering past sexual partners. Hellinger repeatedly emphasized that children often emotionally replace their parents' past sexual partners. For example, if a child's mother left a man before getting involved with the child's father and that man harbored strong resentment towards the woman, the child may start to resent the mother on his behalf. These are unconscious processes that govern the dynamics of family systems. From this, we can draw very interesting conclusions regarding the psychology and psychotherapy of relationships between men and women. It is important to consider the fact that any sexual partner we have had, to some extent, becomes connected to our family. Depending on how our relationship with them ends, our subsequent sexual relationships will take shape. If our previous partner resents us, the next partner will, to some extent, sooner or later resent us as well. The same applies in reverse. If the previous partner is grateful to us and experiences positive emotions, the next partner will sense it within the family field and react accordingly.

Naturally, a significant portion of the problems that arise within and outside the family system are directly related to a disruption in the balance of "giving and taking."

For example, in a partnership, if a man gives too much to his wife, it can destroy the relationship just as effectively as giving too little. The more one partner provides various goods of different qualities, the more the other partner will feel guilty about it.

The disruption of this balance can lead to various negative consequences. A man who gives too much to his wife will eventually betray her. It is worth noting that the perceptions of how much each partner should give and take from each other can significantly differ and be strongly influenced by the conscience of the ethnic and family systems to which the partners belong. This conscience embodies deep rules that the social system follows. If an individual, as part of this system, begins to violate these rules, it can produce various symptoms at the psychological, physical, and social levels.

Some symptoms in a person belonging to a family system can create a lack of empathy towards a particular family member. Stronger symptoms may arise in cases of hatred. Particularly intense symptoms occur when there is hatred towards deceased family members.

Let's consider an example from a supervision session conducted by Bert Hellinger at a seminar in Florida in 2003. A female psychotherapist approached him and shared a story about her patient who developed a very rare symptom after 35 years: elephantiasis. The symptom appeared after the patient decided to find her father, whom she had never seen before. She discovered his whereabouts and went to his house, but when she arrived, she found out that he had already passed away. After some time, the symptom began to actively manifest.

Hellinger conducted a constellation and placed two key elements in it: a representative for the patient and a representative for her deceased father. The patient's representative approached the father's representative and started yelling at him with fury. Her scream seemed somewhat insane. Hellinger immediately halted the constellation.

In this case, the symptom actively developed after the patient began to transmit the dormant hatred within her. The strong negative emotion became a trigger for her connection to her deceased father. In a way, she entered the "realm of the dead," while the symptom itself, which creates significant problems for spatial movement, prevented her from moving or rather, from moving into her father's home. In this case, the patient violated the rule of hierarchy by aggressively reacting to the father figure and disregarding the need to accept the deceased as they were.

Hatred towards the dead brings the hater closer to the dead, and the intensity of the feeling generates a certain symptom. In this situation, we observe another rule directly related to the dynamics of social systems: "We are free from what we accept as it is. What we hate enslaves us and holds us back." Hatred is a prison. Hatred towards a deceased family member is a prison with severe consequences.

A somewhat similar situation occurred in our private practice. A patient came to us who had never seen her father. During the course of psychotherapy, we discussed extensively the importance of establishing contact with the parental figure if it had not been established before. Hellinger believes that such contact can be highly beneficial for the child, regardless of the feedback received from the parental figure.

The patient found her father in another city, visited him, and established a connection. The contact was emotionally normal, and her father was glad to see her. However, the new wife of the father most likely was not. After seven months of communication, the father wrote to her that he could no longer stay in touch, terminating the contact. Presumably, this was at the request of his wife.

Our patient was overwhelmed with intense hatred. For several weeks after that, she experienced aggressive outbursts, and then, while riding a bicycle, she was involved in a hit-and-run accident. She was admitted to the hospital in serious condition with a fractured collarbone and a severe head injury. The head trauma was localized in the left temporal-parietal area of the brain, causing her to experience letter agnosia for the first four days after the injury. Ordinary text appeared to her as if it were written in a foreign language.

In this case, the intense hatred she felt towards her living father led to such an outcome.

Love and hatred are concepts that are somewhat similar in our psyche and physiology. Indifference, rather than love or hatred, represents their opposite.

Observing various patients, we repeatedly confirm the idea that hatred within a family gives rise to symptoms, and hatred towards deceased family members leads to very severe symptoms, both psychological and physical. Sometimes, symptoms manifest causally, at the level of cause and effect, when a person, after violating certain family rules to which they belong, feels drawn to situations where they may experience certain traumatic events.

Helinger reveals very interesting ideas regarding the emotional changes that need to occur within an individual before they are capable of establishing a fulfilling romantic connection with a person of the opposite sex. He explains that in order for a bond to be stable, a man needs to emotionally detach from his mother and move closer to his father figure. If this does not happen, the man's heart will be occupied by the mother figure, and he will be unable to form genuine relationships with women.

Based on our observations, men who are very close to their mother figure frequently engage in infidelity towards their partners. They are more inclined towards short-term relationships and often state that they cannot love or do not know what it means to love other women. These men also rarely desire marriage or children. In general, they exhibit irresponsibility in their sexual and partnership relationships. Excessive closeness to the mother figure often predisposes a man to criminal tendencies. All of our patients who, to some extent, were involved in criminal activities were "mommy's boys." The overwhelming majority of male patients who sought the services of prostitutes were also "mommy's boys."

However, we have also frequently observed that men who are emotionally closer to their mothers can deeply immerse themselves in the religious, spiritual, and scientific spheres. In order to feel comfortable, the "mommy's boy" needs to rebel against existing rules and go beyond their boundaries. Naturally, going beyond these rules can have both constructive and destructive consequences. Therefore, the fate of a man belonging to this profile can be highly unpredictable. Yet the quality of their lives is directly linked to their ability to detach from the sphere of maternal influence.

The necessity of accepting parents as they are has nothing to do with blind compliance with their will. After reaching maturity, a person must learn to make decisions independently. We have observed numerous examples where adult men seeking advice from their mothers regarding complex life situations experienced a strong sense of helplessness. Overcoming this feeling can be achieved through distancing from the mother figure and symbolically or directly aligning oneself with the father figure. By being close to his father figure, a man gains social strength and the opportunity to effectively grow within society. Despite this rule, we have encountered a significant number of "mommy's boys" among our patients who have managed to achieve certain social heights. However, what unites them all is that their achievements were built upon the violation of moral or legal rules rather than their observance.

On the other hand, men who are emotionally closer to their father figure are more inclined to adhere to various social rules. They are often oriented toward family values and tend to be more orthodox. This applies to various spheres of life. "Mama's boys" and "daddy's boys" cannot understand each other. They often have completely different values and goals in life, with different vectors and focuses of attention. As an analogy, a "mama's boy" is more like the captain of a pirate ship, while a "daddy's boy" is the captain of a state ship. The "mama's boy" naturally gravitates towards women who are closer to the father figure, finding the connection he lacks.

A similar situation exists in the structure of relationships with parents for women, but with some modifications. If a man needs to distance himself from the mother and get closer to the father figure to mature, a woman needs to first distance herself from the mother and get closer to the father figure, learning how to maintain a psycho-emotional connection with him, and then move away from the father and get closer to the mother again.

If a woman remains emotionally attached to her father, there will be no room in her heart for another man. Such a woman will prefer short-term romances over long-term relationships. This preference can exist on both a conscious and unconscious level. In other words, a woman may consciously desire long-term relationships, but for some reason, they do not work out, and she intentionally changes sexual partners frequently.

The situation of a "daddy's daughter" becomes significantly exacerbated if the father is a socially significant person, holds a high position, or has other significant achievements. In our experience, in such cases, it is almost impossible for her to emotionally distance herself from her closeness to the father figure. Such a woman is capable of being in a long-term relationship only with a man who has lower status than her. However, if she persists in staying close to a high-status man while maintaining a strong emotional bond with her socially significant father, it will generate a strong conflict within her, which can manifest through symptoms of various qualities and directions.

Very often, such women find a husband who is significantly less socially prominent than her and her father and start to cheat on their spouse. The less prominent husband is perceived as a complement to the father figure. If the father is cruel and aggressive, it often leads the "daddy's daughter" towards sexual promiscuity or even engaging in prostitution in various forms. The "daddy's daughter" always prefers "mama's boys" when searching for a partner, finding in them the connection they lack themselves. A long-lasting sexual bond between a "mama's boy" and a "daddy's daughter" is extremely rare. Only mutual emotional detachment from parents of the opposite sex can sustain and make it genuinely comfortable for both parties.

It is important to distinguish between the concepts of accepting a parent and being close to them. Accepting parents allows a child to establish a connection with the resources present in the family system, both masculine and feminine. Sometimes, due to various reasons, another family member may replace the lost parent. For example, a grandfather may act as a substitute for a father. In such cases, the child can effectively establish a connection with the image of masculine behavior. However, if the connection with the masculine or feminine image is completely lost within the family, the likelihood of neuroticization can significantly increase. In such circumstances, in order to rectify the situation, the child needs to find a new father or mother independently. By this, we mean a person who will serve as a role model for the child's desired type of behavior. There should be at least a minimally empathetic bond established between this person and the child. Then, the child will be able to integrate within themselves a complete image of masculine or feminine behavior.

Excessive closeness to a parent keeps a person's ego in a more infantile position, which will to some extent generate feelings of guilt. The older the person, the stronger the sense of guilt will be, which will shape other symptoms within their personality. For instance, male alcoholics and drug addicts often belong to the category of individuals who are excessively close to their mothers but do not fully accept them.

There is another interesting characteristic of our personality: we are capable of accepting a parent only when they maintain a certain distance from us. Being too close quickly turns into rejection. Increasing the distance allows acceptance to emerge but does not guarantee it. If we specify the appropriate and most suitable distance between a child and a parent, it is important to consider that it varies during different stages of development. The older the person, the greater the distance required for them to feel comfortable.Beliefs about the distance from the parental figure heavily depend on the conscience of the family and the ethnic system to which the person belongs. For example, in some families and cultures, a close bond between a child and their parents in adulthood may not evoke strong neurotic feelings, while in others, the dynamics can be diametrically opposite. Therefore, it is extremely challenging to establish clear criteria for the necessary distance. The emergence of certain symptoms serves as a calibration criterion for understanding the distance that needs to be established from the parent in order to improve the individual's condition.

Excessive closeness can generate the same symptoms as close distance. For example, the closer a man is to his mother, the more likely it is that he will prefer short-term relationships with women, probably avoiding marriage and fatherhood. His attitude towards women will be primarily sexual, lacking emotional closeness. Such men easily separate from women and often do not experience sentimental feelings about it. However, if the distance significantly increases, the man's attitude towards women can change dramatically. He will seek not a mistress but a wife, and marriage often becomes his primary goal in relationships with the opposite sex. These men genuinely desire children and express strong positive emotions upon their arrival. They do not shy away from responsibility. In general, this profile describes a husband rather than a lover.

However, different challenges arise in this case. Intense passion is rarely accessible to these men. Their love is more moderate, calm, and stable. Over time, the sexual attraction towards their permanent partner may diminish or even be completely reduced. On the contrary, it may increase towards other women, often leading to the search for a mistress. Nevertheless, the man continues to emotionally love his wife and rarely leaves her. This occurs due to the unconscious need of the man to transform his wife into the mother figure he lacks.

As a result of these processes, the dynamics of partnership relationships can be metaphorically represented as walking a tightrope, where a strong inclination in one direction or the other signifies a fall. Maintaining this balance to some extent is an art that can be learned by understanding the principles of family system dynamics.

Similar processes occur in women who are too close to their father figure.

Such women are more consciously or unconsciously oriented towards sexual relationships than family and children. This profile corresponds more to that of a mistress than a wife.One vivid metaphor that effectively illustrates balanced parent-child relationships is the metaphor of our planetary system. Life on any planet is likely to emerge only if it is at a sufficient distance from the Sun for its warmth to foster life. If the distance is too great, it will be too cold, and the likelihood of life arising in such circumstances is also doubtful. In our view, this metaphor is highly applicable to describing relationships with parental figures who have the capacity to give life to their child while maintaining the appropriate distance.

Let us provide an interesting example from our work with patients. A 28-year-old man came to us with severe stuttering symptoms that had developed in early childhood. In our work with him, we discovered his strong attachment to the maternal figure, his dependence on her opinion, and a series of difficulties in asserting his own positions. Professionally, the patient is a doctor with excellent musical and programming skills. He has a developed and intellectual personality.

Through therapeutic work involving specific exercises from body-oriented therapy, we were able to quickly help him develop the ability to speak almost stutter-free. For instance, we provided him with breathing techniques and techniques of bodily response to emotions through hand strikes on a punching bag. The man was amazed by the changes that occurred in him. However, these changes were only short-lived. As soon as he returned home, where he lived with his mother, the symptoms returned.

He continued to come to us, and we regularly managed to demonstrate to him that body-oriented psychotherapy exercises could quickly and effectively restore his fluent speech. When the symptoms reappeared after some time, they did so with less intensity than before, but there was no complete recovery. We explained to him that the main part of the symptoms was being caused by excessive attachment to his mother and that full healing would only be possible if he significantly distanced himself from her. Several years later, our prognosis proved to be entirely accurate.

He moved to Germany to work as an anesthesiologist, living there for some time. As a result of breaking the constant close bond with his mother, the symptoms diminished and eventually disappeared. When the patient returned to his hometown for a while and came to talk to us, his speech was fluent and rapid. There was nothing interrupting his thoughts. In this case, we can observe how effective it can be to maintain the necessary distance from a parent.

Another vivid metaphor that effectively illustrates balanced parent-child relationships is the metaphor of our planetary system. Life on any given planet is likely to emerge only if the planet is at a sufficient distance from the Sun, allowing its warmth to generate life. If the distance is too great, it will be cold, and the likelihood of life emerging in such a case is also doubtful. In my opinion, this metaphor is highly applicable to describe relationships with parental figures who can give life to their child while maintaining the proper and appropriate distance.

Let's provide a fascinating example from our work with patients. A 28-year-old man came to us with severe stuttering symptoms that had developed in early childhood. In our work with him, we discovered his strong attachment to the maternal figure, his dependence on her opinion, and a series of difficulties in asserting his own positions. Professionally, the patient is a doctor with excellent skills in music and programming. He has a developed and intellectual personality.

Through therapeutic work with specific exercises from body-oriented therapy, we were able to quickly develop his ability to speak almost without stuttering. For example, we provided him with breathing techniques and techniques of somatic emotional response through hand strikes on a punching bag. The man was amazed by the changes that occurred within him. However, the changes themselves were only short-lived. As soon as he returned home, where he lived with his mother, the symptoms resurfaced.

He continued coming to us, and we regularly demonstrated to him that body-oriented psychotherapy exercises could quickly and effectively restore his fluent speech. When the symptoms returned after a while, they were less intense than before, but complete healing did not occur. We explained to him that the main part of the symptoms was produced by hypercontact with his mother, and full recovery was only possible if he distanced himself significantly from her. Several years later, our prognosis was fully justified. He moved to Germany to work as an anesthesiologist and lived there for some time. Due to the disruption of his constant close bond with his mother, the symptoms diminished and eventually disappeared. When the patient returned to his hometown for a visit and came to talk to us, his speech was fluent and rapid. There was nothing in his consciousness that interrupted him. In this case, we can see how effective maintaining the necessary distance from the parent can be.

Therapeutic Intervention Model

This model is a set of speech patterns that a psychotherapist utters to the patient during the therapeutic process. Bert Hellinger defines these phrases as "strong," meaning they exert a significant influence on the conscious and unconscious processes of the patient when applied correctly by the psychotherapist.

The model comprises 12 different speech patterns, each serving various purposes. Sometimes the therapist utters the phrases while the patient simply listens, but a much more effective approach is for the patient to literally repeat the phrases. The patient does not necessarily need to fully comprehend the meaning of the phrases. They operate at a deep, abstract level, lifting and activating a significant part of the profound experience. Moreover, they possess a trance-like effect, making them interdisciplinary and applicable during hypnotic induction.

It is crucial to understand that it is the appropriateness of the phrase itself that can create the desired effect. Merely employing a straightforward, algorithmic approach guided by rational reasoning often fails to yield the expected substantial changes. These patterns can be easily utilized in independent therapeutic work. Meditations incorporating these patterns can have a profoundly transformative effect.

Delegation of Responsibility / Identity Perception

This pattern focuses on declaring a volitional impulse and delineating certain psychological and behavioral boundaries. It can activate unconscious processes that were previously stagnant or functioning improperly.

A crucial criterion is the delineation of emotional boundaries within the individual's personality. Often, if we fail to establish clear boundaries, our unconscious can behave unpredictably, frequently leading to discomfort and provoking uncontrollable behavior.

Examples of interventions based on this pattern include the following:

- "**I leave this here with you.**" This intervention is applied in relation to individuals or the experiential space.
- "**I let go of this.**" For instance, a problematic situation or experience.
- "**This is my/your/his/her/their responsibility.**" This is applied to specific members of a family or organizational system to which the individual belongs.

In the latter case, various other terms can also be used, such as "experience," "emotions," "desires," "boundaries," "trauma," "pain," and others.

Boundaries can also be delineated in the following ways:

- "**You can sort this out among yourselves.**" This intervention can be used, for example, when separating a child from negative feelings between conflicted parents. Quite often, on an unconscious level, the child interferes in the parents' conflict, even while formally remaining detached. Again, on an unconscious level, the child aligns with the side that provided more for them.
- "**I (identity), you (identity), they (identity).**" For example, "I am the son, you are the father, they are members of our family."
- "**Now you can speak for yourself.**" Some explanation is required here. The formation of symptoms in an individual is often linked

to a rejection of certain deceased or excluded family members. As a result, symptoms become a means of "speaking" for these rejected and excluded individuals to some extent. In the process of constellation work, after accepting such rejected individuals, this intervention may be appropriate. The acceptance itself can be facilitated through the phrase from the acceptance pattern: "**Now I see you**," and through the phrase from the inner space pattern: "**There is a place for you in my heart**."

- "**Living with the living, dead with the dead.**" This phrase becomes relevant when, during the dynamics of constellation work, it is observed how images of deceased family members significantly interfere with the conscious and unconscious processes of the living.
- "**My place is with the living.**" This phrase can be applied when an individual unconsciously attempts to align with deceased family members.
- "**I look at them for you.**" For example, the dynamics may be as follows: if a parent does not want to look at a close family member, such as the father, the child will empathize with that person on a deep level, often manifesting it through various symptoms. In such cases, the child or a representative of the child in the constellation needs to say to the mother's representative, "**I look at him for you**." Verbalizing the deep unconscious process often changes it, making it more manageable and consequently less pathological.
- "**I make the decision - me/you/them**." This pattern helps declare and delineate zones of personal responsibility if they have been violated or incorrectly perceived.

Gratitude / Respect / Value

This pattern provides an opportunity to express feelings that, for various reasons, have not been realized. These interventions are excellent for summarizing various internal processes. These phrases can activate strong abreactive processes, releasing deeply blocked emotions.

Examples of interventions:

- "**Thank you for life**." This phrase is appropriate for parents or individuals who have saved the patient's life.
- "**I respect your boundaries.**" This phrase can be applicable in various contexts, but we believe it can be particularly relevant when parents address their children.
- "**To me, you are the best (only one)**." This phrase can be used for many family members, often parents or more distant ancestors.
- "**You are my treasure**." It can be addressed to a group of individuals within the family or to the entire family system as a whole.
- "**I respect what you do**." Applicable to many family members, often children addressing their parents.

The phrases we have listed, when applied in the appropriate context, can uplift the deep intention that may underlie a patient's symptom. Once verbalized, this intention loses some of its power or ceases to function altogether. Despite the apparent simplicity of these patterns, their impact can be astonishing.

Hierarchy / Equality

Within various social systems, there is always a distinct hierarchy determined by rules. Hellinger comments that those participants who entered the system earlier, who are older, and who adhere well to the system's rules, giving more than they take, potentially occupy a higher position in the hierarchy. There can be many examples of violating the systemic hierarchy, such as when a child places themselves above their parents, a younger sibling disrespects an older sibling, a subsequent sexual partner despises the previous one, and so on. In the case of violating the hierarchy of the system to which an individual belongs, they immediately feel a sense of guilt and shame. This process is directly influenced by the unconscious interaction of the individual with the members of the system. To exist comfortably within a particular family system, one needs to strive to understand the existing hierarchy. Observing the hierarchy deprives a person of feelings of guilt and thereby removes symptoms.

Examples of interventions can be found as follows:

- "**You are big, and I am small**." The intervention is directed from the child to the parents or more distant ancestors.
- "**You give, and I take**." The intervention is directed from the child to the parents or more distant ancestors, but often the focus is on the figures of the father and mother.
- "**You are equally good to me**." The intervention is most often directed by the child to both parents. This intervention can be particularly effective when the child excessively favors one parent. Typically, if a child does not empathize with one parent, they eventually take their place, replacing them. Sometimes the process of replacement can be halted through therapeutic work, including the use of phrases from this model. However, in some cases, the process of replacement has a deeper nature, and therapeutic work can do little to change it. Rather, it can set the direction for therapy that the patient may pick up.
- "**Now you are one of us**." This phrase is used when a particular family member has been excluded and then returned.
- "**With you, we are equals**." The phrase is appropriate in relation to any family member who occupies an equal hierarchical position. For example, from a husband to a wife.

Planning the Future

The application of this pattern provides an opportunity to create a more conscious perception of future events and direct a person's behavior and emotions in the desired direction. Emotional connection with the future also provides additional support for the individual, allowing for more rational thinking and action.

Examples of interventions can be found as follows:

- "**Now I will do something good with this**." This intervention is relevant when therapy reveals a negative situation that, in a literal sense, cannot be resolved.
- "**I will remember**." This is applicable in relation to any negative past experiences within the family system.
- "**I will accept everything you reveal**." This phrase expresses readiness to accept the secrets of a family member and shows respect for them.
- "**I will take care of myself**." The phrase is directed from children to parents or more distant family members, and it can be a promise.

Acceptance of the Present

Different phrases about accepting and acknowledging the present can allow for a more vivid and accurate awareness of the situation. These phrases can also serve as truisms - truths that are difficult to consciously resist, making them even more trance-inducing.

Examples of interventions:

- "**I have come to terms with this**." The phrase implies accepting the situation in the family system as it is. Only after that is it possible to take any action.
- "**I accept you as you are**." Similar to the previous phrase, but the focus of attention is on a specific individual within the family system.
- "**Now you are with us**." The phrase is about accepting family members who were previously excluded.
- "**This is part of life**." The phrase is about accepting the situation as it is with the maximum generalization to the entire life context.

As Bert Hellinger said, "What we reject holds us back. What we accept sets us free." These phrases bring us as close as possible to the practical embodiment of this belief.

Acceptance of the Past

Acknowledging and accepting the past is just as important as accepting the future and the present. Until a person is able to accept their past, it holds them back and prevents them from moving forward. However, acceptance in this case means agreement and readiness to properly conclude what was left unfinished.

Examples of interventions:

- "**I ran away from you.**" This phrase is directed toward significant family members from older generations. It is spoken when a descendant, for various reasons, avoids their ancestors.
- "**I shared the responsibility/emotion/secret.**" This phrase acknowledges the process of specific bonding between family members in the past.
- "**You were forgotten.**" This phrase is directed at a specific family member who was excluded in the past for various reasons.

Acknowledgment of Perception / Thinking / Emotion

This pattern allows for a deeper awareness of various psychological processes that may be actualized during the therapeutic process. Consciously actualizing these psychological processes allows for a better understanding, management, and control of them. Additionally, uttering these interventions can create a connection between fragmented experiences that were previously unconnected for various reasons.

Examples of interventions:

- "**Now I see you.**" This can be applicable to any family member, living or deceased, who, for some reason, was not the focus of attention.
- "**I don't know your depths.**" This phrase acknowledges the fact that some of the patient's ancestors may have had secrets that cannot currently be revealed for various reasons. It also creates an atmosphere

of acceptance and respect for the person it is directed at.

- "**This is the truth**." The phrase is aimed at acknowledging certain facts related to the family system that were hidden or ignored for various reasons.
- "**For me, this is happiness**." Any integrative processes occurring within the family system, consciously or unconsciously, can be significantly enhanced by this phrase.

Internal Space Allocation

A person's symptoms are directly related to their resistance to various processes in life, circumstances, people, emotions, and so on. The longer we fail to accept someone or something from our family system, the more the fact of non-acceptance creates a certain alternative that we cannot ignore. Sometimes, acceptance itself requires time and a certain transformation of personality, without which proper integration may be impossible.

These phrases create an important vector of conscious movement that, under certain appropriate circumstances, can yield magnificent results. One of the particularly strong observed consequences of these phrases is a sense of relief and tranquility. Sometimes a person's anger and resentment towards others prevent them from reconciling with themselves by accepting certain facts of reality. In such cases, it is necessary to release the situation and allow the patient to make the decision on their own.

Examples of interventions:

- "**For you/you all/this, there is a place in my heart**." This phrase can be directed towards any family member, a group of people within the family, significant emotional processes, or current events.
- "**For you, there is a special place in my heart**." This phrase serves the same function as the previous one but, among other things, emphasizes the particular significance of a specific element within the system. This can be important, for example, in relation to a person

in the family who has been excluded and unaccepted for a long time. The balance rule in the family system states that the more something is rejected, the more persistently it will be accepted. Quite often, we can observe a pattern of non-acceptance and acceptance spanning several generations. For instance, what parents strongly reject, their children start actualizing. In this process, the family system finds balance. However, it should be noted that balance cannot be achieved without understanding polarities.

- "**You also have a right to a voice within me**." This phrase is aimed at the conscious actualization of the process of manifesting someone who has been excluded from the family system through the patient's consciousness and body. Uttering this phrase can partially or completely weaken the symptom's power.
- "**Only you are dear to me. There is no place in my heart for others**." Sometimes, certain images of deceased family members become the primary focus of the patient's unconscious processes. Sometimes the person may be aware of this, sometimes not. The best way to rectify the situation is to give the image what it wants. That is, verbally accentuate its maximum value. Afterwards, the dynamics usually change, partially or completely. However, if significant changes do not occur, it is pointless to force the situation. The intervention sets the vector of consciousness movement, and further actions should be left to the wisdom of the family unconscious.
- "**You will always live in my heart**." This phrase allows for emphasizing that the act of acceptance will also take place in the future. Such an action usually leads to a deeper integration of meanings.

Request

Requests and blessings have the ability to actualize and align hierarchical positions within the family system, initiate the correct vector of emotional processes, and unleash the potential of current resources. The provided phrases are particularly effective when directed at family members from older generations.

Examples of interventions:

- "**Please.**" This phrase can be relevant when addressing an older relative who may be upset with the patient for something or simply not paying attention to them.
- "**I request you.**" The purpose of this phrase is similar to the previous one.

Blessing

Phrases requesting blessings have the power to establish or enhance the connection between younger and older generations. Hellinger commented on his understanding of good parents and good children. In his view, a good parent is one who is capable of giving, while a good child is one who is capable of receiving.

Parents pass on specific resources to their children, which can be perceived by the children as either something good or something bad. However, if a child is able to perceive what comes from their parents as a blessing, it empowers them. Rejecting what comes from the parents weakens a person. But it's important to remember that literal acceptance is not mandatory. The child can transform everything they have received in their own way. In ancient alchemy, this process was called "sublimation" — the alchemists referred to it as the process of turning lead into gold, that is, transforming something base into something noble.

Unfortunately, not all children receive "gold" from their parents. But if a child can independently turn "lead" into "gold," it significantly strengthens them. Merely rejecting the "lead" yields no fruit. The best choice is to accept what comes and, if it is disliked, subject it to transformation, processing, and subsequent assimilation.

Examples of interventions:

- "**Bless me.**" This phrase is uttered by a child in relation to their parents or older relatives.

- "**I bless you.**" This phrase is spoken by a member of the older generation towards someone from the younger generation.
- "**Peace be with you.**" This phrase can be directed at various family members or their group. It is worth noting that this phrase has the ability to create a sense of proper completion of a particular process within the family system.

Accentuation of Value

Assigning significance to important systemic processes occurring within the family system strengthens them and makes them more resilient. When the significance of certain important aspects or parts of the family system is not emphasized, some or all family members will take responsibility for it, and this will manifest in various symptoms. Each element of the family system plays an important role. Some elements may be more coherent and balanced, while others may exhibit different symptoms. However, the coherence of some elements and the symptoms of other family members are interconnected and dependent on each other. Therefore, each element of the family system holds value. Naturally, these values can have different meanings.

Examples of interventions:

- "**Dear (father, mother, son, daughter, etc.)**" This phrase directly accentuates the significance of a specific family member.
- "**I value you.**" This phrase conveys a similar meaning to the previous one and serves as its logical continuation.
- "**You are priceless.**" This phrase places special emphasis on significance. It is appropriate when referring to a person who has been excluded from the family system for an extended period.

Indication of Perception / Action

Phrases of this pattern emphasize the transformative process that may occur in the patient during therapeutic work. They reinforce it, contribute to the patient's growing confidence in the correctness of what is happening, and actualize a more intense expression of suppressed emotions.

Examples of interventions:

- "**Just observe/listen/feel/absorb/breathe**." This phrase is suitable for any transformative process within the context of therapy.
- "**Allow your body to surprise you**." This phrase is effective when a moment of revelation occurs in therapy, revealing a mystery that has not been expressed for various reasons.
- "**Just let this have an impact**." This phrase is useful when the patient has already gained some experience in the therapeutic process but has not fully grasped it yet.
- "**Open your heart to everything that lies between you, and begin to grow together**." This phrase initiates deep processes of assimilation and integration of the experiences observed by the patient within the therapeutic context.

Pathopsychological Profiles and Drama Therapy

It is worth noting from the outset that drama therapy in psychotherapy is one of the most suitable approaches for almost all pathopsychological profiles. The variations lie more in the details of how each profile representative reacts to the process of dramatic therapy.

Hysteroid Profile

For hysteroid patients, participation in the dramatic form of psychotherapy is often perceived as being in their element. Hysteroids themselves are actors, and here they are provided with such a splendid sublimation context. However, practicing therapists should not forget that some of the emotional and behavioral reactions to histrionics involve exaggeration and sometimes even falsehood. Based on our experience, histrionic personalities almost always create the greatest impact on the audience in the dramatic form of psychotherapy. Some cases of working with such patients can leave a deep impression and be remembered for years. Moreover, in my opinion, the dramatic approach to working with histrionic patients becomes effective only when the therapist can identify the patient's true emotional reactions, a skill that comes with time and consistent practice. It is important to always remember that, on a deeper level, histrionics are not interested in concluding therapy, especially in a dramatic manner. Just as an actor is unlikely to want to end their career after a good performance, a histrionic is interested in creating a strong emotional impact on others. However, most of their games operate on an unconscious level.

Paranoid Profile

For paranoid patients, immersion in dramatic forms of therapy is rare. The presence of unfamiliar or little-known individuals often triggers anxiety and distress in them. The ability for open and sincere communication also significantly suffers. Paranoid individuals may constantly believe that anything others see or hear about them during group work will eventually be used against them. It is virtually impossible to convince such personalities otherwise. However, if paranoid reactions are not exaggerated, a paranoid individual can gain valuable and significant insight through dramatic therapy.

Psychopathic Profile

In our observation, pure psychopaths will ignore the opportunity to participate in dramatic group work. If they do participate, they often have a poor understanding of what is happening before them due to problems with abstract thinking. A psychopath usually cannot grasp the abstract core of a dramatic session, making it difficult for them to draw any conclusions for themselves from what they have seen, heard, and felt. Much more often, in a dramatic group, one can find patients with a mixed pathopsychological profile, where psychopathy comes along with, for example, a histrionic profile. The combination of psychopathic and histrionic profiles can occasionally be seen in dramatic groups, while other combinations are extremely rare.

Obsessive-Compulsive Profile

According to our observations, individuals with an obsessive-compulsive personality adapt excellently to the dramatic therapeutic process and draw numerous insights and inspiration from it. Participation in a dramatic session can deeply address their problems at times. Patients with this profile usually do not exhibit strong resistance to this form of psychotherapy.

Schizoid Profile

Initially, individuals with schizoid personality often experience difficulties adapting to the dramatic context. However, as they realize that they are accepted in the group, they begin to behave differently. This is closely related to the intensity of schizoid manifestations. The more intense they are, the slower the adaptation process becomes. We have observed various examples of behavior and dynamics among schizoids in dramatic groups. Some may consistently attend sessions for a year or more, while others may only participate once or a few times. We have discovered that the dramatic group can have positive effects on schizoid personalities, particularly if they remain in the group for a longer period. However, even a single session can provide an opportunity for better self-understanding.

Epileptoid Profile

According to our observations, individuals with an epileptoid personality feel great after dramatic therapy. They are not prone to excessive dramatization like histrionics, excel in playing assigned roles, and are highly receptive to the information received during therapy. We have found that dramatic therapy is one of the best forms of therapeutic work for epileptoid personalities. However, it depends on the individual and other personality characteristics.

Manic-Depressive Profile

Bipolar patients are highly responsive to dramatic works and can easily assimilate psychotherapeutic material. However, in my opinion, dramas are sometimes insufficient for them to reach the core emotions underlying their personality profile. More rigid, abreactive cathartic methods are likely required, which can be applied in parallel with dramatic works. However, manic-depressive patients most often appear in a dramatic session during the manic phase when they accumulate a lot of energy. Sometimes they may join the group during the interphase. During the depressive phase, patients are usually unable to motivate themselves to attend therapy in general, and specifically the dramatic form of it.

7

Psychedelic Therapy

This vector of psychotherapy encompasses specific treatment methods for neurotic and psychotic patients, utilizing a combination of various verbal and somatic therapeutic modalities along with substances that alter the state of consciousness. Currently, psychedelic methods are very rarely employed in practice. The vast majority of substances used in these treatments are classified as narcotics and fall under Category A, which means they are considered substances that cannot be used in medical practice. However, some countries and certain symptoms make exceptions, allowing for the application of psychedelics. For example, in Austria, the legal use of LSD-25 for pain management in stage-four cancer patients is possible.

Nevertheless, this kind of attitude towards psychedelic treatment methods was not always present in the medical field. Therefore, in order to fully explore this topic, it is necessary to trace the history of the emergence and development of this psychotherapeutic vector.

LSD Therapy

It is best to start with the year 1938, when Austrian chemist Albert Hofmann, working at the Sandoz chemical-pharmaceutical laboratory in Basel, Switzerland, synthesized a significant number of different alkaloids from the parasitic fungus called ergot, which grows on wheat spikes. This plant was often used in folk medicine, and its decoction was administered to women in labor to stimulate contractions before childbirth. During his work, Hofmann tested the obtained alkaloids on laboratory mice, but the results only provided a conditional understanding of the substance's influence on them. In 1938, Hofmann did not find anything particularly interesting among the laboratory material obtained and set it aside in the archives. Five years later, he felt the desire to return to the research on ergot and conduct several tests. He selected one alkaloid that he considered most suitable for testing and began performing specific analyses.

Albert Hofmann

After some time, he began to feel unwell and decided to return home. He left the laboratory, got on his bicycle, and started his journey. As he rode, his condition became increasingly strange and unusual. Numerous sensory distortions started to appear in his consciousness. Hofmann couldn't comprehend what was happening to him but began to suspect that he might have accidentally ingested the alkaloid he had been working with. He remembered that he may have rubbed his eye with his hand while wearing rubber gloves during his work with the extracted alkaloid. There was a high probability that a particle of the substance remained on the glove and later came into contact with his eye's mucous membrane. Hofmann eventually made it home. The sensory distortions he experienced were accompanied by various delusional states. In his book "LSD: My Difficult Child," Hofmann writes that he started having delusional ideas, such as that his neighbor was a witch who wanted to enchant him. He also describes his state in detail: "Upon arriving home, I lay down and entered into a not unpleasant, intoxicated-like condition characterized by an extremely stimulated imagination. With my eyes closed, fantastic images of extraordinary plasticity and vividness surged toward me, accompanied by an intense kaleidoscopic play of colors. This condition gradually passed after two hours while I remained stunned."

After some time, the symptoms almost disappeared. The next day, he returned to his laboratory to test the substance on himself again, in order to fully convince himself that yesterday's state was indeed caused by it. He chose the minimal dosage he believed to be suitable—250 micrograms (later it was discovered that this dosage was more average than minimal; LSD-25 can have an effect on a person even at a dosage of 25 micrograms)—and ingested it. As he had anticipated, his state from the previous day recurred.

Hofmann identified the substance he obtained as LSD-25 (diethylamide tartrate of d-lysergic acid). This substance is semi-synthetic and does not exist in its pure form in nature. Hofmann, Stoll, and Troxler describe the formula of LSD as follows:

After Hofmann conducted further experiments on himself with the substance he found, he decided to share his discovery with psychiatrists who, in his opinion, could derive some benefit from patient treatment.

Hofmann contacted the son of his supervisor, Walter Stoll, who was a psychiatrist at a psychiatric clinic in Zurich, and handed over his findings. Stoll concluded that LSD-25 could be promising for further research and conducted the first study involving both healthy volunteers and mentally ill patients. Stoll published the findings of his research in 1947, which caused a sensation in the scientific community and sparked a wave of new

LSD-25 studies in various countries around the world.

The majority of LSD-25 research was related to the "model psychosis approach." The fact that even microscopic doses of 25 mcg of LSD-25 could already slightly alter a person's state prompted the emergence of the biochemical theory of schizophrenia and other psychotic disorders of personality, as well as behavioral and thought disorders. Various hypotheses were formed, suggesting that the onset of the schizophrenic process could be attributed to different endogenously synthesized substances or even specific metabolic cycles. One of the most notable hypotheses was the serotonin hypothesis, proposed by Woolley and Shaw. The key aspect of their hypothesis was the assumption that the profound influence of LSD-25 on human consciousness occurred due to its interference with the functioning of serotonin receptors in the human brain.

Another area in which LSD-25 found application was self-administration experiments by psychiatrists, psychotherapists, psychologists, and students in these fields. At that time, it was believed that LSD-25 could provide a kind of excursion into the world of a schizophrenic, which could become much more understandable after experiencing it firsthand.

One of the first clinical experimenters with LSD-25 on himself was the Czech physician and psychiatrist Stanislav Grof, who would later have a significant impact on the development of this method of psychotherapy and its dissemination worldwide. Grof writes that he underwent his first LSD-25 session in a clinical setting in 1956. He also comments that he was part of an interdisciplinary team that investigated various consciousness-altering substances in a clinical context. This team was led by Dr. Milos Voitechovsky, who introduced him to the fundamental ideas and methods of working with consciousness-altering substances that existed in psychiatry at that time.

Stanislav Grof

Various attempts were made to classify the category of substances to which LSD-25 belonged. The following names were proposed:

- **Hallucinogens:** substances that *induce hallucinations.*
- **Psychomimetics:** substances that *simulate psychosis.*
- **Psychodisleptics:** substances that *disrupt the soul.*
- **Psychedelics:** substances that *open the soul.* The term was coined by Humphry Osmond. This particular term gained the most popularity and, according to many experts, most fully reflects the essence of the substance's impact on human consciousness.

In 1949, just two years after Stoll's publication on the initial clinical trials of LSD-25, Crowley suggested using the compound as a full-fledged psychotherapeutic agent. In the following years, numerous independent researchers, apart from Crowley, began employing LSD-25 as an adjunct to their psychotherapeutic work. As a result, notions were formed regarding how this compound should be administered, in what quantities, and under what conditions.

After the discovery of LSD-25, the overwhelming majority of research focused on exploring the "model psychosis" hypothesis and its influence on the minds of both healthy individuals and patients with various mental disorders. It aimed to observe how patients with different psychiatric conditions reacted to the compound. Stanislav Grof writes that the pioneers and trailblazers of this research were Frederick in West Germany, Sandison, Spencer, and Whitelaw in England, and Bush, Johnson, and Abramson in the United States.

During the course of working with the compound, many researchers discovered that its use yielded highly successful and inspiring results with patients suffering from the following symptoms:

- Narcotic addiction
- Alcoholism
- Sexual deviations
- Depressive personality disorders
- Sociopathy and criminal psychopathy
- Various personality disorders

In the early 1960s, it was also found that LSD-25 could have an impact on cancer patients. For patients with this symptom, 1-2 sessions of LSD-25 could significantly alleviate their emotional suffering and provide long-lasting relief from physical pain. Even cancer patients who had no religious affiliations and were atheists could discover a new, profound understanding of death and what might await beyond. Thus, in this case, we can observe how engagement with transpersonal experiences through the use of LSD-25 was capable of transforming the personality of the patient. In some of his books, particularly "The Ultimate Journey," Grof provides several examples of his work with terminally ill cancer patients and the full spectrum of changes they experienced throughout this practice.

The development of LSD-25 therapy was centered in Europe and North America. European psychotherapists established the European Medical Society for Psycholytic Therapy. This society began formulating general guidelines for conducting LSD sessions and developing training standards to prepare psychotherapists to work with LSD. In North America, specifically in Canada, the Association for Psychedelic Therapy was established, with its theoretical framework and application methodology potentially differing significantly from those of their European colleagues.

Stanislav Grof writes that numerous international conferences were held to discuss the peculiarities and specificities of applying LSD-25 in clinical settings. He also provides a list of cities and dates where these conferences took place:

- Princeton in 1959
- Göttingen in 1960
- London in 1961
- Amityville in 1965
- Amsterdam in 1967
- Bad Nauheim in 1968

The 1968 ban on the use of LSD-25 put an end to any further research in this direction and almost any form of clinical application.

Some researchers have suggested that the effect of LSD-25 on emotional and physiological processes in the human body can be compared to the effects of electroconvulsive therapy, insulin shock, or electroshock therapy.

A phenomenon of LSD-25's impact on depressed patients was discovered, wherein they could experience a significant number of euphoric states during the course of their interactions with the compound. Studying this phenomenon, Kondrou proposed the deliberate use of LSD-25 for the treatment of depressed patients, initially employing an approach reminiscent of the old methods of opium treatment. In other words, he administered small doses of LSD-25 to his patients, gradually increasing the dosage each day in anticipation of a psychotherapeutic effect. However, clinical trials with this approach proved unsuccessful. LSD-25 did not exert a direct pharmacological influence on depression.

Subsequently, it was found that the influence of LSD-25 could only manifest itself through proper psychotherapeutic work by the therapist and the patient. It was the targeted work of the psychotherapist that laid the foundation for qualitative changes in the patient's personality.

The pharmacological vector of using LSD-25 was abandoned, and the therapists who explored this topic focused on determining the specific psychotherapeutic work that needed to be carried out during the administration of LSD-25 to facilitate substantial changes in the patient's condition.

Researchers have found that LSD-25 often induces strong age regression in patients, leading them to experience cathartic feelings and release emotions that were previously suppressed. Sometimes, patients would have states interpreted as memories of past incarnations, and such reports were quite common when working with high doses of LSD-25.

The theoretical foundations for describing the findings made by therapists studying their patients' states were largely borrowed from the concepts of Freud and his disciples. These theories postulate that emotional suppression contributes to the development of muscular tension, which conceals unexpressed affective energy. This energy, when not manifested at the appropriate time and place, constantly seeks various ways of release, often manifesting through various psychological, physical, or social symptoms. Once the emotional energy behind the muscular tension is realized, the symptoms arising from the tension should disappear or significantly diminish.

Stanislav Grof describes in his book "LSD Psychotherapy" that at the time of its writing (1979), most therapists agreed that the outcome of a psychotherapeutic session using LSD-25 depended to a significant extent on several non-pharmacological factors, such as the therapist's personality, the setting, musical accompaniment, the conversation between the therapist and the patient, and so on. The compound itself allows for the amplification and manifestation of the processes that already occur in the patient's conscious and unconscious mind.

Grof also writes that LSD-25 qualitatively differs from other drugs in its ability to enhance and expedite the psychotherapeutic process. It is similar in efficacy to several other substances, such as psilocybin, psilocin, mescaline, ibogaine, MDMA, DPT, and some others, which have occasionally been used in clinical practice.

In the context of LSD-25 application in the clinical field, a large variety of therapeutic styles emerged, each differing in their approaches regarding dosage administration, frequency, setting, and manipulations performed on the patient to optimize the quality of work. Here is a list of these styles and their respective creators:

- Psycholysis — Ronald A. Sandison;
- Psychedelic Therapy — Humphry Osmond;
- Symbolysis — Jan van Rhijn;
- Gebesynthesis — Harold Abramson;
- Lyserganalysis — Roberto Givernetti and Federico Gregoretti;
- Oneiroanalysis — Jean Delay;
- LSD Analysis (Anaclitic Therapy) — Joyce Martin and Pauline McCririck;
- Transintegrative Therapy — Duncan MacLean;
- Hypnodelic Therapy — Sidney Cohen and Arnold Ludwig;
- Psychosynthesis — Salvador Roquet.

Unfortunately, the majority of materials on the works of these authors are not freely accessible and are challenging to find. Through descriptions of the theoretical aspects and practices of some of them, we can gain an understanding of how these variations of LSD implementation took place in a clinical context.

There were forms of LSD-25 administration where the patient received microdoses ranging from 25 to 50 mcg. During the session, the patient maintained verbal contact with the psychotherapist and freely associated. In this case, the compound was used as an amplifier of the regular psychodynamic process. The primary focus of exploration was the patient's personal, more or less conscious experience. Such dosages often did not lead to experiences of a perinatal or transpersonal nature.

According to Grof, this approach to working with LSD-25 can be combined not only with analytical therapy but also with Jungian analysis, bioenergetic analysis by Alexander Lowen, various neo-Reichian practices, gestalt therapy by Frederick Perls, and others.

Therapists also experimented with applying such low doses of LSD-25 in group psychotherapy. In these groups, all participants, except the therapist, would be under the influence of a small dose of LSD-25. The motivation behind creating such groups was the assumption that accelerating individual personal dynamics with LSD-25 could also accelerate group dynamics. However, as Grof describes, the therapeutic outcomes in such groups were not very favorable. Participants could function adequately in the group only when given microdoses of the substance. Once therapists attempted to increase the dosage, patients would disconnect from the group dynamics and retreat into their own experiences, causing the group to become disorganized.

After some time, this form of LSD-25-assisted psychotherapy was abandoned due to its insufficient effectiveness.

Psycholytic Therapy

Psycholytic therapy, developed by Ronald A. Sandison, involved the use of LSD-25 in doses ranging from 75 to 300 mcg during patient sessions. The term "lytic" in the method's name derives from the Greek word "lysis," meaning "dissolution." The author believed that the goal of therapy was to alleviate tension and resolve conflicts present in the patient's psyche.

LSD-25 sessions were typically conducted once every one to two weeks. The number of sessions varied significantly based on the quality and intensity of symptoms, averaging between 15 and 100 sessions. Psychotherapists practicing psycholytic therapy often shared Freud's views on conscious and unconscious processes, classifying any experience that could be characterized as transpersonal as an attempt to escape the exploration of significant analytical material or as a manifestation of schizophrenic tendencies.

Grof comments that some therapists attempted to analyze the transpersonal experiences of patients and work with them, contrary to psychoanalytic notions.

Grof lists various representatives of this approach to LSD-25 application. In addition to Sandison, they included Spencer, Whitlow, Bakman, Ling, and Blair from England; Andersen-Heyn and Van Rijn from the Netherlands; Johnson from Norway; Hasner, Tauterman, Ditrich, and Sobotkiewiczova from Czechoslovakia.

Many specialists claimed that the main drawback of psycholytic therapy was its excessive duration. Although one well-known practitioner of psycholytic therapy in Europe, H. Leuner, believed that this form of therapy could reduce the duration of the typical psychoanalytic process by at least threefold. It is worth mentioning that Hanscarl Leuner is now famous in the field of psychotherapy for his method of symbol drama, which, naturally, is largely based on his theoretical and practical experiences during the practice of psycholytic therapy. Unfortunately, this fact is not mentioned in any books on symbol drama.

If we compare the effectiveness of psycholytic and psychedelic therapy, Grof writes that no comparative studies have been conducted on this matter. Therefore, on this topic, so only hypotheses can be suggested in this area.

Psychedelic Therapy

In contrast to their European counterparts, psychotherapists from North America developed a different approach to the theoretical and practical application of LSD-25 in clinical settings. This approach became known as psychedelic therapy and subsequently became synonymous with working with consciousness-altering substances in clinical conditions. This method was developed based on psychotherapists' observations of patients' experiences, which had a distinct mystical, spiritual, and religious dimension. The creators of this method, Hoffer and Osmond, developed a treatment program for alcoholics using LSD-25 in Saskatchewan, Canada, in the early 1950s. The method drew inspiration from the hypotheses of Ditman and Weitlisi from the United States, suggesting that the effects of LSD on human consciousness and the body bear some resemblance to the state experienced during delirium tremens.

Hoffer and Osmond observed alcoholics who stopped drinking after experiencing delirium tremens. Their initial intention was to simulate a delirium tremens-like experience in the consciousness of alcoholics using high doses of LSD to achieve a therapeutic effect. The results of their tests were quite promising, but it seems that the key transformative element of the intervention was not the simulated delirium tremens experience, but the profound transpersonal experiences that patients encountered during psychedelic sessions. This experiment laid the foundation for the theory and practice of psychedelic psychotherapy, which would later be actively developed and applied to patients suffering from various mental and behavioral disorders.

As the method itself evolved, its key postulates and goals were formulated. The main goal became the dissolution of the ego during peak transpersonal experiences, in which the boundary between the individual and the perceived world fades away. There is a sense of connection and unity with the world and all living beings.

Grof comments that these experiences can be accompanied by visions of the brightest white or golden light, various rainbow colors, intricate patterns, and more. Experiences with various archetypal figures related to specific mythological and religious traditions may arise. Grof also recounts that during his psychotherapeutic practice, he repeatedly observed phenomena where patients, despite not being religious at all, could, under the influence of high doses of LSD-25, have intense mythical and religious experiences.

The dosage of LSD-25 used in psychedelic therapy is significantly higher, ranging from 300 to 1500 mcg. Another notable distinction in psychedelic therapy is the increased attention given to selecting the environment in which the psychedelic session takes place. Preferred settings include spaces that encompass the following elements:

- Beautiful furniture
- Flowers

- Paintings
- Captivating photographs
- Sculptures
- Various natural elements
- Fresh and dried fruits and vegetables
- Various natural incenses

The most optimal locations for conducting sessions are buildings situated near:

- Ocean
- Mountain ranges
- Forests
- Lakes
- Other places that exude the aesthetics of nature

Sound design holds great importance. The space should have a powerful stereo system, and prearranged playlists with carefully selected music should be prepared in advance.

During psychedelic sessions, the following types of music are most commonly used:

- Classical music
- Ethnic music
- New Age music
- Ambient music
- Trance music

Preference is given to musical tracks that either have no lyrics or contain foreign language lyrics for patients undergoing psychotherapy. Verbal communication is entirely halted during the psychedelic work. If the need for communication arises, nonverbal forms of interaction are encouraged.

Grof reports that psychedelic therapy has never been popular in Europe and has been embraced by only a few European colleagues. He also lists notable practitioners of psychedelic therapy in Canada, including Hoffer, Osmond, Hubbard, Smith, Chwelos, Blewett, MacLean, and MacDonald. In the United States, practitioners such as Sherwood, Harman, Stolaroff, Fadiman, Mogar, Allen, Leary, Alpert, Metzner, Ditman, Hayman, and Whitless are mentioned.

Psychedelic therapy has shown its greatest effectiveness in working with:

- Alcoholics
- Drug addicts
- Patients suffering from depression
- Cancer patients

To achieve the full effect, the treatment of symptoms related to psychoneuroses and psychosomatic disorders during a psychedelic session should be accompanied by comprehensive verbal processing.

A significant challenge of psychedelic therapy is the absence of a guarantee that individuals who undergo this form of therapy will have a profound transformative experience. Grof mentions that the effectiveness rate fluctuates between 25% and 78%. He further reports that the highest percentage of transformative experiences was observed in drug addicts, followed by mental health professionals, alcoholics, and cancer patients, while neurotic patients had the lowest level of transformative experiences.

LSD Analysis (Anaclitic Therapy)

This particular application of LSD in patient treatment was developed by two female psychoanalysts from London, Joyce Martin and Pauline McCririck. The term "anaclitic" (anaklinein) translates from Greek as "to lean on something." In the context of psychotherapy, the term refers to the early childhood strivings oriented toward the maternal figure.

The authors of the method primarily used a combination of ideas from LSD therapy sessions at the psycholytic school and supplemented them with their own interesting findings. In contrast to many other psychoanalytically oriented psychotherapists who believe that manifestations of physical contact with the patient can worsen the quality of psychotherapy, Martin and McCririck used excessively close contact with the patient to help satisfy various unmet needs that may have been formed during the early stages of infancy and personal development.

The authors of the method created a new template for the interaction between the psychotherapist and the patient, in which they would be in close proximity throughout most of the LSD session, leaning against each other and separated only by a blanket. The psychotherapist and the patient could embrace each other. Through such "contact," patients often experienced strong age regression, even to an infantile state. When the therapist noticed that the patient had already regressed, they would take a prepared bottle of milk and feed the patient from it, simulating the process of breastfeeding.

The dosage of LSD-25 in anaclitic sessions was relatively small, typically ranging from 100 to 200 mcg. This dose was often sufficient to induce the desired age regression, bringing the individual closer to an infantile state, but not enough to fully reveal the contents of the archetypal part of the person's unconscious. However, it should be noted that the depth of the experience can significantly vary from patient to patient.

Patients who underwent this therapy described their subsequent impressions. For example, they experienced a sense of symbiotic merging with the maternal image. They felt like infants during the lactation process, receiving nourishment from the mother's milk. They experienced identification with the oceanic feeling of unity with the womb. Occasionally, they could engage in experiences with archetypal overtones, where the patient observed representations of mother nature and the image of the Virgin Mary in various cultures.

Martin and McCririck commented that they were able to achieve good results in a relatively short period of time while working with patients with severe neuroses and borderline mental disorders. The authors presented their method at various scientific conferences and even produced a documentary film about it. Colleagues reacted to Martin and McCririck's practice in very different ways, with some expressing admiration and others expressing disapproval. However, the reactions were often emotionally intense.

This form of LSD therapy did not have widespread development and appears to have been practiced solely by its creators. Stanislav Grof mentions his experience undergoing anaclitic therapy with Martin and McCririck and speaks of it in the highest regard, considering it a unique experience.

It is worth commenting on this technique and stating that, in my opinion, this approach can yield excellent results in cases of deep rapport between the therapist and the patient and compatibility of their personalities. Unfortunately, this is not accessible to every patient. It is also important to consider the numerous potential pitfalls that may arise during this type of work. This is particularly relevant when it comes to the potential for the therapeutic process to become sexualized if the therapist and patient are of different genders.

Hypnodelic Therapy

This form of LSD-25 therapy in clinical settings was developed by Levin and Ludwig, combining the administration of LSD-25 with the use of hypnotic suggestion. The name was coined by combining the words "hypnosis" and "psychedelic." During the initial session, the patient's personal history, including significant symptom manifestations, is typically collected and discussed. The therapist also attempted to hypnotize the patient to assess their hypnotizability and the specific behaviors exhibited under hypnosis. Hypnosis was often induced in the old European style using the Lafontaine-Braid technique, where the patient's attention was focused on a shiny object held above their head. If the first session went well, with the therapist gathering sufficient information about the patient and the patient demonstrating adequate hypnotizability, they would reconvene after 10 days to initiate full hypnodelic therapy. Levin and Ludwig typically administered 125–200 mcg of LSD-25 for client work.

Initially, the patient was given a dose of LSD-25, and almost immediately, they were induced into a hypnotic trance to align the effects of LSD and the hypnotic trance temporally. Because the effects of hypnosis do not contradict and often coincide with the effects of LSD, the transition was usually experienced by patients as relatively gentle.

Levin and Ludwig primarily used hypnodelic therapy with alcoholics and drug addicts. According to their observations, combining hypnotic and psychedelic techniques yielded more noticeable results compared to using these forms of psychotherapeutic work separately.

It is also important to comment on the studies by Vogel and Hoffer. In their work, they reported being able to suspend the effects of LSD and induce LSD-like states in patients using hypnosis on days when they did not take LSD.

Group LSD Therapy

This form of LSD therapy is based on therapists' attempts to develop a methodology for working with a group of different patients who take moderate to high doses of LSD-25. There is minimal coordinated interaction between the therapist and patients in this style of therapy. Most often, each participant goes through their own experience independently, although they can interact with each other if necessary. The motivation behind this method was largely rooted in saving therapists' time. During the sessions, participants typically lie down and listen to music as part of the psychotherapeutic process. Different therapists may vary the rules of group interaction.

Salvador Roquet's Psychosynthesis

One variation of collaborative group LSD therapy was Salvador Roquet's psychosynthesis, although Roquet used not only LSD-25 but also various other psychedelics, more commonly of plant origin, in his work. Roquet was unique in combining his psychiatric and psychoanalytic expertise with his deep knowledge of healing practices among indigenous people who had used peyote cactus, hallucinogenic mushrooms, and other substances for ritual shamanic purposes for many centuries or even millennia.

Roquet often assembled groups of 10–28 individuals. The patients selected for these groups came from diverse backgrounds. They could have different symptoms, be at different stages of treatment, and be of different genders and ages. Such a mix was created to facilitate a more comprehensive group analysis process. The more diverse the participants in the group, the greater the likelihood that each member would be able to project the contents of their unconscious and engage in constructive interaction with it. Roquet's patients were often outpatients under his care, and they underwent 10–20 sessions of this type of psychotherapy.

It is also important to note that Roquet's psychosynthesis has no relation to the similarly named psychotherapy developed by Roberto Assagioli in Italy.

Patients Raised in Families With Religious Fanaticism

Therapists have made a number of interesting observations. It turns out that patients who were raised in families with a lot of religious fanaticism and narrow-mindedness exhibited numerous anti-religious tendencies during LSD sessions.

During the therapeutic process itself, the internal processes in patients begin to intensely project onto the therapists and medical staff. In the eyes of the patient, they may be perceived as criminals, murderers, sadists, perverts, or demonic entities. Conversely, there can also be a tendency where the projections involve the patient's "superego" rather than the "id." In such cases, people in the patient's surroundings may become police officers, judges, prison wardens, or executioners. At times, the entire process of psychotherapy may be perceived as a scene of sexual orgies, a brothel, a harem, a concentration camp, a courtroom, or a death row. Unfortunately, Stanislav Grof, when describing such projections by his patients, does not comment on the specific psychodynamic aspects of their personality that could explain the reasons for the formation of these particular sensory and semantic distortions.

Grof explains that, similar to Freud's perception of dreams as the via regia (royal road) to the unconscious, working with LSD can be interpreted in the same way.

Levels of Personal Experience During LSD Sessions

During an LSD session, the depth of experience can vary greatly depending on factors such as dosage, the severity of personality disorders, the activity of defense mechanisms, the session setting, and the psychiatrist's personality. Grof identifies three main levels of experience:

1. **Psychodynamic Level**
2. **Perinatal Level**
3. **Transpersonal Level**

Psychodynamic Level

At the psychodynamic level, a person confronts deep representations of their childhood experiences. Various problematic situations can unfold and be experienced here. Different complexes can be worked through. For example, a patient may work through feelings associated with the Oedipus or Electra complex, such as fear of castration, envy of the penis, and so on. This level of experience is most often actualized at low doses of LSD. If the dose is too high, the patient may bypass such an experience and delve into the realms of perinatal or transpersonal levels.

Perinatal Level

Stanislav Grof identified four basic matrices of condensed experience that a person can undergo during LSD sessions. He refers to these matrices as basic perinatal matrices (BPM) and numbers them from one to four, according to the order of their emergence. Key experiences at this level involve birth, death, pain, agony, and more. Importantly, these experiences are often not metaphorical but directly felt as real processes. Various sensory and semantic representations of these processes can emerge, such as involvement in combat, being in concentration camps, witnessing accidents and decaying bodies, being in cemeteries, participating in mourning ceremonies, and so on. Significant somatizations can occur. The patient may feel suffocated and experience intense trembling, spasms, convulsions, and severe vomiting. Let's describe all four perinatal matrices that arise at this level of experience.

First Basic Perinatal Matrix

The first BPM encompasses the entire period of the infant's presence in the womb, from conception to the onset of labor contractions. This perinatal matrix is experienced as a vision of paradise, oceanic bliss, and cosmic ecstasy and can evoke real sensations of being in the womb. If there were significant stress factors during pregnancy, the picture may be altered. Representations of cosmic engulfment, a sense of poisoning, and minor spasms can arise.

Second Basic Perinatal Matrix

The second BPM begins with the onset of labor contractions and ends with the onset of the fetus's descent through the birth canal. This experience is directly associated with various adverse experiences that can be interpreted as war, torture, accidents, imprisonment, and physical violence of various kinds. The infant may feel surrounded by various monsters who want to harm them. More often than not, this is accompanied by a sense of helplessness and an inability to escape the problematic context. Scenes of being in hell, confinement in a cage, apocalyptic visions, feelings of inadequacy, inferiority, oppression, pressure, a sense of persecution, and the feeling that the torment will never end, along with ominous mystical omens, can occur.

Third Basic Perinatal Matrix

This perinatal matrix begins with the infant's entry into the birth canal and ends with their emergence from it. The experience within this perinatal matrix is interpreted as a fight, battle, assault, rape, sexual orgy, various combinations of aggression and sexuality, being in a nightclub or amusement park, and a literal reenactment of birth in women. Scenes of murder, bloody sacrifices, and the reliving of death and rebirth may occur. Spasms, convulsions, sweating, and chills can manifest.

Fourth Basic Perinatal Matrix

Stanislav Grof comments that this perinatal matrix begins with the infant's exit from the womb and extends for approximately the first five hours of life outside the womb. This perinatal matrix can be experienced and perceived as visions of vast spaces, spectra of beautiful colors, enhanced perception of everything, a desire to help and support others, and a decrease in pressure. Feelings of grandiosity and manic behavior, as well as sensations such as pain in the umbilicus, fear of death and castration, and severe shortness of breath, may occur.

Transpersonal Experiences

Grof believes that a distinguishing feature of this experience is its specific category, in which an individual transcends the boundaries of their ego and undergoes various encounters with other objects and phenomena. In most cases, individuals deal with experiences they have never had under ordinary conditions or that they rarely experience under special circumstances.

Experiences related to this category can be interpreted by patients as deep regression and exploration of the biological and spiritual past. According to Grof, embryonic prenatal memory can be activated, allowing individuals to re-experience their existence in the form of a sperm or an egg during the conception period. A deeper level of regression can involve transgenerational experiences, where individuals may be associated with the experiences of their family members and witness various fragments of their lives. Grof admits that sometimes these narratives could be verified for accuracy. At times, what a child saw accurately reflected the experiences of their ancestors, even if the ancestors themselves never shared such situations with anyone.

Regression can go even deeper, in which case patients may access their ethnic or collective unconscious. Consciousness can also undergo identification with animal and plant archetypes, as well as various natural phenomena. Additionally, there can be intriguing associated reenactments of organs and cells within one's own body. Many patients are capable of voicing memories from past incarnations. Stanislav Grof provides numerous descriptions of such experiences in his books.

Main Stages of LSD Psychotherapy

According to Grof, the absence of strict time constraints is ideal for LSD therapy. The number of sessions with different patients can vary greatly. Stanislav Grof describes three main stages of LSD psychotherapy:

1. **Preparation stage**
2. **Psychedelic sessions**
3. **Integration of the experiences**

Preparation Stage

This stage involves a specific period of working with the therapist without the use of LSD-25. During this stage, symptoms are discussed and explored using various verbal techniques of psychotherapy. Depending on the therapist's professional orientation, the content of the exploration can vary significantly.

The number of sessions in this stage can range from 5 to 20 hours, depending on the depth and intensity of the issue. A crucial factor is the establishment of a deep rapport and trust between the therapist and the patient, as this can influence the course of the entire therapeutic series. When possible, the patient's personal experiences are analyzed, and key psychotraumatic situations that they have encountered in different periods of their lives are identified. Information about the patient's time in the womb and the process of their birth may also be analyzed if the patient has such information.

Hypnoanalysis can be used to explore important unconscious information if necessary. However, if the LSD session is conducted for self-exploration, seeking inspiration, or professional training purposes, this stage can be significantly shortened and include only a few hours of therapeutic conversation.

Psychedelic Sessions

Grof asserts that ideally, psychedelic sessions should take place in a specially designed therapeutic unit or apartment, preferably on the ground floor. The location should be equipped with a small kitchen and easily accessible bathroom facilities. If the session space is part of a larger working center, good sound insulation is necessary. It is highly beneficial to have direct access to nature, such as a forest or ocean. According to Grof, it is best to start the session in the morning. If it starts later, for example, after lunch, the altered states associated with therapeutic work may continue until late in the evening, causing difficulties with sleep.

Some other psychotherapists, like Mexican psychiatrist Rokuet, the creator of psychosynthesis, followed a slightly different regimen for psychedelic work. Following shamanic traditions of working with psychedelic substances, consumption often began late at night. We cannot provide significant data on the differences in effectiveness between one time period and another.

Grof comments that fasting for one to two days before taking the substance can have several advantages, including reducing the likelihood of vomiting during the session, intensifying and enriching the experiences, and decreasing the chances of negative experiences. If the session is conducted without prior fasting, a light dinner the night before and only a liquid breakfast in the morning before the session is recommended. If the session takes place at a different time, it is better not to consume any food three to four hours before it.

Consuming heavy or large amounts of food can affect the depth and content of the session. This especially applies to the consumption of red meat (beef, pork), which, if taken before the session, may increase the likelihood of negative experiences.

The effects of the substance usually begin within 20 to 40 minutes. After that, the patient is advised to lie down with a blindfold on and remain in that state for the next four to five hours. The schedule may vary depending on the therapeutic school's beliefs and the therapist's personality. The patient wears headphones playing specially selected music. Therapist-sitters are present next to the patient throughout the session, usually one or two individuals. If it is two people, it is recommended to have a man and a woman to fully actualize paternal and maternal transferences. The sitter's goal is to assist the patient when necessary and maintain the most favorable framework for the therapeutic process. It is best to refrain from engaging in any conversations during the session, as it can adversely affect the depth of the experience. Excessive talkativeness from the patient during this period may indicate resistance to the therapeutic process. Communication is only maintained in cases of special need.

Integration of Experiences

After the session, it is recommended for the patient to get a good sleep. The patient can sleep as much as they want. Upon waking up, it is possible to listen to the melodies that played during the therapy session again, and it is preferable to engage in a lengthy conversation with the therapist to discuss various details of the experience. Patients may find various forms of creative self-expression beneficial. Drawing pictures, mandalas, clay sculpting, writing poetry, stories, engaging in dance improvisation, and more can be excellent options. Sometimes, it is through creative self-expression of the re-experienced material that significant emotions can be integrated.

Another technique that can be used for integration is the technique of lung hyper-ventilation. After the legal prohibition of using LSD-25 in clinical settings, this hyper-ventilation technique became the primary substitute for psychedelic work. Stanislav Grof, along with his wife and collaborator Christina Grof, named this form of work "holotropic breathwork."

Usually, hyper-ventilation is used after an LSD session if the patient experiences a blockage in responding to certain residual emotions. When the effects of LSD are waning, there may simply not be enough energy to release some emotionally suppressed products that were not addressed in other sections of the psychotherapy session. Typically, the patient is asked to lie down with their eyes closed, and the music is replayed through headphones or speakers. They are then instructed to breathe as quickly and deeply as possible. This type of breathing usually lasts for 30 to 60 minutes. Often, emotional reactions occur during the process of hyper-ventilation.

Group therapy can be a good choice for working through the experiences obtained during a session with the use of LSD-25.

Psychedelic Therapy with Cancer Patients

Stanislav Grof and his wife, Christina, initially assumed that their patients would be emotionally "normal" individuals. However, they later discovered that this was not the case. Grof writes that at times, the emotional issues of the patients were so severe that he began to suspect a close connection between these issues and oncology. During psychedelic sessions, it was found that cancer patients could have a strong psychological defense that significantly hindered the full unfolding of their experiences. Only by establishing a deep rapport between the psychotherapist and the patient can this situation be changed.

The general content of psychedelic sessions with cancer patients is largely similar to working with patients such as neurotic individuals, alcoholics, drug addicts, and so on. However, LSD sessions with cancer patients have their own specific characteristics, as they tend to be more preoccupied with their bodies.

During the initial stages of an LSD session, various patients may experience nausea, vomiting, tremors, heart problems, and breathing difficulties. In addition to these "common" symptoms, cancer patients may exhibit symptoms indicating a direct connection to the disease and reflecting various deviations that can occur in the patient's body. This can include severe nausea and vomiting in patients with stomach cancer, urinary and fecal incontinence in patients with tumors in the pelvic area, or metastases in the spinal cord.

Grof stated that, based on his observations, LSD sessions were perceived as much more exhausting for cancer patients compared to other categories of patients. They often experience a longer period of fatigue after the sessions.

Grof reports that some cancer patients were able to achieve a sense of self-awareness at the level of their body tissues and cells during an LSD session. Other patients attempted self-healing and the release of emotional blocks in the areas where tumors were growing. In this spontaneous approach to clearing emotional blocks, the foundations of Chinese medicine, which claims that diseases arise due to the blockage of Qi energy in specific areas of the human body, were evident.

Some patients attempted to rid themselves of emotional blockages on their own, while others admitted that they wanted to visualize what they believed to be healing colors. They used colors such as golden, blue, and green. Yet others employed various visualization techniques and attempted to influence the progression of the disease through their internal efforts.

Some participants expressed the desire to complete various unfinished tasks, let go of resentments, express gratitude to their loved ones for what they had done for them, and so on. They could also experience connections with deceased relatives during the session.

Perspectives on Psychedelic Psychotherapy

For over 40 years, starting in 1967, the psychedelic form of therapeutic work was prohibited in almost all countries worldwide. After LSD-25, attempts were made to find a legal substitute for it, but as soon as something similar emerged, the substance would eventually find its way to the streets and be used recreationally within the drug culture. Subsequently, it would be legally prohibited for clinical use.

For instance, a similar fate befell MDMA (3,4-methylenedioxy-N-methylamphetamine) in the mid-80s, which some therapists adapted for working with excessive emotional problems. Although this substance, in combination with therapy, could have an astonishingly positive impact on the psyche, it also had some issues. In particular, it created a regular euphoric backdrop, which led MDMA to become one of the most prevalent club drugs and continues to be so to this day.

Unfortunately, it is true that uncontrolled street use of substances like LSD-25, MDMA, psilocybin, and DMT has led to the prohibition of their clinical application. However, recently (as of 2012), the attitude towards psychedelic therapy in the scientific and clinical communities has gradually started to change. Some American and European psychotherapists have occasionally made attempts to reintegrate the use of these substances into clinical practice.

Additionally, the laws in the United States have been gradually becoming more accommodating toward research involving psychedelic substances. For example, in 2012, during a seminar in Moscow, Stanislav Grof revealed that at that time, students at seven universities in the United States were able to participate in legal research with the use of LSD-25.

Ketamine Therapy by Evgeny Krupitsky

In the Soviet Union and later in Russia, a prominent advocate of psychedelic therapy was Evgeny Mikhailovich Krupitsky (born in 1959), the chief narcologist of the Leningrad region, a psychiatrist, and a doctor of medical sciences. He served as the head of the laboratory of clinical pharmacology of addictive states at the A.V. Valdman Institute of Pharmacology, part of the I.P. Pavlov St. Petersburg State Medical University.

Evgeny Krupitsky

Krupitsky was a member of various international societies, such as the American Society of Addiction Medicine, the International Society of Addiction Medicine, the Research Society on Alcoholism, and more.

The primary focus of Krupitsky's scientific interests was the development and implementation of new therapeutic agents for addictive pathology and the study of the pathogenesis of addiction to psychoactive substances. Krupitsky asserted that significant scientific discoveries were made during the study of psychedelic therapy in the 1950s and 1970s that can be effectively applied in modern clinical practice. He believed that the state of catharsis achieved by patients in the context of psychedelic therapy contributes to positive personality changes and can lead to personal growth and the transformation of one's views on oneself and the surrounding world.

Krupitsky initiated his clinical research on psychedelic work in 1984–1985, using ketamine as the primary medication. Ketamine, commonly used as an anesthetic for anesthesia induction, was employed in exploring the effects of ketamine-assisted psychedelic therapy (KPT) on patients suffering from alcoholism. In the process, he demonstrated that profound psycho-spiritual experiences that could arise in patients during the use of ketamine have the potential to create profound personal transformations. To objectively assess changes in the psycho-spiritual states of his patients, he developed and validated a scale for evaluating changes in the level of spiritual development. This scale was based on the self-assessment scale of spirituality by C. Whitfield, designed to capture changes in the spiritual development of members of Alcoholics Anonymous groups, and the "Life Values Changes Questionnaire" by K. Ring, created to assess changes in values and meanings experienced by patients who underwent clinical death.

During his research, Krupitsky observed three groups of people. The first group consisted of 25 alcoholics after ketamine-assisted psychedelic therapy (KPT), the second group included 21 alcoholic patients who underwent autogenic training, and the third group comprised 35 healthy volunteers who completed a four-month meditation course. Conducting the study, Krupitsky found that alcoholics experienced a significant increase in their level of spiritual development during KPT. Similar changes were observed in the healthy participants who underwent meditation training.

In contrast, patients undergoing autogenic training demonstrated significantly fewer positive changes. Krupitsky discovered that KPT transformed the life goals and beliefs of the patients, effectively influencing their life choices and predisposing them towards a more sober lifestyle. Even in small doses, ketamine enabled patients to access their transpersonal aspects of personality and engage in mystical experiences. Apart from treating alcohol dependence, Krupitsky also examined the impact of ketamine-assisted psychedelic therapy on heroin addicts. However, due to stricter regulations regarding the use of ketamine in the medical field, Krupitsky's research on KPT was discontinued.

Ketamine Psychotherapy (KPT) Method

Ketamine-assisted psychedelic therapy consists of several main stages. Let's list them.

Preparatory Stage

During 1-3 sessions of verbal psychotherapy, patient preparation takes place. The mechanism of undergoing KPT is explained. The patient's expectations, anticipations, and fears are discussed. The psychotherapist informs the patient that they will be able to see, hear, and feel during the psychedelic experience. It is explained that ketamine will actualize repressed and suppressed content in the patient's unconscious. It is also cautioned that the patient may symbolically comprehend the causes of alcohol dependence under the psychedelic substance's influence. This can lead to various insights that can significantly change the patient's life. This stage proceeds as a friendly dialogue between the physician and the patient, creating an atmosphere of trust. The conversation should not adopt an authoritarian or mentor-like tone.

Psychedelic Session

During this stage, the patient is administered intramuscularly with ethimizole (3 ml / 0.10 ounces of a 1.5% solution) to enhance the quality of imprints in long-term memory. Then, a ketamine-containing anesthetic is administered intramuscularly in subanesthetic doses (2–3 mg / 0.07 - 0.10 ounces per kilogram / 2.2 pounds of body weight), followed by intravenous administration of bemegride (5–10 ml / 0.17 - 0.34 ounces of a 0.5% solution). Bemegride is used to potentiate emotional experiences and visions. Ethimizole and bemegride also enhance the functional activity of the cerebral hemispheres, significantly improving the quality of the psychedelic session.

Then a musical background is created, which can effectively enhance emotional experiences. Partial verbal contact may be maintained between the physician and the patient during the session.

The psychotherapist also exerts a specific influence on the patient based on the information obtained during the conversation. The conversation aims to establish a mindset of sobriety and psychological non-acceptance of alcoholism, as well as address specific life tasks that may be relevant to the patient's life. During the patient's profound hallucinatory experiences, the physician may induce the sensation of the smell of alcohol to emotionally and sensorially negate the experience and elicit a negative reaction towards it. The KPT session is always conducted by two physicians—a psychotherapist and an anesthesiologist—in the conditions of an intensive care unit. These conditions are necessary to ensure patient safety, as ketamine administration may lead to complications such as increased blood pressure, respiratory depression, and others. The contraindications for KPT include:

- Endogenous mental disorders
- Epilepsy
- Hypertensive disease of grade II-III
- Ischemic heart disease

- Increased intracranial and intraocular pressure
- Severe renal dysfunction
- Pregnancy

Final Stage of KPT

At this stage, prolonged group therapy is conducted with 4-5 patients who have undergone the psychedelic work. During the interval between the second and third stages, which typically lasts 1-3 days, patients receive an assignment from the psychotherapist to describe in writing, in as much detail and clarity as possible, everything that happened to them during the psychedelic session.

At the same time, they are not supposed to share their experiences with anyone until the beginning of group psychotherapy. This is done to elevate the significance of the acquired experience. During the actual group therapy session, patients share their experiences, comment on various details, and discuss the symbolic content.

The psychotherapist assists patients in interpreting their psychedelic experiences, relating them to their current life situation in general and alcohol dependency in particular. The conversation reinforces the mindset of a sober lifestyle. The psychotherapist strives to help patients adopt a new attitude towards themselves and the surrounding world through the prism of the experience gained during psychotherapy.

Clinical Effectiveness of KPT in Alcohol Dependency Treatment

Krupitsky describes his research involving 111 men suffering from alcohol dependency. The KPT procedure itself was carried out at the completion of a three-month treatment course in a narcology clinic. All study participants were volunteers. The control group consisted of 100 individuals with alcoholism who received conventional treatment methods. The following data on the effectiveness of the KPT method was obtained over time. During a one-year follow-up period, remission was observed in 65.8% of patients who underwent KPT. In the control group, remission was observed in only 24% of patients.

Krupitsky highlights several key elements of the therapeutic potential of the KPT procedure. The first is the associative attachment of the smell of alcohol to the patient during negative experiences that may occur during the therapy session. Krupitsky comments that when alcohol was presented during KPT sessions, patients consistently exhibited grimaces of disgust. The re-experiencing of such aversion at a deep level was fixed in the patients' memory. In this case, we see that Krupitsky employed techniques from behavioral psychotherapy aimed at creating a negative emotional attachment to a stimulus related to the object of dependency.

The second important aspect of KPT is its suggestive potential. According to Krupitsky, during the work with ketamine, patients are highly susceptible to various suggestions that the therapist can create. Krupitsky also notes that the level of suggestibility during KPT is higher than in conventional hypnotherapy. Suggestibility likely increases due to the vivid imagery and intense emotional coloring of psychedelic experiences.

According to Krupitsky, the third aspect of therapy effectiveness is the use of subanesthetic doses of ketamine during the therapy session, which allows for the maintenance of two-way verbal contact between the psychotherapist and the patient. Krupitsky emphasizes that this promotes individualization and a more personalized approach to psychotherapeutic interventions.

Another important aspect is that ketamine enables patients to be more emotionally open and candid during the session, touching upon topics that are difficult to acknowledge in a normal state. This provides an opportunity to influence changes in the patient's values and beliefs, contributing to the formation of attitudes towards taking responsibility for their actions and their lives. Yet another significant factor is the existential orientation of the psychotherapy process, where one of the key elements of influence is the process of meaning-making. This process contributes to creating a foundation for change and transformation in the individual.

Krupitsky also emphasizes the importance of the patient's direct involvement in the psychotherapy process. This involvement primarily applies to the initial stage of therapy and its concluding stage, where patients participate in group psychotherapy.

KPT in the Treatment of Substance Dependence

Krupitsky reports that individual clinical studies indicate the potential applicability of KPT to patients with substance dependence. Similar to working with alcoholics, the method of using small doses of ketamine is presumed to be more effective. This allows for a dialogue with the patient during the therapy session, thereby creating a mindset of abstaining from drug use. Krupitsky warns that KPT should be conducted with caution when dealing with drug addicts to avoid triggering uncontrolled ketamine use. It is necessary to initiate transformative processes in the patient that can change their orientation towards a drug-free life.

Application of KPT for the Treatment of Neurotic Disorders

Krupitsky emphasizes that ketamine psychedelic therapy is not only conducted for patients with alcohol and substance dependence. Pilot studies have demonstrated the effectiveness of KPT in treating various neurotic disorders. The most effective outcomes of psychedelic therapy have been observed in the treatment of depressive personality disorders and PTSD (Post-Traumatic Stress Disorder). KPT has shown slightly lower effectiveness in working with patients with OCD (Obsessive-Compulsive Disorder) and phobic neurosis. The greatest resistance to KPT was observed among patients with hysterical neurosis.

Psilocybin Psychotherapy

Psilocybin and psilocin were synthesized in the 1950s by Albert Hofmann, who had previously discovered LSD. Psilocybin was frequently used in clinical studies as part of psychedelic therapy before it was placed under prohibition along with LSD. These substances naturally occur in various species of mushrooms, and the ritual use of such mushrooms in certain ethnic groups dates back thousands of years.

Among the most renowned scientists and mycologists dedicated to studying psilocybin mushrooms were Robert Gordon Wasson and his wife, Valentina. Another notable researcher of psilocybin mushrooms is mycologist Paul Stamets, who has made significant contributions to reintroducing the medical application of psilocybin through extensive scientific research.

Paul Stamets

Recent studies conducted at Johns Hopkins University have shown that psilocybin, found in mushrooms, can significantly reduce anxiety and depression in cancer patients. Moreover, this effect can persist for up to six months following a single high dose of psilocybin. The researchers emphasize that the findings should not be considered separately from the medical context. It is worth noting that psilocybin is still classified as an illegal narcotic substance in most U.S. states, and any claims about its positive effects can be perceived as drug propaganda. However, it is important to mention that an increasing number of states in the U.S. are starting to legalize the use of psilocybin in clinical research.

Robert and Valentina Wasson

The next experiment conducted by the Johns Hopkins Institute regarding the use of psilocybin involved 51 participants selected from a pool of 566 volunteers. Prior to the study, each participant underwent a comprehensive psychiatric evaluation. During the experiment, half of the participants received a moderate or high dose of psilocybin, while the other half received a placebo. Over a period of five weeks following the administration of psilocybin or placebo, the researchers observed various states experienced by the participants. Additionally, the participants underwent different forms of testing to assess manifestations of depressive states, attitudes towards quality of life, death, meaning, optimism, and other criteria.

After the completion of the study, the results indicated that the group receiving psilocybin experienced a significant reduction in depressed mood, anxiety, and fear of death, while demonstrating improved indicators of life satisfaction and optimism. In the longer term, approximately 80% of the participants who received psilocybin continued to show clinically significant reductions in depression and anxiety six months later. Furthermore, 83% of the patients reported increased satisfaction with their lives.

One of the researchers involved in this experiment, Roland Griffiths, highlights the astonishingly long-lasting effect of psilocybin, which can persist for several months. Griffiths comments that conventional psychotherapy for cancer patients, aimed at reducing anxiety and depression, often takes weeks or months and sometimes yields no positive results at all. The application of psilocybin to alleviate negative emotional states in cancer patients shows great potential, judging by the experimental data obtained.

MDMA-assisted Psychotherapy

MDMA is a semi-synthetic substance belonging to the amphetamine class and classified as a phenethylamine. It is also known as "ecstasy," "Adam," XTC, and others. MDMA was first synthesized by the German chemist Anton Köllisch in 1914 at the pharmaceutical company MERCK and patented. At that time, the synthesis of MDMA aimed to discover new substances that enhanced blood clotting. However, in the first half of the 20th century, MDMA remained unused in the pharmaceutical industry.

Only a few studies on humans involving MDMA and its derivative, MDA, were conducted in the 1950s and 1960s by order of the U.S. Army under the MK-Ultra program, which aimed to investigate consciousness manipulation using psychoactive substances. After one of the project participants died from an MDA overdose, the research was terminated, and MDMA was once again forgotten.

Its resurgence and widespread use came about thanks to the American chemist and researcher of psychoactive substances, Alexander Shulgin. Shulgin, following a recommendation from one of his students, Mary Clieman, successfully reproduced the complete synthesis of MDMA in his laboratory and began testing its effects first on himself and then on volunteers, gradually increasing the dosage step by step.

Alexander 'Sasha' Shulgin

Shulgin discovered that MDMA possesses a pronounced euphoric and relaxing effect, gently altering a person's state of consciousness and making empathy and sympathy more pronounced. Individuals were able to vividly recall various forgotten episodes of their lives and express emotions that had been hidden in the depths of their consciousness much more easily.

Shulgin and his wife began attempting the first trials of MDMA therapy with some acquaintances and achieved very positive results. Sometimes, in just one MDMA therapy session, they were able to address symptoms in clients who had been seeing psychotherapists for a long time, often without success.

For instance, Shulgin describes the case of a client who had suffered from severe panic attacks during flights for many years. Psychoanalysis and hypnoanalysis had not helped him. Key memories that triggered the panic attacks were blocked in his memory. During MDMA therapy, the client was able to regress to his childhood, specifically a moment when he was in school during a lesson. The ceiling collapsed in the classroom, and many children were injured. The client's father was the school principal. After this incident, his father often repeated to him, "We will never speak of this again. We forget about this incident." Thus, the father created a strong hypnotic amnesia in his son regarding the key traumatic experience, which later in adulthood manifested as a fairly serious neurotic symptom resistant to conventional forms of psychotherapy. During the MDMA session, the client was able to deeply engage in the emotional re-experiencing of the traumatic event and express suppressed emotions. According to Shulgin's comments, the client's panic attack symptoms disappeared after the session.

However, Shulgin and his wife were not practicing therapists and did not aim to create separate forms of psychotherapy. Therefore, in the late 1970s, Shulgin decided to introduce MDMA to his friend, psychotherapist Leo Zeff. By that time, Leo Zeff was planning to retire, but after experiencing the effects of MDMA on himself and his patients, he not only returned to full therapeutic practice but also traveled across America, conducting training seminars for other therapists on how to effectively apply MDMA in psychotherapeutic practice.

Leo Zeff gave the name "Adam" to MDMA, believing that this substance could restore a person to a state of innocence that precedes feelings of guilt and shame instilled in individuals during the process of socialization and personal growth. In the early 1980s, many American therapists began actively using MDMA in their therapeutic practices. However, due to the memory of the fate of LSD, which was completely prohibited in the 1960s, the use of MDMA was not extensively publicized in scientific publications and was not widely discussed in public. As a result, no comprehensive scientific studies on the application of MDMA were published, and no research on its specific effects on human consciousness was conducted.

Despite the careful use of MDMA by therapists, the substance extended beyond therapeutic applications. In the mid-1980s, MDMA became one of the most popular club drugs, leading to its eventual prohibition, similar to that of LSD.

In the early 1980s, when MDMA was still not prohibited in America, MDMA therapy showed particular effectiveness in working with patients suffering from post-traumatic stress disorder (PTSD) and depression. It was especially successful in working with Vietnam veterans.

In Los Angeles, at the University of California, full-scale studies on the safety of MDMA use in psychotherapeutic work were conducted from 1993 to 1995. Similar studies were subsequently carried out in Israel, the United States, Canada, and Switzerland. The main subjects of the research were individuals suffering from PTSD, war veterans, victims of sexual violence, and others. Over 130 patients participated in the studies. The research revealed that MDMA has long-term effectiveness in correcting the aforementioned symptoms. However, discussions regarding whether MDMA should be accepted as a full-fledged medication for psychotherapeutic work continue.

Subsequent comprehensive studies on MDMA followed. For example, in 2016, the FDA granted permission for the organization of a large-scale clinical trial of MDMA, which was supposed to involve the participation of 230 patients. The results obtained from this study showed that the use of MDMA in psychotherapy was more effective than placebo by a factor of two. As a result, in 2017, the FDA designated MDMA-assisted therapy as a "breakthrough treatment" for post-traumatic stress disorder (PTSD). Subsequent clinical trials of the method were initiated.

The trials demonstrated greater effectiveness of active doses of MDMA (75–125 mg) in working with PTSD compared to control dosages (30 mg). According to researchers, after the conducted trials, there is a high probability of submitting an application for the inclusion of MDMA in the lists of medical drugs through an expedited and streamlined procedure. The sooner this happens, the better, as PTSD itself is challenging to correct and often leads to suicide, while drugs that effectively heal this condition are not frequently synthesized. A comprehensive decision on the applicability of MDMA-assisted therapy will likely be made in 2021.

Thanks to the active stimulation of dopamine secretion in brain cells, MDMA has the potential to be used in the treatment of Parkinson's disease, specifically hand tremors that occur with this condition. In Parkinson's disease, dopamine levels significantly decrease in certain areas of the brain. Currently, MDMA-assisted therapy for this diagnosis is used unofficially.

In addition to the treatment of Parkinson's disease, oncologists have become interested in MDMA because it has been found that this substance can induce apoptosis in lymphoma cells, and MDMA derivative compounds have demonstrated good potential for chemotherapy in studies.

Ibogaine Psychotherapy

Ibogaine treatment can rightfully be classified as part of the psychedelic approach in psychotherapy, although this treatment method is not widely practiced. Ibogaine itself is an indole alkaloid found in the iboga shrub, which grows in Central and Western Africa, particularly in Gabon. The iboga plant and especially its roots have been used since ancient times and continue to be used in the existing pagan Bwiti cult for ritual purposes. The iboga consumption ritual in Gabon is a spiritually initiatory procedure and is widely practiced in the country. Bwiti shamans have long used iboga and its properties to heal various ailments. Ibogaine possesses strong hallucinogenic properties.

Initially, ibogaine was used in Europe as part of the Lambarène preparation and was used as a stimulant for central nervous system activity and muscle function. It was also used to alleviate fatigue and depression. The use of ibogaine had a place in the realm of sports doping; however, these substances did not gain widespread popularity due to ibogaine's ability to induce deep muscle relaxation after short-term stimulation.

The history of ibogaine's use as a tool in psychotherapy begins in 1962 with a man named Howard Lotsof, who suffered from severe heroin addiction. Lotsof took ibogaine to have a new psychedelic experience, but the 30-hour ibogaine trip yielded very interesting results. Lotsof discovered that after taking ibogaine, he completely lost the urge to use heroin. The desire for it was absent, and withdrawal symptoms were nonexistent, which greatly surprised him. Lotsof began administering ibogaine to various heroin addicts and consistently encountered similar results: a loss of the desire to use heroin and a lack of subsequent withdrawal symptoms. Lotsof attempted to create specific charitable foundations focused on rehabilitating drug addicts using ibogaine but did not find the desired social response and support. Later, Lotsof established the company NDA

International, which obtained all the necessary patents for treating drug addiction with ibogaine. The company began rehabilitating drug addicts using ibogaine.

However, by the late 1980s, ibogaine had been placed on the list of banned substances in the United States as Schedule I, causing the company's operations to move to the Netherlands. There, in collaboration with Dutch psychotherapist Jan Bastiaans, Lotsof conducted a successful experiment with thirty volunteer drug addicts. In 1993, the United States Food and Drug Administration (FDA) granted permission for clinical trials of ibogaine, but an unforeseen event occurred shortly after that disrupted the rehabilitation program.

Howard Lotsof

In the Netherlands, during the ibogaine treatment for drug addiction, one of the participants died. Subsequent investigation confirmed that her death was not due to negligence on the part of the leading rehabilitation project. Most likely, the cause of death was the participant's continued secret use of heroin during ibogaine rehabilitation. However, financial disagreements arose between the project organizers, followed by legal proceedings, leading to the closure of the project. Subsequently, ibogaine research ceased, and Lotsof's company went bankrupt.

Despite this, the ideas and practice of rehabilitation with ibogaine found their place in many private clinics, especially in third-world countries, where doctors specializing in addiction medicine began charging significant sums for ibogaine therapy. This therapy emerged in unlicensed clinics in Panama, Costa Rica, St. Kitts, Mexico, and Europe. Prices ranged from $4,000 to $10,000.

Currently, centers that have been working with ibogaine therapy for a long time have accumulated extensive experience in its application. However, fatal outcomes during therapy did not go smoothly. Over the past 15 years, 12 cases of death due to ibogaine ingestion have been officially registered, and there are serious grounds to suspect that there may be many more unreported cases. Subsequently, statistical data showed that the probability of death from ibogaine intake is 1 in 300.

Since 2007, deaths from this substance have ceased to be recorded. The potential cause of death may be the presence of cardiovascular diseases in patients undergoing therapy. It is worth noting that the ibogaine trip itself lasts for about 30 hours, which puts a significant strain on the heart. Additionally, it should be taken into account that some drug addicts may continue to use opioids during ibogaine treatment, which also ends tragically. The influence of other health-related factors that could not be fully documented and statistically studied should also be considered.

It is important to note that no serious and comprehensive studies on the impact of ibogaine on human body functioning have been conducted. Therefore, there could be numerous factors that contribute to fatal outcomes.

The format of ibogaine therapy bears many similarities to the basic format of psychedelic therapy, where the psychotherapist acts as a sitter in clinical conditions, assisting and providing support to the patient when necessary. Various techniques and practices related to different therapeutic traditions can be employed in the process. It is highly desirable for the therapist to understand the possible experiences and specific emotional states the patient may encounter and to know what actions can be taken in response to those experiences and crises. It should be noted that ibogaine administration can induce strong vomiting and other physiological reactions; thus, the sitter should possess resuscitation skills to provide qualified assistance if needed.

Prior to the clinical use of ibogaine, it is important for the patient to undergo at least minimal verbal psychotherapy in which the psychological issues to be addressed are discussed.

Patients should be informed that the use of ibogaine carries a relatively high risk of fatal outcomes.

Patients with severe mental disorders and cardiovascular diseases are not recommended to undergo ibogaine therapy.

In the process of clinical application, the following information regarding the dosing of ibogaine has been obtained. When using pure ibogaine hydrochloride, it should be administered at a dosage of 10 mg/kg for men and 9 mg/kg for women. In the case of heroin addicts undergoing ibogaine therapy, the dosage should be doubled, as opioids may partially block the effects of ibogaine. It is highly undesirable to consume any narcotics or alcohol at least 24 hours before the ibogaine session, as it may have unpredictable consequences.

At the beginning of the ibogaine intake, the effects of the substance typically start manifesting approximately 30 minutes after administration and gradually develop over a period of two hours. Various bodily, auditory, and visual representations can occur. Tinnitus, coordination difficulties, and heightened perception of sounds and colors may be experienced. Vomiting can occur around three hours after ibogaine intake.

The ibogaine therapy session itself lasts a very long time, sometimes spanning 20 to 30 hours, and in some cases, it may extend over several days. Meaningful communication with the patient during the session can be quite challenging. The patient can drink water, but the consumption of food is likely to be impossible, so it is best to refrain from it.

Two main phases of the ibogaine trip are distinguished: the oneirophrenic and the processive phases. During the oneirophrenic phase, the individual sees a multitude of flowing images and experiences with closed eyes. It can resemble watching vivid and colorful movies. These intense visions often directly relate to the patient's life memories, presented in a direct or symbolic form. This phase typically begins around 1 to 2 hours after the start of the session. The processive phase is a phase of processing and understanding the acquired experience, where cognitive processes and analysis become more active. The onset of this phase occurs approximately 3 to 6 hours after ibogaine intake and can last from 8 to 14 hours.

In many cases, a single ibogaine session is sufficient to induce constructive changes in consciousness and physiology. However, there may be a need to duplicate the ibogaine therapy session. In such cases, it is recommended to maintain a minimum of one month between the two working sessions.

After the ibogaine therapy session, the intake of melatonin and B-group vitamins is recommended.

Finally, it is worth reminding and emphasizing that in West Africa, specifically in Gabon, where the tradition of iboga root consumption originated, ibogaine is used by the shamans of the Bwiti cult as a universal therapeutic and initiatory agent for balancing the mind and body. Iboga "therapy" in Gabon is by no means limited to drug addiction but offers a broader spectrum of correction for mental and physical disorders.

Modern neurological research has shown that the consumption of iboga root stimulates the abundant production of a neurotransmitter in the brain, which has been named "ibogaine." It is believed that the abundant secretion of the ibogaine neurotransmitter in the brain somehow "overloads" the synthesis of basic neurotransmitters, resulting in a state of balance in the mind. However, this is just one hypothesis that still requires verification and validation. For now, it is important to consider that the effect and therapeutic impact exist, and further research is needed to determine precisely how ibogaine affects the human brain and body.

Post-psychedelic Forms of Psychedelic Therapy

After the prohibition of psychedelics in clinical practice, many doctors and scientists turned to developing legal therapeutic methods that, on the one hand, do not involve the use of prohibited chemical substances but, on the other hand, can provide benefits comparable to those of psychedelic therapy. In the context of this book, we will describe three prominent representatives of the post-psychedelic culture who actively worked with individuals using psychedelics before their formal prohibition. These individuals are Stanislav Grof, John Lilly, and Hankskarl Leuner.

Stanislav Grof's Holotropic Breathwork

Stanislav Grof was born in 1931 in Czechoslovakia. He completed his medical degree at Charles University in Prague in 1956 and specialized as a clinical psychiatrist. At the beginning of his career, he primarily focused on the clinical application of psychoanalysis.

In 1959, Grof was awarded the Karel Kuffner Prize for his outstanding contributions to the field of psychiatry.

Grof underwent training in psychoanalysis with Fedor Dosuzkov, his psychoanalytic teacher. However, Grof's psychoanalytic ideas were significantly transformed by his involvement in the clinical use of LSD-25, which was gaining momentum in the late 1950s. While working with patients using this substance, he regularly observed feedback from them that did not fit into traditional psychoanalytic concepts. Faced with this dilemma, he had to choose between considering the feedback from LSD-taking patients as the product of the mind's immersion in a state of profound intoxication, a hallucination devoid of practical value, or regarding the experiences as significant information that significantly expands our understanding of the psyche. Grof chose the latter path and dedicated himself entirely to working with LSD-25 for many years. He defended his dissertation on the subject of LSD's application to obtain his Ph.D. in Philosophy in 1965 at the Czechoslovak Academy of Sciences.

However, following the prohibition of clinical use of LSD-25, he was compelled to seek other means to clinically actualize transpersonal experiences in patients. After some time, Grof, along with his wife Christina, developed the method of Holotropic Breathwork, which, in terms of effectiveness, is similar to the practice of using LSD-25 but with specific differences. Since then, Grof has been teaching the technique and practice of Holotropic Breathwork to this day (2019).

In 1969, Grof became one of the founders of the "Journal of Transpersonal Psychology." That same year, he joined an experiment on the use of psychedelics at the Spring Grove facility, which was being conducted at the Maryland Psychiatric Research Center.

Grof's first marriage ended in 1975. Afterward, he married Christina Hill, who later took his surname. It is with her that Grof has been conducting seminars on transpersonal psychotherapy and holotropic breathwork for many years.

In 1977, Stanislav Grof, along with Michael Murphy and Dick Price, founded the International Transpersonal Association, of which he served as president from 1978 to 1982.

In 1993, Grof received the Honorary Award from the Association of Transpersonal Psychology.

In 1995, he became a professor at the Department of Psychology at the California Institute of Integral Studies.

In 2007, Grof was awarded the title of Honorary Professor by Moscow State University. He also became an Honorary Member of the Russian Psychological Society.

In 2014, his wife and collaborator, Christina Grof, passed away.

In 2016, Stanislav Grof married psychotherapist Brigitte Aschauer, who took his surname.

As of 2019, Grof continues to work, conduct seminars on transpersonal psychology, and contribute to the development of humanity's scientific potential.

Some of Stanislav Grof's most famous books include "Realms of the Human Unconscious," "The Cosmic Game," "The Holotropic Mind," "The

Holotropic Breathwork," "Spiritual Emergency," "Beyond the Brain," "Psychology of the Future," "The Stormy Search for the Self," and others.

Stanislav Grof, while observing patients undergoing psychedelic therapy, discovered that their experiences could be categorized into distinct blocks. Part of the experience patients had was directly related to the infantile, or what is commonly referred to as the "Freudian" unconscious. In this case, patients dealt with various childhood memories, unresolved traumas, and associated emotions. Another significant sphere that Grof observed in many of his patients was the realm of prenatal development. He found that through LSD-25 therapy and later through holotropic breathwork, individuals could vividly recall and resurrect in their consciousness various emotional experiences in general and psychotraumatic situations in particular that might have occurred during their time in the maternal womb. The mapping of this experience was so extensive that Grof had to divide it into four basic perinatal matrices (BPM).

We partially explore the topic of BPM in the chapter dedicated to the psychedelic dimension in therapy, where we delve deeply into Stanislav Grof's contributions to LSD therapy. In this section of the book, we touch upon these topics only briefly.

By the first BPM, Grof understood the experiences accumulated by a person during their time in the maternal womb—the entire period of pregnancy before the onset of labor and childbirth. This experience is often remembered as "oceanic bliss" and unity with the "cosmos." Problems can arise if the mother experienced any psychotraumatic events during pregnancy, desired to abort the child, suffered physical trauma, and so on. In such cases, each of these experiences leaves emotional imprints on the child and, to some extent, influences their personality dynamics.

The second BPM occurs when contractions begin, the placenta tears, but the birth canal has not yet dilated. This state almost always leaves strong negative impressions in the individual's consciousness, although the duration of the child's stay in this phase can have significant importance. When recalling such an experience, a person may see images of various beings threatening to attack them, monsters, or the dead who want to torment them, render them helpless, and so on.

The third BPM actualizes the experience of actively passing through the birth canal. A person may recall this experience as passing through a tunnel, the walls of which are adorned with knives and dagger blades. It can be an image of a tunnel, corridor, cave, and so on. In any case, there is a motif of struggle and resistance present. Aggressive and sexual feelings are often actualized during this stage.

Grof identified the fourth BPM as the experience of liberation from the confinement of the womb during the first five hours after birth. Feelings of weightlessness, freedom, and completeness are actualized, and images of carnival processions, grand celebrations, and collective rejoicing may be seen. Sometimes, if the birth was very difficult, the fourth perinatal matrix may take on connotations of sorrow and the process of dying.

The third level of the unconscious that Grof identified, working with the feedback from his patients, was the transpersonal level. The content of this level lies beyond the literal experience of the individual. It encompasses the experience of collective memory of the group to which the person belongs, ancestral memory, and even archetypal content that relates to all of humanity as a whole. Carl Jung referred to this level as the collective unconscious. Here, a person can recall the experiences of their past incarnations and associate them with the experiences of various animals, natural elements, and material objects.

Grof considered these three levels of the human unconscious as systems of condensed experience (SCEs), which, in his opinion, are three key links in human consciousness.

The term "holotropic," which Grof used in relation to the name of therapeutic breathing, can be translated from Ancient Greek as "directed towards wholeness." The technique of holotropic breathing is quite simple and is likely borrowed from yogic breathing techniques (pranayama). In pranayama, breathing techniques similar to holotropic breathing are called kapalabhati and bhastrika. Both types of breathing involve the use of lung hyperventilation techniques.

It is also worth noting that before Grof, Wilhelm Reich, a disciple of

Freud and the creator of vegetotherapy, as well as his students, including Alexander Lowen, could have used intensive breathing techniques in their work with patients. However, neither Reich, Lowen, nor their followers made hyperventilation a central technique in their therapeutic methods.

Leonard Orr independently used hyperventilation techniques in the process of psychotherapy and called his method "rebirthing." Currently, it is quite difficult to trace whether Grof borrowed techniques from Orr or vice versa because both holotropic breathing and rebirthing emerged in the mid-1970s. Despite their general similarities, the methods can differ significantly in details.

When working with holotropic breathing, the patient is instructed to lie on the floor on a soft mat and begin breathing intensively through the mouth. There are no strict rules for breathing, but fast and deep breathing is preferred. The faster and deeper the breathing, the more likely it is to induce an altered state of consciousness. From a physiological perspective, during intensive breathing, carbon dioxide is flushed out of the person's blood, and the blood vessels in the brain constrict, leading to the inhibition of the functioning of the cerebral cortex. Additionally, the limbic system of the brain becomes activated, which, in turn, triggers a range of diverse experiences, such as deep euphoria, various illusions and hallucinations, profound inner experiences, and access to bodily sensations that are often inaccessible in the usual state. It is also worth noting that blood pH increases, causing respiratory alkalosis, which is a disturbance in the acid-base balance of the body.

However, despite this, the breathing technique itself does not entail any serious negative consequences for the body, although some critics of holotropic breathing claim otherwise, suggesting that brain cells can die during asphyxia. However, there is no scientific evidence to support this claim. Many practitioners who have undergone tens or even hundreds of hours of holotropic breathing sessions have not experienced any illnesses. Stanislav Grof commented that over more than 30 years of actively conducting holotropic breathing seminars, he has facilitated this form of therapeutic work with over 30,000 people, and the variety of feedback he has received from them can truly be impressive.

The foundation of holotropic breathwork therapy draws heavily from the structure of working with patients in psychedelic psychotherapy. The preferred format of work is group therapy, with the number of participants ranging from 4 to 20, although Grof does not set an upper limit on the number of participants. For instance, when conducting holotropic breathwork seminars in different countries, he has worked with groups consisting of more than 50 participants.

Before the breathing session begins, participants are instructed by the therapist regarding the session itself, what might happen, the specific experiences that may arise, and what to do in case of any negative experiences. It should be noted that depending on the individual neurophysiology of each participant, sensory experiences can vary greatly and may focus on specific sensations.

Some participants may have multiple visual experiences during the breathing process, which may include sensory distortions or sequentially meaningful experiences. Others may place greater emphasis on external and internal sensations, while some may experience increased motor representation of sensations, such as waving their arms and legs, hitting the floor, experiencing vibration, spasms, limb paralysis, and so on.

During holotropic work, some participants may produce various sounds, often reflecting specific emotional states that are not constructively expressed in ordinary states of consciousness. These sounds can include laughter, screams, crying, uproarious laughter, hissing, prolonged vocalization of vowels, and so on. Olfactory and gustatory representations are relatively rare.

Participants are informed that almost any form of sensational expression is a form of emotional release, and it is highly undesirable to restrain these expressions during the breathing process. The only fundamental limitation is the prohibition of directly involving other group members in reacting to one's own emotions.

If the group consists of more than 4–5 individuals, it may be optimal to divide it into sitters and breathers during the breathing session. The sitter acts as an assistant to the therapist and remains next to the breather, providing support if necessary throughout the session, which usually lasts from 45 to 90 minutes. Then, at the end of the breathing session, the sitter and breather switch places.

Sometimes, during the breathing process, there may be a need to work with the patient's body, for example, when excessive motor representation becomes evident. In such cases, when the patient is moving too intensely and cannot control their movements, the therapist may approach the patient and temporarily block their intense movements with their hands or their entire body, allowing the patient to experience resistance and express their emotional response in a more concentrated manner.

In this way, the therapist helps the patient "exhale" more quickly. Once the intensity of the energy begins to diminish, the therapist releases the patient and allows them to continue breathing. Sometimes, the sitter with experience in this form of patient interaction may directly work with the patient's body.

An integral part of the holotropic breathwork session is the use of music. The playlist for the breathing session is often composed of classical and ethnic music, New Age music, a combination of ethnic and light electronic music, ambient soundtracks, and so on. It is undesirable to use tracks with lyrics or songs in the language spoken by the participants themselves. Soundtracks without lyrics or with minimal lyrics are preferable. The fewer semantic associations the patient receives through words in the music, the better. In addition to musical accompaniment, various world incenses are used during the holotropic breathwork session to create a favorable and calming state for the patient. Some therapists may also play various ethnic shamanic instruments, such as the shamanic drum, bongos, jew's harp, didgeridoo, and so on, in addition to the regular musical accompaniment.

As the breathing session approaches its end, the music gradually fades, and participants are asked to lie down for a while, aligning their breathing and avoiding quick movements. When all the patients have returned to a normal state, a group sharing session begins. They share their experiences and discuss the emotions they encountered during the breathing process. Typically, the therapist does not conduct an in-depth analysis of the patients' experiences, although in some cases, specific analytical comments may be appropriate. However, in the holotropic breathwork approach, special emphasis is not placed on analyzing the experiences. If patients manage to access the transpersonal realm of their personality and experience certain archetypes of the human unconscious, the therapist may recount stories from myths and legends that contain the images seen by the patient. Naturally, in such cases, the therapist must be knowledgeable in the fields of mythology and religious studies.

Each holotropic breathwork session can significantly differ from previous ones, offering unique insights, emotional responses, and a specific understanding of oneself, others, and the world. The holotropic breathwork technique itself can be effectively applied as a standalone method of psychotherapy or as a valuable complement to other therapeutic approaches.

Hanskarl Leiner's Symboldrama

Hanscarl Leuner (1919–1996) was a German psychotherapist, professor, and medical doctor. He was the creator of:

- Catathymic-imaginative psychotherapy, also known as "symbol drama"
- The International Society for Catathymic Imaginative Experience and Imaginative Methods in Psychotherapy and Psychology
- The European Medical Society for Psycholytic Psychotherapy

Leuner also served as the head of the psychotherapy and psychosomatics department at the psychiatric clinic of the University of Göttingen in Germany. He was born in Bautzen, Germany, into a merchant family. During his studies in Germany, he aspired to become a physician and psychotherapist.

There is an amusing story about Leuner's decision to seek advice regarding his future profession from Fritz Künkel, a renowned psychotherapist at the time in Germany. Künkel ironically told him that in order to become a good psychotherapist, he would first have to complete medical school and then forget everything he had been taught there. Considering Leuner's significant success in his profession, we can assume that he took his "guru's" recommendation to heart.

Hanskarl Leiner

In 1937, Leuner graduated from high school. In 1939, he enrolled in the medical faculty of Frankfurt University. That same year, he was called to the front and served as a radio operator in the tank troops until 1941. Due to a shortage of doctors in Germany in 1941, he was sent back from the front to study at the medical institute.

In 1946, after the war, he passed his state exams at the University of Marburg. In 1947, Hanscarl Leuner defended his dissertation. From 1947 to 1948, he underwent training in Jungian psychoanalysis under Gustav Schmalz, who was a disciple of Carl Jung and had himself undergone analysis with him. During that period, the attitude towards Jungian analysis was quite skeptical, as Jung's psychotherapeutic contributions were considered more products of his intuition than forms of scientific experimentation. Nevertheless, Leuner recognized the effectiveness of Carl Jung's therapeutic method and began working on experiments that could validate Jung's theories and make them clinically adaptable.

From 1948 to 1954, Leuner attempted to improve Jung's method. In the process of this "improvement," he developed his own comprehensive psychotherapy method, which was later named "catathymic-imaginative psychotherapy" or "symbol drama." Naturally, this method was rooted in Jungian analysis, but in theory and practice, it differed significantly from it.

In his works, Leuner describes working with the motives of symbol drama, such as "Meadow," "Stream," "Mountain," "House," "Name," "Important Person," "Hitchhiking," "Bog Hole," and "Entrance to the Cave." Additionally, Leuner introduced practices such as working with "fixed images" and "transformation phenomena" into his therapeutic work.

From 1955 to 1957, Leuner developed a practice of working with symbolic beings in the imagination. Its foundation naturally lies in Jungian active imagination practice.

Leuner proposed specific motifs of imagination that could facilitate interaction with these "beings." He would ask his patients to imagine a bog hole or the entrance to a cave. Then, for some time, the patient was instructed to simply contemplate the given motif.

Afterwards, Leuner would give a directive command: "Now, some creature or person will emerge from the hole; observe it." Frequently, the images that appeared in the patients' imaginations greatly frightened them. Leuner referred to this emotional phenomenon as the "horror of the Gorgon."

Despite the intense negative emotions, Leuner encouraged patients to observe the images. Over time, the images themselves became less intimidating and threatening. This therapeutic process took up to 30 minutes of session time.

When the goal was achieved, Leuner would instruct patients to approach the visualized object, touch it, or simply stroke it. According to Leuner, this process allowed for the release of suppressed affective tension in the patient's psyche and the integration of the experience behind it.

In 1959, Leuner began researching the active imagination of symbolism in various landscapes. He attempted to identify specific fixed criteria that differentiated the visualization of landscapes in individuals with different neurotic pathologies from those in a normal state of consciousness. He discusses his work on this topic in the article "Landscape Image as a Metaphor of Dynamic Structures."

In 1959, Leuner worked at the psychiatric clinic of the University of Göttingen, where he led the department of psychotherapy and defended his doctoral dissertation in psychiatry and neurology.

In 1960, during one of the seminars conducted by Leuner, a discussion emerged that subsequently influenced the development of the associative method in symbol drama.

From 1963 to 1973, Leuner continued his psychoanalytic education at the Educational Center for Psychotherapy and Psychoanalysis in Göttingen. During this period, he underwent supervision with Franz Haygler and analyses by Haygler-Evers and Werner Schwidder.

In 1964, Hanscarl Leuner published his article "The Associative Method in Symbol Drama."

During the same year, he founded the European Medical Society for Psycholytic Psychotherapy (EPT). In 1965, he obtained the title of professor. In 1974, he established the Society for Catathymic Experience of Images and Imaginative Methods in Psychotherapy and Psychology (AGKB). In 1975, he assumed the leadership of the Department of Psychotherapy and Psychosomatics at the Center for Psychological Medicine at the University of Göttingen. In 1978, he created the International Society for Catathymic Experience of Images and Imaginative Methods in Psychotherapy and Psychology (IGKB). He retired in 1985. In 1996, he passed away from pneumonia in Göttingen.

Throughout his prolific career, Hanscarl Leuner conducted numerous lectures and training programs in various cities in the United States and Europe. He was one of the pioneers in the study of LSD-25 and its effects on the psyche and consciousness. He was regarded as one of Germany's leading experts in this field of research. There were various styles of applying LSD-25 in psychotherapy and psychiatry.

The psycholytic method, actively utilized by Leuner, was particularly popular in Europe. Its distinct feature was the use of small dosages of LSD-25 and a large number of therapy sessions. During the psychotherapy process, patients could undergo over 100 sessions involving the administration of LSD-25 over several years.

The psychedelic method gained significant popularity in the United States and Canada, focusing on the use of higher dosages of LSD-25 and a smaller number of psychotherapy sessions, usually no more than ten.

The method of symbol drama spread to many countries worldwide and found its application in various domains of psychotherapeutic practice.

Pathopsychological Profiles and Psychedelic Therapy

When describing the influence of psychedelic substances on patients with different pathopsychological profiles, we specifically mention LSD-25. It is important to consider that the reactions of individuals belonging to specific profiles to other substances may be quite similar. The majority of the statistical data we relied on in writing this work was directly related to LSD-25. That is why we selected this particular substance as a reference point.

Hysteroid Profile

In patients with a hysteroid personality profile, LSD sessions often reveal intense and profound experiences, even with small dosages. Internal sensory representations span a wide range of visual spectra, producing a multitude of diverse images. The behavior of these patients can appear extravagant and exalted. All unconscious processes within the hysteroid personality become more intensified. What would take several dozen psychotherapy sessions to unfold in a hysteroid individual can be condensed into a single session. There is a high likelihood of an erotized transference toward a therapist of the opposite gender, as well as the emergence of numerous fantasies involving the therapist, sitter, or other individuals present during the LSD session. Hysteroid individuals more frequently generate strong and inflated sexual transferences. The patient may perceive the therapist as the embodiment of the "id," such as an Arab drug dealer, a native Aborigine, Casanova, a crime lord, or a great seducer. Transferences related to the "super-ego" may also occur, such as the image of a holy person, the world's best therapist, Jesus, Mohammed, Buddha, a hero saving the world, and so on. Hysteroid personalities, more often than other patients, recall past incarnations, remembering that the therapist had a connection to them, that they have met many times, and so forth. Such patients enjoy discussing these topics, elaborating on the details of their experiences, and withholding nothing. They tend to exaggerate the positivity of the changes more frequently than others.

Paranoid Profile

The behavior of paranoid patients during LSD-assisted therapy reflects their unresolved tendency towards delusional negative interpretations of reality more intensely. Grof comments that his observations of patients with a paranoid personality profile can likely confirm a connection between homosexuality and paranoid behavior. Latent homosexual feelings may surface and be projected onto the therapist of the same gender. In male patients, this realization of latent homosexuality can be accompanied by strong fears and panic attacks. Particularly, this can be aggravated by experiencing sexual feelings toward the opposite gender. Grof reports frequently observing feedback from male patients stating that during LSD-25 therapy, they felt a female body and experienced clitoral and vaginal orgasms. He also notes similar occurrences in female patients, where they described experiencing male-type orgasms. However, such cases were much less frequent in male patients.

Psychopathic Profile

Stanislav Grof has written extensively about how LSD therapy can significantly alter the psychopathic symptoms of patients. However, the experiences these individuals undergo during LSD-25 sessions are often intense and distressing. Patients frequently recount experiences of being in hell and enduring various tortures. The intensity of these experiences may prompt the patient to request that the session be interrupted (for which the drug naloxone is typically used). Unbearable mental anguish can transition into shifts to alternative personalities. For instance, Grof describes a case in which he worked with LSD-25 with a woman who had an antisocial personality, had been incarcerated multiple times, engaged in heavy drug use, and identified as a lesbian. Her symptoms of antisocial behavior closely resembled the concept of a psychopathic personality profile. During the therapy, the patient shifted into an alternative personality, identifying herself as a devil and threatening Grof, promising him many troubles if he didn't stop helping her. This part of her personality dissipated after the LSD session ended. Subsequently, Grof observed significant changes in her. She stopped using drugs, managed to find adequate social work, and even established heterosexual relationships. However, unfortunately, she couldn't maintain them for long and returned to homosexual relationships. Grof admitted that after this incident, he started considering having a Christian crucifix present during sessions with patients, just in case. Similar processes, in different forms, can occur in other psychopathic patients.

True psychopathic individuals are incapable of experiencing guilt and shame. However, when we talk about a psychopathic accent, the feeling of guilt and shame may not arise in certain life situations.

For example, in relationships with the opposite sex, in business relationships, etc. On a physiological level, psychopathy is manifested by weak activity in the anterior and posterior cingulate gyrus, which is directly related to the capacity for empathy and compassion. It seems that LSD-25 is capable of awakening these brain regions. During an LSD session, the psychopath, in a way, comes face to face with their conscience, which they have suppressed for a long time or their entire life. The various "hellish" experiences they go through likely reflect their actions. Thus, the integration of personality fragments takes place.

According to the current legislation in most countries worldwide, psychotherapists are not allowed to conduct LSD sessions with their patients. However, thanks to Stanislav Grof's developed technique of holotropic breathing, which is completely legal and recognized in many countries, we can observe effects similar to those of LSD sessions. A similar pattern emerges when psychopathic patients, undergoing deep breathing processes, often confront a very difficult and unpleasant integration, which unequivocally indicates the fragmented nature of their personality. Unlike schizophrenic personality disorder, where fragmented parts can simultaneously exist within consciousness, the psychopath is only aware of one aggressive part. The sacrificial part is constantly projected onto other people to make them feel good, continuously causing pain and suffering to others.

Obsessive-Compulsive Profile

Grof describes working with LSD-25 and obsessive-compulsive patients as quite challenging. These patients exhibit a high level of resistance to the substance. It seems that they can withstand doses of over 500 mcg, only reporting some unpleasant sensations in their bodies. Sometimes, multiple LSD sessions are required for the patient to weaken their psychological defenses and allow unconscious material to be released calmly.

Grof also reports that increasing the dosage usually leads to no significant results. He observed a case where a patient was given a dose of 15,000 mcg intramuscularly, which had little effect. As we can see, increasing the dosage is ineffective. Psychiatrists have found a dosage limit of 400–500 mcg. If a patient does not respond to this dose, further increases are unlikely to have any effect. Obsessive-compulsive patients express numerous anxieties and fears about the upcoming session, which, of course, creates strong tension during the LSD session and hinders the free expression of unconscious material. The patient may literally struggle against the effects of the substance. There is a strong need for total self-control. Visual sensations are almost absent, and bodily representations are more common. Various complaints such as headaches, nausea, sweating, and unpleasant sensations are frequent. The session becomes a constant inner struggle, leading to profound fatigue.

This self-struggle has a pronounced psychodynamic aspect, which can shed light on the underlying cause of the symptom, rooted in powerful resistance and rejection of one of the parental figures. Often, it is the father figure.

Schizoid Profile

Resistance from schizoid individuals towards psychedelic work can be very strong. The level of resistance may resemble that of patients with obsessive-compulsive symptoms.

Epileptoid Profile

Individuals with an epileptoid character are capable of strongly unveiling unconscious processes, which is reminiscent of the demonstrative profile but without excessive exaggeration of effects. They often experience greater comfort working with higher doses. If we specifically discuss epilepsy as a disease, working with epileptic patients can be problematic because LSD-25 can trigger an uncontrollable series of epileptoid seizures that are difficult to control. This is why working with such patients can be life-threatening.

Schizophrenic Profile

LSD-25 has been tested on patients suffering from schizophrenia by various psychiatrists in different countries. In Europe, there were even specialized clinics dedicated to treating schizophrenic patients with this drug and similar ones in terms of quality. Numerous studies have been conducted, showing that the drug could create positive dynamics for some patients.

Manic-Depressive Profile

Symptoms of manic-depressive psychosis, like symptoms of depression, are closely related to serotonin secretion in the human brain. In such disorders, serotonin secretion significantly decreases. LSD-25 has the ability to activate serotonin receptors in the human brain. Therefore, the use of LSD in such patients can cause significant remissions. Formally, depression is the symptom that was well addressed during the clinical trials of LSD-25. LSD sessions are often accompanied by strong euphoria, laughter, and joy in depressive patients. Some observations have led to the assumption that even a single administration can induce complete remission.

It has also been found that LSD affects patients with exogenous and endogenous depression differently. Grof describes how patients with exogenous depression interact deeply on a profound level. They delve deeply into a wide range of biographical material that holds psychodynamic significance in relation to the symptom. On the other hand, patients suffering from endogenous depression often fixate on specific, profound primal emotions that form the basis of their depression. These patients are at risk of experiencing a temporary exacerbation of symptoms after an LSD session. Grof comments that his observations align with the experiments of Danish psychiatrist Arendsen-Hinsh, who was one of the pioneers in the clinical application of LSD-25.

* * *

It is important to draw the Reader's attention to the fact that currently, various forms of psychedelic therapy are not legal in most countries worldwide. Therefore, the information we present here is based on the accumulated data from our colleagues in the United States and European countries before the prohibition on the use of the described methods of psychotherapeutic work. It is also essential to emphasize that the information in this chapter regarding the use and application of psychedelic substances is strictly commented on in a clinical medical context and has no relevance to their non-professional use outside of medical institutions.

8

Antipsychiatry

Antipsychiatry is not a comprehensive practical methodology for therapeutic work but rather a philosophy. It offers a fresh perspective on the world of mental deviations, presenting new "windows" through which we can gain a deeper understanding of the reality of psychological disorders.

To some professionals, the ideas of antipsychiatry and its proponents may seem insane and disconnected from reality. However, it is important to remember that the concept of illness is always based on a general understanding of health and normalcy. Yet, one must not forget that the notion of normalcy is not static. It changes in accordance with the spirit of the times. What is considered normal in one culture may be perceived as madness in another.

Recognizing the relativity of our notions of normalcy, it is crucial to acknowledge that those individuals who, from our perspective, may appear insane are not always so in the grand scheme of things. Countless examples can be cited by recalling the biographies of various renowned scientists who exhibited peculiarities in their behavior, speech, and thinking.

The ideas of antipsychiatry began to flourish in the mid-20th century, largely due to the efforts of Ronald Laing. Some of his colleagues embraced this new wave in psychiatry and creatively developed its principles.

Ronald David Laing

Ronald David Laing (1927–1989) was born in Glasgow, Scotland, in the United Kingdom. He was the only child of David Park MacNair Laing and Amelia Glen Laing. Laing believed that his childhood was unhappy due to his emotionally restrained and non-affectionate mother. He received his primary education at Hutchesons' Boys' Grammar School in Glasgow. Laing developed a strong interest in philosophy at a young age and read the works of famous philosophers such as Plato, Aristotle, Sophocles, Aeschylus, and others. He was also musically talented and engaged in singing and music, becoming a licentiate of the Royal Academy of Music and a member of the Royal Music Society in 1944–1945.

Ronald Laing

From 1945 to 1951, Laing studied medicine at the University of Glasgow while also working as a hospital orderly in a psychiatric ward. This experience greatly influenced his choice of future specialization, which would be neurology. During his studies, Laing's attention was drawn to ethical questions regarding the relationship between philosophy and medicine. He also became part of a group of amateur researchers who practiced hypnotic suggestion for experimental purposes.

Laing had a passionate interest in sports as well. He engaged in tennis, mountaineering, croquet, and track and field athletics.

He underwent an internship in the neurosurgical department of the Gartnavel Royal Hospital under the guidance of former field surgeon Joe Schorstein, who introduced him to the works of philosophers and psychotherapists such as Kant, Husserl, Kierkegaard, Sartre, Wittgenstein, Freud, Jung, and others.

From 1951 to 1953, Laing served as a military psychiatrist in the Royal Army Medical Corps. In his work as a psychiatrist, he strove to establish a confidential rapport with his patients. Through this trusting relationship, he was able to help many patients regain their connection with life. Rumors circulated that during his service, Laing preferred the company of his patients over that of his colleagues. It was during this time that he gradually developed the belief that madness was more of a philosophical question than a medical symptom. According to Laing, understanding the world of the mentally ill, accepting them "as they are," and engaging in peaceful interactions could initiate unique psychotherapeutic processes within the patient's psyche. From Laing's perspective, madness could be seen not merely as a symptom but as a personal characteristic.

During his military service, Laing met Anne Hann, with whom he began a relationship. The young couple soon got married, and they went on to have five children.

After leaving the army, Laing started working as a psychiatrist at the Gartnavel Royal Psychiatric Hospital in Glasgow, where he conducted one of his experiments with mentally ill patients. This experiment, known as the "noisy room," took place from 1954 to 1955. In this experiment, both the staff and the patients at the clinic remained in their usual attire and engaged in regular interactions and daily activities. Laing aimed to simulate a normal psychological environment, which he believed was a crucial therapeutic factor in working with patients. The experiment proved successful, and indeed, Laing's approach yielded constructive results.

In 1956, Ronald Laing, along with his family, moved to London where he took up a position as a senior registrar at the Tavistock Clinic. He also underwent comprehensive psychoanalytic training at the Institute of Psychoanalysis under the guidance of Donald Woods Winnicott.

In 1958, together with Aaron Esterson, Laing embarked on an in-depth study of families with schizophrenic patients, aiming to uncover the underlying causes of the illness. He began to view schizophrenia not as an individual's disease but as a "knot" within the family system. Laing's term "knot" can be understood as a specific interconnection between the individual and the social group to which they belong. In this sense, schizophrenia started to be interpreted as a problem of integrating the individual into the social environment. The research conducted by Laing and Esterson enabled them to identify typical profiles of the schizophrenic patients' father and mother. In such families, the father is often weak and submissive, while the mother is cold and domineering.

In 1960, Laing opened his private psychoanalytic practice. That same year, one of his most famous books, "The Divided Self," was published, receiving numerous positive reviews and accolades in medical journals. Although the book initially did not gain immediate recognition, it eventually became a full-fledged bestseller. Laing begins his book with the definitions of the "existential-phenomenological foundation of science and personality" and "existential-phenomenological understanding of psychosis." He introduces the term "ontological insecurity," which forms the basis for his model of schizophrenia, as an attempt to preserve the unstable "self" through internal fragmentation and the creation of an external false mask.

In 1961, his second book, "Self and Others," was published, serving as a conceptual and ideological continuation of his previous work.

In 1962, Laing assumed leadership of the Langham Clinic in London.

Laing became one of the psychiatrists who worked and wrote in the spirit of anti-psychiatry philosophy. The central thesis of this philosophy suggests that mental illness is a myth created by society to control individuals who deviate from the majority.

Starting in the mid-1960s, Laing began to appear frequently on television where he presented his views. He hosted a television program dedicated to topics such as madness, health, and family. Laing's rebellious philosophy eventually made him an idol among British youth.

While Laing embraced existentialism and anti-psychiatry in his ideological and philosophical realms, which largely informed his literary works, in practice, in his work with patients, he employed various methods of psychotherapy such as behavioral therapy, gestalt therapy, and existential therapy. As a result, his approach can be considered eclectic.

In 1964, while in the USA, Laing met Timothy Leary, a prominent advocate for the use of LSD. Intrigued by Leary's ideas, he returned to the United Kingdom and began applying LSD to his patients. It is worth noting that, at that time, LSD was not yet prohibited and was seen as one of the therapeutic tools.

In 1965, together with Esterson, Laing established an experimental community for schizophrenic individuals called "Kingsley Hall." The clinic's work was based on Laing's experimental experience with the "noisy room" in Cooper's Community, "Villa 21," and a kibbutz for schizophrenics in Israel that Esterson had studied. At Kingsley Hall, there was no hierarchy, and there was no formal division between doctors and patients. This community existed for five years before it was closed. In many ways, Laing's experiment holds a significant place in the history of psychiatry and has yielded some constructive results. However, due to its extravagance, it did not find widespread acceptance in the field of psychiatry.

The personality of the schizophrenic was neither suppressed nor confined. To some extent, Laing perceived schizophrenia as a psychedelic journey induced by the ingestion of hallucinogens, which could end well in the presence of comfortable and balanced conditions and warm emotional support from the environment. In this regard, Laing partially adopted the practices of psychedelic psychotherapists of that time who believed that the administration of psychedelic substances during psychotherapy could bring about substantial constructive changes in patients, provided there was a good rapport and a supportive relationship between the therapist and the patient.

In the second half of the 1960s, Laing separated from his first wife and married a German woman named Jutta Wernicke, with whom he had three more children—two boys and one girl.

In the early 1970s, the book "Laing and Antipsychiatry," edited by R. Boyers, was published, solidifying the "brand" of antipsychiatry not only with David Cooper, who published the work "Psychiatry and Antipsychiatry" in 1967, but also with Laing.

In 1971, Laing embarked on a journey to Ceylon (now Sri Lanka) with his wife and two children, where he spent two months studying Buddhism, which was gaining popularity worldwide. He then traveled to India, where he explored various Hindu practices, received initiation into the cult of the goddess Kali, and studied Sanskrit. He attended lectures by Buddhist Lama Govinda, who was Timothy Leary's guru.

A year later, Laing returned to London and went on a lecture tour of the United States in 1972. During his time in the US, Laing met Elizabeth Fehr, who applied the technique of "rebirthing psychodrama" in her practice. The goal of this technique was to re-experience the birth process and release symptoms through the expression of repressed emotions.

Laing became interested in this practice, adopted it, and began using it with his patients from 1973 on. This technique shares similarities with Stanislav Grof's holotropic breathwork, which was also actively developing at that time, especially after the prohibition on the use of LSD in clinical settings.

In the 1970s, Ronald Laing published works such as "Knots" (1971), "Do You Love Me?" (1976), "Facts of Life" (1976), and "Conversations with Children" (1978). In 1985, he published his autobiography titled "Wisdom, Madness, and Folly."

In the 1980s, Laing separated from his second wife and met another German woman, Sue Zanghell, with whom he had another son. However, his relationship with Zanghell lasted only one and a half years.

Towards the end of his life, Laing entered into a relationship with his secretary, Margaret, who gave birth to his son in 1988.

Laing passed away from a heart attack that occurred while playing tennis at the French resort town of Saint-Tropez.

Laing wrote about psychological states such as ontological certainty and uncertainty about the self. Ontological certainty about the self can create a foundation for deriving pleasure from interpersonal connections. On the other hand, ontological uncertainty only breeds preoccupation with one's own safety, imposes limitations on social interactions, and hinders genuine satisfaction.

Laing wrote about three forms of anxiety stemming from ontological uncertainty about the self. These are:

1. **Engulfment**: This form of anxiety is associated with fear of any kind of relationship, both external with others and internal with oneself. The individual is frightened by contact, the expression of warm emotions, attachment, and so on. (This anxiety can be referred to as a schizoid conditionally.)

2. **Fissure**: In this form, individuals experience and undergo an existential vacuum, a sense of inner emptiness. Complete contact with external reality is perceived as a potentially traumatizing process capable of generating only problems. Reality, other people, and social events are seen as persecuting the individual. (This anxiety can be conditionally termed paranoid.)

3. **Petrification**: According to Laing, petrification can manifest in three forms:

- A feeling of terror that causes a person to "freeze." It is a particular psychological pain that, once experienced, renders the person insensitive to emotional relationships.
- Fear of being transformed from a living person into an automaton, a robot, or a stone. It is anxiety regarding being used, transformed into a routine element of the world, and preoccupied with external formalities.

- Fear of turning others into "stones," perceiving others as objects, and disregarding their feelings. (This anxiety can be conditionally termed psychopathic.)

Laing discussed two types of personalities in relation to their connection with the bodily aspect. These types do not represent the polarity of mental health and illness; each has its own advantages and disadvantages. They are:

1. **Embodied personality**: By an embodied personality, he meant an individual who has a connection with their body, sensations, and feelings, and considers themselves alive. They sense that they consist of flesh, blood, and bones. For such individuals, the mind and body are inseparable. However, the split within them can occur in other situations. In certain situations, an embodied personality may be much more vulnerable than an unembodied one. Embodiment of personality does not guarantee protection against anxiety, stress, and other mental disorders. (This type is most closely related to the concept of epileptoid personality.)

2. **Unembodied personality**: Such a personality perceives itself separately from its body, which is seen as one of the objects in the external world. The individual becomes an external observer, a dissociated critic, detached from emotions and experiences. (This type of personality is most closely related to the concept of schizoid personality.)

Laing presents his view of personality as a specific norm and the culmination of various psychic mechanisms at work, such as repression, displacement, projection, introjection, splitting, and so on. Some functions of these defense mechanisms can be considered constructive, leading to a balanced control of the individual, while other functions can create destructive experiences that significantly alienate the individual from the structure of existence. Laing believed that the prevailing notion in psychiatry that patients should be changed into inanimate objects rather than accepted as living human beings perpetuates the illness that is diligently being treated. According to him, psychotherapy should strive to restore the fullness of warmth in communication between individuals through their interconnectedness.

One of the terms frequently used by Laing was "metanoia." In Ancient Greek, it translates as a change of mind, a reevaluation, or a change of thought. It signifies a shift in perception accompanied by regret and repentance. In religion, "metanoia" signifies "repentance." In analytical psychology, Carl Jung borrowed this term from Heraclitus and used it as a synonym for another term, "enantiodromia," referring to the process of something transitioning into its diametrical opposite. Laing himself defined metanoia as a schizophrenic psychosis that involves a process of testing and potential rebirth, capable of leading to the true essence of one's personality. Other psychiatrists associated with the anti-psychiatry movement, particularly David Cooper, held similar views.

In his theories, Laing sometimes leaned toward an ultra-radical anti-psychiatric position, explaining that in the context of human socialization, one's consciousness becomes mystified, causing individuals to enter a world of social hallucinations that most people call reality. What is commonly referred to as health is, in fact, a variety of madness that is not easily cured. In this conviction of Laing's, we can see the influence of Buddhism with its philosophy of the illusory nature of the world, the need for enlightenment, and transcending the cycle of samsara. Another strong anti-psychiatric belief of Laing's was that psychiatrists could learn more about the inner world and specific experiences from schizophrenics than the other way around. This belief was also shared by another advocate of the American anti-psychiatry movement, Frank Farrelly, the creator of provocative therapy, who commented during his seminars that his best teachers were his patients.

American psychologist Kirk Schneider claimed that Laing described psychosis as if he were "leading a team of researchers who had visited an abandoned island of psychotics." Kirk believed that Laing was a pioneer in his field. To some extent, he can be compared to the French physician Pinel, the founder of psychiatry in France, who became widely known for his reforms in the treatment of the mentally ill in clinics. Thanks to Pinel, patients with mental disorders were unchained, and he also implemented hospital regulations and doctor visits. Schneider also referred to Laing as an astronaut of consciousness.

Laing wrote in "The Phenomenology of Experience": "If the human race survives, future men will, I suspect, look back on our enlightened epoch as the time when a great many certainties were known to be uncertain and the multitude of dogmas that had been regarded as axiomatic for thousands of years were gradually and sometimes painfully withdrawn. We, of course, cannot feel this future in our bones, but it can be anticipated intellectually."

David Graham Cooper

David Cooper (1931–1986) was one of the creators of the anti-psychiatry movement in psychiatry. He was born in Cape Town and received his medical education there. In 1955, he moved to Paris, where he found his wife, and soon after to London, where he opened a private practice and worked in several medical institutions. One of the significant encounters in Cooper's life occurred in 1958 when he met Ronald Laing, who shared most of his professional views. They began a fruitful collaboration, and in 1964, they co-authored the book "Reason and Violence: A Decade of Sartre's Creative Work."

In 1965, Cooper participated in the establishment of the therapeutic community "Kingsley Hall" founded by Laing. In 1967, Cooper published the book "Psychiatry and Anti-Psychiatry," which formally became the first comprehensive work to introduce the term "anti-psychiatry" and discuss various philosophical concepts related to this movement in psychiatry. Cooper also wrote works such as "The Death of the Family," "The Grammar of Living," and "The Language of Madness."

David Cooper

Cooper advocated for a social model of the development of psychotic disorders, believing that symptoms arise in individuals through socialization. It is primarily Cooper who can be considered the person who popularized the term "anti-psychiatry" in scientific discourse, largely due to his rejection of the clinical psychiatric treatment methods that existed at the time. In addition to the philosophical concept of anti-psychiatry, Cooper was influenced by Marxism, existentialism, and French structuralism and post-structuralism. Cooper held radical and aggressive anti-psychiatric convictions that not only called for reforms in medicine but also provoked revolutionary sentiments. He believed that we were living in a pre-revolutionary period and that the revolution itself should start with a "revolution of madness," that is, the dismantling of psychiatric institutions as they existed before.

In addition to the "revolution of madness," Cooper advocated for a "revolution of love," the liberation of society from puritanical sexual morality, considering the "bed" as one of the secret weapons of the revolution. He saw the potential in a comprehensive social revolution, reformation, and dismantling of the foundations of bourgeois society. The "revolution of madness" was seen by him as the initial link that could trigger further processes of total social transformation.

Cooper developed the concept of "the grammar of the political," which is a specific grammar of power and influence within the context of the psychic and social space. This concept is divided into four levels.

1. **The micro-political level of the inner space of the individual:** Psychic and physical experiences can be seen as political acts. In other words, any form of psychological or physical disorder is a metaphorical expression of a structural problem of communication existing within the group to which the individual belongs. The interconnection between external social aspects and profound internal aspects is explored. To some extent, Cooper attempts to consider the world of an individual's inner experiences as a smaller fractal in relation to larger social processes, highlighting the interdependence of different internal processes and their structural orderliness. This is the internal psychic level.

2. **The micro-political level of the family:** The family system, in which the individual matures, shapes a specific structure of experience that potentially becomes a cause for internal conflicts within a person who does not feel the need for close fusion with others. This level pertains to family systems.

3. **The micro-political level of confrontational groups:** This level encompasses various social institutions and organizations that replicate the functioning structure of the family. A child goes to school, attends college, visits hospitals, and serves in the army—all these social organizations are closely interconnected on a structural level with how the family system functions and what profound values it propagates. This level relates to larger organizational systems.

4. **Macro-political level:** Determines the functioning of all social organizations in society to some extent. The transformation at the macro-political level can bring about changes at all other levels of

social and psychological existence.

We will provide commentary and note that, in general, the conditioning of the levels occurs from bottom to top, meaning from the fourth level to the first. However, despite this, all levels are closely interrelated, so not only does the greater condition the smaller, but the smaller also influences the greater, being an integral part of it. It is important to reiterate that this model is best understood through the lens of Mandelbrot's fractal concept, which suggests that a smaller fragment of a system symbolically reflects the structure of a larger fragment and exists in a specific form of interdependence with it. Thus, Cooper presents a model that considers the sphere of the political and the psychic within a particular holistic continuum, which is a relatively rare phenomenon in psychological and psychiatric models. Typically, these spheres are not integrated into comprehensive concepts and models in most personality theories.

Cooper believed that the structure of the family and domestic life conditioned individuals to always be part of a social group and discouraged solitude. Any manifestation of personal autonomy can be a blow to the organization of the family system. Cooper was convinced that madness is a movement away from a familial mode of existence.

Contact and connection with other individuals are encouraged, as is the pursuit of autonomous existence, where the individual can function as a self-sufficient personality. At the very least, he pointed out certain values actively declared in society that proclaim the integrity of the family system as a criterion of normalcy and adequacy for an individual.

He also believed that schizophrenic disorders were a consequence of the suppression of personality in society. This suppression occurs through the imposition of stereotypical values. Unwillingness to conform to the majority's values is perceived as madness and is not only criticized on a moral level but also subjected to social and institutional pressure. Contemporary psychiatry is a clear example of this.

Cooper, to a large extent, equated madness with rebellion and dissidence. In this sense, a madman acts as a kind of revolutionary whose activity is directed not outwardly toward the social world but toward psychic experiences. In this, we must note Cooper's originality of thought, as he truly directed attention to mental disorders, drawing analogies between internal psychic processes and external politics.

Both Cooper and Laing believed that schizophrenia in an individual was a vivid manifestation of a crisis within the social group they belonged to. The need to break free from the shackles of social pressure finds expression in various psychotic symptoms.

Cooper expressed rather radical convictions that if the structure of family functioning, as accepted in our society, could be destroyed, we would liberate individuals from a behavioral model that potentially triggers schizophrenic symptoms.

He also believed that the schizophrenic process could be a peculiar attempt to regain lost wholeness.

Like Laing, Cooper used the term "metanoia" and perceived it as a form of movement between four states: eknoia, paranoia, noia, and antinoia. In Cooper's understanding, they are interpreted as follows:

1. **Eknoia:** This is the condition of the majority of people who live in society and conform to its rules and norms. Living in a state of eknoia is a constant way of annihilating one's true self, rejecting it for the sake of certain social ideals that are imprinted on a person from early childhood without choice. Sooner or later, the state of eknoia can provoke a deep rebellion within a person, a realization that something is fundamentally wrong or incorrect. However, being devoid of the cards on how to leave one's established place, individuals mostly begin to exhibit certain anxieties and eventually psychotic symptoms.

2. **Paranoia:** In a state of paranoia, individuals become uncertain about the correctness of social organization. They begin to realize that their profound essence is suppressed, and they are unable to fully be who they truly are.

3. **Noia:** In this state, individuals may experience intense depression and sadness due to the process of separating themselves from their social group. The old mask has not yet been fully removed, and the new one has not yet formed, but the irreversibility of specific personal transformations is already felt.

4. **Antinoia:** This state is the transcendence of one's self, the destruction of one's former self, and its complete transmutation and transformation. It is a state that brings the individual closer to a transcendent experience. The psychospiritual journey may be perceived as a form of madness, but in this case, we witness the relativity of such madness. A person who has entered this state may perceive individuals in the state of eknoia as mad.

Each of these states is experienced by an individual sequentially. Each element of the model represents a progression culminating in the fourth stage. With each stage, there is a gradual reshaping and restructuring of the personality.

To a large extent, the process of transitioning from eknoia to antinoia can be perceived as a continuum of a child's impressions during the process of birth. Eknoia is perceived as a state of fusion with the womb, paranoia as the period of the onset of labor contractions along the birth canal, noia as the process of exiting the womb, detachment, and cutting of the umbilical cord, and antinoia as the existence of the individual outside the womb. If we consider Cooper's model in this way, we can note its strong resemblance to Stanislav Grof's model of basic perinatal matrices (BPM). In any case, we must acknowledge that both authors delve into certain profound impressions in the human unconscious using different maps of description.

David Cooper, following the example of Tommaso Campanella and his utopia "The City of the Sun," constructed his ideas about the ideals of a therapeutic society in which the model of solitary existence and the model of interconnectedness with other members of society could coexist harmoniously. Cooper believed that only when an individual learns to be autonomous and experience solitude can they fully engage with others.

Despite the somewhat utopian nature of these models, Cooper managed to conduct an experiment in which he observed the functioning of his "therapeutic society." This project was called "Villa 21" and operated for four years in one of the wards at Shenley Hospital.

The project involved patients between the ages of 15 and 30 with symptoms of schizophrenia, psychopathy, and other personality disorders. The aim of the experiment was to attempt to prove that the classical system of functioning in psychiatric institutions, characterized by rigid regulations and repressive modes of intervention, is not necessary and, moreover, can contribute to the deterioration of patients' conditions. During the experiment, patients were not confined within the usual boundaries traditionally seen in psychiatric institutions and actively participated in assisting and supporting one another. The democratic system of functioning within the ward and the equal relationships between patients and therapists did not compromise the quality of the ward's work. Positive results were obtained, indicating that the adopted structure of relationships is not a significant and obligatory attribute of the ward's functioning. The experience gained from "Villa 21" served as the foundation for the future collaborative experiment of Laing and Cooper in their therapeutic community, "Kingsley Hall."

Unfortunately, the progressive beliefs and long-term experiments of Laing and Cooper did not find widespread application. It can be assumed that their philosophical and practical findings await their time and will unfold to their full potential.

Thomas Szasz

Thomas Szasz (1920–2012) was a renowned American psychiatrist, professor of psychiatry, and prominent figure in the anti-psychiatry movement. He was born in Budapest and was the younger of two sons in a Jewish family. His father was involved in private entrepreneurship. While attending school, Szasz demonstrated diligence as a student and excelled in sports. In 1938, the Szasz family moved to Cincinnati, USA, where Thomas enrolled in college at the university, specializing in the study of physics. In 1941, he completed his bachelor's degree in physics and decided to pursue a new specialization in medicine at the same university. He completed his education in 1944 and entered an internship program. In 1945, he received his medical degree. He then studied psychoanalytic therapy at the Chicago Institute of Psychoanalysis.

Thomas Szasz

Szasz's primary teacher in psychoanalysis was Franz Alexander, the founder of psychosomatic psychoanalysis, whose views significantly influenced Szasz's immersion in the scientific aspects of psychotherapy. Szasz's early scientific articles focused on psychosomatics, specifically symptoms such as hypersalivation, alopecia, constipation, and diarrhea. In 1951, Szasz obtained specialization in psychiatry and also got married. In 1954, he was drafted into military service during the Korean War. In 1956, he became a professor of psychiatry at Syracuse University, a position he held for the rest of his life. Prior to 1956, Szasz's work primarily dealt with issues of psychosomatics and classical psychoanalysis. In 1957, his first book, "Pain and Pleasure: A Study of Bodily Sensations," was published. In 1966, "The Myth of Mental Illness" was published, followed by "The Manufacture of Madness" in 1970. In these latter two books, which made Szasz particularly popular, he actively developed the philosophy of anti-psychiatry, providing a multifaceted historical analysis of it. In 1971, the American Humanist Academy awarded him the title of "Humanist of the Year."

Alongside Laing and Cooper, Szasz is one of the key activists in the anti-psychiatry movement. In his work, he paid significant attention to criticizing the functional structure of psychiatric care, arguing that political systems encourage the use of psychiatry as a punitive social instrument. He fought for the mental rights of individuals, believing that everyone has the right to govern their own mind and body as they see fit, both in terms of internal mental processes and external political matters. Szasz was a liberal and democrat who advocated for the fight for one's rights and ridiculed the absurdity of various social institutions' organizations.

In his book "The Myth of Mental Illness," Szasz comments that we cannot speak of a mental disorder as something real since we cannot directly observe what exactly happens within a person's psyche. In this view, Szasz aligns to a large extent with the philosophy of behaviorism proposed by B.F. Skinner and the concept of the "black box," which refers to certain internal processes that, for the most part, cannot be objectively investigated. Behaviorists aimed to exclude all unobservable mental processes from the realm of research. Unfortunately, this position ultimately led to the almost complete disappearance of behaviorism in its pure form. It is worth noting that Szasz wrote his main works at a time when neurophysiological diagnostics had not yet reached sufficient development. At that time, the scientist could afford not to rely on objective data, such as magnetic resonance imaging, which is capable of qualitatively describing the neurophysiological aspects of mental states and experiences. Szasz's disregard for numerous scientific data obtained through objective research on various disorders discredits his philosophical position. Unfortunately, until the end of his life, Szasz defended ideas that were formed in the late 1950s and early 1960s.

Like Laing and Cooper, Szasz expressed radical anti-psychiatric beliefs and argued that the concept of mental illness should be entirely removed from the classification of clinical medicine. Szasz then shifted to his understanding of the psychiatric institution, stating that it primarily exists as a political instrument and perpetuates the myth of mental illness to maintain positions of power and influence. Szasz even believed that psychiatry had become a parody of medicine and had become something akin to a separate state religion that dictates and predetermines the criteria of normality and abnormality at its own discretion. Michel Foucault, in his 1961 book "Madness and Civilization: A History of Insanity in the Age of Reason," shared Szasz's opinion regarding the dubious authenticity of psychiatry as a genuine science. An interesting observation made by the professor was regarding drug addiction, stating that drug addicts are persecuted in a similar manner to how Jews, Gypsies, witches, representatives of sexual minorities, and others were persecuted in different countries in the past.

Szasz expressed support for the following ideas:

- **Presumption of sanity:** Sanity and insanity should be determined through legal methods, with the right to appeal. A person is presumed sane until proven otherwise.

- **Right to suicide:** Szasz believes that suicide is an expression of personal choice, and the state should not impede it.

- **Abolition of the insanity defense:** According to Szasz, the determination of sanity or insanity by psychiatrists in court should be discontinued. He believes that such assessments are irrelevant to objective reality. By fulfilling this social function, the psychiatrist resembles a priest who condemns and judges.

- **Abolition of involuntary hospitalization:** Involuntary hospitalization, in Szasz's view, is a gross violation of individual rights. In the documentary film "Psychiatry: An Industry of Death," released in 2006, Szasz expressed his opinion that any form of involuntary hospitalization is a crime against humanity.

- **Personal right to drug use:** Szasz considered drug use to be a victimless crime. He also believed that addiction is not a disease. The medical concepts of addiction have no objective relation to reality. The use of substances that alter consciousness is an expression of individual freedom of choice. Substance dependence itself can be seen as a specific social ritual. Examples of this can be found in cultures where the use of consciousness-altering substances is a distinct cultural characteristic that has been present in society for many centuries and even millennia.

Szasz directed his rebellion and protest against the state institution of psychiatry, commenting that his philosophy often has no relation to the psychiatrists, psychotherapists, psychologists, and social workers who practice privately.

Behind Szasz's excessive, sometimes ultraradical, and scientifically unfounded approach to treating the mentally ill, we can trace his deep intention to defend personal freedom, fight for equality, and protect true moral values.

Pathopsychological Profiles and Anti-psychiatric Forms of Psychotherapy

It is important to emphasize from the outset that anti-psychiatric therapy is not merely a set of specific methods but rather a philosophy embraced by the psychotherapist in their practice. It is quite challenging to speak about the specific effectiveness of this therapeutic approach for patients, especially those who do not suffer from severe mental illnesses. It should be understood that in this case, the therapist's personality and the various instrumental practices they intend to employ in their work will play a significant role. However, one can observe a general pattern in the application of anti-psychiatric philosophy towards patients with different pathopsychological profiles.

Hysteroid Profile

Individuals with a hysteroid profile tend to adore indulging in the therapist's philosophical inclinations in order to receive positive feedback and, in turn, become the center of attention. Naturally, if the therapist's philosophical "credo" possesses a certain eccentricity that sets their therapeutic approach apart from others, hysteroids can readily embrace this game and become deeply involved in it. It is important to note that hysteroid personalities are often indifferent to the specific means by which attention is attracted. The therapist's profound conviction in the validity of an eccentric philosophy and therapy can be perceived by the patient as a peculiar and specific form of indulging their neurotic behavior. Therefore, the anti-psychiatric style of working with patients with a hysteroid personality profile should be applied in a measured and moderate manner. Only the proper combination of theory and practice in this case can bring about constructive changes in the patient.

Paranoid Profile

In my opinion, it is better not to apply the anti-psychiatric approach when working with paranoid patients. Most likely, a paranoid patient will construct their own specific and exaggerated paranoid reality based on the therapist's philosophy and behavior, which is unlikely to benefit them. Paranoids see deception everywhere. The likelihood of perceiving this "deception" in the therapist's behavior, who practices the philosophy of anti-psychiatry, will significantly increase in their eyes. Paranoid patients are not particularly fond of eccentric therapists or eccentric psychotherapeutic methods. This must be kept in mind.

Psychopathic Profile

A psychopathic patient may be inclined to play games of anti-psychiatry with the therapist. However, it should not be forgotten that any game involving a psychopathic individual is a game of predator and prey. When engaging in the game, the psychopath will clearly aim to outsmart the therapist. There is no need to indulge in the illusion that the profound philosophical meaning of anti-psychiatric therapy can emotionally touch a psychopath. They simply do not require it. Therefore, in the context of this profile, it is also necessary to state the complete inapplicability of this therapeutic philosophy.

Obsessive-Compulsive Profile

For patients with an obsessive-compulsive profile, the variety of anti-psychiatric philosophy can play a positive role when the instrumental aspects of therapeutic work are applied correctly. The excessive pedantry of such patients, combined with the therapist's appropriate methods, can provide the patient with confidence in their abilities. They may perceive the obsessions inherent in their personality as unique character traits that have not fully found proper social embodiment. In this case, practices aimed at redefining the meaning of the patient's actions can be particularly effective. A significant change in their attitude towards certain neurotic behaviors can serve as powerful support for the patient to develop self-confidence and create a more constructive self-image. Naturally, this will activate positive therapeutic psychodynamics within the individual. Therefore, for this particular personality profile, we recommend the application of anti-psychiatric theory and practice as needed, according to the patient's personality and the appropriateness of the therapeutic context.

Schizoid Profile

Depending on various psychodynamic factors, schizoid individuals will react differently to the practice of anti-psychiatric philosophy. A schizoid person experiences a need for detachment and dissociation from various conventional social routines and is often capable of creating interest-based clubs for fellow schizoids. Anti-psychiatric philosophy accommodates the idiosyncrasies of the patient, allowing them to perceive their symptoms not as deviations from the norm but as alternative versions of normality that can be accepted as given. Therefore, if this type of practical philosophy is applied to a schizoid individual, certain aspects of their personality will undergo constructive changes. If the right notes can be found within the schizoid's soul, working with anti-psychiatric philosophy and practice can create a powerful rapport that potentially becomes a precursor to constructive changes in the patient's personality.

Epileptoid Profile

Based on our observations, the anti-psychiatric approach to therapy is unlikely to be suitable for patients with an epileptoid personality profile and a full-fledged epileptoid disorder due to their inclination towards a more orthodox view of the therapist's work. The epileptoid individual often seeks to see the therapist as a bastion of basic social values that they themselves occasionally ignore. Within society, the epileptoid personality is in a constant state of transition, first engaging in regretful actions and then seeking redemption through specific social institutions, often of a religious nature. Due to this dynamic, the therapist's indulgence in the various negative behavioral manifestations of the epileptoid personality is rarely perceived by the patient in a constructive manner. Therefore, we do not recommend the application of the anti-psychiatric approach in psychotherapy for patients with this personality profile due to its extremely low effectiveness.

Schizophrenic Profile

In fact, the anti-psychiatric approach was specifically developed in the 1950s and 1960s for patients with a schizophrenic personality profile. In this case, the most important aspect is the correctness and accuracy of the therapist's imitation strategy, which creates a mirror of the internal world of the schizophrenic patient. By correctness, we mean behavior with empathy that truly has a powerful healing effect on the patient. Excessive eccentricity in external behavioral forms can have a constructive effect but should not be the basis or the leading factor. The rules can be similar for patients with a schizophrenic accent. However, it is important to remember that deep adjustment through anti-psychiatric work is carried out to create new adaptive mechanisms in the patient's personality, which could potentially help them live more fully. This must be constantly taken into account and worked on, primarily through the prism of this belief.

Manic-Depressive Profile

Based on our observations, the anti-psychiatric approach is often not fully applicable to patients with MDP personality profile. The two key phases that patients go through—manic and depressive—often do not require reinforcement of the adequacy or inadequacy of their social manifestations. However, if we are discussing schizoaffective disorder, which can represent a specific combination of MDP and schizophrenic disorder, anti-psychiatric methods may find their place with proper and constructive application.

9

Integrative Psychotherapy

Many contemporary therapy approaches are related to different vectors, combining some of them. Often, two, three, or sometimes four vectors are involved. However, in my opinion, only a few are able to combine all or almost all vectors to some extent, forming an integrative presupposition in the system for adopting various methods and elegantly combining them.

The initial division into pure psychoanalysis, behaviorism, humanistic therapy, and transpersonal therapy is gradually becoming a thing of the past as different therapists find their way of combining different methods, discovering that the correct combinations can yield excellent results in working with patients. However, we believe that the integrative style of psychotherapy implies that the philosophical foundation of the method itself is based on the concepts of acceptance, borrowing, and coexistence with other methods.

In a sense, the integrative style is not an assortment of different styles but rather a **metastyle** or a model of models that can simultaneously incorporate unique therapeutic methods.

Neuro-Linguistic Programming

Neuro-Linguistic Programming (NLP) has become the primary representative of the integrative vector in psychotherapy. It was created in the early 1970s by Richard Bandler and John Grinder. Richard Bandler was a psychology student who regularly conducted gestalt therapy sessions at the university, while John Grinder was a linguistics professor who once visited Bandler's group and became interested in what he was doing with his patients.

Grinder attempted to create a specific "map" of linguistic patterns used by Bandler during his work. They then joined forces and started working together on what later became known as the meta-model.

John Grinder

They began studying the works of renowned therapists in order to capture the linguistic structure of what they do and the correct questions they usually ask patients to evoke insight and catharsis, thereby manifesting the "magic" of psychotherapy. They focused their attention on five therapists.

Richard Bandler

These were Frederick Perls, the creator of Gestalt psychotherapy; Milton Erickson, the author of non-directive hypnotic suggestion; Virginia Satir, the creator of family therapy; Frank Farrelly, the creator of provocative therapy; and Moshe Feldenkrais, the creator of the Feldenkrais Method. They also actively collaborated with psychologist, ethnologist, and anthropologist Gregory Bateson, who played a significant role as their mentor and consultant. It is worth mentioning that the works of American anthropologist Carlos Castaneda, who studied the shamanic traditions of Mexican Indians, significantly influenced the emergence of early NLP.

Map of the World

Initially, Grinder and Bandler were intrigued by the linguistic structure used by therapists. They based their assumptions on the idea proposed by linguist Korzybski in 1933, that "the map is not the territory," meaning our perception of the world is not the actual world, and the language we use is a way to operate with the "map" of the world. Bandler and Grinder introduced the notion that our language shapes our map of reality, and this shaping occurs through three fundamental processes.

1. **Generalization:** The process by which several different experiences are grouped together in consciousness into one category or, based on a new experience, a separate category can be formed. For example, a child gets an electric shock. Their consciousness generalizes the experience and perceives all other electrical outlets as potentially dangerous and capable of causing pain. We do not need to recheck each socket for the danger of its impact. Experiencing or witnessing it once is enough.

2. **Deletion:** When we acquire a specific experience, we only describe a part of it with our language. We use this part in the process of social communication, conveying it to others. The other part of our perception that is not formulated in words is either omitted and does not become conscious at all, or it is gradually suppressed into the realm of the unconscious. In the context of verbal communication, for instance, the phrase "I'm glad to see you" can have various meanings for a person. The underlying meanings may be hidden behind this phrase. We do not request the specifics that lie behind it; we mostly operate with the "label" rather than the actual object.

3. **Distortion:** A significant portion of the map is formed through the analogization of one experiential block with another, representing something as a metaphor for something else. In ancient cultures, many such analogies were used to compare human qualities with the behavior of different animals. The process of analogization is closely related to the construction of myths and ancient beliefs. By blending different experiential categories together, we gain more opportunities to use them qualitatively in our lives. At the physiological level, the process of distortion can be explained by the emergence of multiple connections between neurons in the brain. It is important to remember that the intelligence of a living being depends much more on the quantity of connections between brain neurons than on their actual number. The process of distortion is closely linked to the process of

personal creativity, allowing individuals to create something new that was not previously represented in their perception.

Based on their understanding of the three fundamental processes of reality mapping, Bandler and Grinder began formulating specific clarifying questions that a psychotherapist can ask a patient to help them fully grasp the deep structure of their experience. We typically use surface structure in verbalization and thinking.

Examples of surface-level experiences can be phrases like "She doesn't love me," "They don't understand me," or "The world is a war." Within each phrase, various meanings can be embedded, significantly differing in the understanding of different individuals. From a set of different clarifying questions that allow for the realization of the deep structure of experience, the first model in NLP emerges—the Meta Model.

The first two collaborative literary works by Bandler and Grinder are dedicated to this model. These two volumes are "The Structure of Magic," in which they extensively explain how this model can be applied in the context of therapeutic work.

Metamodel

Let's explore how different questions can be categorized according to the three processes of reality mapping. We will provide examples of correspondences highlighted by Michael Hall.

Distortions

1. **Nominalization** refers to words that cannot be perceived through the representational systems of perception. They cannot be seen, heard, or physically felt. However, they always carry specific meanings. The key ideas embedded in nominalizations may be identical for everyone, but the secondary ideas and details of the first and second can vary significantly.

Examples of such words include "love," "equality," "brotherhood," "collaboration," "understanding," "harmony," and "freedom," among others. Examining the meaning of these words without interpreting the specifics can lead to a cognitive error.
Clarifying questions to eliminate the cognitive error of nominalization are as follows:
"What exactly do you mean by the term 'freedom'?"
"What specific actions do you perform when expressing your love?"
"By what criteria do you determine that what is happening between you is friendship?"

2. **Mind-reading** involves certain statement phrases that imply the presence of a cognitive process, emotion, or state in the subject of discussion without mentioning the sensory criteria through which this information became part of conscious awareness.
   Examples include "I see that you are a good person," "I think you understand me," and "I feel that we will work well together."
   Clarifying questions can be as follows:
   "What exactly do you see that allows you to consider me a good person?"
   "Based on what thoughts did you assume that I understood you?"
   "Which specific sensations enable you to understand that I am a good person?"

3. **Cause-effect linkage** is a linguistic construction that implies the mention of two events where one is perceived as the consequence of the other. However, the experience that could provide an understanding of why these events are causally linked remains unexplored.
   Examples include "If you eat little, you won't grow", "If you don't listen to me, you'll remain foolish." "If you show off, you won't get candy."
   Clarifying questions can be as follows:

"Based on what specific information did you come to the conclusion that if I don't eat, I won't grow?"
"How did you understand that I would remain foolish if I didn't listen to you?"
"What served as the basis for your belief that if I show off, I won't get candy?"

4. **Complex equivalence** occurs when one nominalization is equated to another. The equation can be perceived literally or metaphorically. Examples include "love is war," "freedom is harmony," and "life is a stream."
Clarifying questions can be as follows:
"What exactly allows you to equate love and war?"
"Based on what criteria do you compare freedom and harmony?"
"What specific experiences in your life allow you to compare life and a stream?"

5. **Presupposition** refers to a statement that contains a secondary implied meaning not explicitly expressed in the message text. There are 29 different types of presuppositions. Here are some examples:
Phrase: "Next time we will do better."
Presupposition: "There have been previous times."
Phrase: "He bought the fifth car."
Presupposition: "Four have already been bought before."
Phrase: "Do you realize that you understand me?"
Presupposition: "You understand me."
Clarifying phrases can be as follows:
"Do you mean that there were previous times?"
"Do you mean to say that four cars were already bought before this one?"
"Do you mean that I already understand you?"

Generalizations

1. **Universal quantifier:** In this case, we are working with predicates that generalize certain experiences. These words include "all," "always," "no one," "never," "nobody," "nowhere," "no way," and so on.
   Example usage of this pattern: "All people are the same," "It always happens like this," "Nobody wants to understand me," and so on.
   Unpacking questions:
   "Name those people whom you consider to be the same."
   "Can we consider these people as 'all'?"
   "What do you mean when you say it always happens?"
   "Does it happen every day, every minute, every second, or are there time limitations?"
   "Who exactly doesn't want to understand you? List them."
   "Is there a possibility that somewhere there are people who can understand you?"

2. **Modal Operator of Necessity:** The use of phrases like "I cannot" and "I must." *Examples*: "I cannot afford to do it today," "I must stay where I am."
   Unpacking questions:
   "What exactly prevents you from doing it today?"
   "Is there a possibility to overcome these factors?"
   "What exactly makes you stay where you are?"
   "Have you ever tried not staying where you are?"

3. **Lost Performative:** A phrase that does not specify the author who created the message or the source from which it was taken.
   Examples: "Men should provide for women," "Women should cook, clean, and give birth to children," "Children are the flowers of life," "Take care of yourself."
   Unpacking questions:
   "Who is the author of this message?"

"Where was the information taken from?"

Omissions

1. **Indefinite Noun**: Inanimate objects without specifying additional information.
   Examples: "I returned to the house," "They bought a car," "Set an alarm clock," "In this case, it's better to take a trombone."
   Unpacking questions:
   "Which specific house did you return to?"
   "Which car did they buy?"
   "Which alarm clock should I set?"
   "Which specific trombone is better for me to take?"

2. **Indefinite Verb**: Verbs without specifying the details and specifics of the action being performed.
   Examples: "They run," "They perform on stage," "He falls asleep," "Someone shouts."
   Unpacking questions:
   "How exactly do they run?"
   "How exactly do they perform on stage?"
   "How exactly does he fall asleep?"
   "How exactly does someone shout?"

3. **Incorrect Comparison**: A sentence that presents a comparison without specifying the basis for comparison or the criteria used for evaluation.
   Examples: "They are better than everyone else," "These students are smarter than the others," "He possesses greater strength."
   Unpacking questions:
   "In what specific way are they better than everyone else?"
   "How did you determine that these students are smarter than the others?"

"How did you determine that he possesses greater strength?"
"How exactly was this strength measured?"

4. **Lost Referential Index**: In this case, words such as "someone," "some people," "they," "doctors," "psychologists," "engineers," "tourists," "volunteers," and so on are used in speech and thought.
Examples: "Someone is waiting for you," "Some people are already at the starting line," "Doctors know a lot about medications."
Unpacking questions:
"Who specifically is waiting for me?"
"Who specifically is already at the starting line?"
"Which specific doctors know a lot about medications?"

Michael Hall's Metamodel

Michael Hall expanded upon the Grinder and Bandler model by introducing additional cognitive distortions inherent in human thinking and speech.

1. **Identification:** This metamodel pattern clarifies any unspecified identification used in speech. In the alternative meta-model, we will consider two specific forms of the identification pattern. In this case, we view the model element as the most abstract form.
Examples: "liberal," "party-goer," or "judoka."
Unpacking: "What specific meaning do you attribute to the word 'liberal'?"

2. **Statistical Terms:** This pattern unpacks phrases that rely on statistical data. Formally, this pattern is a variation of the lost referential index in the classic NLP metamodel.
Examples: "English scientists have proven that...." "Scientific research confirms the validity of our hypotheses."
Unpacking: "Which specific English scientists are you referring to?"

3. **Over / Under - Defined Terms:** This pattern reveals excessive descriptions of an object or process, creating a specific representation of the discussed object, or simply inadequate descriptions that do not provide a complete understanding of the subject matter.
   Example of excessive description: "I really wanted to do what I had been dreaming about." "Given the conditions of my life, I was not able to do it." "So, I decided to take a step that could change my life."
   Unpacking: "Please specify more clearly: what specifically motivated you and what action did you take?"
   Example of inadequate description: "This largely determined the course of events."
   Unpacking: "Which specific course of events did it determine?"

4. **False verbal dichotomies:** Occur when there is a direct denial of the influence of one process or phenomenon on another.
   Example: "My financial well-being has nothing to do with the political situation in the country."
   Unpacking: "Based on what criteria did you come to the conclusion that your financial well-being has nothing to do with the political situation in the country?"

5. **"Either-Or" Words:** This pattern presents an ultimatum, offering only two possible choices while ignoring other potentially viable options.
   Example: "Either you listen to me or you leave."
   Unpacking: "What other possible courses of action exist for me in this situation?" "What are the reasons for this strict limitation of choice—either one or the other?"

6. **Pseudowords:** In this case, words with vague and sometimes absurd semantics are used, which can significantly differ in meaning when used by different people.
   Example: "You're crazy."

Unpacking: "What exactly do you mean when you say I'm crazy?"

7. **Multilevel Statements**: This pattern involves a phrase in which the logical level that should determine the meaning of the message is not specified.
   Example: "How can you allow yourself to do this?"
   Unpacking: "Could you clarify the meaning you attribute to the question?" "What answer or action would you like to receive in response?"

8. **Personalizations:** This pattern occurs when a person takes someone else's action or emotional reaction personally without considering real sensory criteria. Actions are often interpreted negatively, making this cognitive error predominantly characteristic of paranoid personalities.
   Example: "You don't look at me during our conversation, so you must be plotting something against me."
   Unpacking: "Based on what reliable sensory information do you form your judgment?"

9. **Metaphors:** The use of analogies and metaphors in communication does not fully reveal the true meaning of the message but rather diverts from it and often misleads the interlocutor regarding the actual content of the message.
   Example: "He grew up like a weed by the roadside."
   Unpacking: "What do you mean when you say he grew up like a weed by the roadside? Does this metaphor objectively describe the process of his growth?"

Initially, Bandler and Grinder did not think that their work could take a separate direction in psychotherapy. In their work "The Structure of Magic," they comment that the model they describe can be perceived as auxiliary to any form of therapeutic work, and they do not claim to form a separate direction in psychotherapy. But time proved otherwise. They continued studying the works of various therapists and began forming notions about the structure of other therapeutic mechanisms. Different people gathered around them, actively participating in their research and studying the structure of personal experience and expertise.

A short time later, when the seminars conducted by Bandler and Grinder became quite popular and when they started teaching not only the meta-model but also new models, there arose a need to somehow name what they were doing. There is an amusing legend about how the name NLP itself emerged. Whether it is true or fiction is hard to judge, but it is not of substantial importance. Before one seminar, Richard Bandler, John Grinder, and their associate Frank Pucelik were sitting in a car, contemplating what to call their field of activity. They actively discussed the topic for some time but could not reach a consensus. Soon, one of them noticed a stack of books lying in the car. One was about neurology, another was about linguistics, and the third was about programming. The combination of these three key words gave the name to the method that is still known as neuro-linguistic programming.

Although NLP itself was formed in the context of modeling by well-known and successful psychotherapists, it was not essentially psychotherapy but was defined by its creators as the "science and art of modeling subjective human experience." That is, it could effectively apply to various spheres of human activity. It is precisely because of this that NLP has spread widely to other areas of human endeavor, such as politics, advertising, business communication, interpersonal communication, etc.

Formally, the meta-model was intended for correcting cognitive distortions that may occur in an individual's experience, and in this sense, the meta-model work closely resembled cognitive therapy by Aaron Beck and rational emotive therapy by Albert Ellis, although it had some differences. Due to the initial focus on cognitive correction, it can be said that the primary vector in which NLP developed was the cognitive vector.

Anchors

The next significant vector was the behavioral one. The creators of NLP borrowed the concept of acquiring a conditioned reflex from Ivan Pavlov. A similar term used by behaviorists, particularly John Watson and B.F. Skinner, was "operant conditioning." Both imply the ability to elicit an old response through a newly established stimulus.

For example, Pavlov did this with dogs by creating an association between food consumption and the activation of a light bulb in their physiological reactions. Later, when only the light bulb was presented to the dogs, the scientist observed the secretion of gastric juice. Or how Watson did it with the little boy Albert. He showed him a white rat, and when the boy laughed, the experimenter struck an iron gong behind his back to induce fear. After a certain number of repetitions, Albert began to display fear in response to the white rat.

In this case, we see the restructuring of a response, where the previous stimulus is replaced by a new one. Naturally, based on the works of Pavlov, Watson, and other scientists, therapeutic methods were developed. Behavioral therapy, which applies the restructuring of old responses to new ones through operant conditioning, became widely known in America. Most likely, it was from behavioral therapy that NLP borrowed the concept of "anchors."

Anchors can be of various types:

- **Natural anchors**: Imprinted in our physiology, they are reflexive. For example, it can be a reflex to pull your hand away when touching something hot.

- **Spontaneously created anchors:** For instance, when you were in the company of pleasant people and heard a new musical track, two stimuli became associated. After some time, when you hear that track again, the state of pleasant interaction you had previously experienced reappears in your consciousness.

- **Artificially created anchors:** In this case, states are intentionally linked. For example, when a patient experiences a resourceful state that needs to be anchored, the therapist touches a specific point on their shoulder and applies consistent pressure for 5–15 seconds. Then, when there is a need to reproduce the state, the therapist simply presses on the same point again to activate the desired state.

Types of anchors:

- **Visual anchors** can be external or internal. A typical example of an external visual anchor is a fixation on the image of a familiar person that evokes a stable positive reaction. The response to an internal image involves visualization. For instance, you imagine that there is a party awaiting you tomorrow, and pleasant sensations arise in your body.

- **Auditory tonal anchors** can be both external and internal. With an external anchor, you may hear a loud noise and experience anxiety. With an internal anchor, you create certain sounds yourself that change your state. For example, humming a children's song that puts you in a humorous mood. The effect of an auditory tonal anchor is directly related to the sound itself, not the literal semantic meanings that words and phrases may carry.

- **Auditory discrete anchors** elicit a response not to a simple sound but specifically to the semantics of a word or phrase. It can also be external or internal. With an external anchor, you may hear the phrase "Get up!" and automatically jump out of bed. With an internal anchor, your state changes when you articulate a specific semantic construction or simply do it solely on the level of thinking and inner dialogue.

- **Kinesthetic anchors** are activated when there is any touch on the body, such as stroking, a strike, or a push, etc. For example, if you experience anxiety and are slapped on the shoulder at that moment, a subsequent slap on the shoulder can trigger the anchored state of anxiety. Kinesthetic anchors can also include taste and olfactory stimuli.

- **Motor anchors** are activated through the repetition of specific motor dynamics or statics. For example, while in a specific posture, you experience a strong sensation. Later, when you assume the same posture again, the sensation returns. Similarly, the dynamic aspect can come into play. For instance, you memorize a particular sequence of movements, let's say a dance routine, in a fixed state. Then, when you repeat the sequence of movements, the anchored state returns.

These types of anchors are specifically used in brief therapy sessions to evoke positive changes in patients.

One of the classical techniques in NLP that utilizes anchoring is "collapsing anchors." In this technique, a negative state is associated with one anchor, which is then targeted for therapeutic work, while one to three positive statements are associated with another anchor to counterbalance the negative anchor.

The negative anchor is activated first, reestablishing the negative state, and while it persists, the positive anchor is activated. Both anchors are held simultaneously for a period of time, after which the negative anchor is released, followed by the positive anchor. This pattern is fundamental for working with kinesthetic anchors, although a similar anchoring method can be effectively applied to other representational modalities.

The downside of working with kinesthetic anchors is that direct physical contact with the patient or interlocutor is required, unless in a therapeutic context. In some cases, these physical touches may be somewhat inappropriate. It is important to consider this factor, especially when dealing with patients who belong to certain psychopathological profiles and may not be receptive to physical contact. Schizoid personalities serve as a striking example of such profiles.

In such cases, the use of visual and auditory anchoring may prove effective. For example, during a conversation with the patient, one can inquire about resourceful states in their life. While the patient comments on these states, subtle fixed gestures can be made with the hand or another body part, thereby creating a visual anchor for that particular state.

Later, when the conversation touches on sad topics, the visual anchor can be subtly reproduced to introduce the resourceful state into the negative context, thereby overriding it. Similarly, auditory anchoring can be employed by using rhythmic tapping on the table with fingers or an object instead of a hand gesture.

Changing Personal History

A highly intriguing therapeutic technique in NLP is the technique of altering personal history, which is rooted in psychoanalysis and hypnoanalysis. In this technique, the therapist guides the patient into the past to work through their traumatic experiences.

The classical approach utilizes anchor techniques for this purpose, although other methods of state change can also be employed. Initially, the therapist elicits the patient's concern or issue, such as the fear of public speaking. Then, step by step, the therapist assists the patient in traversing their personal timeline, identifying when this fear originated in their life. Gradually, they aim to reach the root cause of the fear, uncovering when it first emerged and under what circumstances, thus reviving it in the memory during the therapy session.

Subsequently, the therapist dissociates the patient from the current problem and inquires about three resourceful states that were lacking in all the contexts associated with the fear of public speaking. The patient determines the necessary states, and the therapist helps them locate instances of experiencing those states in their own life. These states are then anchored.

Moving forward, the therapist re-associates the patient with the earliest manifestation of the traumatic experience and activates the resource anchor. Finally, the patient gradually progresses along the timeline to the traumatic experience that has been recalled. In each subsequent negative experience, the positive anchor is also activated. Once the overlaying of negative states with positive ones is completed up to the present moment, an additional practice can be introduced.

The therapist asks the patient to shift into the future and imagine themselves speaking publicly. When the patient successfully recreates this future scenario, the therapist also activates the resource anchor, thus programming the anticipation of the experience yet to come. There are numerous variations of this technique, and its execution should be calibrated to suit the individual patient and their specific needs. A dry and mechanical execution may fail to yield comprehensive therapeutic results.

Submodalities

Working with submodalities is an intriguing practice in NLP. Submodalities represent the qualitative characteristics of the primary modalities of perception - visual, auditory, and kinesthetic.

Visual submodalities	Auditory submodalities	Kinesthetic submodalities
Brightness	Loudness	Intensity
Contrast	Tone	Temperature
Focus	Intonation	Pressure
Color image	Reverberation	Pain sensitivity
Black and white image	Echo	Location of occurrence
Image mobility	Mono/Stereo	Volume of sensations
Image static	Spatial sound positioning	Sensory differentiation
Spatial image position	Sound intensity	Direction of movement of sensations
Presence of frame on the image	Classification of sound source	Onset and decay rate
Direction of image movement	Sound quality	Diversity of sensations
Image movement speed	Sound refraction	Cyclicity of sensations

This table lists the most basic submodalities, but there may be more of them. Submodalities encode our experience. Depending on the specific sub-modality code, we react differently to past, present, or future experiences. For example, we can discuss submodalities that associate a person with an experience or dissociate them from it, thereby increasing or decreasing the intensity of emotional experience. In other words, the more experience encoded by associating submodalities, the more intense the emotional reaction will be, and conversely, dissociating submodalities can nullify emotional intensity.

For example, a large, bright, moving image that is closely related to your possible future achievement is likely to evoke strong positive emotions. Meanwhile, a small, dull, static, and distant image will not evoke any emotional reactions.

Naturally, it has been discovered that we can instrumentally change one submodality of experience to another, thereby creating new emotional reactions and recoding existing or potentially possible experiences. The application of submodalities, like anchors, has a very wide range of applications in NLP and can be used in various contexts.

The simplest example of working with submodalities in practice is the direct transference of submodalities. For example, you recall an experience that evokes negative emotions and place the image of that memory to your left. Then you focus on the key submodalities that encode that image. Next, you recall an experience that consistently evokes positive emotional reactions. You place the image of that experience on the right side of your imaginary screen. This image is also analyzed to determine the predominant key submodalities. Once the main submodalities in the two images are identified, there is a sequential recoding of the negative image into a positive one, where the image itself does not change but its submodal code does. For example, if the positive image was in color and the negative one was black and white, we would transform the negative image into a color image. However, it should be understood that direct transference of resource submodalities is not always suitable for therapy. If we simply want to improve our relationship with someone, submodality recoding of their image into a more positive one may be appropriate. But if we are working with an image of an animal attacking the patient, it would be more appropriate to apply dissociating submodalities to the image, making it small, distant, and black and white.

A simple one-time change of submodalities in some cases will have a strong effect, while in others it will not. There is a concept that, in our experience, so-called critical submodalities can take place. When a critical submodality is activated, an experience that used to evoke a fixed emotional reaction undergoes a radical change in quality and starts producing a stable, different emotional reaction.

Each person may have their own personalized critical submodality, but an example can be provided. One of the best options, in my opinion, is the critical submodality of a bright flash. First, the patient is asked to recall a negative experience that consistently triggers a negative emotional response. Then they are asked to recall a bright light from a welding machine. After that, they are instructed to overlay the image of welding fire onto the image of the negative experience and hold it there for some time. If done correctly, the negative image seems to fade away, and when attempting to access the negative emotional experience, the patient experiences difficulties. Either the emotional intensity significantly decreases or disappears altogether.

The effect of using critical submodalities is often quite strong and stable.

Reframing

In the original NLP, two main types of verbal reframing were considered. The term "reframing" can be interpreted as "shifting into new frames," reforming, changing the frame, or transferring meaning from one frame to another. Primarily, it refers to frames of meaning. Initially, NLP founders identified two types of reframing: context reframing and content reframing.

Context Reframing

Context reframing involves transferring a specific behavior from one frame of meaning to another, where the meaning of that behavior changes significantly and can even become diametrically opposed to what was characteristic in the previous context. For example, behavior involving physical aggression on the street is potentially disapproved of. However, when placed in the context of a boxing ring, it can acquire positive and socially acceptable meanings.

Content Reframing

In content reframing, the context itself remains unchanged, but meanings are selected in such a way that the evaluative judgment of the behavior changes and becomes diametrically opposite. A typical example of content reframing could be the phrase, "He is not slow but rather thoughtful and unhurried."

Language Patterns by Robert Dilts

Robert Dilts extensively explores the topic of reframing in his book "Language Patterns." Essentially, Dilts' model is an enhanced and expanded version of the reframing model proposed by Grinder and Bandler. He identifies fourteen reframing patterns. Let's list each of them and briefly discuss their application.

1. **Intention:** The question is posed as to whether a certain behavior has any positive intention that can influence the process. An example of a positive intention could be the desire to attract attention through the manifestation of an illness.
   Example: "When he is sick, he receives enough attention."

2. **Redefinition:** In this case, a different definition is given to a behavior, process, or belief, thus radically changing the emotional reaction to it.
   Example: "He is not cowardly but rather a very cautious person."

3. **Consequence:** Attention is shifted to the positive consequences of a negative process or belief.
   Example: "Even though you lost your bag, you clearly gained some vigilance."

4. **Separation:** In this case, attention is directed toward certain details

of a negative process or belief. By focusing on them, the frame's meaning can change dramatically.
Example: "Even though you were late for work, you heard the song of such a beautiful bird."

5. **Unification:** The question is asked: "What larger logical element of the class to which the process or belief belongs can shift its qualitative perception?" In simplified terms, the question is: "If this is bad, what is good?"
Example: "Even though you were very scared during the parachute jump, you still went through with it."

6. **Analogy:** An analogy or metaphor is chosen that, on the one hand, suits the description of the process or belief, but on the other hand, qualitatively shifts its assigned meaning.
Example: "Hercules also cleaned the Augean stables" (to someone who is tired of cleaning a room).

7. **Frame resizing:** Temporal, quantitative, or qualitative characteristics of the process or belief are changed, creating new constructive meanings that differ from the original ones. For example, we take and expand the potential time frame based on which the negativity of an event ceases to be perceived as significant.
Example: "When you look at the current problem from the perspective of your entire life, you only see it as experience."

8. **Alternative outcome:** It is indicated that there are other, different from the ones presented, possibilities for the development of a situation related to the process or belief.
Example: "Sometimes being fired becomes a stimulus for a person to start their own successful business."

9. **Alternative outcome:** In the context of this reframing pattern, an

alternative perspective on the process or belief is offered, one that is inherent to someone with an alternative worldview.
Example: "From a psychiatrist's point of view, you represent a very interesting case."

10. **Reality strategy:** The sequence in which a person experiences sensations in order to perceive the process or belief as negative is determined. Then, an alternative strategy is suggested.
Example: "Even though he looks terrible, his speech is so pleasant and warm!"

11. **Opposite example:** It is indicated that any exception confirms the rule. The result of the process or belief may be something diametrically opposed.

12. **Hierarchy of criteria:** Attention is focused on the existence of some other criterion related to the process or belief that can significantly alter its perception.
Example: "It's not about who wins or loses; it's about the game continuing."

13. **Self-application:** The question is posed: "Is it possible to logically apply the meaning of the process or belief to oneself?" Thus, a paradoxical logical process is created.
Example: A patient says that he is very afraid. The therapist responds, "Okay, can your fear be scared?"

14. **Metaframe:** It is assumed that there are other beliefs or processes based on which the current belief or process can undergo significant semantic transformation. Formally, it all comes down to considering which belief holds a higher hierarchy, and attention is fixed on it.
Example: "Today he behaved terribly, but being truly best friends means accepting each other with all the pros and cons."

Six-Step Reframing

A well-known technique in NLP is "**Six-Step Reframing.**" It aims to create a trance-like state in the patient, where the work primarily involves their unconscious mind.

The first step involves identifying the request that the therapist will work with. In the second step, an "analog signal" is established as a non-verbal communication system with the patient's unconscious mind. The patient's unconscious mind is directly asked to raise the index finger of their right hand if they want to answer "yes" and the index finger of their left hand if they want to answer "no." After this, the unconscious mind is asked if it wants to interact in any way at the moment, and if it responds "yes," the process moves to the third step.

The third step involves addressing the symptom that the therapeutic work will focus on. The symptom is asked whether it has a "positive intention." It is worth explaining and commenting on the fact that NLP presupposes that behind every symptom lies a positive intention. In other words, the manifestation of a symptom is simply a way of not knowing how to do something optimally. For example, a person who overworks and exhausts themselves at work, despite knowing that they are pushing their limits, is ignoring their body's signals. Once their unconscious mind "realizes" that the body won't get any rest, it forms a symptom that forces the person to stay at home, rest, and not work. The positive intention behind the symptom is fundamentally beneficial, and if a constructive outlet can be provided, the symptom itself can be eliminated. Often, in the third step, the part of the person's personality responsible for the symptom answers "yes" to the question related to the positive intention.

Following this, the process moves to the fourth step. In this step, the therapist addresses the creative part of the patient's personality and suggests creating three or more new ways of fulfilling the positive intention for the part of the personality responsible for the symptom and then transmitting these methods to it. If the creative part of the personality agrees to do this, the process moves to the fifth step, where the part of the personality responsible for the symptom is asked, "Are you willing to accept these methods if they are suitable?" If it agrees and accepts the new methods, the process moves to the sixth step, where a request is made to the entire unconscious mind of the patient to determine if there are any other parts of their personality that may hinder the implemented solutions. If the response is positive and such a part exists, a new cycle of the technique is applied from the third to the fifth steps. If everything is going well, the technique concludes.

There may be other additional steps in this practice. For example, upon completion, it is possible to express gratitude to the unconscious mind for its cooperation, thus demonstrating therapeutic courtesy. This technique has many nuances that are challenging to describe in detail due to the considerable variability of responses to the technique among different patients.

Rapport Building

One of the key background practices in NLP is the technique of rapport building during the process of psychotherapy, which Bandler and Grinder borrowed from their teacher, Milton Erickson. Although such a practice can also be found in the works of other psychotherapists, Erickson used this technique as one of the key elements in establishing rapport with his patients. Through rapport building, he was able to establish deep trust even with psychotic patients.

We explore Milton Erickson's work in more depth in the chapter dedicated to the hypnotic and provocative approach in psychotherapy.

Rapport building when working with patients can take various forms and include a multitude of nuances. Let's consider several types of rapport-building.

- **Breath mirroring:** During communication with an individual, it is important to synchronize one's breathing with theirs. The key criterion for successfully practicing this technique is maintaining a rhythm in the breath. People who breathe in a rhythm similar to ours are perceived as close and friendly individuals.

- **Posture mirroring:** Directly mimicking someone's posture in regular communication is not suitable for rapport building, as the patient may perceive it as literal parody on a conscious level, which can trigger resistance. However, partially mirroring posture by reflecting the main contours of body positions can have a positive influence on the communication process.

- **Gesture mirroring:** When mirroring gestures, it is not advisable to immediately start with a full replica of the interlocutor's movements. It is sufficient to replicate the general outlines of the gestures, as if tracing them, and it can also be beneficial to reproduce the repetition with a slight delay of 3–15 seconds to make the mirroring less noticeable to the interlocutor.

- **Speech pattern mirroring:** In this type of mirroring, tone of voice, intonation, volume, and timbre are most commonly mirrored. Copies of intonation markers can be recreated.

- **Value and belief mirroring:** In this case, the therapist should initially identify any key values and beliefs held by the patient and then directly or indirectly validate them through verbal and non-verbal communication. For example, if it is discovered that the patient is interested in art and painting, occasionally mentioning famous artists and their works can be effective.

Each type of rapport building has numerous intricacies in its application, and when used correctly, it can yield remarkable results in working with patients as well as in everyday interpersonal communication.

Eye Accessing Cues

The calibration technique in NLP is used to gather various verbal and non-verbal information for subsequent analysis and qualitative utilization in psychotherapeutic work. One of the most popular calibration models in NLP is the eye-accessing cues model, which has been extensively explored and developed by Robert Dilts. This model involves using information about the six main directions of the interlocutor's gaze, which often have specific, fixed meanings.

Eye movements play a significant role in our cognitive processes, particularly in the construction and recall of sensory experiences. They can provide valuable insights into how we visualize and remember visual images, construct sounds or speech, and connect with our bodily sensations. In this section, we will explore the different eye movements and their corresponding cognitive functions.

Let's examine these directions in more detail.

Upward and to the right gaze: When we shift our gaze upward and to the right, it is often associated with the construction of visual images. This cognitive process involves mentally creating or manipulating visual representations in our mind. It allows us to vividly imagine and construct new visual scenes or scenarios.	Upward and to the left gaze: On the other hand, when we direct our gaze upward and to the left, it is linked to the recall of visual images. This cognitive process involves retrieving previously stored visual memories, enabling us to remember and mentally recreate past visual experiences.
Rightward gaze: Turning our gaze solely to the right is related to the construction of sounds or speech. This cognitive function allows us to mentally generate or manipulate auditory stimuli, such as constructing inner dialogues or imagining different sounds.	**Leftward gaze:** Conversely, when we shift our gaze solely to the left, it is associated with the recall of sounds or speech. This cognitive process involves retrieving auditory memories, enabling us to remember and mentally replay past sounds or conversations.
Downward and to the right gaze: When we look downward and to the right, it involves connecting our visual experiences with bodily sensations. This cognitive function allows us to integrate or associate visual images with physical or sensory feelings, enhancing our overall sensory experience.	**Downward and to the left gaze:** Directing our gaze downward and to the left is linked to internal dialogue and reflection. This cognitive process involves engaging in introspection, self-reflection, or internal conversations with ourselves.

Table of Eye Accessing Cues Vectors

Understanding these various eye movements and their corresponding cognitive functions provides valuable insights into how our minds process and represent information. By studying these mechanisms, we can further comprehend the complex interplay between our sensory perceptions, memories, and internal cognitive processes.

According to Robert Dilts' assumptions, this pattern holds true for 70% of right-handed individuals. In the case of left-handed individuals, the right and left columns may be reversed. There are cases of specific individual variations, so this pattern should not be perceived as entirely universal. In the vast majority of cases, the following remains constant for this model: if a person's gaze is directed upward, it means they are processing visual images. If the gaze moves horizontally, the person is processing auditory or verbal representations. If the gaze is lowered, it indicates engagement with kinesthetic sensations or that the person is immersed in internal dialogue.

Representational Profiles of Personality

One of the key models of personality profiling in NLP is the representational systems model. There are four main representational profiles of personality: visual, auditory, kinesthetic, and digital. Belonging to a specific profile means that one's perception emphasizes a particular representational system. Pure profiles do not exist; we always utilize all sensations in our body. However, in some individuals, the emphasis is significantly shifted, allowing for the identification of distinct profiles. It is common to observe individuals who combine characteristics from different profiles.

Characteristics of individuals belonging to different representational profiles:

Visual

- Has a tendency to use visual language and expressions.
- Focuses on images, appearances, and visual aesthetics.
- Demonstrates a strong visual memory and vivid imagination.
- Pays attention to visual details and stimuli in their environment.

Auditory

- Uses auditory predicates and expressions in speech.
- Relies on sound, tone, and rhythm in communication.
- Has good auditory memory and a musical inclination.

- Notices and remembers auditory details and sounds in their surroundings.

Kinesthetic

- Prefers kinesthetic predicates and expressions.
- Values physical sensations, touch, and bodily experiences.
- Relates to emotions, feelings, and physical comfort.
- Demonstrates sensitivity to physical space and tactile stimuli.

Digital

- Utilizes cognitive and abstract predicates in speech.
- Emphasizes logical thinking, analysis, and categorization.
- Prefers intellectual discussions and problem-solving.
- Focuses on concepts, ideas, and mental processes.

Predicates of Speech

One of the earliest topics actively explored within the NLP tradition was speech predicates. The founders of NLP discovered that individuals who actively perceive and interact with the world through specific sensory modalities tend to use speech predicates corresponding to those modalities. The distribution of predicates across sensory modalities can be as follows:

Visual Predicates	Auditory Predicates	Kinesthetic Predicates	Digital Predicates
See, view, watch, observe, light, color, perspective, notice, examine, scrutinize, brightness, contrast, dimness, contemplate, review, gaze.	Listen, pay attention, sound, melodic, noisy, loud, ringing, buzzing, speaking, shouting, resonant, tone, intonation, timbre, noise.	Feel, sense, warm, soft, fluffy, smooth, springy, rigid, flexible, rough, touch, stroking, impact, push-off.	Calculate, transform, convert, ponder, reflect, contemplate, add, subtract, multiply, divide, compute, and create.

Table of Speech Predicates 1

In addition to the four main categories of predicates, within the realm of kinesthetics, we can distinguish completely separate and independent categories. These include motor, gustatory, olfactory, and vestibular predicates.

Motor Predicates	Gustatory Predicates	Gustatory Predicates	Vestibular Predicates
Move, shift, slide, walk, run, jump, approach, take off, fall, move.	Taste, taste, anticipate, deliciousness, sweet, bitter, salty, sour, overly sweet, spicy.	Smell, sniff, scent, fragrance, aroma, stench.	Balance, equilibrium, balance, rotate, spin, unwind, twist.

Table of Speech Predicates 2

The use of speech predicates related to motor actions allows us to describe and communicate experiences involving physical movement and actions.

Gustatory predicates involve the perception of taste and flavor, enabling individuals to express their sensory experiences related to different tastes. Olfactory predicates are used to convey the sense of smell and the perception of different odors. Lastly, vestibular predicates pertain to balance, equilibrium, and the physical sensations associated with movements and rotation.

By understanding and utilizing these various speech predicates, therapists can better align their communication with the sensory modalities and subjective experiences of their clients, facilitating effective therapeutic interventions.

There is a greater number of predicates that correspond to each representational system than we present in the tables. The more developed a person's particular representational system is, the more frequently they use predicates that align with it, and the greater the number of predicates within that representational system they employ. Predicates associated with the preferred representational system evoke positive, sometimes euphoric, states in individuals. Predicates from a less-utilized representational system may have no impact on the person at all. If a visually oriented individual prefers the phrase "I see bright prospects for our communication" in their communication, a kinesthetic individual is more likely to say, "I feel that we have a significant number of points of connection." By knowing a person's preferred representational system, we can automatically establish rapport with them by using predicates that correspond to their system. The study of various speech predicates is applicable in the context of trance induction. If a hypnotherapist utilizes a wide range of speech predicates during the trance induction process, it can create a unique volume and depth of the hypnotic trance.

Sensory Strategies

While examining how people utilize their sensations in perceiving the world, the creators of NLP discovered that individuals tend to employ specific chains of sensations to achieve fixed outcomes. These chains of sensations are referred to as sensory strategies, and there exist a multitude of such strategies among individuals. Some strategies yield successful, constructive outcomes, while others do not. Let's explore these sensory strategies:

1. **Decision Strategy:** This involves the sensations an individual experiences when making a specific decision. For example, a person may first need to visualize an image and then feel the sensations that arise in their body. If the sensations are positive, they proceed with the action; otherwise, they halt the action.

2. **Reality Strategy:** This strategy enables individuals to judge the reality or unreality of their perceptions. For instance, how can we differentiate between what is real and what is not? Memories of yesterday or a dream that occurred last night? The sensory strategies for this test can be highly diverse. For example, a person may recall a series of past images that evoke a positive kinesthetic response, indicating those with the highest likelihood of being real. Then they recall an image that is subjected to the test of realism. Subsequently, a kinesthetic test is performed for this image to determine the difference in kinesthetic response compared to the images that are considered highly realistic. If there is a clear match, the image is categorized as real; otherwise, it is deemed unreal.

3. **Creativity Strategy:** This strategy pertains to how a creative individual generates something new. An example of this strategy can be seen in Salvador Dali's creative process. He would sit in front of a canvas, place a metal basin in front of him, and hold a spoon above the basin. He would then wait for drowsiness to set in, reaching a semi-dream state. When he fell asleep, the spoon would fall into the metal basin, creating a loud clang. Dali would wake up, derive images, and start painting based on the sensations and states that arose from this experience.

4. **Motivation Strategy:** This strategy explores how we can motivate ourselves to take action. A powerful motivational strategy was discovered by boxer Mike Tyson. Describing his experience, he said, "When I hit rock bottom and had no strength or desire to continue my training, I would look into my future and tell myself: if you don't get up and keep going, tomorrow will be even worse."

5. **Memory Strategy:** This is the ability to memorize blocks of information. John Grinder once proposed an interesting strategy for remembering the names of unfamiliar people. According to his suggestion, during an introduction, upon hearing the person's name, you first visualize the name written on their forehead, then pronounce the name aloud several times, and finally make a hand gesture as if you are writing their name on paper.

6. **Thinking Strategy:** An example of a thinking strategy is the approach to solving life problems or gaining understanding. For instance, the creator of provocative therapy, Frank Farrelly, mentioned that during a therapeutic session, numerous internal monitors appear in his mind, each showing a variation of behavior that can be employed in working with the patient. When he makes a choice, he associates it with the corresponding image and proceeds to manifest what he has envisioned.

By incorporating these sensory strategies into our understanding, we can gain insights into how individuals perceive and interact with the world around them. Moreover, recognizing and utilizing these strategies can enhance communication and facilitate the achievement of desired outcomes.

We have provided only five examples of sensory strategies, but there are a multitude of existing strategies in total.

Sensory strategies can be modified, thereby bringing about significant behavioral changes in individuals. By transmitting one person's strategy to another, we can effectively teach them to perform certain tasks with greater proficiency and efficiency. The strategies we have described may involve both sensory structures, which are literal sequences of sensations, and fixed meanings associated with the context of their implementation. In its literal sense, a sensory strategy refers solely to a sequence of sensations. During the process of modeling sensory experience in NLP, sensory strategies are marked by a sequence of Latin letters, representing the utilized representational systems.

To effectively understand and analyze sensory experiences, it is essential to have a comprehensive system for encoding and representing sensory strategies. The following table presents the coding system for sensory strategies, along with their representative systems.

Notation	Representative System
Ve, Vi	Visual External, Visual Internal
At, Ad	Auditory Tonal, Auditory Discrete
K	Kinesthetic
M	Motor
G	Gustatory
O	Olfactory
Vs	Vestibular
N	Nociceptive (Pain)

Table of Encoding for Sensory Strategies

*The letter "**e**" represents external sensory experiences, while "**i**" denotes internal sensory experiences. The letter "**t**" signifies tonal or auditory aspects, while "**d**" represents discrete or digital elements.*

By utilizing this notation system, we can categorize and describe various sensory strategies. Here is an example of a sensory strategy notation and its potential interpretation:

Example: Ve → Vi → K → Adi → Ade

Interpretation: The individual visually perceives an external image → mentally represents possible future actions or interactions with the image → experiences a kinesthetic response to the perceived image → reflects on the sensations evoked → articulates a conclusion.

Sensory strategies can vary in complexity, ranging from simple combinations of a few elements to intricate algorithms with multiple branches and steps. Understanding and deciphering these strategies is crucial for comprehending how individuals process and respond to sensory information.

Neurological Levels

One of the most widely used models in NLP at present is the model of neurological levels (NL), which provides insights into the logical levels of personality and their semantic content. The term "neuro" suggests that the process of structuring personality and various cognitive and behavioral processes associated with this structuring have a direct relationship to physiological processes, particularly neurological processes. This model is effectively employed in the process of modeling the experiences of different individuals and in the development of various therapeutic techniques aimed at constructive personality change.

Neurological levels provide a framework for understanding the different levels of human experience and identity. Each level corresponds to specific aspects of a person's being and can offer insights into their deeper motivations, values, and beliefs. The following table outlines the key characteristics associated with each neurological level. The NL model encompasses six core levels.

Level	Key Characteristics
6. Mission and Vision	This level addresses the larger abstract roles that can be inherent to a person's identity. It delves into existential, transpersonal, and philosophical aspects of the self. Question: "**Who am I in a broader sense beyond the social roles I play?**"
5. Identity	This level pertains to the specific identities and roles that shape an individual's sense of self. Question: "**Who am I?**"
4. Values and Beliefs	This level explores the values and beliefs that underlie one's manifested behaviors. Question: "**What is important and valuable?**"
3. Capabilities	This level focuses on specific qualities of behavior and performance. Question: "**How does something happen?**"
2. Actions	This level involves the immediate actions or behaviors being exhibited. Question: "**What is happening?**"
1.Environment	This level considers the context and circumstances in which events occur. Question: "**Where and when does something happen?**"

Neurological Levels Table

Understanding these neurological levels provides valuable insights into the various dimensions of the human experience. By examining these levels, we can gain a comprehensive understanding of an individual's identity, motivations, and the underlying factors that shape their behavior.

One practical application of NLP is the classification of patient therapy requests. Each request can be attributed to a specific neurological level, and based on that level, specific therapeutic techniques can be selected that are most appropriate for addressing the request. For example:

1. **Environment-level request**: "I'm fed up with the people around me."
2. **Action-level request**: "I want to get rid of anxiety."
3. **Capabilities-level request**: "My spouse doesn't treat me well."
4. **Values and beliefs-level request**: "I don't understand why women don't like me."
5. **Identity-level request**: "I want to fully mature as a person."
6. **Mission and vision-level request**: "I want to contribute something special to the world."

By classifying therapy requests according to their corresponding neurological levels, therapists can tailor their approach to address the specific needs of each patient. This targeted application of NLP techniques enhances the effectiveness of therapy interventions.

One example of therapeutic application using NL is the practice of "aligning neurological levels." It is believed that all NLs are closely interconnected, with higher levels influencing the lower ones. Thus, if a patient's request is received at a lower NL, the therapist can help the patient move to a higher level of personality. This process involves exploring the necessary states and insights that can be brought to the lower logical levels. It can serve as a resourceful element for transforming both symptoms and the individual as a whole.

Neurological alignment can be conducted through regular conversation, but the classic approach involves using anchoring techniques for anchoring and the subsequent introduction of states.

For example, if a patient's request is at the Behavior Level and stated as "I want to get rid of anxiety," the therapist can systematically elevate the patient to higher levels.

Transitioning to the Capabilities and Skills Level activates the specific details of how anxiety arises within the individual and its nature.

Transitioning to the Beliefs and Values Level brings awareness of their content in the context of personal anxiety.

Transitioning to the Identity Level allows full recognition of the social roles in which anxiety manifests.

Transitioning to the sixth level provides awareness of the larger purpose behind fulfilling these social roles. Sometimes it is necessary to reach the sixth level, while in other cases, activating the fifth level may be sufficient. When the fifth or sixth level is reached, its state is anchored, often through a kinesthetic anchor.

Naturally, before anchoring, it is necessary to ensure that the achieved state is resourceful and serves as a "meta" state in relation to the stated condition. With the anchored meta-state of a higher NL, the descent is carried out sequentially to a lower one. If the sixth level has been reached, the descent is made to the fifth; if the fifth level has been reached, the descent is made to the fourth, and so on. During the descent to a lower NL, the anchor of the meta-state that was reached earlier is activated. Thus, the therapist and the patient descend to the symptom-level NL and introduce the meta-state there as well. If necessary, it is possible to go to lower levels than the one from which the request was expressed and introduce the meta-state there. This is an approximate description of how neurological alignment can occur. This practice may have nuances and specific features that need to be taken into account when working with patients of different psychological profiles.

Milton Model

The two main founders of NLP, Richard Bandler and John Grinder, were introduced to one of the most renowned American hypnotherapists, Milton Erickson, through their friend and mentor, Gregory Bateson.

According to legend, they studied with him and modeled his skills for approximately 11 months, after which they started incorporating numerous patterns of his work with patients into NLP.

The modeled therapy patterns of Milton Erickson were subsequently named the Milton Model and included patterns specifically related to hypnotic interactions with patients.

It is worth noting that Erickson did not limit himself to the use of hypnosis alone; thus, his range of therapeutic methods was significantly broader than what is considered within the scope of the Milton Model.

The Milton Model is mainly adapted for application within the context of hypnotic suggestion.

Let's identify the main patterns of the Milton Model:

1. **Rapport with existing experience:** During trance induction, vague clarifying questions are asked, allowing the interlocutor some freedom of choice.
   Questions like "Isn't it?" or "Isn't it so?"

2. **Double binds:** The interlocutor is offered two or more choices without actually choosing. In other words, no matter what the interlocutor chooses, the choice will always lead to the correct outcome.
   Example: "Will you enter a hypnotic trance right now or when you sit comfortably and relax?"

3. **Conversational presuppositions:** This pattern actively uses modal operators of possibility, giving a sense of freedom of choice and the absence of rigid constraints.
   Example: "Can you allow yourself to enter a trance state? Can your

unconscious start learning? Is healing possible in this hypnotic trance?"

4. **Extended quotes:** This pattern extends the frame of quoting and prolongs it until the interlocutor's attention is slightly overloaded. Typically, during extended quotes, the contexts of description are sequentially changed, creating additional load on the perceptual apparatus. Due to the overload, what was said earlier gradually fades into the unconscious. This, in fact, is the goal of using this pattern.
   Example: "I recently remembered a patient who told me a story from his childhood. He met a boy who once climbed a mountain and saw an amazing view that immersed him in a very pleasant and relaxed state, akin to a deep and vivid dream that some people can experience..."

5. **Selective violation of boundaries:** In this pattern, we begin to attribute cognitive processes, emotions, states, and sensations to objects that cannot experience them. Thus, two goals are achieved. Firstly, the perception pattern is disrupted, indirectly suggesting what we would like our interlocutor to experience.
   Example: "I wonder what the chair can feel like when someone enters a hypnotic trance on it?"

6. **Uncertainty pauses:** During the construction of a sentence, we pause for a while, allowing the interlocutor's imagination to fill it in independently in their mind, and then we complete it.
   Example: "As you enter a hypnotic trance, you may feel... a special gift from your unconscious."

7. **Utilization:** Whatever happens to the interlocutor during communication, whatever resistance they may exert, it can be utilized. That is, we can gain control without directly confronting the problematic behavior.
   Example, if a patient tells the therapist, "I can't enter a hypnotic

trance," the therapist responds, "That's right, you can't enter a hypnotic trance until you sit in that chair."

8. **Analog marking:** Analog marking can be of three main types: visual, auditory, and kinesthetic. During visual marking, when suggesting certain words, for example, we make a specific gesture visible to the interlocutor. During auditory marking, we change the tone, volume, or intonation of speech. During kinesthetic marking, we may specifically touch the interlocutor. Auditory analog marking is most commonly used during trance induction.

9. **Linguistic linkage:** To create a coherent flow of trance induction, linking words like "and," "but," as well as phrases indicating cause-and-effect relationships, such as "when-then," "if-then," "while," and "during," are used.
   Examples: "As you enter the trance and feel relaxation, you can let go of your thoughts. You may resist and keep your eyes open, but your unconscious has already started to immerse you in a hypnotic trance. When you feel my touch on your shoulder, you will begin to experience something new and unusual."

10. **Temporal ambiguity:** The use of words that establish an indefinite temporal framework.
   Examples: "Sometimes it happens... Occasionally, the unconscious reveals its secrets... There are moments when the trance simply emerges..."

11. **Addressing personality parts:** Direct or indirect addressing of a specific part of the personality. This breaks the interlocutor's perception pattern and significantly enhances the trance effect of communication.
   Example: "I greet your unconscious. Your wise part is ready to manifest. What would your symptom like to tell you?"

12. **Hypnotic approval:** Words of approval for the experience that an individual goes through during hypnotic induction.
    Examples: "Very good... Exactly... That's right..."

NLP, as an integrative psychotherapy, naturally goes beyond existing models and constantly evolves, introducing new models of change and transformation. In NLP, we primarily see not just a psychotherapy system, but rather an operating system that enables more effective interaction with both our conscious and unconscious realms.

It is worth emphasizing once again that NLP is not simply a collection of techniques and models but rather a specific metaphilosophy that allows for more effective interaction with new experiences, qualitatively assimilating them into our consciousness, and transmitting them to others in various life contexts.

Metaprograms

In the early 1980s, when NLP had already been actively developing for many years, it was discovered that different NLP techniques produced rapid and profound changes for some individuals while being less effective for others. This led to the idea that there were certain omissions at the foundation of NLP models. There must be filters that could reliably determine which types of techniques are more or less effective in different cases. Simply dividing people into visual, auditory, kinesthetic, and digital (VAKD) profiles was not sufficient, although these profile filters had significant value. To some extent, the idea of meta-programs was likely borrowed from Osgood's semantic differentials and cognitive styles initially mentioned by Alfred Adler. Although the ideas of cognitive styles were later extensively developed by a range of authors.

Regardless, it is important to highlight the relationship between the concepts of meta-programs, semantic differentials, and cognitive styles since a deeper examination of research dedicated to these concepts can provide a wealth of useful and complementary information. In the next part of this chapter, where we will explore Ken Wilber's integrative model in more detail, we will provide a more comprehensive description of cognitive styles. In the context of the chapter dedicated to NLP, we would like to examine 15 fundamental meta-programs that, in my opinion, are most applicable in practical work. It is worth noting that one of the NLP researchers and trainers, Michael Hall, in his book "The Secrets of Personal Mastery: 51 Metaprograms," describes the corresponding number of meta-programs in its title and provides a detailed analysis.

First and foremost, it is important to note that meta-programs are filters in our perceptual apparatus that allow us to better perceive certain blocks of information while disregarding others. Depending on our understanding of how these filters function, we can more effectively deliver information to individuals and interact with them. In the context of NLP practice, it has been discovered that meta-programs can not only be verified through interaction with individuals but also changed. This has led to the development of new techniques and practices.

List of Metaprograms

1. **Sorting Filters** (people, values, processes/procedures, actions/things):
   What is the primary focus of attention for a person? For example, if you are going on vacation, are you primarily going to be with someone? Or with whom? Or is it important in the context of your life? For example, a pilgrimage to holy places. Or are you going to do something? For example, simply surfing. Or are you going with the intention of improving a skill? Or towards a particular thing or for a specific item? These are all sorting filters. People have them in different combinations. If the sorting filters of two people do not match at all, the likelihood of their meeting can be highly doubtful.

2. **Chunk Size** (big, small):

Some people are accustomed to thinking in large categories of experience and abstract terms, generalizing blocks of their experience into them. Others, on the contrary, love to detail their experience. A vivid example can be a phrase from one person to another: "Buy something tasty." This phrase clearly corresponds to a large chunk size. And a person with a specific metaprogram profile criterion will use it. If a person with a small chunk size hears this phrase, it can greatly confuse them.

3. **Thinking Style** (deductive, inductive, or transductive):
   Some people have a well-developed deductive thinking style, thinking from the general to the specific. For example, if you know that a person suffers from schizophrenia and understand the criteria for its manifestation, you can easily predict how the patient will behave in different situations. Others have a well-developed inductive thinking style, thinking from specific to general. For example, if you are trying to verify if someone is lying in their communication and gather several clear signs of deception, you can label the person as a liar based on the generalization of these signs. And for some individuals, transductive thinking can be well-developed, thinking in terms of analogies and metaphors. For example, if you are a psychotherapist and a patient with depression comes to you, you can quickly recall all the cases when patients with depression came to you or remember cases of depression described in various psychotherapeutic literature. In the case of transduction, you remain at the same logical level of generalization and operate with the information contained within it.

4. **Comparison Focus** (similarity-difference):
   Some people, in the process of communicating with others, more often activate the confirmation filter that looks for similarities between themselves and their interlocutor. Others do the opposite; they constantly seek differences.

5. **Motivation Type** (towards positive or away from negative, towards positive and then away from negative, away from negative and then towards positive):
   For some people, to start moving towards a goal, they need to anticipate the joy of achieving it. For others, they need to feel how unpleasant it would be if they stayed put. For others, they need to first anticipate the benefits and then feel the discomfort if there is no progress. And there are those who are the opposite; for motivation, they first need to experience the potential negative outcome if there is no movement and only then understand that moving towards the goal can yield very good results.

6. **Type of Reference** (internal, external - others, external - world):
   When we experience positive or negative outcomes in our lives, we tend to attribute various causes to these results. Individuals with an internal reference type believe that they are solely responsible for everything, while those with an external reference type, oriented towards other people, shift the responsibility onto others. Individuals with an external reference type towards the world believe that everything happening in the world is related to destiny, circumstances, the intervention of mystical forces, and so on.

7. **Orientation in Time** (past, present, and future):
   In our lives, we can be more or less focused on different temporal periods. Some people derive pleasure from being surrounded by old things and watching old movies, embracing the nostalgia of the past. Others are oriented towards the present moment, interested in what has just been released, the latest trends, or recent updates to stay in sync with the times. Yet, there are those who strive to surround themselves with objects and images that anticipate what the world of the future might be like.

8. **Temporal Inclusion** (inclusion of time, temporal dissociation):

Individuals with temporal inclusion experience a life where fragments of memories are closely associated. They derive more sensations from life but are less inclined to reflect on exactly what is happening or contextually analyze the situation. Conversely, individuals with temporal dissociation are always somewhat detached from their feelings, better analyzing the current life context, their memories, and their potential future.

9. **Temporal Accessibility** (sequential, random):
   Individuals with sequential temporal accessibility constantly strive to bring order to the sequence of their life experiences; they have a preference for order. On the other hand, individuals with random temporal accessibility are not burdened with the need to clearly and structuredly organize their life experiences.

10. **Information Gathering Style** (uptime, downtime):
    People with an up-to-date information-gathering style are predominantly oriented towards the external world. They are highly vigilant, capable of noticing even the slightest differences and changes in the world in general, and in people's behavior in particular. Conversely, individuals with a downtime information-gathering style have their attention focused inward. They find it more difficult to gather new information but possess remarkable abilities to analyze the information they already have, draw accurate logical conclusions, and make inferences.

11. **Perceptual Categories** (polarity, continuum):
    Some individuals tend to perceive the world as a set of rigid polarities. For them, things are either good or bad, completely acceptable or completely unacceptable, excellent or terrible. This perceptual category is characterized by polarity. On the other hand, others are capable of thinking more smoothly and moderately. Such individuals judge something as more or less suitable, to a large

extent uncomfortable, acceptable to 80%, and so on. They have more differentiated scales of evaluation.

12. **Perceptual Resilience** (penetrability, impermeability):
Individuals with the metaprogram of "perceptual resilience and penetrability" experience strong discomfort when even the slightest distractions arise during the process of engaging with or focusing on something. They can be irritated by a slight rustle behind the door, a sudden noise outside, a barely audible conversation in another room, and so on.
On the other hand, individuals with the metaprogram of "perceptual resilience—impermeability" perceive things differently. They can calmly concentrate on solving a task even in an environment with numerous distracting factors. During the task, these factors simply cease to bother them.

13. **Modal Operators** (necessity, possibility):
When we consider the modal operator of necessity as a metaprogram, we refer to situations where a person follows the impulse of obligation, a sense of self-compulsion in certain life situations. For such individuals, a life situation is more of a duty than a freedom of choice, and the dominant phrase is "I must." Conversely, individuals with the metaprogram "modal operator - possibility" perceive the world as an arena of possibilities and freedom of choice rather than duty and adherence to it. Their key phrase is "I can."

14. **Comparison Style** (quantitative, qualitative):
For some individuals, the most significant criterion for task completion is quantitative indicators. For example, they may focus on having dealt with 20 patients, running 50 kilometers, eating 5 apples, and so on. When the metaprogram "comparison style - quantitative" dominates, the quality of the performance itself may not be particularly in focus. On the other hand, individuals with the

metaprogram "comparison style - qualitative" prioritize immediate quality in the execution of tasks. For them, it's not about how many times they perform a certain physical exercise but how well and qualitatively they do it.

15. **Orientation Towards Closure** (completeness, incompleteness): Some individuals are deeply concerned about ensuring that everything they start is completed. Unfinished tasks weigh heavily on them, making them restless. This metaprogram is known as "orientation towards closure - completeness." In contrast, individuals with the opposing metaprogram do not experience discomfort when they initiate a task and leave it unfinished.

In NLP, there are no notions of good or bad metaprograms. There are no boundaries defining correctness or incorrectness. In the context of modeling mastery or pathology, one can create a metaprogram profile of an individual and empirically observe how specific sets of metaprograms can lead to various outcomes.

Integral Philosophy of Ken Wilber

Only a portion of Ken Wilber's life was dedicated to psychotherapy. He is not the creator of any specific school of psychotherapy; however, his integrative philosophical approach has already made a significant contribution to psychotherapeutic practice, in my opinion. Ken Wilber's theoretical models are remarkably capable of organizing the vast conglomerate of experience accumulated by various schools of psychotherapy into comprehensive models and structures. In his philosophy, Ken Wilber is closely aligned with NLP as a form of specific meta-philosophy, although he does not have a direct association with it.

Kenneth Earl Wilber II was born in 1949 in Oklahoma City, USA. Due to his father's military service in the US Air Force, Wilber's family constantly moved when he was a child. Wilber completed high school in Lincoln,

Nebraska. He demonstrated himself as an extraordinary and highly gifted child in school, grasping various subjects effortlessly and even earning the nickname "Brain." Wilber excelled in sports disciplines such as football, volleyball, and basketball. He also showed talent as a gymnast and track athlete.

Ken Wilber

In 1967, at the insistence of his parents, Wilber enrolled in Duke University's medical school to study medicine. However, he quickly became disillusioned with the chosen profession and transferred to the University of Nebraska, where he soon obtained a bachelor's degree in chemistry and biology. Alongside his studies in chemistry and biology, Wilber devoted considerable attention to psychology and Eastern philosophy. After completing his academic education, he made the decision to fully focus on his writing career.

In 1972, Wilber met his future wife, Emmy Watts, whom he married the same year.

At the age of 23, in 1973, he completed his first book, "The Spectrum of Consciousness," which became his initial attempt to create and describe an integrative model that unifies Western and Eastern philosophical perspectives. However, for a long time, many publishing houses refused to publish this book due to its perceived complexity. It was only in 1977 that it was published by the Theosophical Publishing House, "Quest Books." The publication of this book brought recognition to the author in academic circles, enabling him to start delivering various lectures and seminars on the material described in the book.

In 1978, Wilber organized the release of the transpersonal journal "ReVision."

In 1979, his second book, "No Boundary," was published. This was followed by the publication of "The Atman Project" in 1980 and "Up from Eden" in 1981.

In 1981, Wilber divorced his wife, Emmy, and moved to Cambridge, Massachusetts, where he continued publishing the journal "ReVision."

In 1983, Wilber met his second wife, Terry Killam. After marrying Terry, she was diagnosed with breast cancer, which led Wilber to entirely put aside his writing career from 1984 to 1987 in order to dedicate himself to caring for his ill wife. However, Terry's treatment did not yield significant results, and she passed away in 1989. Based on the experience gained during Terry's treatment and care, Wilber published the book "Grace and Grit" in 1991.

In 1998, Ken Wilber founded the Integral Institute, which focused on various research endeavors and the development of scientific inquiries aimed at integration into a theoretical model that allows for the synthesis of scientific knowledge into comprehensive and structured models.

In 1999, Wilber published another book titled "Integral Psychology," in which he attempted to present models that encompassed the diverse psychological knowledge available at that time.

In 2000, Wilber released his next book, "A Theory of Everything," where he conducted an integrative analysis of various spheres of human activity, such as politics, religion, science, and business. He demonstrated how these spheres could be represented through the lens of Clare Graves' spiral dynamics.

In 2006, Wilber published his book "Integral Spirituality," which became a remarkable synthesis of his ideas on spirituality and religion in diverse mystical traditions from around the world. It is worth noting that Wilber not only explored these traditions on a theoretical level but also immersed himself deeply in many of them, gaining practical experience. Thus, we are dealing with not just a theoretical compilation but also a living experience, making the material, in my opinion, even more unique.

Since 1987 and up to the present day, Ken Wilber has been living and working in Denver, Colorado, where he leads the activities of the Integral Institute and University, both of which are actively developing, and whose research findings are increasingly being applied in various spheres of human life.

Ken Wilber's integral approach finds its embodiment in a wide range of scientific investigations, extending far beyond mere philosophy. Wilber introduced the philosophy of integration into areas such as psychology, psychotherapy, philosophy, sociology, politics, economics, religion, mysticism, and more.

Studying various schools of psychology and psychotherapy with their diverse theoretical concepts and practical techniques, Ken Wilber observed that each of them has its own validity. They do not contradict one another but rather complement each other qualitatively. Wilber proposed a spectral model to examine these theories, suggesting that schools of psychology and psychotherapy are like colors in a rainbow, existing within their own spectra. According to him, only by considering the entirety of the spectrum can one obtain a truly comprehensive picture of reality. Due to his deep fascination with various religious and mystical traditions, many researchers have attributed to Wilber the role of a transpersonal philosopher. However, Wilber's orientation was not merely towards the integration of Western and Eastern knowledge. His ideas aimed at integrating experiences from diverse fields of study and religions. Therefore, it would be incorrect to label Wilber as a transpersonal psychologist or philosopher. Wilber is a pure integrative philosopher.

One of the key models created by Ken Wilber is the AQAL model, which essentially became the foundation for his future theoretical and practical constructions. As his knowledge expanded, he further developed this model into AQALALASAT, which stands for "All Quadrants, All Levels, All Lines, All States, All Types."

The model itself, as conceived by Wilber, includes five distinct categories of experience that cannot be simplified and must be considered when examining experiences from an integrative standpoint.

Basic quadrants, also referred to as sectors, are four in total. The first sector is the "**I** - Individual Interior," focusing on the subjective experience of the individual. This sector encompasses realms such as religion, philosophy, subjective psychology, and phenomenology—essentially all areas of activity that primarily deal with subjective, rather than empirical, experience. The second sector is the "**It** - Individual Exterior," encompassing areas of activity that, on the one hand, study the individual but, on the other hand, have a direct relation to empirical, objectively verifiable experience.

This sector includes physiology, medicine, physics, chemistry, objective psychology, and so on. The third sector, the "**We** - Collective Interior," pertains to the study of internal processes of group interaction among individuals. This sector encompasses fields such as cultural studies, sociology, cultural anthropology, and the like. The fourth sector, "**Its** - Collective Exterior," examines forms of activity that study external group social processes. This sector includes economics, politics, theories of system functioning, and the like.

Developmental levels imply a specific sequence of development that an individual or a group of individuals undergo during phylogenesis and ontogenesis. Developmental levels can be diverse. The scales of levels most commonly used by Wilber include the scales of value-motivational hierarchy by Clare Graves, the spiral dynamics by Don Beck and Chris Cowan, and the developmental levels proposed by Jane Loevinger, Robert Kegan, and Jean Gebser.

Developmental lines denote various forms of the ability to apply the intellectual sphere of personality. Each person and group of people, as they progress in their development, advance in their understanding of something to a certain extent. Some individuals excel in interpersonal communication, others solve mathematical equations, and others possess exceptional self-regulation abilities, and so on. Let us enumerate the main developmental lines:

1. **Cognitive** line, or the awareness of what exists.
   Cognitive and mathematical intelligence.
2. **Moral** line, or the awareness of how things should be.
   Moral intelligence.
3. **Emotional** line. Awareness and influence on the spectrum of emotions, self-regulation.
   Emotional intelligence.
4. **Interpersonal** line, the ability to communicate effectively with others.
   Social intelligence.
5. **Needs** line, exemplified by Maslow's hierarchy of needs model: recognition of personal needs and the strategies to fulfill them.
   Needs intelligence.
6. **Spiritual** line. Awareness of the purpose of one's existence.
   Spiritual intelligence.

And numerous other potential developmental lines.

States can occur in all quadrants and can be categorized as states of consciousness—wakefulness, dreaming, and trance (the "**I** - Individual Interior" sector)—and states of energy—gross, subtle, and causal (the "**It** - Individual Exterior" sector). In the context of state analysis, Ken Wilber presents his classification of categories of spiritual states. It is also worth noting that states of consciousness can be peak, altered, religious, or meditative. All these states can be interpreted as spiritual.

Types also exist in all quadrants. A prominent example of a type is the masculine and feminine personality types. It can manifest in individuals or specific groups of people. For example, the masculine type of personality may involve identification with action, rigidity, and aggressiveness, while the feminine type is associated with communication, overall sociability, empathy, and compassion. Here, we can recall Carl Jung's typology of individuals as extroverts and introverts, which he later expanded by adding four more profiles—people of thinking, intuition, sensing, and feeling—and each of these can be viewed through the lens of introversion and extroversion. Based on Jung's typology, the Myers-Briggs Type Indicator and Aushra Augustinavichute's socionics were created. Cognitive styles, which may be inherent to a person, can also be considered as part of personality typology. For example, the Enneagram model and Enneatypes developed by Oscar Ichazo.

Let us now examine in more detail some of the models that Ken Wilber actively considers within his AQAL framework.

Application of Quadrants

The application of quadrants can be utilized in various spheres of human activity, including psychology, psychotherapy, medicine, business, and politics. Quadrants provide a remarkable dimension of attention that can be taken into account when addressing a wide range of tasks.

"**I** - Individual Interior" Quadrant: Psychoanalysis, Gestalt therapy, Humanistic therapy, Provocative therapy.	"**It** - Individual Exterior" Quadrant: Behavioral therapy, Pharmaceutical assistance, Biological feedback.
"**We** - Collective Interior" Quadrant: Psychodrama, Family psychotherapy, Systemic constellations, Group analysis, Alcoholics Anonymous groups.	"**Its** - Collective Exterior" Quadrant: Social support and assistance services, Anonymous helpline services, Programs for predicting various mental disorders and problems with social adaptation.

Four Quadrants of Integral Psychotherapy

(Here, we can observe how various therapeutic practices and schools of therapy are distributed among the quadrants.)

When examining reality through the lens of only one sector, we may fall into various forms of radicalism that can limit our perception of the reality map. Let's consider the examples of the four main radicalisms.

"**I** - Individual Interior" Quadrant: Radical idealism, "Reality is mind".	"**It** - Individual Exterior" Quadrant: Behavioral therapy, Pharmaceutical assistance, Biological feedback.
"**We** - Collective Interior" Quadrant: Radical postmodernism, "Reality is meanings constructed by culture".	"**Its** - Collective Exterior" Quadrant: Radical systems theory, "Reality is the web of life".

Levels of Development by Jean Gebser

Jean Gebser identified five main levels of development that, on the one hand, are reflected in the process of phylogenesis, and on the other hand, can be traced in the context of social development from early childhood to adulthood. He distinguished five stages: archaic, magic, mythical, rational, and integrative stages. They primarily reflect the dynamics of human development based on the dynamics of epochs, millennia, and centuries.

Archaic Stage: The state at this stage is fully identical to the world - a complete merging and undividedness with the world. At the level of personal development, it is the complete symbiosis of the infant with the mother. At this stage, there is no real need to influence anything. Symbiotic connection with the environment is a specific guarantee for solving key life tasks. It is a state of absolute infantilism and innocence. The first early tribes that existed 500,000 years ago.

Magic Stage: At this stage, we already see not a literal identity with the world but unity with it. The first signs of differentiation and separation appear. At this stage, our ancestors existed with a special state of consciousness that had deep connections with nature. Jean Gebser introduces a special term for this stage - "vegetative interpenetration," indicating a subtle sense of interconnectedness among all living things. Vegetative interpenetration constitutes the essence of experiencing the world at this stage of development. In many ways, Gebser equates the state of vegetative interpenetration with Carl Jung's term "synchronicity," which refers to the profound mystical interconnectedness of everything in the world that cannot be grasped through rational constructs and concepts. At this stage, there emerges a mystical confidence in the ability to influence the world, although actions are still infantile. This is the stage of primary magical rituals and the beginning of sympathetic magic, where there may be a conviction that if an image of a deer is drawn before hunting and then struck with a spear, it will make the hunt more successful. Approximate time frame: 50,000–10,000 BCE.

Mythical Stage: At this stage, there is an even greater detachment from the world. Notions of various forms of duality in consciousness emerge, such as good and evil, light and dark, masculine and feminine. Full-fledged mythological descriptions of the world with pantheons of deities arise, whom one can serve and ask for something by performing specific rituals and adhering to rules, making one's life better and more correct. The first signs of the emergence of rational thinking may be observed, but they do not yet dominate or determine the main course of social events. Myth governs human consciousness. When problems arise, people turn to the divine and powerful entities in their beliefs, seeking a personalized factor that can solve their problems. Approximate time frame: 10,000-1,225 BCE.

Rational Stage: This stage is characterized by consciousness and the ego as something separate, differentiated, and autonomous. There is a need for clear temporal ordering in a linear formation. There is a clear demarcation of the past, present, and future. In previous stages, the state of "here-and-now" predominated, and the division into temporal periods was highly conditional. Human attention increasingly focuses on the details of acquired experience and its analysis, giving rise to scientific and exploratory forms of activity. According to Gebser, the approximate beginning of this stage is 1,225 BCE. In 1,336 BCE, according to Gebser, the rational stage enters a certain deficit period. At this stage, consciousness achieves final "liberation" from its origins.

Integral Stage: At this stage, we can observe the manifestation of going beyond the traditional perspective. The source begins to be perceived as something spiritual and tangible, capable of providing a sense of wholeness. Integrative notions of the world and human beings emerge. Various sciences and spiritual traditions gradually move towards integration and the unification of experience.

Levels of Ego Development by Jane Levinger

The origins of Jane Levinger's ideas about levels of ego development can be traced back to Alfred Adler. Adler was the first to express his ideas about the ego's ability to play a dominant role in relation to the realm of motivation. In her model, Levinger describes individual levels of personality maturity and the general tendency toward self-regulation. Levinger directly associates the process of ego development with the gradual acquisition of autonomy skills, which begin to manifest in behavior and constructively shape the surrounding world. In her classification, Levinger avoids rigid attachment to a fixed chronological age. Her model reflects a clear hierarchy of criteria that depicts the dynamics of personal maturation and one's capacity for autonomy. Each stage involves an examination of impulse control, the ability for adequate interpersonal relationships, self-awareness, and an analysis of one's behavior.

Levels of Development According to Levinger

1. **Pre-social stage**: At this stage, the infant gradually distinguishes itself from the surrounding world. There is a slow process of differentiation and self-awareness as a separate entity. Reality is constructed in the mind as a stable world of objects.

2. **Symbiotic stage**: The process of individuation continues. Although a close connection with the mother persists, there emerges a certain communicative sphere through the use of sound analog communication. The key to transitioning to the next stage is the child's ability to express a literal or symbolic "no."

3. **Impulsive stage**: Various physical and emotional impulses that arise in the child's interaction with the external world contribute to their self-assertion as a separate entity. The focus is primarily on aggressive, alimentary, and sexual impulses. According to Levinger, the emergence of the word "why" in the child's lexicon serves as a trigger for transitioning to the next stage.

4. **Stage of self-defense**: The child begins to recognize the existing scheme of potential rewards and punishments and anticipates them. This leads to relative control over their behavior. Such control increasingly helps the child restrain the impulses that previously dominated their behavior in the earlier stage of development. At this stage, self-criticism is still absent, but the concepts of guilt and shame emerge. However, more often than not, the causes of guilt and shame are attributed to someone else or circumstances.

5. **Conformism stage**: This stage begins to actualize when the child establishes a connection between their own well-being and the well-being of the social group to which they belong. The rules of existence within the group become the leading value orientations, and their

violation elicits serious disapproval. Group membership becomes a guarantee of personal safety and further development.

6. **Self-awareness stage**: At this stage, a vivid realization emerges that the ideal self-image may not correspond to the image of the real self. Group stereotypes are gradually replaced by one's own stereotypes. Individual differences in character traits become apparent.

7. **Conscientiousness stage**: According to Levinger, this stage involves a radical complexity of the mechanisms of self-regulation. She also comments that very few individuals reach this stage by the age of 13-14. The stage of conscientiousness often marks the completion of a full internalization of social rules, where conscience, self-criticism, and a sense of responsibility begin to function fully. There is a need to set personal goals and strive to achieve them to the best of one's abilities and opportunities.

8. **Individualistic stage**: This stage particularly highlights the sense of personal individuality and poses challenges regarding emotional connections between people, issues of personal relationships, and ways to resolve them.

9. **Autonomous stage**: At this stage, the ability to embrace internal conflict emerges. It develops within the individual between their needs and the social obligations they undertake. A realistic view of the world, objectivity, and the ability to strive for abstract ideals and goals are formed.

10. **Integrated stage**: The key distinction of the integrated stage from the autonomous stage is the consolidation of a sense of identity. Levinger compares the integrated stage of development to Abraham Maslow's state of self-actualization. According to Levinger, this stage of development is quite rare.

Stages of Human Development According to Robert Kegan

Robert Kegan, a professor at Harvard University, developed the theory of subject-object differentiation and orders of consciousness. Kegan identified a model of human developmental stages, incorporating five main stages into this model.

1. **Impulsive mind:** Early childhood. This stage is observed from birth to 5-6 years of age. The child's existence is determined by their momentary impulsive desires, which dominate over self-control.

2. **Imperial mind:** Adolescence (6% of the adult population).
   The approximate age range is from 6 to 20 years. The individual gradually gains control over their impulses and emotions, but their needs, interests, and desires captivate them. The ability to set specific goals and gradually achieve them emerges, as well as the need to adhere to social rules to avoid group censure.

3. **Socialized mind:** (58% of the adult population).
   This stage begins at the age of 20. The person gradually gains control over satisfying various social needs. They also become fully socialized and organize their life as part of society. At this stage, the influence of society on the individual, with its pros and cons, becomes fully revealed. This stage can continue throughout life.

4. **Self-authoring mind:** (35% of the adult population).
   At this stage, the individual gradually develops the ability to self-form, determine their environment, and follow their own path. They move away from conformist social rigidity characteristic of the previous stage.

5. **Self-transforming mind:** (1% of the adult population).

At this level, fixation on oneself ceases. The individual is no longer consumed by ideas of satisfying their own needs. They perceive everything that manifests in the world and their life as equal and interdependent parts of a whole. This is a period of integrative and holistic perception of existence. These qualities are often found in various spiritual masters, philosophers, and highly intellectual individuals.

Spiral Dynamics by Don Beck and Chris Cowan

(Category of Developmental Levels)

Levels of Spiral Dynamics

1. **Beige**: The main idea of this level is to do whatever it takes to stay alive. It represents the level of physical survival. Instincts are used for survival purposes, and self-identity is very weak. The primary priorities are food, sex, warmth, and safety. It marks the transition from animal to human. Approximately 100,000 years ago.

2. **Purple**: Worshiping the spirits of nature and creating a family hearth. Demonstrating subordination and loyalty to the leader and the group. Preserving sacred oaths. Strict obedience to accepted taboos and seasonal rituals. Basic self-identification emerges as part of the group. The main priorities are family, group affiliation, and adherence to rituals. The formation of tribes, magic, and primitive art. Approximately 50,000 years ago.

3. **Red**: The fundamental rule at this level is to be who you are and do whatever you want, regardless of anything else. Being in a constant state of readiness for battle. Striving for power and dominance over the group and other individuals. Seeking to impose one's own rules on the group in which one exists. The main priorities become power

and dominance. The era of warlords, conquests, and discoveries. Approximately 10,000 years ago.

4. **Blue**: At this level, there is a desire to adhere to group rules and make sacrifices for them. Clear legal order. Subordination is directed more towards the group's rules than to the leader. Formation of clear moral principles. Establishment of bureaucracies. The emergence of a fully developed social matrix with clearly defined roles. Ideas of justice, democracy, and equality gain prominence. Living by the rules now provides the best opportunities for the future. Control of aggressive feelings. Emergence of literature, monotheism, and goal-oriented awareness. Approximately 5,000 years ago.

5. **Orange**: At this level, individuals begin to play their own game within society, aimed at victory and dominance. In some sense, this level may resemble the third level, but with adherence to the fundamental rules of the fourth level. Progress is achieved through understanding and realizing the secrets of the world. The right strategy and tactics enable one to forge ahead and achieve superiority. There is a very clear self-identification, understanding of one's own path and goals. The conditions for individualism are formed, and comprehensive economic structures are established. Approximately 1,000 years ago.

6. **Green**: At this level, individuals start seeking balance in the world, engaging in close collaboration with their environment. Personal selfish goals become less of a concern. There is a need to do something for others to transform the world we live in into a better place. Liberation from greed, prejudices, and dogmatic beliefs. Self-enrichment and the enrichment of the world through spirituality, harmony, and balance. Struggle for human freedom in various manifestations, human rights, and collectivism. Approximately 150 years ago.

7. **Yellow**: Integrative level. Awareness of oneself as part of the world and as an individual entity. Recognition of previous levels of development. Perceiving life as a kaleidoscope of hierarchies and systems. The ability to interact with them effectively and achieve efficient and constructive outcomes. Tolerance towards differences existing at various levels of Spiral Dynamics. Understanding the wholeness and complexity of the world, having unrestricted access to various knowledge and traditions, and constructing a system of holistic interconnections. Approximately 50 years ago.

8. **Turquoise**: Holistic level. Experiencing wholeness through the mind and spirituality. Understanding that human identity, on one hand, is individual, and on the other hand, is a part of a larger spiritual system. Holistic thinking is present. Globalism and the ecology of both the world and consciousness. Approximately 30 years ago.

9. **Coral**: Potentially a higher level of Spiral Dynamics, but not fully interpreted by the authors. Still in the process of emergence.

Each level of Spiral Dynamics is oriented towards either the ego or the group. This progression occurs sequentially. Ego-oriented levels include beige, red, orange, yellow, and coral. Group-oriented levels include purple, blue, green, and turquoise. In the course of personal development, individuals progress through the levels of Spiral Dynamics in a sequential manner. It is worth noting that depending on the level of Spiral Dynamics, one can understand and become aware of both the internal psychological processes occurring within a person and comprehend the nature of their behavior in the external world. This model has powerful multisystem applications in various spheres of human interaction.

Multiple Intelligences by Howard Gardner

In 1983, the American psychologist Howard Gardner presented his concept of multiple intelligences in his book "Frames of Mind." In his work, he categorized individuals into seven types based on their preferred ways of understanding the world and the dominance of a specific intellectual vector. Gardner identified the following types of intelligence: linguistic, logical-mathematical, musical, bodily-kinesthetic, spatial-visual, interpersonal, and intrapersonal. In addition to the seven primary intelligences, he also identified three additional ones: naturalistic, spiritual, and moral.

According to Howard Gardner, the different types of intelligence represent various lines of development throughout a person's life. Working with these lines can serve as an excellent diagnostic tool as well as an instrument for integrative coaching and psychotherapy. However, it is important to note that the applicability of the lines of development and multiple intelligences extends far beyond the context of psychotherapy.

Howard Gardner comments that in his research, he discovered 24 potential lines of development, which can be considered as specific types of intelligence to some extent.

List of Types of Intelligence According to Gardner

1. **Linguistic Intelligence**: Ability to easily learn different languages and understand the structure, rules, and peculiarities of language.

2. **Logical-Mathematical Intelligence**: Ability to think in a logical and mathematical manner.

3. **Musical Intelligence**: Ability to sense, create, and convey musical harmony.

4. **Bodily-Kinesthetic Intelligence**: Excellent control over the body, fine motor skills, and overall body coordination.

5. **Spatial-Visual Intelligence**: Ability to create and manipulate visual images. Creative and artistic thinking.

6. **Interpersonal Intelligence**: Excellent communication skills, the ability to quickly establish rapport with others, and the ability to create and maintain social connections.

7. **Intrapersonal Intelligence**: Ability for self-reflection and self-awareness. Deep understanding of oneself and the world. Philosophical thinking.

8. **Naturalistic Intelligence**: Interaction with the natural environment, concern for ecology.

9. **Spiritual Intelligence**: Engagement with religion and various aspects of spiritual development.

10. **Moral Intelligence**: Ethical and moral aspects of life; advocacy for rights; jurisprudence; defense of social positions.

Spiritual States According to Ken Wilber

Wilber presents distinctions between four primary types of spiritual experiences that can be accessible to individuals:

- **Natural Mysticism**: An example of this experience can be the sense of unity with nature while walking through a forest after rain.

- **Divine Mysticism**: An example can be the experience of encountering a spiritual image during meditation.

- **Formless Mysticism**: An example can be the experience of emptiness, the abyss of consciousness. Here, one can recall Nietzsche and his phrase, "If you gaze long into an abyss, the abyss also gazes into you."

- **Non-Dual Mysticism**: An example can be a unique state of unity of opposites, interconnectedness of all living beings, and their equal value.

Cognitive Styles

The term "cognitive styles" was first mentioned by Alfred Adler to denote the characteristics of stable individual personality traits, cognitive abilities, and various investigative strategies. In Adlerian individual psychology, cognitive styles of personality were viewed as a specific form of individuality, structured by goals and various ways of achieving them.

After Adler, significant contributions to the study of cognitive styles were made by G. Allport, C. Stagner, G. Witkin, V. A. Kolga, M. A. Kholodnaya, and A. Libin.

In Neuro-Linguistic Programming (NLP), there is a concept of personality metaprograms, which are almost synonymous with the notion of cognitive styles. Some metaprograms were discussed in the chapter dedicated to NLP.

Currently, cognitive styles are understood as certain forms of cognitive dichotomies through which we filter our experiences. There is experimental evidence that cognitive styles are closely related to the intellectual sphere of personality, temperament, and motivational aspects. Typically, the literature on cognitive styles describes 10–15 types.

Let's consider some cognitive styles.

1. **Cognitive simplicity or complexity**: Some individuals have a dominant inclination to create clear and simple descriptions of the external world without excessive interpretations. Others, on the contrary, tend to have interpretations filled with excessive details.

2. **Narrow or broad range of equivalence**: Some people tend to differentiate objects in the world based on specific details inherent to them, while others do so based on generalized qualities associated with them.

3. **Impulsivity or reflectivity**: Impulsive individuals make quick and thoughtless decisions and actions, which often lead to a high number of errors. Reflective individuals, on the other hand, take much longer to ponder decisions and approach situations with deeper contemplation. Naturally, the number of life mistakes is significantly lower for reflective individuals compared to impulsive ones.

4. **Focusing or scanning control**: Individuals with focusing control fully concentrate their attention on a specific process or feature during interactions with the world and when solving tasks. As a result, they may ignore a considerable amount of various task-related details. In contrast, individuals with scanning control pay great attention to details, but maintaining complete focus on one thing can be challenging for them.

5. **Low or high tolerance for unrealistic experiences**: Tolerant individuals strive to evaluate their experiences based on their immediate characteristics, subjecting them to constructive analysis. In contrast, intolerant individuals tend to strongly resist experiences that significantly deviate from their core beliefs.

Socionic Personality Types

The term "socionics" was coined by Estonian psychologist Aushra Augustinavichute based on the typology of Carl Gustav Jung and the theory of informational metabolism by A. Kempinski. Socionics is concerned with studying the mechanisms of the psyche through which individuals perceive, filter, and evaluate various types of incoming information -

verbal, non-verbal, discrete, emotional, sensory, and so on. The individual, in the context of socionics, is viewed as a specific system of informational connections that adhere to specific rules.

Augustinavichute first presented her comprehensive ideas about socionics in her book "On the Dual Nature of Man," published in 1980, which was based on her creative reinterpretation of Jung's concepts of psychotypes. Carl Jung identified four main characteristics of personality - thinking, feeling, sensing, and intuition. He believed that there were types of people who were accentuated in one or more of these characteristics. Jung also differentiated individuals into extraverts and introverts. Thus, if we construct a two-dimensional matrix, we have eight primary personality types. Furthermore, to make the descriptions of the types more accurate, Jung introduced an additional, secondary interpretation of the types. The secondary interpretation can be examined within the framework of the following matrix.

Basic Interpretation	Additional Interpretation
Thinking	Sensation
	Intuition
Feeling	Sensation
	Intuition
Sensing	Thinking
	Feeling
Intuition	Thinking
	Feeling

Variability of Personality Types

In this case, we can observe the dual division made by Jung. He interpreted thinking and feeling as rational characteristics that can intersect with sensing and intuition, which are irrational characteristics of personality. Therefore, we can see the emergence of specific combinations, as indicated in the table.

Additionally, as evident from the table, a person can have a dominant rational or irrational characteristic. In her socionics model, Augustinavičiūtė replaced the term "thinking" with "logic" and "feeling" with "ethics." She referred to the combination of the eight primary and secondary functions that Carl Jung presented as "variants of informational metabolism." She began to develop theories that these variants of informational metabolism are specific filters of consciousness that determine and influence the ways of perceiving the world and the nature of interaction with it. They also have a direct connection to a person's character.

Considering the primary function, secondary function, and extraverted or introverted reference, socionics gives rise to 16 main personality types, each possessing its own specific properties and qualities. Augustinavičiūtė believes that all 16 types form a cohesive information structure, which she named "socion."

The peculiarity of the socionics matrix of personality types lies not only in the identification of specific personality types but also in the study of their possible interaction patterns, compatibility, and incompatibility. In her book "On the Dual Nature of Man," Augustinavičiūtė presents an extensive analysis of representatives of each personality type and draws numerous analogies with various well-known historical characters. However, there is a small problem: the assignment of these characters to specific types lacks clear criteria, which undermines the objectivity and validity of her judgments.

Due to these reasons, socionics is not currently recognized as a fully established scientific discipline and is often regarded as a quasi-scientific system. Socionic tests emerged at the early stages of the discipline's development. In addition to tests for determining socionic type, other methods such as interviews, experiments, observations, dossier studies, etc., can be employed.

Despite the various contentious aspects of socionics, its typology has the potential to make an invaluable contribution to the theory and practice of understanding the diversity of psychological personality types.

No.	Primary Function	Secondary Function	Extrovert Introvert	Pseudonym
1	Logic	Sensation	Extrovert	Administrator
2			Introvert	Inspector
3		Intuition	Extrovert	Entrepreneur
4			Introvert	Analyst
5	Ethical	Sensation	Extrovert	Enthusiast
6			Introvert	Conservator
7		Intuition	Extrovert	Mentor
8			Introvert	Humanist
9	Sensation	Logic	Extrovert	Marshal
10			Introvert	Craftsman
11		Ethical	Extrovert	Politician
12			Introvert	Mediator
13	Intuition	Logic	Extrovert	Seeker
14			Introvert	Critic
15		Ethical	Extrovert	Counselor
16			Introvert	Lyricist

Expanded Matrix of Socionic Personality Types

Enneagram and Enneatypes

The concept of the Enneagram and Enneatypes was developed in the 1970s by Oscar Ichazo and Claudio Naranjo. It is worth noting that the ideas of mystic George Gurdjieff also influenced the formation of the Enneagram.

Enneagram (from the Greek words "ennéa", meaning "nine", and "grámma", meaning "written character or figure") is a model consisting of nine personality types and their interrelationships. In essence, the Enneagram model can be compared to the Socionic personality types proposed by Augustinavichiute.

The model describes nine deep unconscious drives that can exist within a person's psyche and how these drives can influence the cognitive, emotional, and behavioral aspects of human existence. They affect character manifestations, transform one's life path, and guide the processes of self-actualization. In addition to the typology itself, the Enneagram pays significant attention to the structure of potential transactions and the system of relationships between individuals belonging to different Enneatypes.

Wilts and Palmer argue that ideas similar to those of the Enneagram can be found in the works of Evagrius Ponticus, a Christian mystic who lived in Alexandria in the 4th century. In his writings, Evagrius described eight thoughts that later formed the basis of the doctrine of the seven deadly sins. He considered "self-love" as the foundational ninth thought, believing that all others follow from it. In a sense, self-love, according to Evagrius, can be seen as a metathought or the thought of thoughts, a specific unifying category. Besides describing the thoughts themselves, Evagrius outlined eight ways to combat and counteract them.

In its modern form, the Enneagram system began to be taught by Oscar Ichazo, a native of Bolivia, in the 1950s. Ichazo referred to his practice as "protoanalysis" and utilized not only the Enneagram but also other symbols and ideas. Claudio Naranjo, upon encountering Oscar Ichazo's Enneagram ideas, began teaching it in the United States in his own interpretation. Subsequently, the teaching of the Enneagram spread and gained popularity among psychotherapists and Christian clergy. Some Jesuit priests started teaching the Enneagram and considering it through the lens of Christian spirituality. However, the official Vatican did not recognize the Enneagram as a suitable tool for spiritual development. Additionally, the Enneagram has gained significant popularity in New Age circles.

One of the existing interpretations of the nine core Enneatypes is presented in the table below (the names in the table are based on the works of D. Riso, R. Hudson, and H. Makan). Each personality type is divided into three subtypes. It is believed that the subtype is directly related to the instinctual drive that dominates a person's life strategies. In the practice of the Enneagram, three primary instinctual energies are distinguished: self-preservation instinct, sexual instinct, and social instinct. Depending on which instinct dominates, different needs begin to prevail in a person.

Correspondence of Needs with Instincts

With a dominance of the self-preservation instinct, needs related to safety, health, and material well-being prevail.

With a dominance of the sexual instinct, needs related to close relationships prevail.

With a dominance of the social instinct, needs related to social recognition, status, and position in society prevail.

Although the Enneagram and the Enneatypes model have gained many supporters among practicing psychotherapists, this model is not recognized in academic circles due to the lack of valid tests that accurately determine a person's Enneatype. Moreover, within the Enneagram method itself, there are different schools of thought that may provide varying interpretations of its theoretical and practical positions. This further complicates the task of validation due to the diversity of subjective views on the subject matter.

No.	Character Role	Passion	Ego Fixation	Basic Desire	Basic Fear	Temptation	Virtue
1	Perfectionist	Anger	Resentment	To be good, ethical, balanced	To be bad, unethical, flawed	Hypocrisy, excessive criticism	Serenity
2	Helper	Pride	Flattery	To be loved	To be unloved	Neglecting one's own needs	Humility
3	Achiever	Self-deception	Vanity	To feel valuable	To have no worth	Striving to always be the best	Authenticity
4	Individualist	Envy	Melancholy (Lack)	To be authentic	To have no identity	Indulging in imagination in the quest for self-discovery	Equanimity
5	Observer	Avarice	Isolation	To be competent	To be helpless	Replacing direct experience with mental concepts	Generosity
6	Skeptic Loyalist	Fear	Doubt	To have support	To be left without support	Indecisiveness doubts	Courage
7	Enthusiast	Gluttony	Planning, deceit	To be satisfied	To experience pain and deprivation	Feeling that happiness and fulfillment are elsewhere	Sobriety
8	Challenger	Lust	Justice (Struggle)	To be protected and independent	To be controlled by others	Considering oneself completely self-sufficient	Innocence
9	Peacemaker	Sloth	Self-forgetting	To be whole	To be divided, disconnected	Avoiding conflicts	Energy (Wholeness)

Table of Enneatypes

Integral Life Practice

Ken Wilber, based on his theoretical and practical inquiries, proposed a specific type of practice that can largely be referred to as a practice of general self-development but simultaneously has, in my opinion, the most direct relation to psychotherapy.

According to Wilber, Integral Life Practice (ILP) aims to facilitate the realization of the spectrum of potentials that can be inherent in the human personality.

The essence of ILP is quite simple—it involves focusing attention and activity on twelve core dimensions. These dimensions are formed as a matrix through the combination of levels of body, mind, spirit, and shadow, as well as sectors of Self, culture, and nature. The practice consists of key foundational modules.

The "**Body**" module encompasses three fundamental aspects of working with the body, or, as Wilber puts it, the training of the three bodies. This training includes gross physical exercises such as fitness and bodybuilding, exercises with the subtle body, such as qigong and tai chi, as well as exercises for working with the causal-transcendental body, which Wilber describes as "the sense of infinity, cycles of light, and life." Working with the causal body involves certain static and dynamic meditative exercises that may incorporate specific mental work, chanting mantras, or affirmations. For example, paying homage to a Buddha statue can be interpreted as a causal bodily exercise.

In the "**Mind**" module, we can engage in activities such as reading, studying, training intellect, memory, attention, and more.

The "**Spirit**" module may involve various forms of meditation specific to different spiritual traditions, such as prayers, chanting mantras, Zen, Kabbalah, Vipassana, and more.

In the "**Shadow**" module, attention is focused on various forms of psychotherapy, self-exploration, and the exploration of one's repressions and suppressions. Here, a wide range of psychotherapeutic forms, techniques, and practices can be employed, depending on personal preference:

NLP, hypnosis and self-hypnosis, autogenic training, psychoanalysis, art therapy, and others.

Each module of Integral Life Practice offers a unique pathway for personal growth and self-realization. By engaging in practices that target the mind, spirit, and shadow, individuals can delve into different dimensions of their being and gain insight into their psychological patterns, spiritual connection, and the integration of their shadow aspects.

Body (Physical, Subtle, Causal)	**Mind** (Education, Intellect, Memory, Attention)	**Spirit** (Meditation, Prayer, Chanting of Mantras, Contemplation)	**Shadow** (Psychotherapy)
Fitness (Physical) Bodybuilding (Physical) Pilates (Physical) Yoga (Physical and Subtle) Qigong (Subtle) Tai Chi (Physical and Subtle) Ritualistic Body Practices (Causal)	Reading Books Watching Educational Videos Attending Seminars Intellectual Training Memory Training Attention Training	Meditation Prayer Chanting of Mantras Shamanic Contemplation Kabbalah Transcendental Meditation Kundalini Yoga	NLP (Neuro-Linguistic Programming) Hypnosis Psychoanalysis Gestalt Psychotherapy Art Therapy

Matrix of the Four Core Modules of Integral Life

In addition to the four foundational modules of ILP, Ken Wilber includes additional ones such as ethics, sexuality, work, emotions, and relationships. It is suggested that individuals choose at least one practice from each of the four foundational modules and begin engaging in them regularly.

Ken Wilber writes that if the integral AQAL model is applied as a specific guiding coordinate system for organizing and understanding a particular sphere of activity, it can be referred to as an "integral operating system" (IOS). This system allows for a significant increase in the level of effectiveness in interacting with the chosen sphere of activity by adjusting perception filters to accommodate the maximum possible diversity.

In my opinion, the application of ILP in the context of psychotherapeutic work creates new and unique opportunities and methods for utilizing a wide range of existing schools and methods of psychotherapy.

Afterword

In this book, I have provided a brief overview of the main fundamental directions in psychotherapy. I have explored the key and foundational concepts of many authors that have direct and indirect relevance to psychotherapy.

Each book in the series, dedicated to a specific psychotherapeutic approach, will always be accompanied by an examination of the combination of the therapeutic approach and various psychopathological profiles. Information about psychopathological profiles is presented in a condensed form as it goes beyond the scope of this series.

In the future, I will dedicate a separate, comprehensive work to psychopathological profiling, which will serve as an excellent complement to the information presented in this book.

Certain comprehensive topics have intentionally been deferred to future books in the series, such as psychoanalytic and behavioral vectors, among others. This has been done to create new focal points in the work and emphasize the themes of this series that are rarely mentioned in introductory textbooks on psychotherapy. These include provocative therapy, psychedelic therapy, anti-psychiatry, and others.

Whether this is viewed as good or bad is for the reader to decide. However, I have made every effort to make this work truly engaging and informative.

The information presented in the books in this series and subsequent ones is structured in our perception into a specific three-dimensional model. This model allows for easy and rapid utilization of information, understanding its specificity, and capturing the interconnections between its various parts.

Some vectors have been discussed in this series, while others will be addressed in the next one. Additionally, future plans include adding supplements to the vectors already presented in this work.

Psychotherapy Vectors Model

Behavioral Vector	Provocative Vector	Cognitive Vector
Psychoanalytic Vector	Integrative Vector	Hypnotic Vector
Somatic Vector	Humanistic Vector	Existential Vector

Table 1

Drama Therapy	Integrative Vector	Pharmaceutical Vector

Table 2

This is the basic three-dimensional model of psychotherapy vectors, with the integrative vector of psychotherapy as the central intersecting point. In the introduction, we have already discussed the dichotomy of psychotherapy vectors, which you can clearly see in the context of this model.

Thus, in our work, we have not only attempted to explore the spectrum of psychotherapy schools but also specifically organize them in relation to each other. In my opinion, this creates the opportunity to effectively and systematically memorize, store, and utilize the information that has been read and accumulated.

This method of structuring through the prism of a three-dimensional model has evolved over many years. During the course on the fundamentals of psychotherapy in universities, the foundation was laid for our understanding of which information would be more effective in presentation and which would not. Over the years, the course has undergone numerous changes as we constantly strive to improve it, making it more practical and engaging. The outcome of our work is a private school of psychotherapy where I have shaped knowledge into a comprehensive structural model. What you will find in the *Psychology & Psychotherapy Theories & Practices Series* is only a part of this structural model, which encompasses many other important topics that, in my view, are necessary for a systematic understanding of psychotherapy and comprehensive education.

I hope that this work will lead to a new understanding of what psychotherapy is, the various branches it encompasses, and their distinctive features.

A Brief Message from the Author

Understanding complex psychotherapeutic theories and practices can be challenging, but by sharing your thoughts and feedback, you can help others discover the value of this book as a tool for mastering these concepts. Your review could be the encouragement someone needs to deepen their knowledge and change their lives by improving their understanding of psychotherapy.

Thank you in advance for taking the time to share your experience! I wish you ongoing success in your journey to become a master in psychotherapy and expand your knowledge. If this book has been valuable to you, I'd be grateful if you could take a moment to leave a review. **Your positive rating would mean a lot!**

To leave a review, just scan the QR code or click the link below: psychemaster.com/recommends/review-psychotherapy-fundamentals

Bibliography

1. Seminar with Dr. Milton H. Erickson: Lessons in Hypnosis. Edited and commented by J.K. Zeig. Moscow: Independent Firm "Klass", 1994.
2. Radin, P. Trickster: A Study of North American Indian Myths with Comments by C.G. Jung and C.C. Kerenyi. St. Petersburg: Eurasia, 1999, pp. 265-286.
3. Farrelly, F., and Brandsma, D. Provocative Therapy. Moscow: Publishing House "Ekaterinburg", 1996.
4. Haley, J. About Milton Erickson. Translated by V.M. Sarina and Y.A. Khudokon. Moscow: Independent Firm "Klass", 1998.
5. Erickson, M.G. The February Man: Hypnotherapy and the Development of Self-Awareness. Milton H. Erickson, Ernest L. Rossi; translated by E.L. Dlugach. Moscow: Independent Firm "Klass", 1995.
6. Erickson, M. Hypnotic Realities: Induction of Clinical Hypnosis and Forms of Indirect Suggestion. Milton Erickson, Ernest Rossi, and Sheila Rossi; translated by M.A. Yakushina, edited by M.R. Ginzburg. Moscow: Klass, 2000.
7. Erickson, M. The Strategy of Psychotherapy: Selected Works. Authorized translation and editing by L.M. Shlionsky. St. Petersburg: Rech, 2002.
8. Erickson, M. Teaching Seminar with Dr. Milton H. Erickson, M.D.: Lessons in Hypnosis. Edited and commented by Jeffrey K. Zeig; translated by T.K. Kruglova. Moscow: Klass, 2003.
9. Moreno, J. L. (2001). Psychodrama. Moscow: "April Press"; "Eksmo-Press." (Translated by G. Pimochkina, E. Rachkova)

10. Moreno, J. L. (2001). Sociometry: Experimental method and the science of society. Moscow: "Academic Project." (Translated by A. Bokovikov, Ed. by R. A. Zolotovitsky)
11. Moreno, J. (1993). Theatre of Spontaneity. Krasnoyarsk: Mental Health Foundation. (Translated by B. I. Khasan)
12. Satir, V. (2007). You and Your Family. Moscow: April-Press, Institute of General Humanities Studies.
13. Satir, V. (1992). How to Build Yourself and Your Family. Moscow: Pedagogika-Press.
14. Satir, V. (2001). Family Therapy. Moscow: Speech.
15. Satir, V. (2009). Family Therapy: A Practical Guide. Moscow: Institute of General Humanities Studies.
16. Satir, V., Bandler, R., Grindler, D. (2000). Family Therapy and NLP. Moscow: Institute of General Humanities Studies.
17. Hellinger, B. (2006). And It Becomes Easy in the Middle of You. Book for Those Who Want to Find Harmony in Relationships, Love, and Happiness. (2nd ed.). Moscow: Institute of Counseling and Systemic Solutions, Institute of Psychotherapy Publishing House.
18. Hellinger, B. (2015). Success Stories in Life and Profession. Kyiv: Hellinger Publications.
19. Hellinger, B. (2005). The Source Doesn't Need to Ask for Paths. Moscow: Institute of Counseling and Systemic Solutions, Higher School of Psychology.
20. Hellinger, B. (2009). Love of the Spirit. Moscow: Institute of Counseling and Systemic Solutions.
21. Hellinger, B. (2007). We Are Moving Forward. Course for Couples in Difficult Situations. Moscow: Institute of Counseling and Systemic Solutions.
22. Hellinger, B. (2007). Orders of Love: Resolving Systemic and Family Conflicts and Contradictions. Moscow: Institute of Psychotherapy Publishing House. (Translated by Diana Komlach)
23. Hellinger, B. (2006). Orders of Help. Moscow: Institute of Counseling and Systemic Solutions.

24. Hellinger, B. (2009). Happiness That Remains. Moscow: Institute of Counseling and Systemic Solutions.
25. Hellinger, B. (2010). Success in Life / Success in Profession. Kyiv: Hellinger Publications.
26. Gessmann, H.-W. (2011). Textbook of Systemic Therapy. (Translated into Russian by Elena Oladova). Publisher: PIB, Duisburg.
27. Gessmann, H.-W. (2011). Forms of Psychotherapy: An Introduction. (Translated into Russian by Elena Oladova). Publisher: PIB, Duisburg.
28. Gessmann, H.-W. (2014). Subjective Theories of Illness. Translation: E.A. Sheronov. N.A. Nekrasov Kostroma State University, Kostroma. ISBN 978-5-7591-1429-1.
29. Bugental, J.F.T. (1998). The Science of Being: Dialogues Between Therapist and Patients in Humanistic Therapy. (Translated from English by A.B. Fenko). Moscow: Independent firm "Klass."
30. Maslow, A.G. (1999). Motivation and Personality. Translation: A.M. Tatlybaeva. St. Petersburg: Eurasia.
31. Perls, F. (1994). "Inside and Outside the Garbage Can." Publisher: "St. Petersburg XXI Century", St. Petersburg.
32. Perls, F. (2007). Gestalt Seminars. (Translated from English). Moscow: Institute of General Humanitarian Research. ISBN 5-88230-202-1.
33. Rogers, C. (1986). Towards a Science of Personality. In "History of Foreign Psychology. Texts." Moscow, pp. 200-230.
34. Rogers, C. (2002). Client-Centered Therapy. Moscow: Refl-Book, Kyiv: Vakler.
35. Rogers, C. (2000). Several Important Discoveries. In "Bulletin of Moscow State University. Series 14. Psychology", No. 2, pp. 58-65.
36. Fromm, E. (2011). Escape from Freedom. Moscow: AST. (Philosophy).
37. Fromm, E. (1998). Psychoanalysis and Ethics. Moscow: AST. (Classics of Foreign Psychology). 10,000 copies.
38. Fromm, E. (2010). The Art of Loving. An Investigation into the Psychological Problems of Ethics. Moscow: AST.
39. Fromm, E. (2010). Psychoanalysis and Religion. Moscow: AST.

(Philosophy. Psychology).

40. Fromm, E. (1998). Man and Woman. Moscow: AST.
41. Shostrom, E. (1992). Anti-Carnegie, or Man, the Manipulator: The Inner Journey from Manipulation to Actualization. Minsk: TPC "Polifact."
42. Shostrom, E., Brammer, L. (2002). Therapeutic Psychology: Foundations of Counseling and Psychotherapy. Moscow: Eksmo. (Psychological Collection).
43. Shostrom, E. (2008). Man, the Manipulator: The Inner Journey from Manipulation to Actualization. Moscow: April-Press, Psychotherapy.
44. Charlotte Bühler: Self-presentation. In: Ludwig Pongratz et al. (Eds.): Psychologie in Selbstdarstellungen. Volume 1. Huber, Bern et al., 1972, ISBN 3-456-30433-1, pp. 9-42.
45. Porter, E.H. (1950) An Introduction to Therapeutic Counseling. Boston: Houghton Mifflin.
46. Porter E.H. (1962) Parable of the Spindle. Harvard Business Review, 40, 58–66.
47. Porter E.H. (1964) Manpower Development. New York: Harper & Row.
48. Porter E.H. (1971, 1996) Strength Deployment Inventory. Carlsbad, CA: Personal Strengths Publishing, Inc.
49. Porter E.H. (1973, 1996) Relationship Awareness Theory, Manual of Administration and Interpretation, Ninth Edition. Carlsbad, CA: Personal Strengths Publishing, Inc.
50. Maslow A. Dominance, Self-Esteem, Self-Actualization. California, 1973.
51. Böadella, D. Biosynthesis. Streams of Life: [Translation from English]. Ed. Berezkina-Orlova, V.B. Moscow, 2016. 448 p.
52. Ginzburg, T.I. "Breath Techniques. Integration Methodology." Moscow, 2010. "Psychotherapy."
53. Gershon, A. Stories Told by the Body. Practice of Authentic Movement. Minsk: 2008, 128 p.
54. Karvasarsky, B.D. Psychotherapeutic Encyclopedia. St. Petersburg: Piter, 2006. ISBN 5-318-00694-9, 5-8046-0152-0.

55. Kurtz, R. Body-Oriented Psychotherapy. Hakomi Method. M.: Nezavisimaya firma "Klass", 2004. 304 p.
56. Lowen, A. Therapy That Works with the Body. Speech, 2000. 272 p. (Practical Psychotherapy). ISBN 5-9268-0001-3.
57. Reich, W. The Function of the Orgasm. Moscow: "AST", 1997. 304 p. ISBN 5-7914-0015-2.
58. Rank, O. The Trauma of Birth and Its Significance for Psychoanalysis. Moscow: "Kogito-Center", 2009.
59. Smith, D. "Diseases of the Nervous System: Textbook of Neurology and Psychiatry" (1915).
60. Stolyarenko, L.D. "Psychology. Textbook for Universities." St. Petersburg, 2008. PITer Publishing House.
61. Fedorova, G.M., Bazhurina, V.B. "Holistic Massage." St. Petersburg: Nevsky Prospect, 2001. ISBN 5-94371-052-3.
62. Feldenkrais, M. Awareness Through Movement. Moscow: Transpersonal Institute Publishing House, 1994.
63. Yanov, A. PRIMARY SCREAM. Series: Philosophy. Publisher: AST. 2009. ISBN 978-5-17-045903-2.
64. Alexander, M., FM. Man's Supreme Inheritance, Methuen (London, 1910), revised and enlarged 1918, later editions 1941, 1946, 1957, scholarly edition Mouritz (UK, 1996, reprinted 2002, ISBN 0-9525574-0-1).
65. Alexander, M., FM. Conscious Control, Methuen (London, 1912), revised and incorporated into the 1918 edition of Man's Supreme Inheritance.
66. Alexander, M., FM. Constructive Conscious Control of the Individual, E. P. Dutton (USA, 1923), Methuen (London, 1924), revised 1946, scholarly edition Mouritz (UK, 2004, ISBN 0-9543522-6-2).
67. Benedek, T. (1964), "In Memorian Franz Alexander 1891–1964.", Journal of the American Psychoanalytic Association 12: 877–81, 1964 Oct.
68. Boyesen, Gerda; Boyesen, Mona Lisa, "Biodynamische Theorie und Praxis", in: Hilarion G. Petzold [Ed.], Die neuen Körpertherapien, 1st

ed. Paderborn: Jungfermannsche Verlagsbuchhandlung, 1977, pp. 140–157.

69. Browning, T. "Gentle Miracles — Holistic Pulsing" (1992).
70. Dunbar, H. F. Symbolism in Medieval Thought and its Consummation in The Divine Comedy, Yale University Press (New Haven), 1929.
71. Eckardt, M. H. (2001), "Franz Alexander: a unique outstanding pioneer", The Journal of the American Academy of Psychoanalysis 29.
72. Hanna, Thomas L. (1970). Bodies in Revolt: A Primer in Somatic Thinking. Holt, Rinehart and Winston.
73. Knaster, Mirka (1996). Discovering the Body's Wisdom: A Comprehensive Guide to More Than Fifty Mind-Body Practices. Bantam. pp. 178–81. ISBN 9780307575500.
74. Levine, A. (1998). The Bodywork and Massage Sourcebook. Lowell House. pp. 159–171. ISBN 9780737300987.
75. Liedloff, J. The Continuum Concept: In Search of Happiness Lost ISBN 0-201-05071-4.
76. Rosen, M., Brenner, S. Rosen Method Bodywork: Accessing the Unconscious through Touch. California: North Atlantic Books Berkeley, 2003. ISBN 978-1-55643-418-1.
77. Roth, G. Maps to Ecstasy: Teachings of an Urban Shaman, 1990.
78. Stillerman, E. (2016). Modalities for Massage and Bodywork (second ed.). Mosby. pp. 402–14. ISBN 9780323239318.
79. Trivieri, Larry, and Anderson, John W. Alternative Medicine: The Definitive Guide. Berkeley, Calif: Celestial Arts, 2002.
80. Binswanger, L. (2014). Existential Analysis. Moscow: Institute of General Humanitarian Research. (ISBN 978-5-88230-520-7)
81. Binswanger, L. (1999). Being-in-the-World. Moscow: KSP+; Yuvanta. (ISBN 5-89692-024-5)
82. Kierkegaard, S. (2011). Either/Or: A Fragment of Life (2 volumes). St. Petersburg: Russian Christian Humanitarian Academy; Amphora. (ISBN 978-5-367-02005-2)
83. Kierkegaard, S. (2009). Philosophical Crumbs, or Fragments of

Wisdom. Moscow: Institute of Philosophy, Theology, and History of St. Thomas. (ISBN 978-5-94242-048-2)

84. Kierkegaard, S. (2018). Conversations and Reflections. Moscow: Ripol-Classic. (Philo-Sophia). (ISBN 978-5-386-10661-4)
85. Meneghetti, A. (1993). Introduction to Ontopsychology. Perm: Horton Limited.
86. Meneghetti, A. (2001, 2002). Woman of the Third Millennium. Moscow: NNBG "Ontopsychology."
87. Meneghetti, A. (2001). Cinema, Theater, the Unconscious. Vol. 1. Moscow: NNBG "Ontopsychology."
88. Meneghetti, A. (2002). Psychosomatics. Moscow: NNBG "Ontopsychology."
89. Meneghetti, A. (1996). System and Personality. Moscow: "Silver Threads."
90. Meneghetti, A. (2007). Textbook on Ontopsychology. Moscow: NNBG "Ontopsychology."
91. May, R. (2004). The Discovery of Being. Moscow: Institute of General Humanitarian Research. (ISBN 5-88239-137-8)
92. May, R. (1997). Love and Will. Moscow: Refl-Book; Vakler.
93. May, R. (2005). The Meaning of Anxiety. Kyiv: PSYLIB.
94. May, R. (1999). The Art of Psychological Counseling. Moscow: Independent Firm "Class."
95. May, R. (2001). Power and Innocence. Moscow: "Sense" Publishing House.
96. Sartre, J.-P. (1953). Existentialism is a Humanism. Moscow: Foreign Literature Publishing House.
97. Sartre, J.-P. (1956). Nothing But the Truth. Moscow: Art.
98. Sartre, J.-P. (1966). Words. Moscow: Progress.
99. Sartre, J.-P. (1967). Plays. Moscow: Art.
100. Sartre, J.-P. (1992). The Wall. Selected Works. Moscow: Political Literature Publishing House.
101. Sartre, J.-P. (1992). Gerogastrat. Moscow: Republic.
102. Jaspers, K. (1991). The Meaning and Purpose of History. Moscow:

Politizdat. (Thinkers of the 20th Century).

103. Frankl, V. (1990). Man's Search for Meaning: A Collection. Moscow: Progress.
104. Frankl, V. (1997). Doctor and Soul. St. Petersburg: Yuvanta.
105. Frankl, V. (2000). The Basics of Logotherapy. Psychotherapy and Religion. St. Petersburg: Speech.
106. Frankl, V. (2000). Man's Search for Ultimate Meaning. Moscow: April-press-Exmo-press.
107. Frankl, V. (2001). Psychotherapy in Practice. St. Petersburg: Speech.
108. Frankl, V. (2001). Theory and Therapy of Neuroses: An Introduction to Logotherapy and Existential Analysis. St. Petersburg: Speech.
109. Frankl, V. (2004). Saying Yes to Life: A Psychologist in a Concentration Camp. Moscow: Sense.
110. Frankl, V. (2015). Memories: What is Not in My Books. Life Memories. Moscow: Alpina Non-fiction. (ISBN 978-5-91671-445-6)
111. Frankl, V. (2016). Logotherapy and Existential Analysis: Articles and Lectures. Moscow: Alpina Non-fiction. (ISBN 978-5-91671-542-2)
112. Yalom, I. (1999). Existential Psychotherapy. Moscow: Class.
113. Yalom, I. (2016). Inpatient Group Psychotherapy. Moscow: Eksmo.
114. Jaspers K. The Meaning and Purpose of History. Translated from German. 2nd edition. Moscow: Republic, 1994. 527 p. (Thinkers of the 20th Century).
115. Jaspers K. General Psychopathology. Translated from German by L.O. Akopyan. Moscow: Practice, 1997. 1056 p. ISBN 5-88001-021-X. Archived copy from December 20, 2011 on Wayback Machine (Allgemeine Psychopathologie, 1913).
116. Jaspers K. Strindberg and Van Gogh: An Experiment in Comparative Pathographic Analysis with the Involvement of Cases of Swedenborg and Holderlin. Translated from German by G.B. Notkin. St. Petersburg: Academic Project, 1999.
117. Jaspers K. A Global History of Philosophy. Introduction. Translated by K.V. Loschevsky. St. Petersburg: Nauka, 2000.
118. Boss M. On the Question of the Hereditary Biological Significance of

Alcohol. Monthly Journal of Psychiatry and Neurology, Volume 72, 264–292 (1929).

119. Boss M. Psychologico-Characterological Investigations of Antisocial Psychopaths Using the Rorschach Test. Journal for the Entire Neurology and Psychiatry, Volume 133, 544–575 (1931).
120. Boss M. Hallucinations in statu nascendi. Swiss Archives of Neurology and Psychiatry, Volume 32/2, 1–4 (1933).
121. Boss M. The Psychic Dynamics of Sleep Walking in Schizophrenia. Swiss Archives of Neurology and Psychiatry, Volume 36/2, 209–220 (1935).
122. Boss M. Indications and Effects of the Sleep Cure. In: Extracts from the Proceedings of the Congress of Alienists and Neurologists of French-Speaking Countries. 1–4 (Masson, Paris, 1936).
123. Boss M. The Fundamental Principles of Schizophrenia Therapy in Historical Perspective. Journal for the Entire Neurology and Psychiatry, Volume 157/3, 358–392 (1937); also in Boss, M.: From Psychoanalysis to Daseinsanalysis, 11–53 (Europa Verlag, Vienna, 1979).
124. Boss M. Individual Pre-treatment for Collective Work Therapy in Severe, Chronic Schizophrenics. Swiss Archives of Neurology and Psychiatry, Volume 62/1, 15–26 (1938); also in Boss, M.: From Psychoanalysis to Daseinsanalysis, 55–70 (Europa Verlag, Vienna, 1979).
125. Grof, S. (1980). LSD Psychotherapy. (Translated by Georgiy Valeriyevich). [Self-published, available in electronic libraries]
126. Grof, S. (2009). LSD: Doorway to the Numinous: Groundbreaking Psychedelic Research into the Realms of the Human Unconscious.
127. Hagenbach, D., & Werthmüller, L. (2013). Mystic Chemist: The Life of Albert Hofmann and His Discovery of LSD. Synergetic Press. ISBN 978-090779146-1.
128. Hofmann, A. (1979). "LSD, My Problem Child."
129. Roberts, A. (2008). Albion Dreaming: A Popular History of LSD in Britain. Marshall Cavendish, U.K. ISBN 978-1905736270/190573627 4.

130. Shulgin, A., & Shulgin, A. (1991). "PiHKAL: A Chemical Love Story." Berkeley: Transform Press. ISBN 0-9630096-0-5.
131. Shulgin, A., & Shulgin, A. (1997). "TiHKAL: The Continuation." Berkeley: Transform Press. ISBN 0-9630096-9-9.
132. Winkelman, M. (2007). "Shamanic Guidelines for Psychedelic Medicine." In Winkelman, M., & Roberts, T. B. (Eds.), Psychedelic Medicine: New Evidence for Hallucinogenic Substances as Treatments. Westport, CT: Praeger Publishers. ISBN 978-0-275-99023-7.
133. Grof, S. (1994). Realms of the Human Unconscious: Observations from LSD Research. Moscow: MTM. (240 pages)
134. Grof, S. (2000). Beyond the Brain: Birth, Death, and Transcendence in Psychotherapy (3rd ed.). Moscow: Institute of Transpersonal Psychology, Institute of Psychotherapy Publishing. (504 pages) ISBN 5-93509-004-X, 5-89939-012-3. Available in libraries.
135. Grof, S. (2013). Holotropic Breathwork: A New Approach to Self-Exploration and Therapy. Moscow: Ganga. (352 pages) (Transpersonal Psychology) ISBN 978-5-906154-38-5.
136. Leuner, H. (1996). Catathymic Imagery. Translated by Ya. L. Obukhova. Moscow: "Eidos."
137. Leuner, H. (1996). Fundamentals of Depth Psychological Symbolism. Translated by Ya. L. Obukhova. Journal of Practical Psychologist, No. 3, 4.
138. Leuner, H. (1996). Directed Affective Imagery. In: Anthology of Depth Psychology, compiled by L. A. Hegai. Moscow: CheRo. Vol. 1, pp. 154-176. (C. G. Jung and Modern Psychoanalysis) (5000 copies) ISBN 5-88711-008-2.
139. Cooper, D. (1964). Reason and Violence: a decade of Sartre's philosophy. Tavistock.
140. Cooper, D. (1967). Psychiatry and Anti-Psychiatry (Ed.). Paladin.
141. Cooper, D. (1968). The Dialectics of Liberation (Ed.). Penguin.
142. Cooper, D. (1971). The Death of the Family. Penguin.
143. Cooper, D. (1974). Grammar of Living. Penguin.
144. Cooper, D. (1978). The Language of Madness. Penguin.

145. Laing, R. D. (1960). The Divided Self: An Existential Study in Sanity and Madness. Harmondsworth: Penguin.
146. Laing, R. D. (1961). The Self and Others. London: Tavistock Publications.
147. Laing, R. D., & Esterson, A. (1964). Sanity, Madness and the Family. Vol. 1. Families of Schizophrenics. London: Penguin Books.
148. Laing, R. D., & Cooper, D. G. (1964). Reason and Violence: A Decade of Sartre's Philosophy, 1950—1960. London: Tavistock Publications Ltd.
149. Laing, R. D. (1965). Mystification, Confusion and Conflict. In Boszormenyi-Nagy, I., and Framo, J. L. (eds.), Intensive Family Therapy. New York: Harper & Row.
150. Laing, R. D., Phillipson, H., & Lee, A. R. (1966). Interpersonal Perception: A Theory and a Method of Research. London: Tavistock Publications, New York: Springer Pab. Co, 1966.
151. Laing, R. D. (1967). The Politics of Experience and the Bird of Paradise. Harmondsworth: Penguin.
152. Laing, R. D. (1970). Knots. London: Penguin.
153. Laing, R. D. (1971). The Politics of the Family and Other Essays. London: Tavistock Publications.
154. Laing, R. D. (1972). Knots. New York: Vintage Press.
155. Laing, R. D. (1976). The Facts of Life. London: Penguin.
156. Laing, R. D. (1977). Conversations with Adam and Natasha. New York: Pantheon.
157. Laing, R. D. (1978). Do You Love Me? An Entertainment in Conversation and Verse. New York: Penguin Books.
158. Laing, R. D. (1979). Sonnets. London: Michael Joseph.
159. Laing, R. D. (1982). The Voice of Experience: Experience, Science and Psychiatry. Harmondsworth: Penguin.
160. Laing, R. D. (1985). Wisdom, Madness and Folly: The Making of a Psychiatrist 1927—1957. London: Macmillan.
161. Laing, R. D. (1995). The Divided Self. Kyiv.
162. Laing, R. D. (1995). The Self and Others. Saint Petersburg: Belyy

Krolik.

163. Laing, R. D. (2002). The "I" and Others. Moscow: Nezavisimaya firma "Klass."
164. Laing, R. D. (2002). I and Others. Knots. Moscow: Eksmo-Press.
165. Laing, R. D. (2005). Phenomenology of Experience. Lviv: Initsiativa.
166. Laing, R. D. (2012). Madness. Family Roots. BookMir.
167. Szasz, T. S. (1974). The Second Sin. Doubleday.
168. Szasz, T. S. (1975). The Age of Madness: A History of Involuntary Mental Hospitalization Presented in Selected Texts. London: Routledge & Kegan Paul Ltd.
169. Szasz, T. S. (1988). Psychiatric Justice. Syracuse, New York: Syracuse University Press.
170. Szasz, T. S. (1988). The Ethics of Psychoanalysis: The Theory and Method of Autonomous Psychotherapy. Syracuse, New York: Syracuse University Press.
171. Szasz, T. S. (1988). Pain and Pleasure: A Study of Bodily Feelings. Syracuse, New York: Syracuse University Press.
172. Szasz, T. S. (1988). Schizophrenia: The Sacred Symbol of Psychiatry. Syracuse, New York: Syracuse University Press.
173. Szasz, T. S. (1988). The Theology of Medicine: The Political-Philosophical Foundations of Medical Ethics. Syracuse, New York: Syracuse University Press.
174. Szasz, T. S. (2001). Pharmacracy: Medicine and Politics in America. Westport CT: Praeger Publishers.
175. Szasz, T. S. (2002). Liberation By Oppression: A Comparative Study of Slavery and Psychiatry. New Brunswick, New Jersey: Transaction Publishers.
176. Szasz, T. S. (2004). Words to the Wise: A Medical-Philosophical Dictionary. New Brunswick, New Jersey: Transaction Publishers.
177. Szasz, T. S. (2008). Psychiatry: The Science of Lies. Syracuse, New York: Syracuse University Press.
178. Szasz, T. S. (2009). Antipsychiatry: Quackery Squared. Syracuse, New York: Syracuse University Press.

179. Andreas, S., Faulkner, C. NLP: New Technologies of Achievement. Kyiv: Sofia; Moscow: Helios Publishers, 2001. ISBN 5-220-00392-5.
180. Augustinavichyute, A. Socionics: Psychotypes. Tests. Compiled by L. Filippov. Moscow: AST Publishers; St. Petersburg: Terra Fantastica, 1998.
181. Byron, A. Lewis. The Magic of Neuro-Linguistic Programming Revealed. St. Petersburg: Petersburg-XXI vek, 1999.
182. Bandler, R., Grinder, J. The Structure of Magic. St. Petersburg: Prime-Evroznak, 2004. Volume 1: ISBN 5-93878-151-5.
183. Bandler, R., Grinder, J. The Structure of Magic. St. Petersburg: Prime-Evroznak, 2004. Volume 2: ISBN 5-93878-152-3.
184. Bandler, R., Grinder, J. Patterns of Hypnotic Techniques of Milton H. Erickson from the Perspective of NLP. Simferopol: Renome, 1999. ISBN 966-7198-31-6.
185. Bandler, R., Grinder, J. Frogs into Princes: Neuro Linguistic Programming. Moscow: Flint, 2000. ISBN 7-256-37680-9.
186. Grinder, J., Delozier, D. Turtles All the Way Down. Moscow: Prime-Evroznak, 2005. ISBN 5-93878-165-5.
187. Grinder, J., Bostic St. Claire, C. Whispering in the Wind: The New Code of NLP. Moscow: Prime-Evroznak, 2005. ISBN 5-93878-188-4.
188. Dilts, R. Sleight of Mouth: The Magic of Conversational Belief Change. St. Petersburg: Piter, 2000.
189. O'Connor, J., Seymour, J. Introducing Neuro-Linguistic Programming. Chelyabinsk: "Library of A. Miller", 1998.
190. Wilber, K. No Boundary: Eastern and Western Approaches to Personal Growth. 1998, 2003. ISBN 5-17-018322-4.
191. Wilber, K. Atman: A Transpersonal View of Human Development. Moscow: AST Publishers, 1999, 2004. ISBN 5-17-021069-8.
192. Wilber, K. Spirit: An Integral Vision for a World Gone Slightly Mad. Moscow: AST Publishers, 2002. ISBN 5-17-014321-4.
193. Wilber, K. One Taste: The Journals of Ken Wilber. 2004. ISBN 5-17-021067-1.
194. Wilber, K. Integral Psychology: Consciousness, Spirit, Psychology,

Therapy. 2004. ISBN 5-17-021067-1.

195. Wilber, K. A Brief History of Everything. Moscow: AST Publishers, 2006. ISBN 5-17-036016-9. Reprint: Moscow: Postum, 2015. - 624 p. - ISBN 978-5-91478-035-4.
196. Wilber, K. Grace and Grit. Moscow: Otkryty Mir, 2008. - 656 p. - 3000 copies. - ISBN 978-5-9743-0127-8. Reprint: Moscow: Postum, 2013. - 656 p. - 3000 copies. - ISBN 978-5-91478-025-5.
197. Wilber, K. Integral Vision. Moscow: Otkryty Mir, 2009. ISBN 978-5-9743-0156-8.
198. Wilber, K. A Theory of Everything. Moscow: Postum, 2013. ISBN 978-5-91478-027-9.
199. Wilber, K. Integral Spirituality. Electronic edition. Moscow: Ipraktik, 2013. Google Books.
200. Wilber, K. Boomeritis. Electronic edition. Moscow: Ipraktik, 2013. Google Books.
201. Wilber, K. Eye of Spirit: Flesh, Mind, and Seeing. Integral World. Moscow: "RIPOl classic", 2016.

About the Author

Dr. **Artem Kudelia**, a psychologist with a PhD and a practicing therapist, has extensive expertise in integrative approaches. He possesses comprehensive knowledge of a wide range of psychotherapeutic methods, including humanistic and existential theories, as well as the practical application of cognitive-behavioral therapy (CBT) to effectively address issues such as anxiety, depression, obsessive thoughts, compulsions, social phobias, and complex emotions. His books are valuable resources for professionals and individuals interested in managing their mental health. In addition to managing symptoms, he helps his clients toward self-actualization in various aspects of their lives, including social, career, and personal aspects.

You can connect with me on:

- https://facebook.com/psyche.masters
- https://instagram.com/psyche.masters
- https://threads.net/@psyche.masters
- https://youtube.com/@psyche.masters
- https://tiktok.com/@psyche.masters
- https://pinterest.com/psychemasters

Subscribe to my newsletter:

✉ https://psychemaster.com/early-reader-signup

Also by Artem Kudelia PhD

The ***Psychology & Psychotherapy Theories & Practices*** series offers a detailed examination of the history, theoretical foundations, and practical applications of fundamental approaches in psychotherapy. It is an indispensable resource for psychologists, medical professionals, psychology students, and anyone interested in understanding these complex subjects.

Additionally, the ***Cognitive Behavioral Therapy Self-Help Guide: 15 Steps to Mental Health*** series provides actionable guidance for overcoming various psychological challenges, such as anxiety, depression, excessive anger, obsessive thoughts, compulsions, social phobias, health anxiety, and intricate emotional struggles. These topics were chosen because many individuals facing these challenges often lack awareness of the underlying dynamics. By gaining insight into these processes, individuals can make informed decisions about seeking help, reinforcing the idea that knowledge is a powerful tool for personal empowerment.

Together, these series offer invaluable resources for those interested in psychology, whether for academic study or personal development, by providing comprehensive insights and practical tools that contribute to improved mental well-being.

Hypnotherapy Fundamentals
Complete Guide

Are you ready to uncover the secrets of hypnotherapy?

This comprehensive guide immerses you in the ***theory** and history of hypnosis*, providing a solid foundation for understanding the principles underlying hypnotherapy.

Explore the various techniques and approaches used in *hypnotherapy **training*** through ***practice exercises***, including the art of *suggestion* and deepening *hypnotic trance states*, the creation of therapeutic propositions, and the utilization of the power of the subconscious mind.

Learn how to effectively apply *hypnotherapy techniques* to address a wide range of issues, from managing stress and anxiety to overcoming phobias and habits.

Gain an understanding of the transformative potential of hypnosis and its applications for personal growth and well-being.

Unlock the secrets of harnessing the power of the mind and creating positive changes in yourself and others.

▼

https://books2read.com/Hypnotherapy-Fundamentals

Psychology of Love & Death
Therapeutic Path to Fundamental Balance in Life and Relationships

How to Achieve Fundamental Balance in Life and Relationships?

Explore dualistic nature of human consciousness, along with the profound impact of seeking balance between fundamental continuums of *love and death*, *instinct and spirituality*, *masculinity and femininity* in shaping our experiences and relationships.

Explore the psychopathological profiles and manifestations of love and death, including profiles such as hysteria, paranoia, psychopathy, and others.

Uncover different types of love, from eros to agape, and study the *three-component Theory of Love*.

Familiarize yourself with *real-life psychotherapy cases* that illustrate the complexities of love, death, and therapy and gain *valuable insights* into the human experience and its challenges.

▼

https://books2read.com/Psychology-of-Love-and-Death

Breathwork Therapy Seminar
Holotropic Journey to Unconscious Mind Secrets

Tap Into the Wisdom of Transpersonal Psychology!

This book is the transcript of a seminar that addresses the profound questions of *subconsciousness*, offering a unique perspective on personal growth and healing.

Gain profound insights into the workings of your mind and explore the mysteries of human consciousness.

Access practical exercises and *techniques* to facilitate personal growth, healing, and self-awareness through *breathwork*.

Written for seekers of self-awareness, psychology enthusiasts, and anyone curious about the depths of the human mind.

Explore the integration of spirituality and psychology, uncovering your inner potential.

https://books2read.com/Breathwork-Therapy

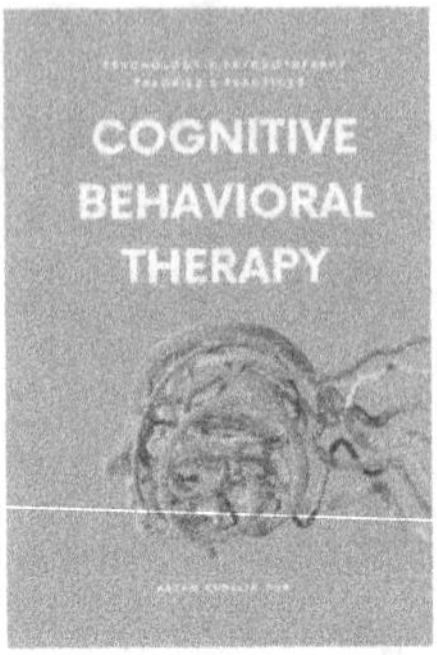

Cognitive Behavioral Therapy
Managing Anxiety and Depression

Explore the roots of anxiety and learn why it's a fundamental aspect of the human experience.

An in-depth exploration of *Panic Disorder*, addressing the irrational fears associated with it.

Examine the nuances of *Social Anxiety* and its impact on personal and professional spheres.

Dive into the world of *Obsessive-Compulsive Disorder*, unraveling its complexities.

Understand the genetic predispositions and learn effective strategies to manage obsessions and compulsions.

Explore *PTSD* from its roots to its biological manifestations. Delve into the trauma cycles, and discover therapeutic techniques for stabilization and overcoming trauma.

Grasp the degrees of *Depression*, from mild to severe, debunking common myths.

▼

https://books2read.com/Cognitive-Behavioral-Therapy

Healing Anxiety and Overthinking
Proven CBT Strategies for Lasting Relief

Are you exhausted from the relentless cycle of anxiety and overthinking?

Discover the 15-step program that will transform your mental health and bring peace of mind.

Millions of adults struggle with anxiety and overthinking, feeling trapped in a cycle of worry and stress. But it doesn't have to be this way. "*Healing Anxiety and Overthinking: Proven CBT Strategies for Lasting Relief*" offers a comprehensive guide to breaking free from the grip of anxiety using practical, proven **Cognitive Behavioral Therapy** (**CBT**) strategies.

♥ ***Imagine waking up every day with a clear mind, free from the constant barrage of anxious thoughts***

This book is your roadmap to achieving that transformation in just 15 steps. You'll learn to understand the nature of your anxiety, identify its triggers, and apply effective techniques to manage and overcome it.

Take Control of Your Mental Health

Don't let anxiety and overthinking rule your life. With "*Healing Anxiety and Overthinking*," you'll gain the tools and confidence to achieve peace of mind and live the life you deserve.

Mastering Intrusive Thoughts
Practical CBT Techniques for Managing OCD

Is ***OCD*** *ruling your life with intrusive thoughts and compulsions?*

Take back control with scientifically-proven CBT techniques designed to help you regain peace of mind.

Millions of adults struggle with obsessive-compulsive disorder (OCD), caught in a relentless cycle of intrusive thoughts and compulsive behaviors. "Mastering Intrusive Thoughts" is your step-by-step guide to breaking free from the grip of OCD using practical, evidence-based Cognitive Behavioral Therapy (CBT) techniques.

♥ ***Picture yourself waking up with a calm, focused mind, no longer burdened by the constant anxiety of unwanted thoughts.***

In this book, Dr. Artem Kudelia offers a clear and actionable path to mastering your thoughts in 15 manageable steps. Whether you're new to CBT or have tried other methods without success, this guide provides the tools you need to finally achieve relief.

✔ **Take the First Step Towards Mental Freedom**

You'll gain the knowledge and confidence to conquer your **OCD** and reclaim your peace of mind.

The Anger Solution
A CBT Program for Emotional Balance

Are you tired of living with persistent anger and overwhelming stress?

Discover a practical, 15-step program designed to bring lasting peace and transform your emotional health.

Millions of adults struggle with anger and stress, feeling trapped in a cycle of frustration and tension. But it doesn't have to be this way. "The Anger Solution" offers a comprehensive guide to breaking free from the grip of anger using practical, proven Cognitive Behavioral Therapy (CBT) strategies.

♥ ***Imagine waking up every day with a calm mind, free from the constant barrage of anger and stress.***

This book is your roadmap to achieving that transformation. With clear, actionable steps, you'll learn to understand the nature of your anger, identify its triggers, and apply effective techniques to manage and overcome it.

✔ **Take Control of Your Emotional Health**

With "The Anger Solution," you'll gain the tools and confidence to achieve emotional balance and live the life you deserve.

Health Anxiety Mastery
30 Proven CBT Steps to Peace of Mind

Is health anxiety controlling your life with constant worry and fear?

Regain peace of mind with proven CBT techniques designed to help you overcome health-related anxiety and reclaim control.

Millions of people struggle with health anxiety, trapped in a cycle of physical symptoms, endless reassurance-seeking, and intrusive thoughts about their well-being. *"Health Anxiety Mastery"* offers a clear, step-by-step approach to breaking free from these patterns using practical, evidence-based Cognitive Behavioral Therapy (CBT) techniques.

❤ Imagine waking up each day calm and confident, no longer overwhelmed by fear and obsessive thoughts about your health.

In this book, you'll find 30 actionable steps to help you reduce anxiety, challenge limiting beliefs, and develop healthier thought patterns. Whether you're just beginning your journey or have tried other approaches without success, these practical tools will guide you toward lasting relief.

✔ Start Your Journey to Balanced Mental Health

How to Get Over Social Anxiety
CBT Strategies for True Confidence and Deep Connection

What if 15 proven steps could free you from social anxiety and help you connect?

Uncover a 15-step CBT program to overcome fear, stop avoidance, and build true self-confidence. Millions struggle with social anxiety, but you don't have to face it alone. This guide provides a clear, evidence-based path to transforming your social life and connecting authentically.

♥ **Imagine engaging in conversations fearlessly and forming genuine relationships free from judgment or rejection.**

With insights from proven cognitive-behavioral techniques and relatable examples, this book offers the practical tools and encouragement needed to face your fears and succeed socially.

✔ **Begin Your Journey to Confidence**

Start transforming fear into connection and reclaim control of your social life with "*How to Get Over Social Anxiety*."

Discover More by Artem Kudelia
Scan the QR code or click the link to access his author page and full collection. Each book provides detailed insights and practical guidance, exemplifying his contributions to psychology and psychotherapy.

books2read.com/Artem-Kudelia-PhD

www.ingramcontent.com/pod-product-compliance
Lightning Source LLC
LaVergne TN
LVHW052016200926
848481LV00005B/1505